An

Introduction

to

Early Childhood Studies

SAGE has been part of the global academic community since 1965, supporting high quality research and learning that transforms society and our understanding of individuals, groups, and cultures. SAGE is the independent, innovative, natural home for authors, editors and societies who share our commitment and passion for the social sciences.

Find out more at: **www.sagepublications.com**

Third
Edition

An

Introduction

to

Early
Childhood
Studies

Edited by
Trisha Maynard and Sacha Powell

Los Angeles | London | New Delhi
Singapore | Washington DC

2014 000 064

Los Angeles | London | New Delhi
Singapore | Washington DC

SAGE Publications Ltd
1 Oliver's Yard
55 City Road
London EC1Y 1SP

SAGE Publications Inc.
2455 Teller Road
Thousand Oaks, California 91320

SAGE Publications India Pvt Ltd
B 1/I 1 Mohan Cooperative Industrial Area
Mathura Road
New Delhi 110 044

SAGE Publications Asia-Pacific Pte Ltd
3 Church Street
#10-04 Samsung Hub
Singapore 049483

Editor: Kate Wharton
Assistant editor: Emma Milman
Production editor: Nicola Marshall
Copyeditor: Gemma Marren
Proofreader: Sarah Cooke
Indexer: Silvia Benvenuto
Marketing manager: Catherine Slinn
Cover design: Lisa Harper
Typeset by: C&M Digitals (P) Ltd, Chennai, India
Printed and bound in Great Britain by Ashford
Colour Press Ltd

Editorial arrangement, introduction and part introductions © Trisha Maynard and Sacha Powell 2014

Chapter 1 © Joanne Westwood
Chapter 2 © Yordanka Valkanova
Chapter 3 and 12 © Nigel Thomas
Chapter 4 © Helen Penn
Chapter 5 © Jackie Marsh
Chapter 6 © Ruth Ford
Chapter 7 © Tricia David with Sacha Powell
Chapter 8 © Thea Cameron-Faulkner
Chapter 9 © Justine Howard
Chapter 10 © Marilyn Fleer
Chapter 11 © Sonia Jackson
Chapter 13 © Iram Siraj-Blatchford
Chapter 14 © Dendy Platt
Chapter 15 © Sally Robinson
Chapter 16 © Siobhan O'Connor
Chapter 17 © Helen Moylett
Chapter 18 © Alison Clark
Chapter 19 © Angela Anning
Chapter 20 © Carol Aubrey

The first edition was published in 2004 and reprinted in 2005, 2007 and 2008.
The second edition was first published in 2009 and reprinted in 2010 and twice in 2012.
The third edition was published in 2014.

Library of Congress Control Number: 2013938617

British Library Cataloguing in Publication data

A catalogue record for this book is available from the British Library

ISBN 978-1-4462-7066-0
ISBN 978-1-4462-7067-7 (pbk)

CONTENTS

Contents

NOTES ON EDITORS AND CONTRIBUTORS

Editors

Trisha Maynard is Professor of Early Childhood Spaces and Director of the Research Centre for Children, Families and Communities at Canterbury Christ Church University. Trisha taught at an infant school before joining the Department of Education at Swansea University in 1991 where she helped to establish a Department of Early Childhood Studies. In recent years Trisha's research has focused on outdoor play, child-initiated learning and wellbeing. She is currently co-directing the 'Evaluation of the Foundation Phase for Wales'.

Sacha Powell is a Reader in Early Childhood in the Research Centre for Children, Families and Communities at Canterbury Christ Church University. She has been involved in many research and evaluation projects on many topics, primarily concerned with early childhood and the provision of services for young children. These have included 'Learning for Life', which explored foundations of character development, and 'The Baby Room Project', which examined the processes and practices of day care for babies. Recent publications include *The Baby Room: Principles, Policies and Practice* (with Kathy Goouch, 2013). She maintains a long-term interest in early childhood provision in China.

Contributors

Angela Anning is Emeritus Professor of Early Childhood Education, University of Leeds. She worked as a teacher in all phases of primary, secondary and tertiary education. She was involved in primary teacher education, childhood studies and professional development at Leeds University. Her research interests are the professional knowledge of those working in early childhood services, multi-agency teamwork, early childhood curricula and in particular art education/children's drawing. She was one of the core team involved in the National Evaluation of Sure Start. She has published extensively in the field of early childhood services and education.

Carol Aubrey is Professor Emeritus at the University of Warwick and Visiting Professor at Birmingham City University. She trained as a primary school teacher and educational psychologist and spent a number of years in primary teacher education, with a particular focus on the early years, first at University College Cardiff and then at the University of Durham. While at Canterbury Christ Church University she led the Centre for International Studies in Early Childhood (CISEC). Her research interests lie in the policy-to-practice context of early childhood education and care and include multi-agency working, leadership, early learning and development, with an interest in mathematics development and inclusion/special educational needs.

Thea Cameron-Faulkner is a Lecturer in the School of Psychological Sciences at the University of Manchester. She taught Linguistics and English Language for six years before studying for a PhD in Psychology. Her research is situated within a constructivist approach to language development and focuses on the role of the linguistic input in the early stages of the developmental process.

Alison Clark is a Senior Lecturer in Childhood Studies at the Open University. Her research interests include children's experiences of place and the development of participatory research methods. Working with Professor Peter Moss at Thomas Coram Research Unit she developed the Mosaic approach for listening to the perspectives of young children and has since adapted the approach for research with young people and adults. Her research studies have included a three-year longitudinal study exploring young children's involvement in the design of learning environments. Publications include *Transforming Children's Spaces* (2010) and co-editing *Understanding Research with Children and Young People* (2014).

Tricia David has worked in the field of early childhood education and care for over fifty years, if one counts being a Sunday School 'teacher' at seventeen, when one four year old really did produce a picture of 'Mary and the Babe and flea [sic]' – which she wishes she had kept. Having officially retired, she is honoured to have been awarded the titles Emeritus Professor at Canterbury Christ Church University and Honorary Emeritus Professor of Early Years Education at the University of Sheffield (2004–2009) and the Lifetime Achievement Award 2011 from *Nursery World*. Tricia's publications have included studies of international comparisons, works on multi-professionalism, the review for *Birth to Three Matters* and the OECD survey of provision in the Netherlands.

Marilyn Fleer holds the Foundation Chair of Early Childhood Education at Monash University, Australia, and is the President of the International Society for Cultural Activity Research (ISCAR). Her research interests focus on early years learning and development, with special attention on play, pedagogy, culture, science and technology.

Ruth Ford is a Senior Lecturer in Developmental Psychology at Griffith University in Brisbane, Australia, and her research focuses on the development of memory and thinking skills during early childhood. Ruth is especially interested in socio-cultural theories of cognitive development and the implications of such theories for efforts to raise the educational attainments of disadvantaged children through early intervention. While working in the United Kingdom, Ruth was instrumental in founding a Sure Start project that was successful in developing the self-regulation and school readiness of low-income pre-schoolers by increasing their experience of one-on-one, scaffolded interactions with their primary caregiver.

Justine Howard is a Senior Lecturer in the College of Human and Health Sciences at Swansea University and the Programme Manager for their MA in Developmental and Therapeutic Play and MA in Childhood Studies. She is a Chartered Psychologist and Associate Fellow of the British Psychological Society. Her research focuses on children's play, specifically evidencing its role in supporting children's development and emotional wellbeing. She is well published and speaks on the topic of play at a national and international level. Recent books include *Play and Learning in the Early Years* (2010), *Play in Early Childhood* (Sheridan et al 2011) and *The Essence of Play* (2013).

Sonia Jackson is Professor Emerita at the Institute of Education, University of London and Swansea University. Before moving into university teaching and research, she worked as a clinical psychologist, teacher and social worker. She is co-author of *Childminder: A Study in Action Research* (1979) and *People Under Three: Young Children in Day Care* (2004) which has been translated into five languages. The third edition (with Ruth Forbes) will be published in 2014. Sonia ran a course for leaders in early years settings for ten years and set up the first UK degrees in Early Childhood Studies at the Universities of Bristol and Swansea. She has published extensively on childcare and the care and education of looked after children. She was awarded the OBE for services to children in 2003.

Jackie Marsh is Professor of Education at the University of Sheffield. She has been involved in numerous research projects that have explored young children's engagement with popular culture, media and new technologies in homes, early years settings and schools. Jackie is currently conducting research on the history of the relation between play, media and commercial culture from the 1950s to the present-day, based on the archival collection of Iona and Peter Opie, located at the Bodleian Libraries. Recent publications include *The Sage Handbook of Early Childhood Literacy* (2nd edn, with J. Larson, 2012) and *Children's Virtual Play Worlds: Culture, Learning and Participation* (edited with A. Burke, 2013).

Helen Moylett is an independent early years consultant and writer. She has been an early years teacher, a local authority senior advisory teacher and a senior lecturer in primary and early years education at Manchester Metropolitan University. In 2000 she left academia to become head of an early years centre. In 2004 she joined the National Strategies. She was centrally involved in developing the Early Years Foundation Stage (EYFS) as well as many of the National Strategies materials associated with it. Helen is currently President of the British Association of Early Childhood Education (Early Education) and a Visiting Fellow of Oxford Brookes University.

Siobhan O'Connor is a Senior Lecturer in Early Childhood Studies at Canterbury Christ Church University with particular responsibility for supporting year one students in their transition to successful study in Higher Education. She has designed and leads teaching on a range of modules including 'being, belonging and becoming', 'diversity and inclusion' and 'values into action'. Her research interests include the development of an inclusive curriculum for early childhood studies degree programmes, notions of professionalism in the early years and the concept of quality in early childhood care and education.

Helen Penn is Professor of Early Childhood in the Cass School of Education, University of East London (UEL), UK, and co-director of the International Centre for the Study of the Mixed Economy of Childcare (ICMEC) at UEL. She was previously a teacher and a senior administrator of ECEC services, before becoming an academic. She has worked for a number of international organisations including OECD, EU and UNESCO and on large-scale international aid projects in Southern Africa and in Central Asia. Her latest book, co-edited with Eva Lloyd is *Childcare Markets: Can They Deliver an Equitable Service?* (2013). She has written widely on global issues, most recently on 'The Rhetoric and Realities of Early Childhood Programmes Promoted by the World Bank' in Afua Twum-Danso Imoh and Robert Ame (eds), *Childhoods at the Intersection of the Local and the Global* (2012).

Dendy Platt is a Senior Lecturer in Social Work at the University of Bristol. He teaches on qualifying and post-qualifying Social Work courses, and on the BSc in Childhood Studies. He has worked as a social worker and team leader in local authority social services departments, as a community worker with Save the

Children and as a family centre manager with Barnardo's. He has undertaken research and writing on social work assessments and decision-making in relation to children and families, on family support and on social workers' engagement with families.

Sally Robinson is a Principal Lecturer who leads the Health Promotion and Public Health team at Canterbury Christ Church University, and an experienced external examiner to other universities. Sally's research has included investigating children's perceptions of eating and body image, healthy early years settings, healthy eating and language learning in European schools, children's views of older people, childhood obesity, and the needs of teachers who are working with children with life limiting or life threatening conditions. Her publications include *Healthy Eating in Primary Schools* (2006). She also works with young children as a play therapist.

Iram Siraj–Blatchford is Professor of Early Childhood Education at the Institute of Education, University of London. Her recent research projects include 'Evaluation of the Foundation Phase across Wales' and she is principal investigator of the major DCSF sixteen-year study on Effective Pre-school, Primary and Secondary Education (EPPSE 3–16) Project (1997–2013). She is working on longitudinal studies in a number of countries including Australia and Ireland. Iram is a former President of the British Association for Early Childhood Education and has published over sixty major reports and books, and over 150 peer-reviewed articles and chapters in scholarly books.

Nigel Thomas is Professor of Childhood and Youth Research at the University of Central Lancashire and founding Co-Director of The Centre for Children and Young People's Participation in Research. He is also a Visiting Professor at the Centre for Children and Young People, Southern Cross University, New South Wales. His research interests are principally in child welfare, children's rights and participation, and theories of childhood. His publications include *Children, Family and the State: Decision-Making and Child Participation* (2002), *Social Work with Young People in Care: Looking after Children in Theory and Practice* (2005), *Children, Politics and Communication: Participation at the Margins* (2009) and *A Handbook of Children and Young People's Participation: Perspectives from Theory and Practice* (with Barry Percy-Smith, 2010). He was from 2005 to 2011 co-editor of the journal *Children & Society* and is now Chair of the Editorial Board.

Yordanka Valkanova is Senior Lecturer in Childhood Studies at Canterbury Christ Church University. Previously, she was Lecturer at University of Roehampton and Assistant Professor at Plovdiv University, Bulgaria. She is a co-editor (with

John Eade) of *Accession and Migration: Changing Policy, Society and Culture in an Enlarged Europe* (2009), the author of numerous articles as well as of the book *Cognitive Development through Manipulative Activities in Children* (Plovdiv, 2001). Her research has focused on history of childhood in Russia and Eastern Europe and digital literacy.

Joanne Westwood is a Senior Lecturer in the School of Social Work at the University of Central Lancashire and Co-Director of The Centre for Children and Young People's Participation in Research, which focuses on promoting and researching children's participation, inclusion and empowerment. Joanne is a qualified social worker and worked with children, young people and their families in both statutory and voluntary agencies. Her research and teaching interests include advocacy, law and child welfare policies and practices. She has undertaken research on migrant children, global childcare systems and children's experiences of domestic violence in the UK.

INTRODUCTION

Trisha Maynard and Sacha Powell

In the introduction to the previous editions of this text (2004 and 2009) it was noted that early childhood appears to command a much higher place on the agenda of politicians and policy makers in the UK. In 2013 this has not changed; indeed, if anything, the global recession and the increasing gap between the most advantaged and disadvantaged children, families and communities has ensured that there is a recognition (by some campaigners at least) that the health, wealth, education and wellbeing of young children and their families really do matter.

This growing recognition of the importance and significance of early childhood is also reflected in the wide range of private, statutory and voluntary organisations, professional roles, and education, training and continued professional development opportunities relating to work with young children and their families. The interest in early childhood spans many disciplines, encompassing diverse areas of study that include scientific interest in the growth and functioning of young brains to research about infants' musicality; some are large-scale, longitudinal studies that evaluate the effects of particular early childhood 'programmes', while others may examine in minute and rich detail the nature of a sibling relationship. Young children are increasingly recognised as potential participants in studies, and methods to engage them ethically and equally in research are gaining prominence. Babies and young children are an everlasting source of interest, intrigue, surprise and delight!

The primary purpose of this book is to provide a core introductory text for the many undergraduate students who are now studying early childhood. While numerous texts now exist, we felt that there was the need for a text that would introduce students to the significant ideas in each of the key areas of study, so providing them with a sound basis for further reading, thinking and research. Of equal importance, we reasoned, was the need for a text that would introduce students to a number of interwoven themes within the field of early childhood studies, and would help to show how these themes are reflected and played out within different areas. This seemed to be of particular importance given that most undergraduate courses are now modular; it can be hard for students to make the links between the various topics or modules studied.

As well as being useful to students, we hope this text will also be of interest to those already working with young children. We believe that all practitioners need to have a sound knowledge of a range of different theoretical perspectives if they are to evaluate and attempt to improve their own practice. That is not to suggest that the theory–practice relationship is straightforward; indeed, the characteristics of the 'reflective practitioner' (Schön, 1983) have been debated for many years. There does appear to be a consensus, however, that practical experience, while essential in developing expertise, is not in itself sufficient.

So what are the key themes addressed in this text? We have identified four: political, social and economic changes; the social construction of childhood and children's rights; the impact of globalisation; and dominant and competing theories.

1 Political, social and economic changes

As many of our authors note and as Sonia Jackson summarises in Chapter 11, keen political attention to early childhood is now commonplace in many countries worldwide and among international organisations like UNESCO and the World Health Organization (WHO). The reasons for this interest are diverse and contested but arguments include a moral responsibility for young children's welfare, legal duties to make certain provisions for them and long-term aspirations about the contribution of citizens to a country's economic growth and stability in a globally competitive 'marketplace'. Although there is wide variation in the proportions of GDP (Gross Domestic Product) that are reportedly invested in early childhood services in different countries (see, for example, UNICEF, 2008; ACPF, 2011; OECD, 2011), there can be no doubt that there has been significant and growing financial investment in provision for the first years of life, including the months before birth. But there is also disparity within countries and across the world in terms of equality of access to good standards of care, welfare and education for young children and their families at home and in their communities. As Sally Robinson notes in Chapter 15, a 'life course' perspective not only exposes social, economic and environmental determinants of (health) inequality but also attempts to redress these by advocating policies that support a progressive universal approach to the re-configuration and re-distribution of services for families with young children. These may be provided by individual agencies but the last decade has seen increasing policy emphasis on integrated working across agencies, between professionals and bridging the private, statutory and voluntary sectors. Moving out of professional silos is notoriously troublesome, whether at departmental level in government or within a community-based 'team around a child/family'. Angela Anning discusses some of the commonly encountered problems in Chapter 19.

In the second edition of this book, it was noted that changes resulting from devolution had become more significant since the first edition of the text was published. This remains the case, with increasing divergence between policies and between the types, and arguably the levels, of provision available in the nations of the UK. This is noticeable, for example, in the ways that the four nations' policies conceive of and differentiate between 'phases' within early childhood.

With increasing policy emphasis on 'school readiness', which many commentators have criticised for its narrow and normalising educational aims and potential for translation to 'instruction' of very young children, early years practitioners are faced with a challenge of blending the demands of meeting assessment requirements with their own pedagogical orientations, which may jar on a philosophical or theoretical basis. Part 4 of the book attempts to offer some support in untangling these kinds of challenges and dilemmas with exemplars and suggestions that are deeply rooted in theory.

2 The social construction of childhood and children's rights

A second prominent theme throughout this edition, as in previous editions of the text, concerns childhood as a social construct. From a social constructionist perspective, what we think we know and believe to be true is not fixed and simply internalised; our beliefs are the product of our experiences and social interactions and are (re-) constructed by and through these (see Chapter 16). Consequently, many authors in this edition reflect how 'childhood' is a concept that exists and is characterised in particular ways by historical (Chapter 2) and contemporary beliefs (Chapters 4 and 5) and is not simply a 'natural' aspect of human existence. So what constitutes childhood in different cultures – if indeed the first years after birth are constructed as such – varies in time and place. Differences can be found around the world in relation to what babies and young children are believed to be, to be capable of doing, are permitted or enabled to do, are prohibited or protected from and this is not purely a response to biological immaturity (Chapter 1). It is also dependent on the existence of a construct of 'adulthood' and how childhood is conceived in comparison. This is starkly evident in discussions of children's rights (Chapter 12). But it can also be seen throughout the book in relation to social processes and discourses that perpetuate the distinction of childhood, for example in specific ideas about children's needs (Chapter 14), policies about them and services provided for them (Chapter 11) and/or which distinguish them from other children and especially from older people – adults.

3 The impact of globalisation

The social construction of childhood can be linked to a further issue noted by several writers: the increasing emphasis on and effects of globalisation (see, in particular, Chapters 1 and 4). The opening up of the world – enhanced by the development and rapid expansion of digital technologies (Chapter 5) – allows us to find out about different childhoods and so challenges our perceptions about what we consider to be 'normal' and thus 'good' practices and approaches – for example, good models of parenting (see Chapter 4). It even facilitates the 'borrowing' of early childhood policies, provision or practices from different cultures and countries. However, while a critical engagement with alternative ideas may be viewed positively, concerns have been raised about the export of theories and practices, and with them particular embedded values, especially when this is from the relatively wealthy North to the relatively poor South (Chapters 1 and 4). A specific anxiety for some writers is the imposition of what are seen as dominant theories of child development (Chapter 1) that may infer that there is a 'universal' child. These theories, along with concepts such as 'culture' and 'quality', are now being explored and problematised (see, for example, Chapters 1, 3 and 4).

4 Dominant and competing theories

Despite, or rather alongside, these concerns, it goes without saying that 'dominant' theories – particularly dominant theories of child development (Chapters 6 to 9) – are both extremely powerful and also increasingly challenged by some writers who offer alternatives to developmental approaches (Chapter 10). An understanding of these theories, along with the ability to be critically reflective (Chapters 16 and 20), to listen to the voices of children (Chapter 18) and the development of skills in, for example, child observation (Chapter 17), are seen as imperative for a highly qualified early childhood workforce.

However, given that they derive from different disciplines, within each area of interest different theories are often in tension (or competition) with one another. Within this text, for instance, some writers consider a range of perspectives and propositions when discussing a particular issue – for example, when exploring children's cognitive development or how they acquire language (Chapters 6 and 8). However, it is also possible to identify competing theories when pursuing an area of interest across different chapters. This is well illustrated in relation to the issue of play. For example, it is maintained that play is fundamental to young children's learning, health and development – cognitive, social and emotional (Chapters 6, 7 and 9) – as well as to the development of adaptable and flexible thought (Chapter 9). It is also indicated that play is central to an inclusive curriculum (Chapter 16). We are warned, however, that not all play promotes learning and development and that when considering children's education, the prioritising (and even the existence) of 'free play' is challenged (Chapter 13). Indeed, when considering play in a global context, the idea that children should be allowed simply to play, rather than making a contribution to the family and community, is raised for consideration (Chapter 4).

Of course, these tensions between competing theories and discourses remind us of the demands and significance of inter-agency and multidisciplinary working (Chapter 19). They also emphasise the complexity, challenges and excitement of the interdisciplinary study of early childhood!

Organisation of the book

This edition of the text is edited by Trisha Maynard with a new co-editor, Sacha Powell, whose field of interest is in the influence of children's rights and the policies and practice of day care for babies. Thanks go to Nigel Thomas for his significant contribution to the first two editions; his ideas and words still resonate through this book.

The twenty chapters between them cover a very extensive territory, ranging from the history of childhood to the place of play in the early years curriculum. In order to make the text more manageable and accessible we have organised the book into four parts:

1. Perspectives on childhood.
2. The developing child.
3. Policy and provision for young children.
4. Developing effective practice.

We do not suggest that these four dimensions are in any significant way independent of each other. Readers will find that the inter-relationships between child development, historical and cultural perspectives on childhood, local and national policy and the nature and quality of provision, and the implications of all this for professional practice, are emphasised throughout the text.

In summary, Part One considers how childhood differs culturally, historically and globally, examines childhood in a digital age and introduces sociological approaches to the study of childhood. Part Two includes chapters on cognitive, social and emotional development, language acquisition and play and also includes a chapter that offers an alternative, more holistic way of viewing child development: that is, as a cultural process. Part Three includes an overview of early years policy and services, as well as specific chapters on children's rights and the law, education, welfare and child protection, health and wellbeing, and inclusion. Finally, Part Four focuses on some particular aspects of practice – child observation, undertaking research with children, the early years workforce, inter-agency and multidisciplinary working and leadership. Each part of the book begins with a brief editorial introduction that explains what is in the chapters that follow and which draws attention to some common themes and to differences of emphasis.

Each individual chapter aims to introduce its subject to an intelligent reader with limited previous knowledge, and also to indicate some of the important areas of debate within the field. Some chapters include case examples or practical exercises. All conclude with some questions or ideas for further work, and with suggestions for further reading. The full list of sources is at the end of the book.

For this third edition all the chapters have been updated; we are grateful to Nigel Thomas, Helen Penn, Ruth Ford, Tricia David, Thea Cameron-Faulkner, Justine Howard, Sonia Jackson, Iram Siraj-Blatchford, Alison Clark and Carol Aubrey for doing this. Some chapters have been totally re-written by new authors: our thanks go to Joanne Westwood, Yordanka Valkanova, Dendy Platt, Sally Robinson, Siobhan O'Connor, Helen Moylett and Angela Anning. We are also grateful for the two new contributions by Jackie Marsh and Marilyn Fleer which we think have strengthened the book considerably.

Each author is an expert in their own field. Their professional backgrounds are diverse, reflecting the multidisciplinary nature of the subject and the strong interchange between theory and practice. Although there are differences of emphasis in the chapters that follow, one perspective still runs through the whole book. This is our theoretical and practical commitment to respecting the rights of children and seeing children as active participants in all matters relating to their health, care, welfare and education. As has been noted in the previous editions, children, we are convinced, should be seen *and* heard!

PART ONE

PERSPECTIVES ON CHILDHOOD

This first part of the book is concerned with perspectives on childhood and how children grow up. It is essentially underpinned by questions such as: 'Is childhood a distinct stage of life and if so when was it invented or discovered?', 'How long should childhood last?' and 'Is childhood as we know it "disappearing" and should we be concerned about this?'. In relation to this final question we were aware that one of the major concerns – 'moral panics' – voiced in the media in recent years has been young children's access to and use of digital technologies. In a new chapter for this edition, therefore, Jackie Marsh considers the nature of childhood in the digital age.

That childhood differs in important ways according to where in the world we are, what period of history we are in, or which social group we are considering, is not in dispute. What is sometimes disputed, however, is whether we can use the words 'childhood' and 'children' to apply to what we find in different times and places or among different social groups. Unsurprisingly, some authors speak of a multiplicity of 'childhoods' rather than a single 'childhood'.

It is now generally accepted that childhood is, in a significant sense, socially constructed – that is, it is something produced in social interaction and discourse rather than being a purely natural phenomenon. That is not to say that there is not a physical and biological base to some of the important characteristics that distinguish children from adults – but the form that these differences take is a social production. In no way is this more evident than in the enormous variation between the appearance of childhood in different times, places and social settings.

In Chapter 1, Joanne Westwood starts with an exploration of globalisation and culture, exploring the anthropological concepts of 'ethnocentrism' and 'cultural relativism'. Westwood's central argument is that globalisation and the international migratory movements of people that bring with them different patterns of child rearing demand that we take a close look at our own belief systems as well as those that inform institutional practices with children. While maintaining that there are universal stages of development (as in Erikson, 1995) Westwood notes that these are also culturally and socially defined. Westwood sees the challenge for practitioners is to recognise and embrace the differences between different cultural beliefs and practices.

In Chapter 2, Yordanka Valkanova examines different historical interpretations of childhood and identifies and evaluates some of the dominant discourses that have surrounded the major traditions of research into childhood. Focusing her discussion within a Euro-American context, and foregrounding education and schooling, she argues that it is the general tension between the existing social and material world, and the possibility for changing this world, that have had an effect on the conceptualisation of childhood throughout the ages.

In Chapter 3, Nigel Thomas reviews developments in the sociological study of childhood and the potential of sociology for advancing our understanding in this area alongside other disciplines. He shows how theoretical models such as Corsaro's 'interpretive reproduction' help us to understand how children can be at the same time determined by their culture and society and active in making meanings and transformations. A strong message is that children do not simply exist in relation to the family or the school, but may have to be understood differently in different settings. This echoes the point made earlier that there is not one 'childhood' but a multiplicity of childhoods, and that children themselves help to define and make those childhoods what they are.

In Chapter 4, Helen Penn argues that while it is possible to identify some general features of early childhood, all of them are shaped and modified by cultural contexts to the extent that, rather than searching for what is shared, it may be more useful to understand what is particular: that is, local conceptions of childhood. Penn argues that views of childhood from the Euro-American context are often seen as universal and attempts are made to export these to the global South, even though there are profound differences in ideas about child development and child rearing practices. Penn notes, however, that while there are concerns that models from the North may be inappropriate, given that globalisation has resulted in the migration of women from rural areas to cities, there is, at the same time, a pressure to provide early childhood education and care (ECEC).

Finally, in Chapter 5, Jackie Marsh explores the nature of childhood in the digital age. She considers the moral panic surrounding children's use of technology and, in relation to this, the conflicting constructs of children and childhood found in the media. Marsh adopts an ecological perspective to consider research on children's use of digital technologies in homes and communities and demonstrates that children's experiences of technology will be shaped by the particular contexts in which they live. As digital technologies are becoming an increasing and more visible part of children's worlds, Marsh maintains that, while we need to be alert to the inherent risks, we also need to acknowledge the opportunities they bring to strengthen and extend what are essential and significant elements of childhood.

1

CHILDHOOD IN DIFFERENT CULTURES

Joanne Westwood

Contents

- Introduction
- Globalisation
- Culture, ethnocentrism and cultural relativism
- Childhood and child rearing in cross-cultural contexts
- The loss of childhood: work and migration
- The United Nations Convention on the Rights of the Child (UNCRC) and children's rights
- Conclusions

Introduction

The perception of childhood as a period of dependence and innocence has a long history. Being strongly associated with the Romantic Movement of eighteenth-century Europe it resonates with more recent Western theories of child development, ideas about child rearing and policies relating to the care and education of children. The advent of a global society, however, demands that we examine and reflect on our own belief systems and those which inform our individual and institutional practices with children. This chapter begins with a discussion of globalisation and culture (see Chapter 4) and then sets out reasons why a cross-cultural understanding of childhood, children and child rearing is a prerequisite for any form of intervention in children's lives. Understanding the importance of culture can challenge our own preconceived ideas about childhood in a global context and help us to determine what we expect from children and their place and rights in society.

Globalisation

Globalisation is the extension of relationships and patterns of social practice and meaning across the world space; what happens in one part of the world has an impact somewhere else (Ritzer, 2008). Globalisation is a layered and uneven process which connects the local to the global (James, 2006) and in doing so brings a range of concerns and issues to the local context. The process of globalisation shifts societies and individuals closer together through the mediums of technology, transport and communication, moves both resources and people and is tied to consumption. Global products and brands and the (re)location of Western business interests to the developing world are all the outcome of globalisation, and the mechanics of globalisation mean that Western business and financial interests drive forward trade and exchange, arguably at the expense of the interests and benefits of local economies. The impact of globalisation is felt by non-developed and non-industrialised countries and it is maintained that power is retained by Western countries (Ritzer, 2008), although critics suggest that this perspective unhelpfully renders consumers as passive and powerless (Buckingham, 2007).

While there are clear benefits of globalisation, particularly in relation to communication and speed, there are disadvantages: specifically the 'hegemonisation' which occurs when one world view or one product/brand dominates. The US burger chain McDonald's provides a good example of hegemony at work in a global market. For example, McDonald's opened stores in China which had a big impact on the ways that families spend their disposable income. Marketing was child-oriented in the early days and China's 'Little Emperors' (a result of the so-called One-Child Policy) began to make demands of their parents in hitherto unseen ways. This changed traditional family dynamics and hierarchies and McDonald's not only brought a form of hegemony and change in dietary intakes but also cultural change that was more akin to family life in the USA than traditional Chinese families (Guo, 2000). Buckingham (2007: 44) suggests that: 'rather than relying simply on physical occupation, the US is now seen to sustain its hegemony through a process of ideological and cultural domination'.

As we can see, hegemony in a global context is not restricted to commodities but also extends to beliefs and ideas about social and cultural practices. There is thus potential for conflict in relation to childhood and ideologies and theories of child development and practice, where dominant views emanating from Western traditions and beliefs stifle local, traditional and culturally specific practices.

Culture, ethnocentrism and cultural relativism

Cultural theory suggests that a universal human culture is shared by all societies and that social practices support societies' structures (i.e. families, faiths) and fulfil individual needs. How then is culture defined?

Culture (see also Chapter 4) is how individuals understand who they are and how people give their lives meaning. Culture defines social groups – that is, the cultural group people belong to (macro culture). Culture is also understood as a set of practices, beliefs, plans and rules which a social group agree upon and which mark them out as unique. Culture gives groups a sense of identity and belonging and pride; it is learned, can be taught and acquired by members of the group (Rai and Pannar, 2010). Children acquire culture through exposure to, and observation and adoption of, behaviours and activities, as well as participation with their community and individuals, and by verbal and non-verbal communication.

Culture provides security and familiarity, is transmitted from one generation to another and is therefore dynamic: one generation may add or develop aspects and ideas about the world depending upon the context. Culture is patterned, uses symbols to convey meaning and continues over time, it is innovative and creative and can change in response to wider influences and societal demands (Rai and Pannar, 2010). For example, the provision of day care for pre-school children became the norm in the UK when the labour market required women to enter the workforce. The culture of child rearing practice being carried out largely by women in the home during the post-war period changed as the economic and political pressures were focused on female employment. This was not a straightforward process, as the development of day care for pre-school children was ideologically and politically opposed (Lewis, 2012) but by the start of the twenty-first century a childcare industry was fully established to provide a range of day care options for families, reflecting a significant cultural shift (see Chapter 11).

Cultures and cultural practices are studied by anthropologists; for example, Mary Douglas (1966, reissued 2006) studied the rituals and cultural practices and behaviours we know as taboos of the Lele tribe in Africa. Douglas argued that rather than being bizarre and primitive, beliefs about taboos, particularly those related to personal hygiene and the protection of females, developed to protect vulnerable members of the social group and to assure its future. Hendry (2008) explores cultures, traditions and their meaning and symbolism more widely drawing on anthropological research in Mexico, Japan and Morocco. Initiation rites, for example, vary widely but exist across many societies to signify a stage of development in childhood or in the transition towards adulthood. In some traditions these rites are gruelling physical tests or mutilations but they provide continuity and familiarity to the social group, tribe or clan.

It is not always easy for a 'newcomer' to learn the rules of the group; consider the example of a child in the UK who has been looked after at home before entering a reception class. In education settings children may, for example, have to learn that in whole class activities they need to signal their desire to speak and then wait to be asked or that they need permission to visit the toilet.

'Ethnocentrism' and 'cultural relativism' are concepts which also require definition if we are to understand how culture and cultural practices are both defended and criticised.

What is ethnocentrism?

Ethnocentrism is the belief that one's own culture and way of behaving is the correct way; all others are judged by this standard. Ethnocentrism generally legitimates a Western 'gaze' or interpretation of a problem or issue – concealing and, in doing so, preventing the articulation of indigenous responses. An example might be where there are concerns about HIV orphans in sub-Saharan Africa; whereas the local community may assert that the care of orphans lies with the extended family and kinship network, Western responses may include the development of institutionalised care. In cultures where extended family members (aunties, uncles, grandparents) traditionally provide care for children this ethnocentric response is deeply flawed as it disrupts customs and practices which have long ensured cultural and community continuity.

Issues related to working children also challenge our cultural perspectives about childhood and what is deemed acceptable and appropriate. Children who work transgress the boundaries and notions of childhood; indeed, the issue of child work/labour has been a longstanding point of conflict and tension in the West with international agencies and institutions at the forefront of the activity to remove children from the workplace. However, while there are good reasons to prevent exploitative child labour there are some benefits for children and their families and communities particularly in the case of poverty where children feel pride at being able to make a contribution to their family or when their work pays for their education.

What is cultural relativism?

James and James (2012: 35) define cultural relativism as:

> The recognition that societies differ in their cultural attitudes towards social phenomena and therefore no universal criteria can be applied to compare one cultural view with another. Culture can therefore only be judged through reference to their own standards.

They provide an example of the age of marriage which varies across Europe, with a fairly standard age of 16. In the Indian sub-continent it is not unusual for girls to be married at 12. In the Western context this may be seen as abusive and exploitative and campaigners suggest that early marriage leads to earlier child birth which impacts on the health of females. However, the cultural practices of early and arranged marriage have been practiced as a means to bring families and kinship groups closer together and ensure the continuance of the tribe, clan or group.

It is important to ensure that when we accept and defend cultural practices, we are not legitimating harmful behaviours. An example of this is found in the Laming enquiry (2003) where the concerns about Victoria Climbié were not expressed or communicated, as the deferential behaviour she presented when with her aunt was accepted by the professionals she had contact with as the norm in her culture (see Chapter 14). The child was clearly frightened by the presence of her aunt, but the extent and reasons for these fears were only articulated after Victoria's death.

The complexity of cultural relativism can be seen in relation to the practice of female circumcision which is common in some parts of Africa. The practice in some cultures is related to transition from childhood to adulthood and beliefs about healthy childbirth. Campaigning organisations in the 1970s and 1980s renamed the practice 'female genital mutilation' and drew political attention to the physical harms caused by the practice (Keck and Sikkink 1998). The practice is now condemned by activists from within the culture and so its legitimacy as a rite of passage for girls is challenged (James and James, 2012).

Childhood and child rearing in cross-cultural contexts

As indicated above, our own views of childhood will have been formed within a particular cultural context and will therefore often be seen as how things 'are' and 'should be'. However, there are many reasons why as practitioners we should broaden our understanding of child development and child rearing practices and also extend what we know about childhood in other cultures.

First, if we accept that developmental theories are contextually and culturally specific (see Chapters 6 to 10), then we can see that there are limits to how these theories are applied. The concept of the self as connected to others which is common in many African cultures develops as part of a rich socialisation process which begins after birth. The mother of the infant communicates the heritage and kinship lineage, emphasising the uniqueness and nobility of his or her birth. Members of the kinship network live in close proximity to facilitate continued social support including childcare between members, as well as retaining links to ancestral heritage (Gbadesgin, 1998 cited in Owusu-Bempah, 2007). This is in contrast to the early experiences of infants in Western cultures who live in a nuclear family with (usually) two parents and develop attachments exclusively with them.

Attachment theory, based on the work of John Bowlby ([1953] 1965) (see Chapter 7), has been challenged as being overly reliant on Western notions of the family, disregarding the varying ways in which global communities, tribal groups and societies rear children. Notions of reciprocity, and the significant role kinship networks undertake, are marginalised in the dominant child rearing theories with which Western education and science are aligned. Owusu-Bempah (2007) argues that socio-genealogical connectedness is crucial for children's adjustment to separation from their family or kinship networks. This theory can assist us in our interventions with children who have experienced their parents' divorce and separation as well as more permanent 'endings' they experience through international migration, long-term fostering and adoption. Understanding that children need to have information and culturally rich experiences which respect their heritage and history is a relevant issue for children who may be brought up by carers who do not share their culture, and as such care givers and practitioners would need to ensure that children's environments and activities draw on multiple cultural experiences.

Second, ecological models of child development have supplemented more traditional theories of attachment and incorporate the notion of the child interacting with, and adapting to, the environment. Erikson's (1995) life stage development theory, for example, suggests that all children go through similar stages or sequences, and each culture has developed its own way of both monitoring and protecting children as they transit each stage. The ecological perspective (Bronfenbrenner, 1979) also suggests that culture and the environment are important factors to consider and development tasks are adapted to suit the environment in which children are reared. More recently, Owusu-Bempah (2007) suggests that child development relies as much on the environment and the nurturing that children receive as it does on the knowledge and understanding they have about their heritage, cultural origins and the sense of being connected to their genealogical roots (see Chapter 10).

Timimi (2009) illustrates the way in which Islamic cultural practices and traditions assist children through various stages of development. These stages have been linked to children developing an understanding of the importance of truthfulness and co-operation and the sophisticated cognitive abilities to discern, show respect and demonstrate social skills. Once these understandings are attained, the child is deemed ready to move to the next phase of development. Within this culture, Timimi points out, indulgent parenting in a social environment that is characterised by high acceptance, low pressure and low competitiveness encourages children to want to show respect to adults and to demonstrate obedience. This is in contrast to Western traditions of child rearing which often over emphasise the importance of individuality, independence and self-esteem in children.

Timimi (2009) maintains that non-Western societies welcome children's acceptance of a range of childhood behaviours and more consensual and hierarchical interpersonal relationships. Children in these social systems are accepted just for being who they are, rather than what they may become, or in achieving certain developmental milestones. Although it is also important to consider that in many faiths, cultures and practices of child rearing the normality of heterosexuality predominates and so the gendered socialisation of children emphasises the reproduction of normative gendered behaviours (Kehily, 2009).

The third reason for examining child rearing and childhood in other cultures is that if we value one cultural perspective or approach to child rearing over another this inevitably leads to 'ethnocentrism' – the belief that one's own way of life is the only or superior way – and this precludes respect for and integration and/or adoption of traditional practices which have worked well in a range of circumstances and environments. In 1930 the anthropologist Margaret Mead published the findings of her study of the Manus people of New Guinea and suggested that modern societies could learn from the child rearing practices of this tribe:

> the successful fashion in which each baby is efficiently adapted to its dangerous way of life is relevant to the problems which parents here must face as our mode of life becomes increasingly charged with possibilities of accident. (Mead, 1954: 13)

This leads to the fourth reason for challenging what we think of as 'taken for granted' knowledge. In many Western societies the family is generally defined through blood relations and it is this family which is morally and economically obliged to care for children. In many non–Western societies the notion of family is broader than blood relations, and includes reciprocity between kinship and extended family networks that have roles and responsibilities towards children and their siblings (see Chapter 4). Some social work interventions for children without parental care have been criticised for transposing Western models of childcare which marginalise and undermine traditional approaches to caring for children (Everychild, 2012). Abebe and Aase (2007) discuss this in relation to the role of the extended family in caring for children whose parents have died from HIV/AIDS in Ethiopia. Child rearing practices in Ethiopia have long included the traditions of sending children to live with relatives distinguished as 'front line' who are blood relations and 'fictive kinships' defined as:

> people who have no blood relationship with each other but have deliberately created social ties that would enable them to co-operate with each other during normal times as well as during periods of stress. (Abebe and Aase, 2007: 2060)

In the UK in recent years family placement work with children who cannot be looked after by their families has started to recognise the important role that wider familial networks play in supporting children and their parents in caring for children, drawing on these and other indigenous approaches found in Africa and New Zealand.

In order to embrace difference and diversity and benefit from the rich sources of knowledge and tradition it brings, we must at all costs resist drawing on our own experience of childhood and our child rearing as the solitary measure of comparison. Mead's work and the work of other anthropologists who study children and their social and cultural life in their own environments bring a wealth of insights to the differences and variations in childhood, family and community life in a global context. We know from the work of Mead that the Manus people looked after their children very well preparing them for later life when they would be responsible for continuing traditions and practices.

However, what are we to make of children being trained for a harsh rural life and their exposure to the natural environment which Western traditions of child rearing would baulk at as dangerous and irresponsible? Mead (1954) reported that Manus children could eat when they liked, play when they liked and sleep when they saw fit. In a Western context this may be seen as neglectful behaviour on the part of the parents and children exposed to this regime would likely be subject to a battery of psychological tests to assess the immediate and long-term damage to them. It thus falls to practitioners to consider how these different approaches may be used to inform and shape our approach to working with and on behalf of children.

The loss of childhood: work and migration

In Western societies, the 'loss of childhood' is often used to describe the way in which children are denied a childhood as they have to assume adult responsibilities. The notion of the 'loss of childhood' is a term often applied to children who work and, as noted above, a Western ethnocentric perspective on child work has led to international calls for the abolition of child labour. However, the reasons for children working are often associated with structural factors and individual aspiration as well as culture and tradition and so global and national attempts to ban children from the workplace may do more harm than good.

Ethnographic research provides a broad cultural context for understanding childhood and children's agency (Nieuwenhuys, 1996; Manzo, 2005) and has informed research on child labour in developing countries and on child work and migration (Liebel, 2004; Hashim, 2006). These studies highlight the role of extended family networks in supporting children's migrations and desire to work. The longer term benefits of migration to children, their families and communities have also been evidenced. Children in Burkina Faso who left their village to work away from home for a year returned with new skills and were more respected by their elders. The migration was often seen by parents and the returning children as *rites de passage* (De Lange, 2005). Busza et al. (2004) found that children's own aspirations and hopes for a better future for themselves and their families were the primary reasons for them to migrate abroad for work. Children's migrations for work were facilitated by intermediaries and extended family members, who often advocated around payment issues and offered support during their migrations in general.

The intervention of states and their agents and attempts to prevent children from working have had negative impacts, for example: children's economic contribution to their family being reduced or removed; children being unable to pay for their education. Western ideals about childhood which inform these interventions neglect to consider the cultural differences which encourage children to make a contribution to their household and education. Western approaches which simply seek to remove children from the workplace and 'give them back their childhood' undermine the social action which children can and do engage in to address structural economic conditions including their bargaining with employers around several issues including working conditions and wages (Liebel, 2004).

UNCRC and children's rights

The UN Convention on the Rights of the Child (UNCRC) (UN General Assembly 1989) provides the framework for a minimum set of universal standards and entitlements for children and signatory countries agree to base their national legislation on these standards. The UNCRC recognises children as holders of rights, rather than being objects of international law (see Chapter 12). In relation to the focus adopted in this chapter, however, the UNCRC may be criticised on several counts.

First, many countries have used the UNCRC to measure progress in improving the life chances and opportunities for children (Twum-Danso, 2009). However, the UNCRC might actually undermine the expectations, aspirations and ambitions of children who can never hope to realise the idealised rights enshrined in the Convention. The monitoring committee (Committee on the Rights of the Child – CRC) is unable to report on the progress countries are making; developing countries simply do not have the resources to monitor progress and there is a lack of clarity in terms of which national government department is responsible for addressing any issues or challenges which are presented in countries' monitoring reports. The capacity of developing countries to invest in infrastructure services such as health and education is also compromised by the availability of national resources.

A view of children both as having rights but, because of their immaturity and innocence, of being incapable of exercising their rights, ensures that the UNCRC affords children protection as well as equal status with adults (Twum-Danso, 2009). For many children, the realisation of their rights and the Western idealised notions of childhood as a space of freedom, innocence and dependence remain outside their grasp. The situations of children in certain countries have worsened considerably in the last few decades and globally many children lack real economic and political power. Financial and structural interventions and programmes are generated though adult-centred concerns and force children into exploitative labour, while international conflicts, such as in Syria, Afghanistan and Iraq, expose them to poverty and dislocation.

The UNCRC and children's rights perspectives have also been criticised for ignoring the realities of children's lives where they are socio-economic actors. The dominance of developmental discourses which reproduce images of children and childhood as (being in) a state of dependence and immaturity simultaneously mutes the expressions of social action and participation which children demonstrate in the vast range of social institutions which cater to and for them. The UNCRC is individualised and based around entitlement and social justice and is not aligned with the sense of community reciprocity and responsibility which characterises child rearing and concepts of childhood in non-Western contexts (Kjørholt, 2007).

Conclusion

This chapter has outlined key reasons why we should understand the differences children experience growing up in their culture. Studying childhood in different cultures is pertinent given the various impacts of globalisation and the international migratory movements of people who bring with them cultures and traditional patterns of child rearing which are often in contrast to notions of what is accepted as normal in our own cultures. As this chapter has discussed, our understanding of childhood necessarily includes recognition that this is not a fixed, one dimensional phase of life which starts and ends with achieving a particular stage of development; these stages, while arguably universal, are also culturally and socially defined. Instead, we may talk of childhoods and childhood experiences, while also acknowledging that these are socially constructed.

Childhood can be a period of innocence and dependency but this is not the experience of all children and importantly nor should it be. Cultural and traditional beliefs systems which engender responsibility, reciprocity and self-discipline shape different childhoods and ensure the reproduction of culture and community cohesion strategies. Child rearing can take many forms and is defined and fostered through traditional practices and by drawing on a range of development theories, some of which are peculiar to a given culture or social group. The challenge for practitioners is to recognise and embrace these differences and the diversity they bring to childhood experiences.

Questions and exercises

1. What are the most important reasons for studying the cross-cultural context of child development and child rearing?
2. How can we find out about cultural differences in child rearing?
3. What do we mean when we talk about culture?
4. What is 'ethnocentrism' and what is wrong with it?
5. What is 'cultural relativism' and what are the problems with it?
6. What impact does the UNCRC have on child rearing?
7. In what way can the UNCRC help us overcome the problems identified with 'ethnocentrism' and 'cultural relativism'?

Further reading

Bronfenbrenner (1979) provides an introduction to his hugely influential 'ecological systems' theory while Green (2010) critically examines a range of sociological and psychological theories which have informed and influenced child development theory and practice. Owusu-Bempah (2007) raises important issues about the cultural limitations of traditional Western psychological child development theories and introduces socio-genealogical connectedness, a cultural theory of child development which is applied to children separated from their parents and communities. Hendry (2008) provides a wealth of research and case studies which are drawn from her anthropological studies of many cultures and their beliefs. Timimi (2009) engages with globalisation theory and its potential as well as challenging the homogenisation of interventions and practice with children which negate cultural understanding and traditions. Buckingham (2007) examines the globalisation question with regard to children and their media literacy and the Western domination of media which majority world children encounter. Twum-Danso (2009) presents a valuable case study about the UNCRC and its application in non-Western states, specifically discussing the challenges in the realisation of children's rights in Ghana. Finally, globalisation brings the distant to a local audience and the growth of social media in the last decade brings the stories of the lives, experiences and cultures of children across the world into our homes. International organisations such as UNICEF and Save the Children use the media of film to capture the experiences of children, and social media platforms such as YouTube and Twitter provide a window for us to engage with children's worlds. These approaches not only depict the impact on children of war, conflict and invasion but also the lifestyles, cultures and traditions and are useful resources if used critically.

2

CHILDHOOD THROUGH THE AGES

Yordanka Valkanova

Contents

- Introduction
- Towards a conceptualisation of childhood
- The historiography of early childhood
- Conclusion

Introduction

This chapter examines different historical interpretations of childhood and identifies and evaluates some of the salient themes and forms of discourse that have surrounded the major traditions of research into childhood. I will argue that the general tension between the existing social and material world, and the possibility for changing this world, have had an effect on the conceptualisation of childhood throughout the ages. In much previous analyses the emphasis is located on what is commonly perceived as the Western world. Space precludes discussion of childhood outside North America and most of Europe and in an attempt to reach a clear sense of detail, the focus is selective and stresses locations where, due to the documentary sources, the patterns of childhood were more apparent. It is also significantly about education and schooling.

Towards a conceptualisation of childhood

I will begin by offering a necessarily historical account of the scholarly discussion of the notion of childhood. Two centuries ago, it would have been unheard of to begin a discussion with a conceptualisation of childhood. Human infants have a long period of dependency relative to other animals and childhood was defined mainly in terms of biology (James et al., 1998). In the main, children were expected to work as soon as possible which meant that what we call childhood, a comparatively long period free from labour, was unknown. Although ideas about children's education and development are one of the oldest areas of consideration in philosophy (for example, by Plato, Aristotle or Confucius), as many societal expectations of what future adults should look like were involved, the notion of childhood, as we shall see later in this chapter, was an area of intense debate.

Recent interest in the discussion of the ontology of childhood – or what it is – and its epistemology – or how we know about it – can be traced back to the post-modern context of the 1960s, and more precisely to the interest in childhood ignited by the influential book written by Philippe Ariès (1962), a French family historian, entitled *Centuries of Childhood: A Social History of Family Life*. Ariès used representation of childhood in medieval art to support his argument that childhood was socially constructed in the seventeenth and eighteenth centuries, and therefore what it was considered to be varied across time and space; it was not biologically given. Social constructionists, like Philippe Ariès, believe that constructs are social products, but through their application in scholarly or everyday discussions they become real. Nevertheless, since the publication of Ariès's book, this assertion has been questioned by many. Interest in Ariès's work stimulated research into historical interpretations of the concept of childhood and looked at its cultural and social dimensions. However, as social constructionism itself teaches us, the proposition that childhood is constructed implies that it does not exist *per se*.

Nevertheless, it is clear that some historians of childhood have found social constructionism to be a valuable tool that allows them to conceptualise the material properties associated with childhood, their representations and the various discourses of childhood (see, for example, Cunningham, 2005). Moreover, social constructionism has been institutionalised in universities in the sociology of childhood for some time now (see Chapter 3), and it was at Brookline College in New York that the first university programme in Childhood Studies was offered in 1970. Nevertheless, it has not proved possible to produce the meaning of an immaculate conception of childhood.

Grounded in the post-modern discourse framed by the work of Michel Foucault, and later of Bruno Latour, historians such as Neil Postman (1985) employed 'adulthood' as a 'counter concept' to examine the extent to which society sets up markers of childhood, and in addition to this, to acknowledge the proposition that both concepts participate in a semantic battle. Indeed, Postman found it analytically useful to distinguish between them and offered the idea of 'adultisation'. Many early years educators found this especially insightful in the establishment of the concept of childhood (see Cannella, 1997). Postman, following Ariès, further argued that children as young as six and seven were regarded as being no different to adults in the time prior to the Renaissance. The argument was based on the anecdotal assertions that no child rearing institutions were known before then, and that children had no special status in society. Thus, the potential of historical research in enriching the discussion of an ontology and epistemology of childhood requires further exploration.

To understand the impact of the social environment on children's identity construction it is necessary to investigate what mechanisms catalyse the transformational function of the social. The cultural–historical dialectical method grounded in the studies of the Russian psychologist Lev Vygotsky ([1926] 1997), offer a promising tool for social constructionist investigation. More precisely, Vygotsky's theory assumes future-oriented intentions to explain identity development. It would appear that in terms of Hegelian dialectic, from which Vygotsky borrowed his conception, change in identity could be explained through social change and through identifying social contradictions that constitute development. In agreement with Vygotsky's theory, some ideas such as Zelitzer's (1985) proposition that children's 'merit' is determined by the fulfilment and satisfaction their existence brings to parents' lives, and Steedman's (1995) suggestion that childhood is used by the parents as an external locus of their selfhood, are valuable additions to Vygotsky's conception of the self. Seen in this light, childhood would appear as an antagonist to Neil Postman's view, a dialectical contradiction between the view of 'the future' on one side and 'the reality' on the other, as Freud (1924) also observed. Further, in recognition of the child's agency, I would suggest that childhood should be regarded as a process of co-construction of selfhood, a consideration potentially important if we would like to practise the discipline of early childhood studies (see Chapter 3 on the 'new' paradigm).

The historiography of early childhood

Ancient times and the medieval era

Ancient and medieval historiography, as well as the anthropological sciences, suggest that the concept of childhood did not originate with industrialisation or during the Enlightenment, as the social constructionists argued in the 1960s and 1970s. Authors, like Ariès, were apparently unaware of the historical writings on medieval and ancient childhood but interestingly enough, even the general philosophical writing in antiquity made little impact on their thesis.

The Greek philosopher Plato's perception of childhood is a convenient example of a reflection of the discourse that underpinned the contemporary understandings of children and childhood. In his vision of an ideal state, presented in *The Republic*, his most popular book, Plato (2009) paid particular attention to the role that education could have in the functioning of the governance of the state. He postulated three stages of biological and psychological development from early childhood to adult life. At the first stage, from birth to the age of three, the child is vulnerable and needs protection and attention. The adult's general role is to amuse, empower and encourage fearless behaviour. Plato described the nursery stage, from three to six years, as a time for play and storytelling. Education starts at the primary school stage, from six to thirteen years. Then, children should be engaged in the study of a variety of subjects, including numbers, geometry, and cubes, morals, music and gymnastics. Physical exercise, he thought, was good for the mind, body and soul. The third stage, from thirteen to sixteen years, was for more complex studies of mathematics, dialectics and arts. From sixteen to twenty years, young men were to be provided with military training. Plato regarded play as a guided pedagogic principle, applicable in all subjects and ages, and developed the idea that children should not be trained through force, but rather through play. This further indicates Plato's understanding of children's specific educational needs and the role of education in the construction of childhood in the ancient world.

As a result of the influence of the growth of the archaeology of childhood, statements about children as significant social agents in ancient history have become commonplace. Such a display of facts becomes integral to the current historiographical account of multiple contexts, and articulates the complexity of the notion of childhood in antiquity. The representations of childhood apparent in the stories about Theseus, Hercules, Achilles and Perseus (Graves, 1960), and in visual art, discursively construct a sense of heroic identity, built on desirable qualities such as bravery, noble morality, handsomeness and a certain degree of clever ingenuity. However, the archaeological scholarship suggests that there are certain contradictions between the images of the desirable identity offered by the adults, and practices such as play and domestic activities documented in the 'everyday discourse' situated in material culture. Moreover, the female and male staged transition to adulthood is documented in textual sources (see Gaius Petronius' *Satyricon* or Apuleius's *The Golden Ass*), and in ancient Greek and Roman myths.

Medieval childhoods

Relatively precise documented representations of childhood in the Middle Ages do exist today. However, medieval historians suggest that initiation practices, which prepared adolescent girls and boys for their gender roles in their societies, have not been examined closely by the social constructionists. For example, the Jewish Ashkenazy Bar Mitzvah ritual of eating cookies formed as the letters of the Hebrew alphabet and covered with honey could be viewed as a sacred symbol of becoming literate, and therefore demonstrates the power of education in the child's life (for Aleph–Bet rituals see especially Marcus, 1996 and Westerman, 2001). In addition, there were circumcision practices for both boys and girls (see Karras, 2003) that alert us to gender specific expectations in relation to future religious roles in society, but they also could be viewed as consideration of the continuity of childhood, or even as a staged childhood. Furthermore, completely at odds with Neil Postman's thesis that no child rearing institutions existed in antiquity and the Middle Ages, medieval historiography maintains that there were patterns of professional childcare in the Middle Ages. For instance, the rural wet nurses in France (Fildes, 1995) where urban mothers would leave their children in 'baby rooms' could be considered as child rearing 'institutions'. Therefore, to believe that no concept of childhood existed in antiquity and the Middle Ages is a remarkably tenacious misconception.

The Renaissance child

We may gain some insights into the continuity of the traditions of the conceptualisation of childhood by examining the notion of the Renaissance child. The Renaissance was a time of change in Europe, considered largely as taking place between the fourteenth and sixteenth centuries, and initiated in Florence, Italy, with a revival of interest in classical Greek and Roman antiquity. The documentary material of the Renaissance reveals what was special about child rearing in the Renaissance. However, rigid class structure and social stratification in terms of poverty and gender inequality had a profound effect on how Renaissance childhood was experienced.

The admiration of ancient values provided a rationale for the Renaissance conceptualisation of childhood. The main goal of education was a polymath, a *homo universalis*, or a person who was skilled in numerous fields or disciplines (Burke, 2000). Indeed, the mirror of antiquity reflected the concept of the ideal aristocratic child, seen as an essential element in the evolution of society aiming for a new future. In his book *Civil Life*, composed in 1429, Matteo Palmieri, a famous Renaissance humanist, outlined the qualities of the ideal citizen, and among other characteristics of respectable citizenship, Palmieri advocated good parenting. He emphasised the importance of education for active participation in the life of the city. Associating childhood with education, he maintained that education must start from an early age, because early years education was crucial for building human qualities that contribute to the betterment of society. In addition, Renaissance men and women distinguished themselves from the previous generations by developing an ardent interest in the individuality of the child (Klapisch-Zuber, 1987). According to Palmieri, parents must observe children's behaviour in order to understand their development. As he put it: 'The child begins to make known his wishes and partly to express them in words. The whole family listens and the whole neighbourhood repeats his sayings' ([1429] 1825: 233). Furthermore, he maintained, fathers should teach their children the alphabet and reward them with kisses and laugher. This display of a rather 'feminine' notion of fatherhood is apparent in Palmieri's book, but it is also an observable feature in many other sources. One possible explanation of this phenomenon is offered by Klapisch-Zuber (1987) who suggested that the adoration and interest in young children was prompted by the cult of the Virgin Mary, developed in the late Middle Ages. Indeed, a clear psychological distinction between adults and children was embedded in the Renaissance discourses. This public expression of the knowledge of childhood is seen even in the deviation from the humanist paradigm in the work of Giovanni Dominici ([1401] 1927), who designed methods of religious education, where play, including games and toys for children, were included.

Specific social and gender differences were notable in the Renaissance education patterns. While the rich noble families provided their sons with training in rhetoric and instruction in philosophy and ancient languages, the urban merchant classes chose for their boys a more pragmatic mode of education, with an emphasis on learning mathematics to satisfy the practical needs of the family businesses. Girls, generally, were educated at home or in convents. The boys from poorer or artisanal families, as well as the girls, would receive an education that suited their status. The Renaissance childhood, the polymath pattern, therefore, was reserved for the nobles. Also, due to poverty, parental mortality or other unfortunate events, many children experienced childhoods which diverged from the standard biography. However, some children from lower classes were able to become scholars, as is the case with Desiderius Erasmus Roterodamus (1469–1536). Still, the advanced, but ultimately aristocratic ideas of the wholeness of the child, in which personal and civic hopes for a better future were embedded, had an impact on the few, rather than on the many. The concept of Renaissance childhood was pregnant with a dialectical contradiction between the expectations for 'the future' on one side, and the reality on the other.

The child of the Enlightenment

Born in post-Renaissance times, in the seventeenth century, the Enlightenment was a breakthrough in thinking: a cultural movement, characterised by a diffusion of information, secularism and the view that all authority must be subject to the test of reason. The Scientific Revolution played a major role in providing tools for examining the epistemological status of ideas of child rearing and education. 'Nature' was a category that dominated the discourse; however, little attention was paid to the precise use of nature and its cognates. In particular, nature was viewed as a corrective to the general law, an instrument of liberation, a concept around which to create a fairer society (Munck, 2000). Works of philosophers, such as John Locke (1632–1704), Voltaire (1694–1778) and Jean-Jacques Rousseau (1712–1778) challenged ideas grounded in tradition, fostered intellectual interchange and placed emphasis on the rights of humanity. Jean-Jacques Rousseau's ideas conveyed in his book *Emile* ([1762] 1964) placed an emphasis on children's experience, and aimed at educating the natural man. Freedom and love should help children unfold their good nature. According to Rousseau, formal tutoring should be avoided; however, the tutor arranges and manipulates the environment to stimulate self-development. Furthermore, books should play little or no part in the child's education, which he thought should be dominated by doing and activity.

A personal diary written by a boy in the Netherlands, starting in 1791, at the age of ten, and kept for several years, exemplifies the way Rousseau's discourse on natural education served to construct childhood at the time (Baggerman and Dekker, 2009). The child was raised by parents who gave him a Rousseauian upbringing, inspired with admiration for nature and scientific progress. Receiving an education preparing him for the clerical profession, the boy documented in his diary his hopes and desires for the future. However, all he wished was to spend as much time outdoors as possible, and to become a farmer when he grew up. The diary captured insightful reflections of the boy's explorations of the world situated in his paternal home and beyond. His reading, designed for both education and pleasure, was broad and combined classical and religious literature. His growth occurred in a loving, supporting environment, surrounded by siblings, extended family members and friends. This diary shows us an example of establishing childhood as a category in its own right, reflecting the dominant view of child rearing as an agent in changing society.

One of the first systematic contributions to the science of childhood produced during the Enlightenment was the work of Dietrich Tideman (1748–1803), a German philosopher and physician, professor in the University of Marburg. Tideman kept a journal of his son's sensory, motor, language and cognitive behaviour during the first thirty months of the toddler's life. Such attempts to generate knowledge about childhood gave cause for historians to think harder about processes and interactions that were previously hidden.

The Victorian child

The notion of the Victorian child has a variety of aspects. First, Victorian childhood has been interpreted in a Marxist mode (Mabbott, 2010). The arguments centre on the influence the middle classes had during the Victorian age. Queen Victoria's reign (1837–1901) was a time of unprecedented political and economic transformations in England. As a result, the growing capitalist industries needed a cheap labour force to satisfy market demand and achieve international competitiveness. Children were often preferred and employed at low rates and long hours. The Victorian middle classes saw their role as enabling the working classes to realise their potential. Factory reform movements prompted legislative changes to improve children's working conditions and introduce free, compulsory education for all (see the Factory Acts from 1878). Compulsory schooling was highly important in terms of creating a childhood of increasing dependency, and one separated from the world of work (Heywood, 2001). However, the efforts put forward were then applied to satisfy middle-class interests. Such arguments viewed the middle classes as a powerful force, aimed at creating a society based on worth rather than on one's birth (Rose, 1991).

Second, quite often historians of childhood made the effect of romanticism and mysticism on child rearing practices their cornerstone (see Malkovich, 2013; also Austin, 2003). Indeed, the middle classes distinguished themselves from the 'wealthy and corrupt' upper aristocratic classes through constructing individual uniqueness. Authenticity, discovered through a rebirth of the medieval ideas and ideals, was used as an image that represented the middle classes' uniqueness as something that was reliable and genuine, and thus acceptable. Discourses embedded in popular magazines such as *Lady's Magazine* revealed assumptions about the future of society evident in the constructions of the concept of childhood. The romantic themes were also apparent in the discourse associated with the arrival of the German educator Friedrich Froebel's (1782–1852) kindergarten, and his idea of early childhood education in Britain. Froebelian pedagogy, as developed by Froebel and his followers across Europe, America and Asia, involved a number of constituents that help us understand why Victorians found this method attractive. For example, a Froebelian syllabus encouraged reasoning, and stressed 'nature', in relation to the conceptualisation of a rather dialectical unity of subjective and objective. It also emphasised holism over autonomism. Play was the natural activity on which teaching and learning should be based. Especially designed objects – gifts – were used to encourage creativity and technological development while emphasis was placed on self-activity as an essential educational process. These were qualities so important in the Victorian era of social reforms. Although Froebel's method was popular, the kindergartens opened in Britain during that time were largely for middle-class children. Nevertheless, Froebel societies, established across the country, made a very successful attempt to bring Froebelian ideas on early childhood education to the general public through providing a highly professional training to kindergarten teachers, and also through a vast publishing agenda. Romantic discourse, therefore, paved the way for professionalisation of early childhood education and care.

The progressive child

The cultural and industrial transformation at the end of the nineteenth and the beginning of the twentieth century brought about a new conceptualisation of child-hood, in which progressive education had its full share. Progressive education, which is rooted in the works of Jean-Jacques Rousseau, Johann Heinrich Pestalozzi (1746–1827) and Friedrich Froebel, was initiated by John Dewey (1859–1952), an American philosopher, who opened a 'Laboratory School', as he named it, in Chicago in 1896. Previously associated with the romantic ideal, the conceptualisation of childhood now shifted its agenda, under the impact of the rise of psychology and research on children associated with it, and it proclaimed a shared faith in human agency and growing understanding of the value of rationality as an important part of successful social and government reforms. Children were encouraged to construct identities in ways that were associated with socially engaged intelligence and self-activity. Progressivism and the new education gained immense popularity in America and throughout Europe and Asia. Many of Froebel's followers, who embraced the philosophy of the new education, such as Patty Smith Hill in the USA, Emmy Walser in Switzerland and Luisa Schleger in Russia, adapted Froebel's ideas to the new notion of Dewey's school (Valkanova and Brehony, 2006). The progressive ideas of childhood were also accommodated within the Marxist labour school philosophy, elements of which were embedded in the pre-schools established by the Soviet regime in Russia after the Revolution of 1917 (Valkanova, 2009). Dewey's ideas were strongly presented in the discursive construct of childhood in Bolshevik Russia. The Soviet reforms in the early childhood sphere sought to establish an education system, in an attempt to engineer the ideal human being, the 'new man' and the 'new woman'. The consideration of labour as an important activity for the development of the child was proposed by a number of academics, including Lev Vygotsky, who advocated the labour school in his book *Educational Psychology* ([1926], 1997). Like Froebel, he maintained that work emerged from play, especially from manipulative and pretend play. Thus, by emphasising certain traits, the legacy of progressive dis-course brought forth a new construction of the child's role in society and revealed a positive recognition of the child's agency.

The normalised child

The growth of psychology as a science at the end of the nineteenth century, and the subsequent development of an interest in 'intelligence testing', provided those profes-sionals working with young children with a new explanatory model of how diverse phenomena in child development fitted into unifying normative patterns (Beatty et al., 2006; Smuts and Smuts, 2006). Overall, the 'scientific method' came as an alternative to the descriptive 'observation method' that was used until then to make assumptions about developmental characteristics of children. Testing was viewed as a promising device in preparing the child for future adjustment in society. The first attempts to develop reliable scales for measuring capability were made in the middle of the nineteenth century. However, one of the most influential sets of measures was introduced in 1884 and used to identify deviancies in the development of children by the British scientist Francis Galton (1822–1911), a cousin of Charles Darwin. Such tests, as well as the testing method founded by the French psychologist Alfred Binet and his assistant Theodor Simon in 1904, marked the increasing demand for 'meaningful' diversity labels in the search for optimal educational arrangements for challenging children, who deviated from the norm.

Indeed, as a result of the influence of intelligence testing on education practices, statements about normal and abnormal became commonplace. The idea of deviance, viewed as a new trajectory of early years pedagogy, played a central role in the work of the Italian physician and educator Maria Montessori. Montessori applied the above dichotomy to establish the notion of a normalised child, which she regarded as a new level of humanity (Brehony, 2000). As she put it: 'Normalisation is the single most important result of our work' (Montessori, [1949] 1967: 204). Montessori made her idea of the normalised child hugely popular by suggesting some ways in which education acted as a mediator between the child and society (Zener, 1999). According to Montessori, only the normalised child becomes a responsible and productive member of society (Montessori, [1949] 1967).

Unfortunately, the normative childhood was a major impulse behind a controversial episode of human history, that of the eugenics movement. Eugenics, defined by its contributors as the science of 'improving' the human race, emerged at the beginning of the twentieth century. The supporters of the eugenics movement believed that every 'defective' child is a burden. These ideas became popular in the United States and Europe (Mintz, 2004), and many public figures agreed that the state had to remove the 'defects' from the human race in order to build a stronger society. Sadly, the eugenics movement spread to Germany and found a home in Nazi ideology in the 1930s (Searle, 1976; Lowe, 1980).

Most recently, normality has been interpreted in relation to 'school readiness'. This concept, also referred to as 'readiness to learn' and 'readiness for school', has entered the official discourse of pre-school education; with standardised 'readiness assessments' used to identify whether children are fit to enter school in a number of countries. In the United States, in 1994, federal legislation which codified delayed entry to school was passed by the Congress. The validity of the arguments that children should be taught earlier has been intensively questioned in the UK as well (Duncan et al., 2007).

The discourse of normality, therefore, is still influential in constructing contemporary experiences and meanings of childhood. However, it would appear that 'normality' in relation to child development is an unstable concept that relies on contexts for its meaning and interpretations.

Neo-liberal childhood

The neo-liberal child is a concept which conveys assumptions about his or her future role as an agent with the mission to rescue society from obscurity. Neo-liberals attempt to delegate power from the state to the individual and encourage the marketisation of children's services (Hendrick, 2003). In its most general sense, the neo-liberal child is positioned as an active and creative individual. Recently, Vincent and Ball (2007) have offered the metaphor of the Renaissance child in an attempt to explain some neo-liberal middle-class parenting patterns. They highlight parents' enthusiasm for enabling intense extra-curricular support for their under fives. The authors link this passion of parents to a desire to establish clear boundaries between the working and middle classes. Admittedly, Vincent and Ball do widen the scope of the concept of the Renaissance child by referring to 'otherness' in the process of identification, in this case a process of co-identification, if we acknowledge the parents' efforts to help their children establish a middle-class self-definition. Indeed, the construction of the Renaissance child is used as abjection of the working-class self-definition. Skelton and Francis (2012) further show that it is possible to account for the division of education accomplishments on the grounds of masculinity. They apply the concept of the Renaissance child to mount a compelling argument, which shows the important role gender plays in the neo-liberal production of subjectivity. Both examples show that social constructivism can help us reach beyond particular historical contexts, and ultimately transform our understanding of the whole tradition of childhood studies.

Conclusion

This chapter has provided examples of the way in which children have been positioned by diverse discourses concerning the construction of concepts of childhood, schooling and education. As the analysis in this chapter has shown, it would be difficult to find a concept that would not be relevant to any of the contemporary traditions. Significant for understandings of how childhood was conceptualised over the ages is the outline of the subject–object relation offered by Vygotsky's concept of 'the self', which allows us to look at how different identities arose and developed, and how they fitted into the larger system of what is considered as 'manhood'. Consequently, the traditions of studying childhood need to be examined in their continuity. This is why it is so important to pay attention not only to the ideas of childhood produced by the 'great minds', by its nature an ontological exploration, but also to see the development of the traditions in studying childhood as a cumulative process of epistemological understanding.

Questions and exercises

1. Briefly describe some criticisms of Ariès thesis on childhood and family.
2. Why are there many concepts of childhood?
3. What features of the Renaissance child distinguish it from the Victorian child?
4. What do the ideas of Rousseau, Froebel and Dewey have in common?
5. Identify some similarities and differences between Montessori's and Froebel's views of early childhood education.

Further reading

Michael Wyness's (2012) text *Childhood and Society: An Introduction to the Sociology of Childhood* gives a comprehensive account of social constructionism, illustrated with examples drawn from research with children. Peter Stearns's (2011) *Childhood in World History* takes us through international contexts and times, and provides useful insights into the world history of children. Finally, Paula Fass's (2013) edited text, *The Routledge History of Childhood in the Western World*, covers the world's most important events and developments and focuses on how childhood is defined and constructed.

3

SOCIOLOGY OF CHILDHOOD

Nigel Thomas

Contents

- Introduction
- What is sociology?
- Socialisation theory
- Psychologists, sociology and childhood
- Anthropologists, sociology and childhood
- The 'new paradigm'
- Studying children in society
- Recent developments and future directions
- Conclusion

Introduction

The aim of this chapter is to introduce some key elements of the sociological study of childhood and to see how it can help us to achieve a better understanding of childhood and children's lives. We will look first at how sociologists have traditionally studied childhood (or more often, have failed to). We will consider some of the problems with socialisation theory and with views of childhood as a preparation for adult life, and consider the critique of socialisation theory from an interactionist perspective. We will also look at some recent work in psychology and anthropology which has dealt with some of the same issues. We will then review what has been called the 'new paradigm' of the sociology of childhood.

·

The second part of the chapter looks at a number of areas of children's lives to see what can be learned about them through sociological research. This part includes some simple exercises based on research texts, which you can do by yourself or with a partner.

What is sociology?

In general terms, sociology is concerned with the study and understanding of *social processes* and *social structures*. These may be studied at a number of different levels:

1. The 'macro' level is concerned with demographic patterns (population and so on) and with global changes in social patterns and relations.
2. The 'meso' level looks at social institutions – the family, work, leisure, schooling and so on.
3. The 'micro' level studies social interaction – sometimes in a very detailed way.

The key organising concepts used by sociologists include:

1. Ideas about social relations – authority, social cohesion, conflict.
2. Social categories such as class, ethnicity and gender.
3. Broader social processes – for instance, 'modernisation'.

Early European sociologists such as Emile Durkheim and Max Weber, at the beginning of the twentieth century, were interested in social organisation and in the relationship between the individual and society. They asked questions such as: 'What binds people together in social groups?', 'How do people come to share belief systems, and why are belief systems different?', 'Why do people obey authority?' In the middle of the century the dominant voices were American – sociologists such as Talcott Parsons who aimed to build a comprehensive theory that would explain everything from global social structures to the detail of social relations in terms of *function*, and critics such as C. Wright Mills who were more interested in the conflicts of interest between different groups in society. In the 1960s a branch of sociology developed that was concerned much more with social interaction – for instance, Erving Goffmann studied how individuals present themselves in society, and Harold Garfinkel focused on the minute detail of interaction, in particular the rules governing conversations.

More recently the dominant voices have included Michel Foucault, with his complex exploration of power and knowledge and, in Britain, Anthony Giddens. Giddens' central preoccupation is with one of the key tensions in social theory, which he characterises as the relationship between *structure* and *agency*. On the one hand, our lives are governed by social structures and social processes, so that it might be said that we have no existence outside society. On the other hand, these social structures and processes are nothing but the result of human activity. So which is prior – do individuals create society, or does society create individuals? Are we free agents, or are our lives determined? A moment's reflection may suggest to us that in some way both statements are true – but the task then is to explore the relationship between them. Another sociologist of major significance is Pierre Bourdieu, who has responded to this question by developing the concept of *habitus*, by which he means the layers of acquired dispositions from which we draw our routines for thinking, speaking and acting. As he puts it, *habitus* is 'embodied history, internalized as a second nature and so forgotten as history … the active presence of the whole past of which it is the product' (Bourdieu, 1992: 56). So we do make choices, but from a repertoire which is more or less limited by our social positioning and experience.

What has all this to do with childhood? From a cursory reading of much of the sociological literature, one might say 'very little'. Many of the standard texts have in the past had no index entry for childhood, or if they have it has been simply a cross-reference to 'the family' or 'education'. This has begun to change, but only slowly, and it is rare to find any book of general sociology with a chapter on childhood. The questions about social structures and social processes have not been asked specifically in relation to childhood; the questions about social relations, authority and power have not been applied to adult–child relations; and the social categories used – class, ethnicity, gender – have not been extended to include childhood. Where we do find books in the past about 'the sociology of childhood' they tend to be specifically about the process of *socialisation* (for instance, Bossard and Boll, 1966). Children are studied, not as actual and participating members of society, but as *prospective* members. What is interesting about children, from this perspective, is the process by which they are made into adults.

Socialisation theory

A child is born into a world that already exists. From the point of view of society, the function of socialisation is to transmit the culture and motivation to participate in established social relationships to new members (Elkin, 1960: 7).

The central idea of classical socialisation theory (note it is often spelt 'socialization', especially in American texts) is that we are in effect *produced* in childhood by social conditioning. It is only through this process that we become *social*, and because human beings are essentially social animals, this means that it is only through this process that we become fully human. More specifically, we are socialised into understanding and accepting the conventional norms and values of our particular society, and into becoming part of a culture; we are socialised into our particular role(s), social status and social class; and according to some our own individual personality is also the result of a socialisation process. The idea that individual personality is the result of socialisation was put forward most strongly by the behaviourist J.B. Watson, who wrote:

> Give me a dozen healthy infants, well-formed, and my own specified world to bring them up in, and I'll guarantee to take any one at random and train him to become any type of specialist I might select – doctor, lawyer, artist, merchant-chief and, yes, even beggarman and thief, regardless of his talents, penchants, tendencies, abilities, vocations, and race of his ancestors. ('Behaviorism', 1930, quoted in Elkin, 1960: 46)

Socialisation theory identifies a number of socialising institutions or 'agencies of socialisation': principally the family, the school, the peer group and the mass media. Some theorists distinguish between *primary* socialisation, which includes the laying down of fundamental characteristics of personality, basic values and so on; and *secondary* socialisation, representing the continuing effect of group interaction and culture on our habits, thoughts and values throughout life. Most of the attention tends to be on primary socialisation; some conceive of this as taking place throughout childhood and into adolescence, while others confine it to early childhood. For instance, Bossard and Boll argue that 'the social conditioning of the personality during the first years of life is of primary importance ... the basic patterns of personality are laid during the period of childhood', and that 'the sociological processes of personality formation can best be studied during the earlier stages' (Bossard and Boll, 1966: 7–8). From this perspective the family is clearly the most important socialising institution.

Socialisation theory came under increasing criticism in the 1970s from sociologists who took an *interactionist* approach, such as Norman Denzin. Studies of adult–child interaction and child–child interaction, and reflections on them, led to dissatisfaction with 'socialisation' as a model for what was observed to take place. Mackay (in Waksler, 1991) uses the example of an observed interaction between a child and a teacher about the child's understanding of a story, to show how the teacher treats the child as incompetent throughout in respect of the task, but how in fact an analysis of the interaction shows that it presumes a high degree of competence on the child's part to make it work.

Matthew Speier puts the criticism forcefully. He argues that traditional interests in development and socialisation have neglected 'the interactional foundation to human group life':

> The traditional perspectives have overemphasised the task of describing the child's developmental process of growing into an adult at the expense of a direct consideration of what the events of everyday life look like in childhood ... the intellectual and analytic position of sociologists is essentially ideological in the sense that they have used an adult notion of what children are and what they ought to be that is like that of the laymen in the culture. (Speier, 1976: 170)

In other words, it is the job of sociologists to bring distinctive analytic tools, and an open and enquiring mind, to the study of childhood, rather than simply recycle conventional ways of seeing and understanding.

Psychologists, sociology and childhood

The key organising concepts of developmental psychology (see also Chapter 6) are very different from those used by sociology – concepts such as *learning*, *conditioning* or sometimes *unfolding*. Most discussions of child psychology start with Piaget, whose key insight was that the child learns to understand the world better as she or he progresses through a series of developmental stages characterised by increasingly sophisticated conceptual schemes. Margaret Donaldson and others revised Piaget, using research that showed that children were able to understand concepts that had been thought to be beyond their reach, if the tasks were presented in a way that 'made sense' to the child. This linked with the ideas of Vygotsky, an early contemporary of Piaget, about the 'zone of proximal development' – the area into which the child is able to move on with support.

There are other differences between Piaget and Vygotsky. Piaget is sometimes thought to view the child as a solitary learner, and Vygotsky is seen as adding a social perspective on the process of development. In fact Piaget did emphasise a social element in learning, but he also seemed to see what was learned as in some sense *natural* – there is a natural progression from one conceptual framework to another, which it is the child's task to discover. For Vygotsky what the child learns is above all a culture, and therefore the role of other people in learning is indispensable. Building on these ideas, a number of psychologists including Jerome Bruner, Martin Richards and Paul Light began to explore the social dimension of psychological development in more depth.

It might on the face of it appear that psychology has converged with socialisation theory, in that it has gone from seeing development as a natural process of 'unfolding', or of the child discovering what is already there in the world, to a focus on the process of transmission of cultural norms and ways of seeing and doing things. In fact the new psychology is very different from traditional socialisation theory precisely because of what Piaget taught us about the child's active participation in learning, and Vygotsky's revelation of the processes of dialogue and negotiation inherent in cultural learning. These strands in the theory are much more convergent with, for instance, the interactionist perspective of Denzin than they are with classical socialisation theory. Barbara Rogoff (1989) writes of 'the joint socialization of development by young children and adults'; she argues that the child from the earliest age is an active participant in the socialising processes of development (see also Chapter 7).

Anthropologists, sociology and childhood

Anthropology is literally 'the study of people'. It developed as an academic discipline in the late nineteenth and early twentieth centuries. First in the field was physical anthropology (the study of variations in physical types around the world), followed closely by cultural anthropology (the study of habits and mode of life), from which developed modern social anthropology with its focus on kinship relationships and belief systems. From the beginning anthropology developed a distinctive method based on close observation and detailed recording in 'field notes', known as *ethnography*. The focus was very much on 'primitive' or 'tribal' societies – people who are 'different' from 'us' in what were thought to be significant ways, although in recent years the same methods and concepts have been applied to Western societies.

Like sociologists, anthropologists for many years were backward in applying their concepts and methods to children and childhood. Anthropologists tended to rely on adult informants, to study adult behaviours and beliefs, to be interested in the social networks of adults, and to share adult concerns with their subjects. In 1973 Charlotte Hardman delivered a paper which argued that children were a 'muted group' who had been ignored by anthropologists and given no voice in the anthropological record. She suggested that children deserved to be studied in their own right as a group with their own *culture*, their own network of relationships, their own beliefs and their own values (see Hardman, 1978). Gradually more and more anthropologists have turned their attention to childhood and the lives of children. This has been important for the study of childhood for the following reasons:

1. It implies looking at children not just as developing adults or adults-to-be, but as people in their own right.
2. It implies looking at children not just in their families or at school, but in their peer group, in work, in interaction with other children and with adults both within and outside their family group.
3. It implies taking children's own explanations and their beliefs seriously, in the same way that anthropology respects adults' accounts of their own culture.

The 'new paradigm'

The contemporary sociology of childhood is distinguished by two central ideas. The first is that childhood is a social construction. Historical and cross-cultural studies have shown us that the 'nature' of childhood is enormously variable according to the social context, and that childhood is in a sense socially defined and created. The biological processes involved in growing up and getting older are real; but the pattern and the meaning of these changes are structured and mediated by society and culture. The second idea is the increasing recognition we have seen in sociology, psychology and anthropology that children must be seen as social actors in their own right. Children's lack of active presence in society has been mirrored by their lack of active presence in theory.

These two insights, that childhood is a social construction and that children are social actors, are the key elements in what has been called a *new paradigm* for the sociology of childhood.

> A paradigm is a theoretical framework, a fundamental way of understanding reality that underlies specific theories; for instance, when Newton's physics based on gravity was overturned by Einstein's physics based on relativity, a new paradigm was created in which different questions were asked and different kinds of answers were given. This new sociological paradigm was clearly articulated by Alan Prout and Allison James (1990).

They describe it as an 'emergent' paradigm, because it is not yet fully developed but still in the process of formation. Prout and James identify the distinctive features of the new paradigm as follows:

1. Childhood is understood as a social construction. As such it provides an interpretative frame for contextualising the early years of human life. Childhood, as distinct from biological immaturity, is neither a natural nor universal feature of human groups but appears as a specific structural and cultural component of many societies.
2. Childhood is a variable of social analysis. It can never be entirely divorced from other variables such as class, gender or ethnicity. Comparative and cross-cultural analysis reveals a variety of childhoods rather than a single and universal phenomenon.
3. Children's social relationships and cultures are worthy of study in their own right, independent of the perspective and concerns of adults.
4. Children are and must be seen as active in the construction and determination of their own social lives, the lives of those around them and of the societies in which they live. Children are not just the passive subjects of social structures and processes.
5. Ethnography is a particularly useful methodology for the study of childhood. It allows children a more direct voice and participation in the production of sociological data than is usually possible through experimental or survey styles of research.
6. Childhood is a phenomenon in relation to which the double hermeneutic of the social sciences is acutely present (see Giddens, 1976). That is to say, to proclaim a new paradigm of childhood sociology is also to engage in and respond to the process of reconstructing childhood in society (Prout and James, 1990: 8–9).

This perspective has produced a great deal of stimulating research, much of it in Northern Europe and Scandinavia. At the same time sociologists in North America have continued to develop research and theoretical work in understanding childhood. Corsaro (2011) made a substantial contribution to thinking about the relationship between *structure* and *agency* in childhood, with his concept of *interpretive reproduction*. The idea behind this concept is that children work to reproduce themselves, their culture and their social relationships, but that in doing so they interpret them for themselves. As he puts it:

1. Children actively contribute to cultural production and change.
2. They are constrained by the existing social structure and by societal reproduction.
3. Within these constraints, children's participation is *creative* and *innovative*.

Studying children in society

The methods used by sociologists to study children in society vary in relation to a number of different factors, in particular the level of analysis:

1. At the *micro* level research is concerned with the study of children as individuals or in social interaction. Research at this level may be qualitative or quantitative, but is more likely to be qualitative. Such research often favours the use of methods of communication that are accessible to children and elicit their competence – for instance drawing, writing and using stories.
2. At the *meso* level research is concerned with the study of children's lives on a larger scale, in relation to institutions such as school, family or the media, in activities such as leisure, sport or travel, or in terms of 'problems' such as poverty, illness, disability, homelessness, divorce and separation, crime, abuse, pornography, war and famine. Such research tends to use survey methods, statistical data or the compilation of findings from a number of 'micro' studies.
3. At the *macro* level research is concerned with the study of children's lives on a larger scale. This might include historical changes in the nature of childhood and in patterns of child–adult relations, or global and generational relationships between children and adults. This research uses statistical data, or analytical and theoretical work based on existing theory or research.

Most of the research we will consider in this chapter is at the *micro* level, because that is where most of the work in the new paradigm is done. However, there is also some important work being done at the other levels.

Children and their peers

Corsaro (2011) uses his concept of 'interpretive reproduction' in studying children's *peer cultures*. For Corsaro, peer culture is defined in interaction, but this takes different forms at different ages. Children's early participation in peer culture is mediated by adults – for instance, it takes place in pre-school settings to which parents arrange access for their children. In these settings children first encounter ideas of sharing and collective ownership, and of friendship. The central themes in children's 'initial peer cultures', according to Corsaro, are: attempts to *gain control* of their lives, attempts to *share* that control with each other, and the importance of *size* and of the idea of 'growing up'. He explores these themes through studies of play routines, of children's protection of their interactive space, and of sharing routines and rituals. Corsaro shows how children learn about autonomy and control through challenging and mocking adult authority and by confronting fears and conflicts in fantasy play. In contrast to the traditional psychologist's view of children's innate capacities unfolding as they mature, or the traditional sociologist's view of roles and values being inculcated by external social institutions and processes, he emphasises the importance of viewing such phenomena as conflict and friendship as *collective* and *cultural* processes.

In later age stages Corsaro focuses on social differentiation: gender differentiation, status hierarchies, core groups and 'rejected, neglected or controversial' children. He advises caution about assuming that these processes are the same everywhere, arguing that cultural differentiation is always important. However, some themes tend to be consistently present: for instance, in pre-adolescent peer cultures he notices the different patterns and issues that typically emerge in the seven to thirteen age group, the greater stability of friendship patterns and the phenomenon of 'best friends', of friendship groups and alliances and of gossip.

Children in families

Sociologists might ask different kinds of questions about children in families, depending on what paradigm they are using. For instance, someone using a *socialisation* paradigm might ask questions like: How are children socialised? How do families 'raise' children? What difficulties do parents encounter in 'raising' children? What are the different patterns of family socialisation? How does family socialisation interact with school and peer culture?

Someone working within a *family sociology* paradigm might ask questions such as: Why do parents have children? What is the significance of changes in family composition? What are the different patterns of family life and how are they experienced?

On the other hand, for those following the new paradigm of the sociology of childhood the salient questions might be: What is the meaning of 'family' to children? How are the lives of children in families negotiated? What is the relationship between children's lives in their families and children's other social worlds? What is the relationship between how childhoods are negotiated in families and the social construction of childhood?

Exploring the implications of the new paradigm for the relationship between childhood and family sociology, James and Prout (1996) draw attention to the ways in which children construct and manage their identities differently in different settings – school, family, peer group and so on – and also in response to the particularities of individual families. O'Brien et al. (1996), in the same volume, report on research into children's views on what counts as a family. Presented with vignettes of different household types and relationships (married couples with and without children, unmarried couples with children, single parent and step families, separated parents), children were asked to say whether these counted as families or not. Younger children tended to emphasise conventional criteria such as marriage, while older ones placed more stress on quality of relationships. Children's views tended to reflect their own personal experiences, and in discussion children were prepared to adapt their views in response to each other's arguments. Smart et al. (2001) studied children's perspectives on divorce and separation, and used children's accounts of family life to show how childhood is changing and the status of children in families is being transformed.

Regardless of the approach taken, some features will be important from any perspective, illustrating common concerns of all sociologists:

1. Changes in family life.
2. Changes in family composition.
3. Children's place in families.
4. Children who are outside families.

Children in school

Now let us look at the kind of questions that sociologists might ask about children in school. The socialisation paradigm produces questions like: How are children socialised in schools? How do schools inculcate social values and norms in children? How does school socialisation interact with family socialisation? Traditional sociology or social policy approaches, on the other hand, might lead one to ask: What is the nature of the school as an institution – how does it operate, where does the power lie? What are the objectives of schooling, and how are they effectively achieved? What is the effect of schooling on social inequalities (in terms of class, gender, ethnicity)?

In the new paradigm the questions that are asked tend to be: What is the meaning of 'school' to children? How are the daily lives of children in schools patterned? How is the experience of children in schools structured in terms of, for example, age, gender, ethnicity? How is meaning negotiated in the classroom between children and teachers? What is the relationship between children's lives in the classroom and in the playground? How does school have an impact on transitions in children's lives? What is the relationship between how childhoods are negotiated in schools and the social construction of childhood?

To take just one example, Seung Lam and Pollard (2006) analyse the transition from home to kindergarten, in terms of children crossing a cultural boundary and, in effect, commuting between two cultural settings. The authors present a conceptual framework for understanding children as agents in the transition, employing elements from socio-cultural theory such as the concept of *rite of passage*. They conclude that:

> children bring to kindergarten what they learned (including patterns of strategic action, competencies, child identity) at home. They are active in making sense of, responding and adapting to the new kindergarten classroom in terms of separation from caregiver, transition programme, physical environment, play and learning, rules and routines and relationships. This is a dynamic and continuous negotiation process of adaptation. (Seung Lam and Pollard, 2006: 137)

There is a growing body of sociological work on children's relationship with communications and digital media – television and video, the internet, mobile phones and so on (see Chapter 5). Reflecting the preoccupations of the 'new paradigm', much of the focus is on how children use these new media to extend their social networks and their interaction with a wider world, and sometimes on how they adapt technology to new purposes and in unexpected ways. Research also addresses questions about 'risks' to children from electronic media, reflecting public concern in this area. Key authors include Buckingham (2000) and Livingstone (2002) and Marsh et al. (2005).

Children, place and environment

There is a healthy interchange between sociology and geography in the field of childhood studies. The growing sub-discipline of 'children's geographies' has its own (eponymous) journal and many other publications (for example, Holloway and Valentine, 2000). Research here is concerned with children's use of place and space, which, as sociologists and anthropologists have noticed, are key factors in shaping children's lives. Related to this is a substantial body of research and practice around children's relationships with their environments and the part which children may play in environmental change at all levels. The journal *Children, Youth and Environments* is of key significance here.

Recent developments and future directions

The flourishing of new sociological approaches to childhood has tended to be dominated methodologically by small-scale research with children in different settings, and theoretically by an emphasis on children's agency. At the same time there have always been sociologists whose focus was on the bigger picture, and who continued to ask questions about the structure of society and children's place in it (for example, Qvortrup et al., 1994; Qvortrup, 2005). More recently there has been increased questioning of the emphasis on 'agency' (Oswell, 2013) and a renewed interest in the ways in which children's lives are more or less determined by social structure, a growing interest in the concept of *generation* and the relationships between generations (Alanen and Mayall, 2001; Mayall, 2002) and in ideas of children's citizenship (Cockburn, 2013).

In relation to early childhood, there is a growing body of work that applies sociological theory to the understanding of young children's lives, especially in day care and early education settings – see for instance, Clark et al. (2005). There is also continuing interest in the cross-cutting of the category 'childhood' with other kinds of social stratification – gender, ethnicity, (dis)ability and class. Lareau (2000; 2003) has shown in particular how in the USA social class is hugely significant in shaping the patterns of children's lives in the present, as well as their opportunities in the future. There is no reason to suppose that the same does not apply in the UK and other countries.

Other writers are concerned with the ways in which childhood is changing, and the impact of social change on childhood. Lee (2001) argues that as adult lives become more fluid and uncertain the old dichotomy, with childhood seen as a preparation for adult life, becomes increasingly irrelevant, and that arguments for seeing children as 'being' rather than 'becoming' need to be reframed to reflect these changes. Prout (2005) questions the adequacy of a purely social understanding of childhood for understanding lives that are so shaped by technology, and argues that we need to conceptualise the construction of contemporary childhood in ways that take account of the inseparable part played by artefacts and machines. Nonetheless, a sociological framework is still of key importance in understanding contemporary childhood.

Conclusion

We have seen how sociology can help us to understand children's lives and children's place in society in a fuller and more rounded way – especially a sociology that takes as its starting point that children are people and participants in social life, not just 'adults in the making'. The insights being developed by sociologists have a lot in common with recent work in psychology and anthropology and to some extent there has been a convergence between the disciplines. However, the distinctive sociological emphasis on social structures and social processes remains important.

It has only been possible in this chapter to introduce some of the ideas behind contemporary sociological research in childhood, and to look at a few examples of the work that is being done. If you want to find out more about the ideas contained in this chapter, do make use of some of the further reading suggested on the next page.

Questions and exercises

Exercise 1

Take an example of research into children's peer culture and relationships – for instance, the paper 'Children's negotiation of meaning' by Nancy Mandell (1991). Ask yourself (or your partner, if you are working in a pair) the following questions:

1. What aspects of children's lives does the study address?
2. What is the main purpose of the study (what is the author trying to achieve)?
3. What concepts or categories are used in the paper?
4. How might we develop this analysis further?

Exercise 2

Read an account of some research into children's experience of families – for instance, Chapters 1 and 3 in *Understanding Families: Children's Perspectives* by Virginia Morrow (1998), or Chapter 3 of *Connecting Children: Care and Family Life* by Brannen et al. (2001). Ask yourself (or your partner, if you are working in a pair) the following questions:

1. What are the main aims of this research?
2. What concepts or ideas do(es) the author(s) start with?
3. What are the principal methods used in the research?
4. What are the most important findings of the research?
5. What questions are left unanswered (or unasked)?

Exercise 3

Read a research paper on children's lives in school – for instance, the chapter 'Making sense of school' by Margaret Jackson in Pollard (1987). Ask yourself (or your partner, if you are working in a pair) the following questions:

1. What are the main aims of this research?
2. What assumptions does the researcher start with concerning children's lives in school?
3. What methods does the researcher use?
4. What are the most important findings of the research?
5. What questions deserve to be explored further?

Further reading

For sociology in general there are many sound introductory texts, such as Giddens (1993). For the sociology of childhood specifically, the most useful sources are probably James and Prout ([1990] revised edition 1997), Corsaro (2011), Waksler (1991 and 1996), Jenks ([1996] revised edition 2005), James et al. (1998) and Wyness (2012). There are useful research collections edited by Mayall (1994), Pollard (1987) and Qvortrup et al. (1994). A good general book on childhood in society is Hill and Tisdall (1997). For a brief overview of trends in developmental psychology, see Woodhead (1999). For those interested in exploring some of these issues further, Thomas (2002) attempts to link the sociological understanding of childhood to issues of children's rights and participation.

4

THE GLOBALISATION OF EARLY CHILDHOOD EDUCATION AND CARE

Helen Penn

Contents

- How childhoods vary
- Caution about culture
- International perspectives – a view from the global South
- The globalisation of early childhood
- Conclusion

How childhoods vary

One of the most puzzling aspects about how children grow and learn is the importance of context. Take a very simple example, that of food. All children need to eat, but how their food is obtained and prepared, when they eat, what they eat, where they eat, how they eat and what they are taught to think about what they eat is almost entirely determined by where they live and whom they live with. A child living in the UK is likely to have a diet high in processed foods, will graze throughout the day and be petulant about many foods; a child in Italy will be encouraged to savour food and consider its consumption as a social occasion; a child living in France will eat to the clock; and a child living in Spain will also eat to the clock, but the clock will be set to a much later time. The staple food – the bulk – that children eat may be based on wheat, rice, sorghum, barley, maize, millet, potato, yam, or many other kinds of crop. Children living in nomadic groups in very cold regions of the world will thrive on a diet extremely high in animal fat. Those accustomed to one type of food may view another staple food as inedible (I shall never forget being given raw whale blubber in Northern Canada by an Inuit woman, and being told that it was 'soul food' and she always felt better for having eaten it. I could barely swallow it!). In some parts of the world there is a surplus of food, but in many parts of Africa or Asia, a child will typically experience hunger as an everyday aspect of life and will never have a choice about the food she or he eats.

Food preparation and consumption, as Goody (1982) pointed out in his classic anthropological text, are deeply embedded in cultural and geographical contexts. This extraordinary variation in food and eating habits means that it is difficult to set nutritional or any other kind of norms that are possible for all children to follow, except at the very broadest level of generality. Children need certain levels of essential nutrients for growth – although even that minimum level is debatable – but the form in which they obtain them is anything but standard.

The example of food consumption is a metaphor for other aspects of young children's lives. The argument being put forward in this chapter is that while there are some very general features of early childhood, all of them are shaped and modified by cultural context. So much so, that rather than understanding the generalities, it may be more useful to understand the particularities. Bruner argues that 'perhaps even more than with most cultural matters, childrearing practices and beliefs reflect local conceptions of how the world is and how the child should be readied for living it' (Bruner, 2000: xi).

This chapter explores some of these local conceptions of childhood, and then considers how and if they are recognised and acknowledged in the early childhood literature. Ideas and descriptions about early childhood, which are mainly European or North American in origin, are misused to describe childhood everywhere. In describing this process of globalisation in early childhood, that is, the spread of ideas about child development derived from understandings and research in European and Anglo/American countries, I use the terms 'North' (Euro-Anglo/American countries/developed countries/the minority world/rich countries/Western countries) and 'South' (Africa, Latin America, Asia/developing countries/the majority world/the poor countries).[1]

---

[1]These categories are not clear cut: there are some countries which do not fit easily into any categories (e.g. Brunei or Qatar). In most countries there is a small elite who are rich even though their country is poor; and, conversely, there are rich countries with some very poor people indeed among their citizens. The terminology shifts with fashion; relatively few people now use the words 'First World' and 'Third World' which used to be the standard terminology. However, the shorthand of 'North' and 'South' is commonly used to describe the large differences that exist between the richest and poorest countries of the world.

Caution about culture

Right at the beginning I want to give a word of caution about using the word culture. 'Culture' is itself a difficult concept, on the verge of being unusable. 'Culture' describes a set of related beliefs and practices of a particular community, although not everyone in the community will understand or practise them in the same way (see Chapter 1). These beliefs and patterns are manifested in surface differences – diet, games, clothes, eating habits and folklore – but they also draw on implicit and embedded assumptions and values, what the historian Catriona Kelly (2007) calls the 'elusive invisible network'. 'Culture' is usually thought of as belonging to a particular geographical space or country, but from a historical perspective, people are always on the move and calamity is always round the corner. As Nederveen Pieterse (2004) has claimed in his book *Globalization and Culture: Global Melange*, 'cultures' are always porous, hybrid, shifting and contradictory and reflect the frequently forced interchanges of ideas and practices that take place over time. For instance, almost all European countries now have large immigrant populations, and even small countries like Ireland or Finland are changing rapidly, so much so that one commentator has coined the phrase 'super-diversity' in order to describe the changes that have occurred in Europe (Vandenbroeck, 2007). On the other hand, in many countries, the nation state is a relatively recent historical imposition, a reflection of past battles and especially of colonialism and empire. Countries like India, Nigeria, Sudan or Iraq or the (now ex) Soviet Union, brought together – sometimes very unhappily – many very different communities, traditions, languages and religions, and talking about a particular country and its traditions is almost meaningless, such is the arbitrariness of national boundaries. So culture is rarely static or unchanging, it shifts from one generation to the next, from one place to another, and always varies over time. It is displayed differently by one individual to another, but is (just about) coherent enough to be recognised and at least partly described. Rather than use the word 'culture' in this chapter, I prefer to use words like 'local community' or 'cultural context' even though these words, too, should be used with care.

International perspectives – a view from the global South

Much of the work in child development focuses at a micro level, about the understandings and interpretations of what children can do and the kinds of explanations that can account for their behaviour. LeVine and New point out that the study of child development has been largely confined to 'America, Europe and other Western countries who comprise less than ten per cent of all children in the world' (2008: 1).

In their recent book they try to redress the balance by collecting together accounts of anthropologists working in unusual (to us) corners of the world. They sum up these accounts as follows:

- Every human society recognises a distinction between children and adults and the age-linked emergence of children's abilities to learn, work and participate in community activities. At the same time societies vary considerably in the way they interpret children's readiness and ability to do these things.
- Schooling is a relatively recent idea. Until the late twentieth century most children participated in economic and domestic tasks; most were involved in multi-age children's groups; and the distinction between work and play was often blurred.
- Childhood environments differ considerably. In material terms, where children live, whether they have water, sanitation and shelter, what they eat and whether they have enough, what kind of healthcare is available to them; and in cultural terms, who they consider to be part of their family, how they speak and who to and in what language, etc. will vary tremendously between societies.
- The ideas of parents are strongly influenced by culture; norms of parenting reflect and help to sustain the moral standards of a community. Parents have strong views about following these norms, yet they also reinterpret them and adjust them to changing circumstances.
- Children are not passive recipients of cultural practices – they are active interpreters. They acquire the conventions of communication and norms of behaviour that give them entrée to their local social world, but they use and modify them for their own purposes.

Some examples of differences

LeVine and his colleagues are trying to broaden the traditional discussions about child development and to point out the narrowness of the knowledge base. LeVine comments elsewhere (LeVine and New, 2008) that what characterises child rearing in the global North is an extraordinary focus on the individual, on an individual child's needs and wishes and preferences. Over and over again advice to practitioners in early childhood guidance manuals stresses that: 'Every child should be treated as an individual', 'each child is unique', 'each child is different', etc. But there are other communities and contexts where the reverse holds true, where collective obligations are prioritised over personal concerns, and what is important is how a child fits into her or his community. Children are, in the words of the anthropologist Paul Riesman, 'learning to be a relative' (1992: 146). Briefly, some alternative understandings of childhood are outlined on the next pages.

1 Individual – collective

The dichotomy between individual and collective, the extent to which the self is seen as a separate bounded individual, or as gaining identity only from nests of relationships, is one of the classic insights of anthropology (Geertz, 1973). In many societies people define themselves in terms of their relationships – as a mother or father or as a brother or a son or a daughter or a sister, or from a village or a community, but never as a unique and isolated individual making his or her own way in the world. In the global North we think it is important to respect individuality; but for others being an individual – on your own and without the constant intimate presence of others – is the worst kind of punishment. From this perspective, sharing is not something which must be painfully learnt – as in so many pedagogic manuals – but something which is as natural and as human as talking and thinking.

Part of this collective ethos is that children are seen as contributors to the household. Everyone pulls together and small children have tasks to do like everyone else. Serpell (1993) described how in his Zambian village, all children were trained to run errands from the moment they could toddle. Paula Fass (2007), the American historian of childhood, has argued that over time, one of the biggest shifts in the interpretation of childhood has been in the amount of time children are expected to work and contribute to the household, or play and be non-contributors to the household. In rich countries the notions of helpfulness and obligation are rarely seen as an integral part of childhood and child rearing. There is a fraught debate around working children. As Fass remarks, some commentators consider it to be morally wrong to 'exploit' children, whereas another approach might value children's satisfaction and pride in being able to contribute to the economy of their household, and be part of a family or community group however young, and whatever the arduous nature of their tasks.

2 Family – community

As suggested above, life for many young children is intensely collective. Families are diffuse and fused into their local community. Wole Soyinka, the Nobel Prize winning novelist, in his autobiography *Ake* (Soyinka 1989) describes his early childhood in Nigeria, and his experiences of compound life. As a small child he was carried on the backs of many women, and as child he remembers some backs as being decidedly more comfortable than others! His book offers a vignette of an utterly communal, although gendered life, where mothers and children were almost, but not quite, interchangeable. Many children slept with his mother in her room, sharing the bed and mattresses on the floor, some of them relatives, others children of friends or visitors who were staying for shorter or longer periods. Other accounts of African childhoods give a similar picture.

By contrast, childhood in rich countries takes place in small and isolated families. It is not uncommon for a mother to say she has never been separated from her child and has had a continuous responsibility for looking after him or her until nursery offers some relief from the 'burden' of parenting. Families are tiny, inward-looking and self-preoccupied; children themselves have become the individual possessions of their parents, a 'lifestyle' choice and a personal investment which may be wisely or unwisely handled. This particular dyadic and narrow model of parenting is continually re-echoed and re-emphasised in the services we provide and the way we write about them, for example in the burgeoning literature about parenting classes.

3 Independent – dependent

These ideas of community, collectivity and family, and the notion of the inseparability of the child from everyday life, produce an understanding of the child as physically and emotionally independent and robust, at least far more so than would be allowed in developed countries. The Australian aborigine writer Kim Scott, remembering his own Noongar childhood in his prizewinning novel *That Deadman Dance* speaks of the confidence, inclusiveness and sense of play of his *community*, and how this produces a confident outward looking childhood and an appreciation of reciprocity (Scott, 2010). The idea of attachment and the need for a continuous, sensitive caregiver is part of the understanding of infancy in most countries where there is a literature about child development. But in many societies the child is one among many; a child of the community as well as of the family, a person who gives as well as takes. This quotation which I have used many times, because it indicates such an extraordinary difference of interpretation of early childhood, is from the anthropologist Alma Gottleib, who studied the Beng community in the Côte d'Ivoire:

> Chantal, a feisty two-year-old in our compound disappeared from sight many mornings, only to emerge at noon for lunch and then around 5pm for dinner preparations. Although she was too young to report on her day's travels, others would chronicle them for us; she regularly roved to the farthest ends of this very large village and even deep into the forest to join her older siblings and cousins working and playing in the fields. With such early independence even toddlers are expected to be alert to dangerous wildlife such as snakes and scorpions and they should be able to deal with them effectively – including locating and wielding a large machete. (2004: 32)

What Chantal is doing is nearly inconceivable to Euro-American childhood experts preoccupied as they are with adult supervision, physical risk and the need for protective environments in a child's long dependency. Despite her lack of language, at two years old Chantal is secure, autonomous, curious and very capable. She has a sense of direction and a sense of time. She can use tools effectively. She and her parents are confident that if there is any kind of hazard she is sufficiently competent to deal with it, by recognising and avoiding it or by calling upon others to help her.

4 The world of spirits

A pervasive theme of folklore is the spiritual world. Dead ancestors and animal spirits are part of the understanding of family life and community obligation. The joyous Mexican festival of the Day of the Dead in November is a celebration when the dead come back to life and party with the living. There are street festivals in which people wearing skeleton masks parade with the crowds and effigies of the dead as skeletons, which are surrounded by the offerings of the living. In many cultures, children may inherit the spirit of departed relatives. This animist view, nature as a continuous cycle of birth and rebirth, rather than a belief in the distinctiveness and uniqueness of an individual human life, sits alongside more traditional Christian or Muslim beliefs. In Mexico, for example, the Day of the Dead has been absorbed by the Catholic church and fused with the Christian festival of All Hallows or All Saints day; the dead party inside the church as well as outside of it. This animism seems to represent the antithesis of modern scientific thought, although the contemporary ethicist and philosopher Pete Singer (2001) has also suggested that human life is over-valued when viewed as part of the spectrum of living things on earth.

5 Gender, patriarchy and gerontocracy

Wisdom and knowledge come with age and experience (even if energy disappears!). Especially in a society where almost all communication is oral and little is written down, an old person dying is like losing an irreplaceable book. It would be unthinkable for a child to be rude or cheeky to an older person, to ignore the embodied experience and wisdom that an older person represents. Lack of respect is often seen by many people as part of the damage and corruption imposed by the prosperous societies in the global North.

By the same token, gender differences are often marked. Women in many places are seen as living a different life from men, and these differences are enshrined in language, in dress, in visible as well as invisible ways. 'Equal opportunities' may be an improbable goal in many places. Girls and boys are treated differently, although this does not necessarily mean that either is inferior. It is regarded as *practical* to see them as having different roles.

6 Language

Language encapsulates culture and community. Many languages have more tenses than English, and this in turn requires more subtlety in the interpretation and recapitulation of events. Other languages are also more heavily gendered, and have many modes of addressing other people when English just relies on 'you' as a main form of address. Some languages are rhythmic and musical, more given to recitation and performance than to private and solitary reading.

Language structures thinking and communication. In one way, children in the South might be regarded as fortunate; often they grow up in bilingual or multilingual environments (Bloch, 2007). Depending on the language you speak, you see and hear the world differently. English is a global language, 'the new Latin' as it is sometimes called. Because English is now so ubiquitous, most native English speakers see no reason to learn another language. But if ways of thinking and relating to other people are built into language, those who are multilingual are automatically at an intellectual advantage. Those who come from oral traditions tend to be acute listeners and to remember accurately. Pre-school and schooling experiences in the North sometimes damage rather than enhance language learning by inappropriate methods, including a failure to appreciate the importance of oral learning, rhyme, chanting and recitation.

7 Being artistic

In the global North artistic self-expression is seen as a form of individuality, rather than as a community undertaking. So in nurseries we value the daubs of young children as a first attempt at self-expression and expect children to be proud if these daubs are displayed to others. But if the artistic expressiveness is a communal one – for example, weaving or choral singing or intricate group dancing requiring complex rhythmic performance, or indeed writing down an ideographic language which requires careful calligraphy on paper – if it is a skill which requires considerable mastery of form before it is recognisable, then it makes little sense to praise ineffectual efforts. Instead what counts is what Barbara Rogoff (1992) has called 'guided participation', a very careful instruction in the correct way to do things and gentle discouragement of what is wrong. It is learning by example, by watching and imitation, rather than by jumping in spontaneously without any understanding of what may be required. The different learning and artistic strategies used in different cultures for young children remains to be explored.

8 Resourced or resourceless

Every year in the UK various organisations provide estimates for the cost of bringing up a child. Even leaving aside the question of paying for childcare, children are deemed to be expensive. They need lots of baby equipment – cots, pushchairs, nappies, high chairs, play pens, baby clothes, baby books, etc. – and lots of toys, graded according to the child's stage of development. Costs run into tens of thousands of pounds over a few years. Imagine then bringing up a child with no resources, no specialised equipment and not even running water, electricity or sanitation. This is how an overwhelming majority of children in the world are brought up. Their parents make do with the natural resources around them, and children themselves soon become inventive with what exists in their immediate environment. This could be regarded as an impoverished life, and some children are undoubtedly restricted and limited in their opportunities but there are also those who claim that living in the everyday world, whatever it happens to be, is enriching: and on the contrary, being brought up in a sanitised miniaturised child-world is impoverishing. The extraordinary film *Buddha Collapsed Out of Shame* (Makhmalbaf, 2007) about childhood in Afghanistan beautifully illustrates these tensions between the independence and vitality of young children left to get on with their lives, and the truly terrible circumstances of everyday life in a war torn country, which they must negotiate. A number of writers have also tried to track the increasing consumerism of childhood and relate it to changing concepts about play and child rights (Katz, 2004; Fass, 2007).

The globalisation of early childhood

The above examples are just a few of the ways in which child rearing is perceived as profoundly different in the global North and the global South. But globalisation in the sense of the spread of English and the spread of ideas about child rearing takes little notice of such intricacies. In a recent article (Penn, 2011) I track the use of ideas about early childhood by international non-governmental organisations such as the highly influential World Bank, UNICEF, UNESCO, Save US and other agencies which promote early childhood care and education programmes in the global South. There is a remarkable similarity among them, a promotion of standard precepts about children's understanding and children's needs drawn almost entirely from child development research in the global North, especially from the USA.

However, even if there is a misguided attempt to apply ideas about early childhood from the global North to the global South without due consideration of circumstances, nevertheless there is also a crisis for women and children occurring in the global South – partly as a result of economic globalisation. There has been enormous internal and external migration, from rural areas to the cities, and from poor countries to rich ones. The result has been what Pearce (1978) called 'the feminization of poverty'. There are now many millions more women coping on their own, mainly in jobs in the informal sector, as market traders or as servants, or in the 'hospitality trade' in the shanty towns or favelas of big urban cities. As a result, almost every big city in the global South now has extensive numbers of private for profit nurseries or crèches, but these are largely unregistered and unrecorded (Woodhead et al., 2009; Penn, 2013). There is a good deal of rhetoric, much of it from external donors such as the World Bank, about the need for early childhood interventions (Garcia et al., 2008), but the reality is that most provision in the South is provided by private entrepreneurs. People pay for what they can afford, and poor people who cannot afford to pay fees either receive a very poor service or none at all. Jody Heymann (2002), for example, undertook a large survey of the needs of working mothers across a number of countries in the South, and pointed out that up to 30 per cent of working mothers leave their children in the care of siblings, or unattended, with the result that the accident rates for such children are shockingly high.

So, on the one hand, there is pressure to provide early childhood education and care (ECEC) and, on the other, there are local traditions and contexts which suggest that models from the North may be inappropriate. The debate about the need for ECEC generally draws on evidence from the North and ignores the circumstances of most children and the arrangements that are made for them. Yet the view of what constitutes good practice in the North is regarded as being a sound principle for export everywhere in the world. Steiner-Khamsi (2004) argues that educational ideas are never straightforwardly transferred from one country to another, but there is always a mixture of adaptation, incorporation and resistance, according to local contexts. These local contexts are not 'untouched' relics of a traditional past, but are themselves the product of many past influences and current socio-demographic pressures. She uses the example of education in Mongolia to describe how educational reforms prescribed by the World Bank and other international agencies were nominally accepted because of the much needed money being offered, but the reforms were in fact subverted or not implemented. For example, she describes attempts by donors to introduce 'community participation' into schools, but there is no word in Mongolian for 'community'. The nearest translation was 'home-place' which rendered the planned interventions by donors meaningless. The reforms just petered out. Although donors are willing to export ideas, the process is rarely reciprocal, and local ideas are regarded as quaint rather than warranting serious attention.

My own experience is that many of the pre-school interventions sponsored by donors in ex-Soviet countries or countries within the orbit of the Soviet system like Mongolia were subverted because the Soviet system of kindergartens was so very much more comprehensive than anything that was offered in its place. Parents and staff were justifiably resentful of the reforms (parent and toddler groups, part-time provision, etc.) that were being introduced (Penn, 2005). More recently, I describe attempts by the World Bank to introduce early childhood initiatives in Namibia, which bordered on farce because the donors were unable (or unwilling) to comprehend the extent of inequality and poverty in the country, and assumed that a combination of private entrepreneurs and community action would provide a viable Euro-American style early childhood service (Penn, 2008).

For the most part globally imported initiatives and reforms do not work, or do not work in the way that donors anticipate, and the usual response is to blame the recipients. They 'lack capacity' or they are deemed too lazy or dishonest to undertake the work that is necessary. A detailed analysis of policy discourse, policy implementation or actual practice is rarely undertaken to explain the frequent lack of success or lack of sustainability of initiatives. As Popkewitz argues, a detailed examination of global knowledge transfer in education would incorporate a critical view of what knowledge exists on the topic (for example, is it as scientific and empirically based as its adherents claim?) and 'how patterns of thought move through and are transmuted in different layers of the local and global systems' (Popkewitz, 2004: ix). From an early childhood perspective this would involve asking critical questions about practice; for instance, in the example cited from South Africa, how do ideas about child-centred practice sit alongside ideas about learning self-restraint and respect? Or as Jones and Vilar argue in relation to their work in Peru for the *Young Lives* project:

> It is critical to unpack culturally specific understandings of core cultural concepts with which a research project is engaging (such as 'children' 'family' and 'work') and how these are subject to competing interpretations and reinterpretations in societies undergoing rapid social, political, economic and demographic transitions. (2008: 45)

All governments in the North have a national framework for the development and support of ECEC. The emphasis, the financing and the effectiveness with which ECEC is delivered vary considerably, even among rich nations but the commitment is unmistakable, and much of it has to do with providing childcare for working mothers (NESSE, 2012). In the global South the issue of working women has now also become critical. But most of the aid efforts focus on the need for nutrition or parental education (Anglo-American style) for poor communities (Penn, 2013). The challenge is to recognise the range of childhood needs that globalisation has produced in the global South, without reproducing the formats of early childhood services in the global North.

Conclusion

This chapter has discussed the expectations and understandings about young children's lives and what they need and how they should be treated in different cultural contexts. Most of the academic and policy discussion that takes place in early childhood does so in a Euro-American context which is untypical of the situation of most children and does not recognise the range of variation which exists.

This lack of recognition of local context is important because when donors try to export ideas about early childhood (or education more generally) to countries in the

South, they often fail. The chapter also discusses some of the ideas about how knowledge transfer takes place, how ideas – in particular, ideas about early childhood – get transferred and who by, and how the recipients incorporate and transform the projects that are often foisted upon them.

The issue of early childhood in the South is also important because of the very rapid urbanisation that is taking place in most countries of the world. Just as there has been a minor revolution about women's roles in the North, which has prompted the development of ECEC as much as concerns about educational opportunity, so there is a rather different kind of revolution going on in the South. Life in the slums and poor quarters of big cities in the South is very problematic, and the kind of care and education offered to young children who live in potentially hostile environments is a matter of real anxiety for anyone concerned about childhood.

Questions and exercises

1. What do you think are the most important values in bringing up young children? Do you think they would be shared by everyone you know?
2. What difference do you think poverty makes to the way young children think of themselves?
3. Do you think policy makers and practitioners in the global North should know more about the lives of children in the global South? If so, what kinds of issues should they be aware of?
4. Do you think young children in the South know about the lives children lead in the UK? If they do know, what would they think about the standards of provision that we have?

Further reading

The UNESCO handbook on early childhood care and education gives an overview of early childhood throughout the world, with chapters from many contributors from the global North and the global South. It is downloadable from the UNESCO website.

5

CHILDHOOD IN THE DIGITAL AGE

Jackie Marsh

Contents

- Introduction
- The digital age
- Media dupe or media savvy? Media discourses of childhood in a digital age
- Children's engagement with digital technologies in homes and communities: an ecological perspective
- Future developments
- Conclusion

Introduction

This chapter reflects on the nature of childhood in the digital age. It offers an overview of research that has explored children's use of digital technologies in homes and communities and considers the main issues that have emerged regarding this use. The chapter also reflects on potential future developments in this field. The aim of the chapter is to provide an introduction to the key issues and debates in a topic that frequently gives rise to misconceptions, and to signal the research questions that might be important in the years ahead. First, however, the nature of the digital age is considered.

The digital age

The social, cultural and economic changes wrought over the past forty years as digital technologies have developed at a fast pace are wide-ranging. The technological transformations, which have created a paradigm shift as significant as the move from oral to written cultures, or the invention of the printing press, have impacted upon a range of areas. In terms of the economy, the employment landscape has changed exponentially since the industrial age. Given that numerous tasks are now automated through technologies and many aspects of business can be conducted over the internet, a globalised approach has been adopted by many industries, leading to the outsourcing of tasks to countries in which workers have a lower standard of living than Western countries. New forms of employment have arisen in the West, such as the development and management of social networking sites. The 'dot-com bubble', which occurred during the last years of the twentieth century, led to the commercial growth of the internet and e-commerce. The internet is becoming increasingly important in the financial landscapes of ordinary households, with a major shift to online banking and purchasing. The Organisation for Economic Co-operation and Development (OECD, 2012) report that 32 million UK consumers shopped online in 2011 for goods and services including food, clothing, music and holidays.

In a similar fashion, digital technologies have had a major impact on our social and cultural lives. Individuals are now networked with a range of other people, both known and unknown, through the use of text and video messaging, and social network sites, such as Facebook and Twitter. Developments in digital photography mean that it is simple to store and send photographs using the internet and the ease of using digital video recording apps on mobile phones has encouraged many to record and upload videos to video sharing sites such as YouTube. The music industry has been transformed through the ability of consumers to access music digitally, leading to the widespread practice of downloading music illegally. These phenomena have been characterised as signalling a move from consumerism to production, with the growth of the 'produser' (Bruns, 2006) – the individual who is both a consumer of mass media and a contributor to media culture through the production of digital texts and artefacts (see Chapter 18 for the use of such technology in research with children). It is inevitable that these changes have had an impact on young children's lives and in this chapter, an overview of young children's access to, and use of, digital technologies will be provided. First, however, we need to consider the broader social and cultural context which shapes this use. The following section considers some of the key messages given about young children's use of technology by the mass media.

Media dupe or media savvy? Media discourses of childhood in a digital age

Moral panics (Cohen, 1987) regarding children's use of technologies are a recurrent feature of media coverage in the UK. These have included concerns about the perceived negative impact of media on children's emotional, physical, social, linguistic and cognitive development, in addition to worries about the way in which children are becoming positioned as economic targets by multinational companies (Kenway and Bullen, 2001). Moral panics have always occurred in relation to the cultures of children and young people, as Springhall (1999) outlines, but the intensity with which media reports have dealt with this matter in the twenty-first century indicates that there has been a material shift in the moral panic discourse. For example, in January 2008, media reports of a spate of teenage suicides in a town in Wales led to headlines such as 'Police fear internet cult inspires teen suicides' (Britten and Savill, 2008), as many of the teenagers involved had used the social networking site Bebo. Police subsequently denied that they had identified the internet as a key common component across the suicides, but this did not prevent extensive media coverage which suggested that this was the case. Similarly, in 2012, the controversial views of the psychologist Aric Sigman were reported widely in the press. Sigman suggested that, based on his review of research on young children's use of television, children under three should not view screens because of concerns about obesity and impact on brain development (Boseley, 2012). While Sigman's views have being challenged by scholars such as Professor Dorothy Bishop from Oxford University,[1] who has suggested that his use of research data is not robust, they resonate with conservative bodies such as the American Academy of Pediatrics, who also warn parents about the dangers of young children's screen viewing and propose banning television viewing for children under two.

Luke and Luke (2001) suggest that the reactions against children and young people's engagement with new technologies can be traced to the growing gap between the communicative practices of adults and youth, with the former based on traditional print-based practices and the latter moving increasingly to on-screen reading and writing. This argument has some resonance with the discussions regarding 'digital natives' and 'digital immigrants' (Prensky, 2001), in which children are characterised as being digitally competent, in contrast to many adults who struggle with the use of new technologies. However, this notion has been subject to widespread critique, given that age does not always correlate to confidence with and use of technologies (Thomas, 2010). Lankshear and Knobel (2011) have used the concept

---

[1] http://deevybee.blogspot.co.uk/2011/09/how-to-become-celebrity-scientific.html (accessed 14 June 2013)

of 'mindsets' to describe this disjuncture, with the term 'insider mindsets' characterising learners who recognise the changes to communication that technologies have brought and thus transform practices accordingly and the phrase 'outsider mindsets' indicating individuals who have a propensity to continue to treat the world in much the same way as before, with digital technologies failing to promote fundamental changes to practices. The discussion in relation to mindsets enables a nuanced account of generational differences in the digital age, recognising that age cannot always be tied to confidence with and use of technologies.

It can be seen, therefore, that media representations concerning childhood and technology present conflicting messages. On the one hand, children are viewed as digital experts, navigating a range of technologies with intuitive expertise, and on the other they are positioned as the innocent victims of a globalised and highly commercialised technology industry, driven to zombified or aggressive cognitive states through an addictive use of various media. Inevitably, the reality is very much more complex, with patterns of use and competence shaped by individual and social circumstances. The next section of the chapter considers the research on children's use of digital technologies and identifies the ways in which the context of this use is all-important.

Children's engagement with digital technologies in homes and communities: an ecological perspective

Despite the widespread prevalence of digital technologies as they have developed over the last decades, there is still a limited amount of research on young children's engagement with it. There is a small number of large-scale national reviews of young children's use of technologies in the US and England (Rideout et al., 2003; Marsh et al., 2005; Rideout and Hamel, 2006; Ofcom, 2012). A larger number of smaller-scale studies have been conducted across a wide range of countries including Scotland (Plowman, et al., 2010), England (Marsh, 2010a; 2010b; 2011; Wolfe and Flewitt, 2010), Australia (Davidson, 2009) and Qatar (Savage, 2012). In the following discussion, an ecological analysis of children's use of digital technologies is outlined, drawing from the work of Bronfenbrenner (1979), in order to understand the way in which different domains of practice shape children's experiences with digital literacy. Ecological theories indicate that attention needs to be paid to the inter-relation of a range of factors which shape individuals' engagement with technology. Nardi and O'Day (1999: 49), for example, suggest that an ecology is 'a system of people, practices, values, and technologies in a particular local environment'. Interaction with technology is never context-free and the relationships between social agents, tools, technological practices and local contexts are complex and determine the nature of its use.

Bronfenbrenner (1979) suggested that the environment in which a child grew up impacted upon his or her development in a number of ways. He argued that individuals exist within overlapping ecological systems that are 'a set of nested structures, each inside the next, like a set of Russian dolls' (Bronfenbrenner, 1979: 3). The first of these structures is the microsystem; this is the immediate environment surrounding the child or children under study. It refers to the immediate interpersonal interactions with significant others in the environment and this environment can vary according to the unit of analysis, e.g. it can be the home, a classroom and so on. The mesosystem links two different microsystems together. An example of this might be the relationship between homes and early years settings. The third level, the exosystem, consists of settings in which children are not active participants but which impact significantly on children's lives. For example, parents' workplaces might have a significant impact on child rearing practices. Finally, the macrosystem is the larger cultural and social context that impacts on the way in which children live. These systems are not intended to operate in a hierarchical manner but instead overlap to create complex and inter-related planes of experiences which inform children's development.

Microsystem

Microsystems are the smallest unit of analysis and are environments that are closest to the child. The microsystem of the home is one in which, in general, the majority of children in the UK are offered access to digital technologies and are supported in the use of these technologies by parents. For example, in the 'Digital Beginnings' study, which involved surveys of 1,852 parents and carers of nought to six year olds and 524 early years practitioners in England (Marsh et al., 2005), many parents reported that they scaffolded children's learning on a range of technologies, including computers and games consoles (such as PlayStation 2 and the Xbox). Children were keen to engage with technologies in ways that fostered social interaction with parents and siblings. Technology was frequently mentioned by parents as a means of developing shared cultural understandings and for families who spoke languages other than English, the media offered a significant means of engaging with both language and culture. Therefore the home as a microsystem was, for the majority of children, a rich site for technological experiences, although there was a significant minority of children who did not have access to a wide range of technologies at home. In the microsystem, socio-economic status (SES) is a significant factor in the types of technological activities in which children engage. Patterns of access differ across technologies, with children in social groups C2DE, working-class children, being less likely to have access to one or more computers or laptops in the home, but more likely to own console game players and computer games than children in more affluent families (Marsh et al., 2005). Across all social groups, however, the microsystem of the home offers a range of opportunities for children to become competent in the use of a variety of digital technologies. Ofcom (2012), in a survey of children's media use across the UK, report that:

- 97 per cent of children have access to digital television at home.
- 91 per cent of children live in homes with access to the internet through a PC, laptop or netbook.
- 66 per cent of three to four year olds and 78 per cent of five to seven year olds use a DVR/Blu-ray player/recorder.
- 44 per cent of three to seven year olds and 79 per cent of children aged five to seven use gaming devices (e.g. games console/handheld games player).
- 37 per cent of three to four year olds and 58 per cent of five to seven year olds access the internet at home using a PC, laptop or netbook.
- 32 per cent of three to four year olds and 33 per cent of five to seven year olds use a radio set.
- 13 per cent of three to four year olds and 22 per cent of five to seven year olds use a mobile phone.
- 12 per cent of three to seven year olds use a portable media player.
- 9 per cent of three to four year olds and 11 per cent of five to seven year olds use a tablet computer (e.g. an iPad).

Children acquire a range of skills and knowledge as a result of this engagement, including skills in the use of hardware and software and the ability to read/view and produce multimodal, multimedia texts. In Table 5.1, a summary is provided of the range of texts that young children view/read and write using digital technologies in the home.

A further noteworthy aspect of children's experiences of digital technologies in the microsystem is the fact that texts are connected across various media. For example, if a child is interested in the television programme *Peppa Pig*, he or she can also encounter the narrative on a DVD, computer game, internet site or iPad app. Kinder (1993) developed the concept of 'transmedia intertextuality' to describe this process. This phenomenon means that there are various entry points to any text and children's understanding of narrative may be developed in complex ways, as various media offer specific experiences of narrative. For example, a child might listen to a story retold from a third-person viewpoint, such as a narrator, and then encounter the same story through a computer game in which he or she can adopt a first-person perspective. Children's play across digital media is also multi-layered and the toys and artefacts linked to favourite media texts enable children to replay characters and stories in a creative manner.

Table 5.1 Young children's digital viewing/reading and writing in the home

Technology	Texts read	Texts written
Television/DVD/Blu Ray	• Words and symbols on remote control • Electronic programming guide • Text included in games on satellite/cable channels (red button) • Words, signs and symbols in programmes and advertisements	
Computer	• Alphabet on keyboard • Text on websites • Text instructions for programs • Text in programs	• Random typing of letters • Writing of name • Writing lists, letters and stories • Typing words/phrases in online sites such as games and virtual worlds
Handheld computers	• Text instructions for programs • Text in programs	
Mobile phones/PDAs	• Text on screen, e.g. text messages • Signs and symbols on the keypad	• Pressing random letters, pretending to text • Choosing emoticons
Electronic games, e.g. LeapPad	• Alphabet on keyboards and text on screen, e.g. alphabet and word games	• Typing in letters and words
Console games	• Text instructions for programs • Text in programs	
Musical hardware, e.g. CD players/radios/ karaoke machines	• Words and symbols on operating systems • Words on screen with karaoke machines	
GPS technologies, e.g. TomTom	• Text on screen, e.g. navigation page	
Other domestic electronic devices, e.g. microwave, washer	• Words, signs and symbols on the devices	

Children are spending increasing amounts of time online and some of them are gravitating to social networking sites that are aimed at older age groups. In a recent study of the online activities of 180 primary school children aged five to eleven (Burke and Marsh, 2013), it was found that a third of the five to eight year olds stated that they had their own Facebook page, yet the entry age for this site is thirteen years.

However, on further examination, it was clear that the children's Facebook pages had been set up by their parents and that the parents were managing and overseeing the children's use of the site, including their friendships. Seven-year-old Katy, for example, reported how her mum was aware of her of Facebook page as she had set it up and managed her friendship network. Katy used the site to chat to family members, such as her aunties. In this instance, it would appear that Facebook was a family literacy practice and that this was a relatively safe use of the site by Katy and her family. Nevertheless, it cannot be assumed that all parents would have effective oversight of their children's use of the site and there are certainly concerns about introducing children to practices such as online gambling, which are prevalent in such social networking sites. This, therefore, is an example of the way in which children's use of digital technologies can be both productive and potentially counter-productive, dependent upon other aspects of their ecological system.

Mesosystem

In Bronfenbrenner's model, the mesosystem connects the interactions between two microsystems. Children, therefore, can interact with individuals, text and artefacts which relate their home experiences to another microsystem, such as neighbourhood and community groups, or schools. Bronfenbrenner (1979) uses the example of a child learning to read to illustrate this. Children's reading ability is influenced by a number of factors, including the nature of the relationship between home and school attitudes to, and practices of, reading. Children who are supported in learning to read at home are more likely to succeed in the task at school. In relation to young children's use of digital technologies, the mesosystem may provide opportunities for children to extend their digital competences or it may limit them, according to the context. For example, some studies have indicated the way in which early years settings and schools do not always support young children's engagement with digital technologies and this may have a detrimental effect on children's confidence and progression in digital literacy (Levy, 2011). A stark example of the disjuncture between contexts in the mesosystem can be found in Wohlwend's (2009) account of children from print-centric early years classrooms in the US, who longed to play with the new technologies and media that were part of their everyday experiences outside of school. She offers an account of one child who, thwarted by the limitations of digital technologies on offer in the classroom, drew his own mobile phone:

> He gave an oblong piece of paper rounded corners and penciled a 3 by 3 array of squares below a much larger square to represent a numeric pad and an LCD screen. Additional phone features (receiver, compact size) were emphasized by adding play actions: he held

the opened paper flat in the palm of his hand, raised his hand to his ear, talked into the paper for a few seconds, then snapped it shut with one hand, and tucked it into his pocket. (Wohlwend, 2009: 125)

The five- to seven-year-old 'early adopters' in Wohlwend's study used paper and pencil to create mobile phones, iPods and video games in order to bring their own digital microsystems into this early years setting. However, Johnson (2010) suggests that even when children have access to new technologies in the classroom, it might not always lead to enthusiastic engagement. She conducted a survey in which thirty-eight, six- and seven-year-old children in Australia completed a ten-item rating scale on internet use at home and school. Her findings indicate that 'children who frequently use and enjoy the Internet at home avoid using the Internet at school, particularly with respect to email but with the exception of playing games' (Johnson, 2010: 290). The reasons for this pattern could be varied and include sensitivity to the differences in contexts across home and school; for example, children may prefer the privacy of home for the purpose of sending an email, or it may be the case that the technological hardware and software in homes and schools are very different and thus children do not easily transfer their practices across the domains.

Exosystem

The exosystem, according to Bronfenbrenner, consists of settings and contexts in which children are not active participants but which impact significantly on children's lives. This could be traced in the 'Digital Beginnings' study (Marsh et al., 2005) in relation to parental employment outside of the home. It was clear from the data that parents who were in upper and middle social class[2] groups were significantly more likely to state that they knew more about computers than their children. These were parents who were often in employment requiring use of computers, or who had experienced some form of post-compulsory education in which computer use was necessary. Many working-class parents had not had the same opportunities to develop confidence in the use of computers outside of the home and they reported less confidence in the use of computers. Twenty per cent of working class parents in the survey felt that they knew less than their nought- to six-year-old children about computers, whereas this was the case for only five per cent of middle- and upper-class parents. These differences have led to concerns about digital inclusion, as social

[2]Class is determined using the National Statistics Socio-economic Classification scale (NS-SEC) e.g. working class is defined as Analytic classes 6–8.

class differences may impact negatively on subsequent attainment in technology-related activities at school, just as Bronfenbrenner (1979) argued could be the case with regard to reading.

Macrosystem

The final nested structure in Bronfenbrenner's model, the macrosystem, refers to the wider social and cultural context in which the child operates. As the previous discussion in the chapter suggests, influences on this level may be negative, given the emphasis in the mass media and popular writings of many cultures on the perceived harmful effects of the use of technology on children's social, physical, linguistic and cognitive development (e.g. Palmer, 2006). In Plowman et al.'s (2010) case studies of young children's use of technology in the home, some parents expressed anxieties about children's use of technologies, including concerns about the possibility of over-use, perhaps as a result of this mass media bias. In an Australian study (Fox et al., 2011) three teachers and ten parents of pre-school children were interviewed about their views of technology. Teachers were positive about the use of technology, but the mothers were opposed to its use at home. It is of interest that eight of the ten mothers had experienced university, three at postgraduate level. It may be that issues of social class were pertinent here, as in other studies, middle-class parents have been more likely to comment on the potentially adverse effects of technology, while many working-class parents were resistant to negative messages in the media and emphasised the importance of their children developing digital skills relevant for employment in the twenty-first century (Marsh et al., 2005).

Drawing from an ecological conceptual framework (Bronfenbrenner, 1979), it can be seen that children's experiences of technology are shaped by the contexts in which they live, both the contexts in which they are present and those external contexts that shape their immediate environment. Each child's engagement with technology is unique to his or her ecological system and this will inform how children's engagement with technology is shaped. Thus, the task of basing decisions about policy and practice on this information is a challenging one, and one which demands careful assessment of these interlocking structures and systems if early years settings and schools are to respond appropriately to children's technological experiences. Early years educators need to ensure that they attend to the specific circumstances of individual children's interactions with technologies outside of early years settings in order to offer them appropriate provision. For example, practitioners could develop a knowledge base that enables them to determine the confidence levels of parents in the use of technologies and where they identify families in which levels of confidence are lower, offer support such as family learning activities that extend parents' abilities to use technologies alongside their children. In this way, the digital divide that exists due to the interaction of access to technologies with other significant factors, such as the historical technological experiences of family members, can begin to be bridged in some way in order to promote technological competence and expertise in digital literacy for all.

Future developments

Recent research in the field has identified the way in which many young children are increasingly drawn to online play (Burke and Marsh, forthcoming). For example, there are a number of online virtual worlds that offer children opportunities to adopt a virtual avatar (an online representation of self) and live in a virtual home. These virtual worlds, many of them commercial enterprises, such as Disney's Club Penguin, enable children to play games, collect virtual coins to buy virtual artefacts and engage in conversation with other users of the site through chat facilities. Studies indicate that young children engage in a similar range of play activities online as they do offline and that these spaces can be productive sites for social engagement (Marsh, 2010a; 2011). Further, the online sites are connected to a range of offline texts and artefacts. Club Penguin, for example, can be played online and on games console platforms, such as Nintendo, but can also be found in the form of comics, books, toys and clothes. It is not possible, therefore, to make a clear distinction between children's online and offline play and digital literacy practices, as the boundaries between these domains are becoming blurred in the digital age. This trend will develop further in the years ahead, with products developed that will enable children to transfer records of play and activities undertaken offline into online contexts, and vice versa. It is not beyond the realms of possibility, for example, that children will be able to capture an offline play episode using a wearable device, such as a video camera in the form of a watch or necklace, and then transfer the video to an online environment, being able to add to the digital text and extend the play episode. Research will need to focus on the impact of this development on the nature of children's imaginative play and storytelling.

In the years ahead, it is also conceivable that children will be able to play with a wider range of interfaces that facilitate imaginative play. For example, console games have become easier for young children to access because of the nature of sensory technologies, which do not require a handset in order to navigate screens. Games that replicate offline movements online are increasingly popular, such as dance games or games of tennis and bowling. Currently, these games are played using a television screen but, inevitably, similar games will be made for smaller and more mobile platforms, such as tablets, in the future. This will enable children to play interactive games in a range of spaces and they will be able to project themselves into imaginative virtual scenarios. Studies would be required that enable early years educators to understand the impact of these developments on children's play across space and time.

A further development will relate to the increasing role that robots will play in children's lives. Robots are becoming more sophisticated and are already being used in a range of offline contexts, such as servicing the needs of older people. In years ahead, children will be able to program and play with robots in ways that are not possible currently. Some scholars have expressed concern about these developments. For example, Sherry Turkle suggests that an increasing use of robots may impact on children's ability to develop intimacy and trust in offline relationships (Turkle, 2011). Researchers in the early childhood field will need to attend to this and related issues in future studies.

These developments are not inconceivable because they are based on current uses of technologies. What they demand, however, is an understanding that technology is becoming ever more pervasive, mobile and transparent in everyday life and that in years ahead, children's engagement in digital play will take place across a range of environments, both indoor and outdoor, online and offline and across time. Technology will enable these environments to become increasingly integrated, so that it will become necessary to understand childhood as it is played out across these spaces.

Conclusion

This chapter has considered the nature of childhood in the digital age. Given the extent to which many young children are competent and confident users of a range of technologies because of their experiences in the home and communities from their earliest years, it is important for early years educators to understand the implications for research, policy and practice. In many ways, digital technologies have not changed the essential elements of childhood, such as the need for deep attachments to family members, the importance of enjoying a strong face-to-face friendship network and having opportunities to engage in creative and imaginative play using a range of natural and manufactured resources. Rather, developments in digital technologies have provided opportunities to extend these elements and strengthen them across a range of contexts. This is not to suggest that technology has only a positive impact on childhood; of course it brings with it risks such as overuse, online bullying and a potential reduction in outdoor play in natural environments. Nonetheless, what the chapter emphasises is that technological developments also bring opportunities and it is important that early childhood educators take an informed and measured approach to this topic.

Questions and exercises

1. Reflect on your own uses of digital technologies. What is similar and different to the way in which young children use digital technologies? How have things developed since you were a child?
2. How can early years educators find out about the digital experiences of children prior to them attending pre-school education? How can these experiences then be built upon effectively?
3. How can early years educators work with parents to understand both the risks and opportunities associated with the use of digital technologies?

Further reading

Plowman, Stephen and McPake's (2010) *Growing Up with Technology: Young Children Learning in a Digital World*, draws on case studies of research with three- and four-year-old children and considers the implications for learning and development of their engagement with a range of digital technologies. Yelland, Lee, O'Rourke and Harrison (2008) *Rethinking Learning in Early Childhood Education* examine how children's out-of-school technological experiences can be drawn upon in early years settings and class-rooms. Burke and Marsh's edited collection (2013) *Children's Virtual Play Worlds: Culture, Learning and Participation* provides reports on a range of studies of young children's engagement in online virtual play environments.

PART TWO

THE DEVELOPING CHILD

A consideration of the developing child necessarily encompasses an exploration of many different theories. Initially, some of these theories may appear contradictory. We need to recognise that theories may emerge from or reflect the particular interests of the theorist: consider, for example, the relationship between Piaget's theory and his early grounding in biology, or Vygotsky's theory and Marxism. In addition, the promotion or acceptance of theories at particular times in history can reflect the interests of dominant groups in society. However, the approach taken in this text is, in as far as it is possible, to consider and use different theoretical models in a complementary way, taking what each can offer to help build a holistic understanding of children's development.

In this respect we were aware that in previous editions of this text we had tended to emphasise particular, and dominant, theoretical perspectives when exploring children's development. It seemed to us that without considering an alternative view – one that examines development from a more holistic perspective – the picture we were presenting may have been unbalanced. As a result, this edition includes a 'challenging' new chapter by Marilyn Fleer who views child development as a cultural process.

A key theme underlying all of the chapters in this part of the book is the role of children in their learning and development. Children are not viewed as passive beings who are moulded and shaped by those around them but are seen as being active in this process: rather than being passively 'socialised', they are actively 'self-socialising'. Thus the young child is both shaped by and, according to cultural-historical theories, also shapes the social and material world in which he or she lives.

In Chapter 6 Ruth Ford develops these and other themes in her review of theories of cognitive development. Having provided the reader with an overview of Piagetian theory, information-processing approaches, core-knowledge theories and socio-cultural theories, she focuses on two important domains of cognitive development: social cognition (which includes an exploration of theory of mind) and self-regulation – an area, she notes, that has been of particular interest to researchers, and arguably also to policy makers, given its significance for children's performance at school.

In Chapter 7, Tricia David (with Sacha Powell) turns to children's social and emotional development, describing how emotions are closely woven together with all other aspects of development, which depend on how babies experience the world. This includes a growing sense of one's own identity, being connected to others, and the ability to exert some control over one's relationships and surroundings. Although attachments seem fundamental to this development, these are culturally specific; babies *actively* learn how to grow into their particular families and communities, helped by 'mind-mindedness', sensitive and attuned care and experiencing responsiveness to their sociability and preferences.

In Chapter 8, Thea Cameron-Faulkner describes three approaches which have been adopted in the study of language development: behaviourist, formalist and, more recently, constructivist. Within this approach children are again seen as active participants in their learning – this time, in relation to the acquisition of language. But, as Cameron-Faulkner points out, the significance of cultural context is also made clear, language acquisition being viewed as a specific form of cultural learning.

In Chapter 9, Justine Howard highlights the significance of play in early childhood. Howard outlines the numerous theories that have tried to explain why we play and indeed that have attempted to define this activity. She argues that in our attempt to understand play and to measure its developmental potential, we lost sight of its unique qualities. It is through an understanding of children's perspectives that we are able to re-connect with these qualities and recognise that, regardless of cultural context, play affords children the opportunity to learn and to heal.

In Chapter 10, as noted above, Marilyn Fleer aims to go beyond traditional disciplinary theories of development and instead seeks to examine child development from a more holistic perspective. Drawing on a cultural-historical theory of child development, Fleer illustrates what is meant by 'cultural development' and provides a model in which this is framed as a cultural process determined by the society in which the child lives and the child's active engagement in that society.

Together these five chapters provide a picture of young children striving to make sense of the world around them, in particular the world of social interaction, and quickly becoming a part of it – influenced profoundly by their surroundings and by what happens to them, but also exerting their own influence on the world from their earliest days.

6

THINKING AND COGNITIVE DEVELOPMENT IN YOUNG CHILDREN

Ruth Ford

Contents

- Introduction
- Theories of cognitive development
- Development of social cognition
- Development of self-regulation
- Applied issues and future research directions
- Summary and conclusion

Introduction

The term *cognitive development* refers broadly to the growth of children's cognition between birth and adolescence, including perception, attention, language, reasoning and memory (Siegler et al., 2010; Bjorklund, 2011). Because cognitive development has such diverse aspects, it has not yet been explained fully by any single theory. This chapter gives an overview of some of the foremost accounts in the field before focusing on two important domains of cognitive development which have been researched intensively in recent years; namely, social cognition and self-regulation. It concludes by drawing attention to practical applications of cognitive developmental research and directions for future study.

Theories of cognitive development

Theories of cognitive development can be contrasted by their stance on several issues, including: (1) the relative contribution of heredity versus the environment, (2) whether development is steady or stage-like, (3) the role of domain-general versus domain-specific processes, (4) the extent to which children initiate their own learning, and (5) the impact of the socio-cultural context. As will become evident, diverse opinions regarding these contentious matters have led to remarkably different views on the nature and development of children's thinking.

Piaget's theory: the child as scientist

Swiss psychologist Jean Piaget initiated the study of cognitive development in the 1920s. He carried out large-scale studies of children's thinking and detailed examinations of his own children's development. Piaget's pioneering theory has been hugely influential, because it provided many thought-provoking ideas that have stimulated research programmes to the present day. Piaget's theory acknowledges a contribution of nurture as well as nature to intellectual ability, describes continuity and discontinuity in development and stresses the active contribution of the child to its intellectual growth (for example, Piaget, 1952; Inhelder and Piaget, 1958; Piaget, 1965; 1969). Piaget's training in biology and philosophy informed his approach to the study of psychology. His background in biology led to an interest in the relations between evolution and human cognitive development, leading him to speculate that children are motivated to acquire knowledge because such behaviour is adaptive. His background in philosophy, particularly in logic, inspired him to search for internal consistency underlying children's errors in problem solving. Piaget's theory is described as *constructivist* in depicting the child as actively constructing knowledge in response to experiences. Piaget's work began gaining attention during the 1960s partly because it rejected ideas that had dominated psychology for the past thirty years (for example, behaviourist models of learning). The essence of Piaget's theory is the notion of the 'child as scientist', carrying out simple tests to discover how the world works.

According to Piaget, continuity in development arises from three processes: assimilation, accommodation and equilibration. *Assimilation* occurs when new experiences are integrated into existing knowledge, *accommodation* occurs when children modify their knowledge in response to new experiences that cannot be assimilated, and *equilibration* reflects the child's attempts to balance assimilation and accommodation to create stable understanding. For example, a young child might believe that only animals are living things because only animals move in ways that preserve their life. Her ideas develop as she encounters new kinds of animals and assimilates these examples into her 'schema' for living things. However, when she discovers that plants move in ways that promote their survival too she experiences a state of disequilibrium (uncertainty) and then accommodates her knowledge structures to the new information about plants and decides that since this movement signifies life, plants must be living things.

For Piaget, cognitive development is discontinuous with four discrete stages (*epigenesis*). His theory assumes that later stages of development build on earlier achievements and these stages are universal (true for all human cultures) and age-invariant (passed through in the same order by all children regardless of rate of progress).

The first stage is the *sensorimotor* stage, which lasts from birth to approximately the age of two years. During this stage, infants think only about objects and events in their immediate environment. Through assimilation, accommodation and equilibration, infants construct progressively more sophisticated links between sensation and motor activity (sensorimotor schemas), enabling them to develop ideas about time, space and causality. As they grow older, infants integrate simple reflexes such as gazing and grasping to achieve more advanced behaviours such as visually guided reaching, they attain an understanding that objects continue to exist even when they cannot be seen (the concept of object permanence), and they test ideas about cause and effect, for example, by shaking and biting a rattle to discover how to produce a noise.

By their second birthday, most infants have entered the *pre-operational* stage, which lasts until approximately the age of seven years. Children become capable of representing their experiences mentally using imagery and language. Piaget referred to this as *symbolic function* and argued that it could be observed in both their deferred imitation and their frequent engagement in make-believe play. For example, Piaget proposed that a three-year-old girl holding a banana to her ear and speaking into it as if it was a mobile phone indicates that she is capable of mentally representing the banana as something else. Once the symbolic function is in place, Piaget's theory suggests that subsequent cognitive development involves the acquisition of new modes of thinking, known as *mental operations*. Pre-operational children are misled by superficial appearances during problem solving because they lack important mental operations necessary for logical reasoning. For example, until they acquire the ability to mentally undo an action, children are unable to understand that the amount of liquid in a container does not change when it is poured into a container of a different shape (that is, a failure of *conservation*). Three other important features of the pre-operational stage are *egocentricism*, the inability to take another person's point of view, *centration*, the tendency to focus attention on a single aspect of a problem at a time, and *animism*, the tendency to attribute life-like qualities and intentions to non-living things.

During the *concrete operational* stage, typically lasting from the ages of seven to twelve years, children demonstrate the use of logic when dealing with problems involving concrete objects and events, and they succeed in conserving number, volume, mass and area. Children also begin to pass tests requiring *seriation* (i.e. sorting objects along a particular dimension such as length), *transitive inferences* (identifying logical relations between objects) and *class inclusion* (understanding superordinate versus subordinate class membership, such as animal versus dog). However, they do not yet show evidence of thinking in abstract or hypothetical terms and cannot easily combine information systematically to solve a problem.

Finally, on entering the *formal operational* stage of development at approximately the age of twelve years, children are able to consider abstract constructs and to formulate and test hypotheses in a scientific manner. For example, if given a pendulum with varying weights and lengths of string they can then deduce what determines the rate of oscillation. Their ability to think hypothetically also leads them to query the way society is structured and to ponder philosophical questions about truth, justice and morality.

Many of the studies that have been stimulated by Piaget's theory have concluded that he underestimated young children's capabilities because he failed to take into account their memory and language limitations. Whereas Piaget's basic findings in relation to the *sequence* of development have been extensively replicated, other research has challenged his notion of stages of development, his emphasis on domain-general reasoning abilities, and his neglect of the contribution of social interactions to children's thinking. These points have been addressed in turn by information-processing approaches, core-knowledge approaches and socio-cultural approaches to cognitive development.

Information-processing approaches: the child as a computational system

Information-processing theories reject Piaget's ideas about abrupt transformations in cognitive development and instead posit a gradual improvement of basic cognitive processes, memory and knowledge (Halford and Andrews, 2010). In terms of core issues, information-processing approaches assume that development reflects both nature and nurture, is continuous rather than discontinuous, involves active planning and problem solving by the child and that the mechanisms of change can be specified.

Notions about information processing hold that as children grow older they become more efficient at encoding information from the environment, faster in their speed of mental processing, better able to apply learning and memory strategies, and more knowledgeable. For example, knowledge acquisition is associated with significant gains in memory capabilities during childhood – young children become better at remembering novel events as they develop *scripts* or mental representations of the usual sequence of activities for commonly experienced routines like attending a birthday party.

The majority of information-processing theories of cognitive development assume sequential processing of information but connectionist or neural-network models aim to mimic the physiological workings of the human brain by invoking parallel processing (Elman, 2005). Neo-Piagetian information-processing views, which account for stage-like development in terms of continuous improvements in processing capacity, have also been influential. Finally, dynamic systems theories reject ideas about linear causality (where x causes y) and, instead, suggest that mutually interdependent parts of the cognitive system co-operate in a non-linear fashion to produce new, emergent properties (Lewis, 2000).

Core-knowledge theories: the child as a product of human evolution

Similar to both Piaget's and information-processing theories, core-knowledge theories assume that the child is an active agent in their own development who strives to learn. Uniquely, however, such approaches argue that children are born with learning abilities already in place that are specialised for particular domains of thought. Innate forms of knowledge are believed to have arisen in response to human evolutionary history, without which it is presumed infants would have difficulty in beginning to make sense of the world. Innate knowledge is suggested to be crucial to the development of such skills as face recognition, taxonomic classification and language. Core-knowledge theorists assume that innate knowledge is domain specific.

Core knowledge has been argued to provide the foundation for children's intuitive or naïve theories about how the world works (i.e. the *theory* approach to development – Wellman and Gelman, 1998). Naïve theories operate in *core domains* like physics, psychology and biology; for example, from a very early age children appear to understand that the world contains physical objects that occupy space and move in response to external forces, that people's behaviour is driven by their goals and desires, and that objects can be broadly classified as either animate or inanimate. Evidence that young children have surprising competence in particular aspects of their cognitive development is hard to explain in terms of Piaget's domain-general theory.

According to theory approaches, cognitive development proceeds as the acquisition of new knowledge enables children to refine and extend their rudimentary theories to create better ones. Such approaches form part of a larger class of theories in the rapidly growing field of evolutionary developmental psychology. As a whole, this approach seeks to explain how specific cognitive skills have developed in response to environmental pressures (Geary and Bjorklund, 2000). Evolutionary developmental psychology distinguishes between biologically primary abilities (that is, cognitive skills determined by evolution, such as language) and biologically secondary abilities (that is, cognitive skills determined by culture, such as reading). It is assumed that the development of primary abilities requires little nurture from the environment whereas the development of secondary abilities requires a higher level of external support. Finally, the sub-domain of developmental cognitive neuroscience attempts to understand cognitive development in terms of brain structures and functions.

Socio-cultural theories: the child as a social being

The theories reviewed so far have uniformly stressed children's active role in their own development as they identify problems and attempt to solve them independently. In contrast, socio-cultural theories highlight the importance of communicative interactions with other people (Bornstein and Bruner, 1989). Socio-cultural perspectives share the notions of *guided participation* (how adults assist children to achieve higher levels of skills than they would attain on their own) and *cultural tools* (including language and other symbol systems, artefacts, skills and values with cultural significance – Rogoff, 1990).

The socio-cultural approach to understanding cognitive development was initiated by the Russian psychologist, Lev Vygotsky. Although Vygotsky was a contemporary of Piaget, his work received little attention in the Western world until it was translated into English as *Mind in Society* (Vygotsky, 1978). Vygotsky was intrigued by the idea that young children are born into a social world in which adults are motivated to help them learn. Whereas Piaget claimed that a child constructs knowledge by actively engaging with the environment, Vygotsky suggested that development is a joint endeavour between the child and his or her caretakers during social interchanges. Vygotsky acknowledged the contribution of nature to development, believing infants enter the world equipped with basic cognitive functions such as the ability to remember. These basic abilities are nurtured into higher mental functions during social interactions and dialogues between a child and his or her parents, teachers and other representatives of culture. Thus, through these interactions, children internalise increasingly mature and effective ways of thinking and problem solving.

Vygotsky (1986) reasoned that social interactions benefit children's thinking due to the input of language and he postulated the existence of three stages of language-thought development. In the first stage, called *external speech*, thinking comes from a source outside the child. In the second stage, called *private speech*, children talk to themselves as a way of directing their own thinking. In the final stage, called *internal speech*, children have internalised their thought processes.

Vygotsky also introduced the idea of the *zone of proximal development*. This refers to an area of functioning just beyond the child's current level to which they are capable of progressing given appropriate assistance from other people with greater knowledge. Vygotsky defined it as 'the distance between actual developmental level as determined by independent problem solving and the level of potential development through problem solving under adult guidance or in collaboration with more capable peers' (Vygotsky, 1978: 86). Vygotsky thus assumed that in most instances children's potential level of functioning exceeds their actual level of functioning.

Subsequent work in the Vygotskian tradition drew attention to the role of *intersubjectivity* in social interactions, that is, mutual understanding arising from joint attention to the same topic. It additionally described *social scaffolding*, that is, the process by which adults provide a temporary framework to support a child's thinking at a higher level than they can yet reach on their own (Wood et al., 1976). As an analogy, the child can be viewed as a building under construction. Scaffolding takes the form of explaining the goal of the task, demonstrating how the task should be done and carrying out the more difficult aspects of the task. At first, children require extensive support to attain a higher level of thinking about a particular problem but, over time, they come to require less assistance until eventually they can complete the task on their own. Children who receive appropriate scaffolding show faster acquisition of new skills than do children who learn independently (see Chapter 13 for a discussion of adult roles in children's learning).

Vygotsky's theory is an example of a *dialectical theory*; it emphasises the development of cognition under social influence. Other socio-cultural approaches can be described as *contextualist*; they stress the wider influence of environmental contexts on development. Interest in contextualism was prompted by the publication of *The Ecology of Human Development*, by Urie Bronfenbrenner in 1979. As described in Chapter 5, Bronfenbrenner viewed cognitive development as proceeding within a nested series of contexts, reflecting three main levels of the environment. First, the *microsystem* comprises the various settings in which the child directly participates, such as home, school and neighbourhood. Second, the *exosystem* comprises systems that affect the child indirectly by virtue of their influence on microsystems. Such settings include the extended social network of the family. Finally, the *macrosystem* comprises the cultural environment of the child, for example, characteristics of a particular socio-economic or ethnic background. Bronfenbrenner also identified *mesosystems*, which represent interactions between two or more microsystems, and subsequently he incorporated the *chronosystem*, referring to influences on development that are specific to a particular historical period (Bronfenbrenner, 1986). For example, children growing up today differ from previous generations in their extensive exposure to television and computers (see Chapter 5). Notably, Bronfenbrenner advocated a transactional view of development in that he believed children, caregivers and the environment have a mutual influence on one another (Bronfenbrenner and Morris, 1998) and the child is not a passive recipient of environmental forces but to some extent selects their experiences. For example, a child who is raised by parents who encourage reading might develop an enjoyment of literature that later leads them to seek out friends with similar interests.

Development of social cognition

The term *social cognition* refers to the cognitive processes that deal with social information. Such processes underpin all social interactions and, over the last two decades, have been one of the most widely investigated topics in developmental psychology. Tomasello et al. (2005) argued that the extraordinary dominance of the human species over other animals has resulted not from our greater intelligence *per se* but from our ability to create and participate in social groups and institutions. On their account, humans are uniquely disposed to understand and share the intentions of others, making it possible for them to engage in sophisticated forms of social behaviour. *Shared intentionality*, which emerges in infancy, means that children are primed to learn through observation and to co-operate with others in activities that instruct them in new skills. In evolutionary terms, shared intentionality may have been crucial to humans' development of language and other symbol systems, as well as complex tools and technologies.

Further to shared intentionality, effective social interactions appear to involve a *theory of mind* or the understanding that human behaviour is governed by a complex system of mental states, such as desires, knowledge, beliefs and emotions (Wellman, 2002). Such understanding enables us to make sense of what people say and do and is vital for successful interpersonal relations (see Chapter 7 on 'mind reading'). As adults, we are aware that other people may have a view of the world that differs from our own, or from reality. The importance of theory of mind is reflected in our frequent use of mental-state terms in everyday language (e.g. John looked for his keys in his coat pocket because that is where he *thought* they were; John is opening the biscuit barrel because he *wants* a biscuit).

It has been argued that young children lack a fully-fledged theory of mind, as evinced by their poor performance on tests of the understanding of false belief. False-belief tests gauge children's appreciation of the fact that people can possess and act on beliefs that do not reflect reality. One of the most commonly employed false-belief tasks is the unexpected transfer task, devised by Wimmer and Perner (1983). In the original version, children watched a story conveyed by puppets. The story featured a little boy called Maxi who put his bar of chocolate in a blue cupboard in his kitchen and then left the scene. Maxi's mother entered the kitchen and moved his chocolate bar to a green cupboard. Upon Maxi re-entering the kitchen, children were asked to predict where Maxi would look for his chocolate. Wimmer and Perner found that 58 per cent of the children aged four to five years incorrectly responded that Maxi would look for the object in its actual location (the green cupboard), whereas 92 per cent of the children aged six to nine years correctly responded that Maxi would look for the object in its original location (the blue cupboard). Such findings have been widely replicated over the years leading to the conclusion that children younger than five to six years find it hard to acknowledge the existence of mental states that are discordant with the real state of affairs.

Investigations of children's theory of mind have raised the usual issues central to cognitive development. First, there is controversy regarding whether acquisition of theory of mind is continuous or stage-like. Based on the finding that the majority of typically developing children start to understand false belief around the age of four-and-a-half years, some researchers have argued that there is a radical shift in the child's thought processes at this time and that younger children fail to possess a representational understanding of mind (the *representational deficit view* – Perner, 1991). The opposing argument is that the rudiments of theory of mind are evident in infancy and develop gradually over the course of childhood. Supporting the latter view, children as young as thirty-six months of age can pass false-belief tests if critical aspects of such tests are made more meaningful. Given that children younger than four years can engage in pretence and identify a variety of basic mental states and emotions, many researchers prefer to postulate continuity in the development of theory-of-mind capabilities during early childhood.

Second, there is debate surrounding whether theory of mind relies on domain-specific or domain-general cognitive processes. Whereas domain-specific accounts assume the existence of a specialised brain or cognitive system devoted solely to theory-of-mind reasoning, domain-general accounts argue that theory-of-mind problems are solved by all-purpose cognitive mechanisms. Domain-specific accounts include the proposals that theory of mind depends on a dedicated cognitive module (*modular theory* – Scholl and Leslie, 1999) or, alternatively, a set of causal, explanatory rules pertaining uniquely to human behaviour (*theory theory* – Gopnik and Wellman, 1992). Regardless of whether there is an element of domain specificity to theory of mind, a role of domain-general processes is suggested by evidence that young children's performance on false-belief tests is positively related to their working memory capacity and powers of inhibitory control. Such evidence implies that success on false-belief tests depends to some extent on children's ability to remember the sequence of events and to suppress their (salient) knowledge of current reality in order to respond to their (less salient) knowledge of past events (Carlson and Moses, 2001).

Finally, research into theory of mind highlights issues of nature versus nurture. A contribution of heredity to theory of mind is suggested by behaviour genetics studies (Hughes et al., 2005) and by brain imaging studies that implicate a specific network of brain areas (namely, the medial prefrontal cortex and temporal poles) as underpinning theory-of-mind abilities (Frith and Frith, 2001). Nevertheless, environmental influences appear substantial, as indicated by speedier theory-of-mind development in children whose mothers refer more frequently to mental states in everyday conversation (see, for example, Ruffman et al., 2002). Conversely, theory-of-mind development is severely delayed in deaf children from hearing families who have restricted opportunities for communication at home (Peterson and Siegal, 1995). The finding that theory of mind fails to emerge normally in deaf children who are deprived of information about other people's mental activities provides strong evidence for an important contribution of nurture to theory of mind.

Development of self-regulation

The term *self-regulation* refers to the ability to curb impulses and to behave in a careful and considered manner (Garon et al., 2008). Cognitive aspects of self-regulation include the ability to sustain attention to independent goal-directed activity and resist distraction, whereas affective self-regulation represents the capacity to manage emotions and to respond effectively in situations that have important personal consequences (Zelazo et al., 2005). Self-regulation is an important function of the prefrontal cortex, a region of the brain that deals specifically with the effortful control of thought and behaviour and that shows significant maturation during the preschool years (Zelazo et al., 2008).

The development of self-regulation has been of prime interest to researchers given its importance for children's performance at school (Rimm-Kaufman et al., 2000). Several investigations have confirmed the robust role of self-regulatory skills in the academic achievements of young children. In one such study with five- to six-year-olds, Blair and Razza (2007) examined the relations between measures of cognitive and affective self-regulation on one hand, and attainments on tests of mathematics, phonemic awareness and letter knowledge on the other. After controlling for verbal ability and fluid intelligence, they found that cognitive self-regulation was positively correlated with all three domains of academic ability. In a meta-analysis of six longitudinal investigations, Duncan et al. (2007) reported that attention skills at the age of five years continued to predict academic performance throughout elementary school.

In light of such findings, it has been suggested that early intervention programmes for children deemed at risk of educational failure should strive to develop the self-regulatory skills that are needed for successful adjustment to the classroom (Blair, 2002; Noble et al., 2005; Riggs et al., 2006). This seems feasible given evidence of strong environmental influences on the development of self-regulation (Farah et al., 2006; Bernier et al., 2010). Studies have sought to nurture self-regulation using computer-based training (Rueda et al., 2005) and appropriate forms of play and social interaction. As an example of the latter approach, Diamond et al. (2007) evaluated the effects of a specially designed pre-school programme (Tools of the Mind) inspired by the work of Vygotsky. Children whose pre-school teachers encouraged them in interactive dramatic play, and in the use of private speech and external aids to control behaviour, subsequently had better self-regulation than children who followed a standard pre-school curriculum.

Applied issues and future research directions

All theories of cognitive development are agreed that the physical and social environment is an important force in children's learning, highlighting the importance of enriching their pre-school experiences. As already discussed, evidence that social interactions figure largely in the development of theory of mind and self-regulation has led to calls for appropriate interventions for children who show impairments in these domains. Research in the socio-cultural tradition has further revealed that children's cognitive development can be enhanced by programmes that promote responsive parenting and exposure to guided learning interactions (Boland et al., 2003; Landry et al., 2008; Ford et al., 2009).

Theories of cognitive development have profound implications for the education of young children even after formal schooling commences. Education has been heavily influenced by Piaget's theory, with its suggestion that allowing children to interact with the environment will facilitate their learning, its notion of cognitive *readiness* for determining when and what children should be taught, and its detailed analysis of children's emerging concepts about number and physical causality. Information-processing theories have introduced detailed, trial-by-trial methods of exploring learning (*microgenetic* methods – Siegler, 2000), core-knowledge theories have provided important information regarding young children's ability to reason about unobservable causes of events, and discoveries within developmental cognitive neuroscience have indicated ways that stimulating specific brain regions can improve aspects of academic learning. Finally, socio-cultural theories of cognitive development can be credited with drawing educators' attention to the importance of make-believe and socio-dramatic play as well as prompting moves to encourage co-operative learning and peer tutoring in schools. Moreover, a growing awareness of the ecological context of development has led to efforts to involve members of the wider community in the educational system with the aim of developing a culture of learning both within and beyond the classroom.

Summary and conclusion

Theories of cognitive development grapple with issues of nature versus nurture, continuity versus discontinuity, active versus passive development, domain-general versus domain-specific learning, and the role of the socio-cultural context. Pioneering studies by Piaget led him to propose that there are four distinct stages of cognitive development, with progress marked by the emergence of more advanced modes of thinking in each successive stage. Piaget viewed young children as amateur scientists who carry out simple experiments on their world to discover how it works. Subsequent investigation in the information-processing tradition suggested that development is continuous rather than stage-like and that it can be understood in terms of age-related improvements in processing mechanisms, memory capacity and knowledge. Additionally, research into innate competences has indicated that infants are born possessing certain kinds of knowledge that facilitate their learning in particular core domains. Finally, the work of Vygotsky and Bronfenbrenner has implicated a contribution of social and cultural factors to children's learning. Vygotsky argued that cognitive development occurs within social interactions with more capable others that guide children into increasingly mature ways of thinking.

In conclusion, the study of children's thinking and cognitive development is a dynamic and evolving field that covers a diversity of topics. All accounts have important insights to offer and recent writings have emphasised the need for theoretical integration. One aim is to explicate the reciprocal relations between a child's biological make-up and social environment, for example, the effects of a child's temperament on the instructional strategies favoured by their caregivers (Gauvain, 2005; Bjorklund, 2011). Other emerging themes include the nature of environmental influences on brain development, particularly stress, and the interplay between sources of vulnerability and sources of resilience (Shonkoff and Phillips, 2000; Blair, 2010). Increasing our understanding of these important issues should pave the way for improved policy and practice in relation to the education and nurture of young children.

Questions and exercises

1. Evaluate Piaget's contribution to our understanding of cognitive development.
2. Weigh the relative strengths and weaknesses of information-processing and core-knowledge approaches to cognitive development.
3. Give examples of ways that parents can use guided participation and social scaffolding to foster their children's learning.
4. Evaluate evidence of domain-specific and domain-general contributions to children's acquisition of a theory of mind.
5. Suggest ways that parents and professionals can improve young children's self-regulation.

Further reading

Berk (2008) *Child Development* is a comprehensive text about child development that relates theory to practice. Bjorklund (2011) *Children's Thinking: Cognitive Development and Individual Differences* reviews competing theories about cognitive development in relation to children's thinking, perception, language and intelligence. Gauvain (2001) *The Social Context of Cognitive Development* extends Vygotsky's ideas about the role of the socio-cultural context in cognitive development by reviewing recent research into children's problem solving, attention and memory. Siegler et al. (2010) *How Children Develop* is an accessible introduction to the field of child psychology that is designed for readers with little background knowledge and charts both cognitive and social/emotional development.

7

BABIES' AND YOUNG CHILDREN'S SOCIAL AND EMOTIONAL DEVELOPMENT

Tricia David with Sacha Powell

Contents

- Introduction
- The foundations for all other learning: more than 'preparation for school learning'
- Born to be social and to form emotional attachments
- Attachment
- Children and families 'at risk'
- Independence and interdependence
- Belonging
- Mind-reading and mind-mindedness
- Conclusions: adults' roles, personal qualities, education and training

---

Introduction

In January 2013 the government decided to announce that regulations pertaining to settings for early childhood education and care (ECEC) in England should be changed[1] because the high costs of what officials insisted on calling only 'childcare'[2] were prohibitive and thus preventing some parents (usually mothers) from seeking work outside the home. Simultaneously, Elizabeth Truss, the Minister with responsibility, announced that in future childcare staff would be required to have achieved Grade C in English and Maths GCSE exams. This was partly intended as a response to Professor Cathy Nutbrown's (2012) government-commissioned report proposing better levels of qualification for work in the ECEC field, though it did not in fact match those proposals. Many parents were interviewed by the media, claiming that such changes would reduce their children's opportunities for affectionate interactions, with negative consequences. They added that they wanted their children to be loved and that qualifications did not mean staff would necessarily show the warmth and sensitivity they would expect for their child. Many early years professionals and academics were similarly concerned (see *Nursery World*, February 2013 issues).

This chapter explores current evidence from research and the influence of contemporary policy concerning what are probably the most important aspects of a child's development during the first years of life – social and emotional development. Above all, it highlights the crucial nature of close and loving relationships because these are the models which will cast either sunlight or long shadows over a child's future experiences: how and what they learn about themselves and the social worlds they inhabit.

The foundations for all other learning: more than 'preparation for school learning'

Social and emotional development is one of the three 'prime areas' in the new Statutory Framework for the Early Years Foundation Stage (EYFS) (DfE, 2012a) in England. These three areas are thought to underpin others and practitioners are urged to ensure these are secure before expecting children to embark on other curricular areas. A 'life course' perspective underpinning recent policies has been concerned with the development of progressive universal service provision for families during pregnancy and the first five years of their child's life (see Chapter 15). This

---

[1] Ratios of staff to babies, toddlers and young children are to be reduced (DfE, 2013).

[2] Government use of the term childcare rather than the OECD's (2006) term Early Childhood Education and Care seems to tie in with many ministerial statements to the effect that ECEC settings are to prepare children for primary school where 'real learning' takes place, rather than recognising the immense learning potential and achievements of babies and small children through play and appropriate joint experiences.

perspective aims to ensure that early intervention reaches the most vulnerable families in order to promote:

> a child's physical, emotional, cognitive and social development so that all children have a fair chance to succeed at school and in later life. (NICE, 2012: 4)

While a review of historical texts shows that those in the field have long claimed to prioritise social and emotional development (see, for example, Taylor et al., 1972), the new emphasis from government and its bodies (e.g. DfES, 2004; Ofsted, 2005; DCSF, 2008a; Field, 2010; DfE and DH, 2011; DH, 2011a) indicates that such a focus is more than the wish to enable all children to be comfortable in their own skins. Preparation for school is said to be dependent on an appropriate level of social and emotional development, as is school achievement. Additionally, later psychiatric care, involvement in crime and anti-social behaviour – all drains on the public purse (Hummel et al., 2011) – may be long-term results from socially and emotionally impoverished early years. In her paper focusing on emotional wellbeing and mental health, Soni (2012: 180) argues that the introduction of the new EYFS provides a 'golden opportunity for practitioners to link together information, provided via the media, research and government, concerning the increased incidence of mental health problems and the value practitioners can offer in supporting children under five in promoting children's mental health.'

Sad and troublesome babyhoods should concern us all, but not simply because of their consequences, more importantly because we would want all our children to experience joy in themselves, in their relationships and in living.

Born to be social and to form emotional attachments

From the moment of birth, babies are intensely interested in other people. In the first months of life they are trying to form close relationships and they are beginning to develop an individual sense of self. At the same time they are coming to know if those individual selves have any agency, or power, over their own lives. During these early months of life, a baby will learn from interactions with parents and carers, developing an understanding of self and of how relationships work – or do not. Such interactions involve cognitive as well as social and emotional processes. Over twenty years ago Judy Dunn (1999) pointed out that compartmentalising children's areas of development for research purposes was not taking account of their interwoven influences.[3] Books by Goleman (2004; 2007) have provided the field with comprehensive

---

[3]When Professor Lesley Abbott suggested the *Birth to Three Matters* (DfES, 2003a) pack should be structured upon 'Aspects' rather than traditional areas of development, as authors of the literature review (David et al., 2003) we worried for a few moments that the task would be difficult but realised that however it was to be structured, it would involve overlaps.

reviews of research about emotional and social development, including studies from neuroscience, which reinforce the importance of these foundational aspects of young children's lives. Discussing 'webs of attachment' Goleman (2007: 114) writes:

> laughing and crying come spontaneously in primal moments of social connection … Distress at separation and joy at bonding both bespeak the primal power of connection.

So human emotions are the basic building blocks of their entire, holistic development, including the personal and social aspects, and human beings seem to be born to be social. Even in the first months of life, babies make distinctions between people/objects, self/other (Stern, 1985). They appear to need to form *attachments* to the people who are familiar and significant to them (usually a parent or other relative at first) and these *attachments* at four months old are said to be good predictors of their attachments and their ability to regulate their emotions at a year old (Braungart-Rieker et al., 2001). It is in the everyday interactions of being sensitively cared for that they begin to be aware of themselves and despite the fact that researchers a quarter of a century ago argued that children do not develop a sense of self (recognise themselves as separate people with an individual identity) until the second year, more recent research indicates that this amazing feat begins soon after birth (Sigelman and Rider, 2008). These first attachments provide a 'model' which will be drawn upon later in life.

Around two years of age, children begin to realise that others may judge them. Shame and guilt begin to constrain negative or immoral behaviour and empathy to inhibit cruelty. When adults – and older children – adjust their behaviour sensitively to what they perceive as the baby's needs and wishes, we say they are behaving *contingently*, not only showing warmth and affection but also modelling for the younger child.

Attachment

One of the most important figures in Western psychology, John Bowlby, formulated and wrote extensively for decades about his theory of attachment (see, for example, Bowlby, 1951; [1953] 1965). Bowlby proposed that attachment is an innate device intended to protect the immature offspring of a species by attracting adults who will ensure their survival. Later, however, Bowlby (1988) himself agreed that attachment research had shown up flaws in his theory and that instead of the idea of specific, crucial phases of development he had come to prefer a theory of developmental pathways. Bowlby's admission alerts us to the need to be wary of expecting any theory to be capable of explaining 'everything'.

Furthermore, attachment theory was used politically, especially during the 1950s and in a way that was never intended, to discourage women from employment outside the home. It continues to exert an effect to this day, as evidenced by the 'key person approach' in early years policy and practice.

Nevertheless, as Baron-Cohen (2011: 48) states, Bowlby's work was remarkable and his predictions have been 'amply proven' and are extremely important socially. He depicts Bowlby's theory thus:

> what the care-giver gives his or her child in those first few critical years is like *an internal pot of gold* … This … is what gives the individual the strength to deal with challenges … It overlaps with what London psychiatrist Michael Rutter refers to as 'resilience'.

So despite some reservations, attachment remains a useful concept in trying to understand babies' need to relate positively to people closest to them and in recognising how early interactions provide building blocks for a sense of self and models for later social competence. The work of psychodynamic therapists and the contributions of psychoanalysis are also important in thinking about attachment. For example, Shore (2011) suggests that, as a result of new technology, we now know there is a neural site in the orbitofrontal cortex of the brain and its growth is dependent upon a child's experience. A carer's 'attunedness' and responsiveness will result in positive emotional development; lack of such experiences, however, result in limited ability to cope with distress, anger, terror and shame, although sensitive relationships later in life can help to ameliorate this.

Recent research demonstrates that not only can babies form attachments to a number of people, it may be that they are better protected and better equipped to form subsequent relationships by having several primary attachment figures rather than the sometimes claustrophobic (and unnatural in human terms) relationship which can result from long hours spent in the company of only one adult, their mother.

Babies can have a network of attachments made up of different members of 'the family' – all the familiar people who share the baby's life (see, for example, the film *Babies* – Chabat and Balmes, 2009). These social experiences are influential in the process of achieving healthy social development (NICHD, 2006). When they are only a few months old babies start making preferential attachments. They behave in ways that are designed to attract the preferred person's attention – smiling, cooing, trying to make eye contact – and will be pacified by that person's voice, a look from them or the presentation of a toy, for example. Some of these preferred attachment figures will be older children in a household. Different attachment figures will elicit different responses from a baby. Passionate crying by a baby when a parent arrives to collect them from an ECEC setting may indicate the strength of an attachment rather than anything amiss (Davies, 1999).

Research by Trevarthen (2009) and his colleagues over the last thirty years has been especially valuable to the field of early childhood. For example, from two months of age, around the time they also engage in social smiling, infants are sensitive to *social contingency* (responsiveness to the infant's signals), especially to the timing of emotional *attunement* in two-way exchanges. These attuned exchanges indicate the development of *primary intersubjectivity* – the rudiments of turn taking, sensitive timing and responsiveness to the other's behaviour, especially facial expressions. Intersubjectivity is thought to be the foundation of early social interaction. Such early, playful interactions are called 'proto-conversations' and they gradually offer the young child opportunities for anticipating and predicting and they form the basis for social and cognitive advances that occur during the first year.

It is common for attachments to change over time. Adults can change their attitudes/approach towards their children at different ages, preferring particular phases of development. Changes in the mother's approach are likely to initiate particular behavioural responses from the infant which in turn will have an effect on the mother's emotions and her subsequent maternal behaviour (Noriuchi et al., 2008). Further, some researchers suggest attachment is universal, but others argue that it is expressed differently in different cultures (Wang and Mallinckrodt, 2006) (see Chapter 1).

Children and families 'at risk'

Some children may be at risk in terms of their social and emotional development for a number of reasons. For example, children born into families who have been informed soon after their baby's birth that their child has an identifiable impairment or life-threatening illness are often left to deal with powerful emotions which may impact upon the attachment process. Despite two Children Acts (HM Government, 1989; 2004), both of which have stressed the requirement for professionals from different services to work together more effectively in the 'best interests' of children, it appears that England still lags behind other countries in its ability to ensure this in practice (see Chapters 11 and 19). Research, training and resources in this area are said to have been neglected (Atkinson et al., 2002), although Messenger (2012), while agreeing over the need for training, suggests the personal qualities, confidence and experience of those involved are important in this respect.

Another example might be a disruption to the attachment process, likely if a baby needs in-patient hospitalisation or many visits in the first few weeks of life. Fenwick et al. (2008) refer to the significance of physical contact between mother and baby and where this is denied – for example, through restrictions in postnatal access – highlight the impact such deprivation can have on the attachment process. As MacFadyen (2010) emphasises, babies have a right to this contact and it is important that staff in institutions such as hospitals are aware of the potential effects of lack of continuity in early relationships and their key role in supporting parents. It is vitally important that medical staff understand the problems that mothers face when there is limited access to their baby, and also the importance of treating the mother and baby as a single entity (Erlandsson and Fagerberg, 2005).

Children with autism, who may appear aloof and indifferent and who do not seek out meaningful interactions with other children or with adults may also need extra support, because they do not perceive their world in the same way that other children do (Wall, 2010). They are unaware of, or do not understand, others' social interactions, gentle teasing, jokes and feints because they have no sense of what is happening in the mind of another person. Meanwhile, shy children may have overactive amygdalas (Kagan, 2010) and high levels of activity in this brain area can inhibit their ability to cope. They need to be with other children who can cope so that their brain mechanisms develop and overcome these inhibitions. Baron-Cohen (2011) explains that prolonged early stress affects the way the hippocampus functions so that the stress hormone cortisol is released into the blood stream by the adrenal gland. Additionally, in one part of the amygdala the nerve cells start branching more than normal. However, as Kagan (2010) argues, while biology, or temperament, may impact on early reactions and abilities, it need not determine them in the longer term and Karmiloff-Smith (2010) suggests caution in using brain studies, as there is a need to look at neural trajectories over time through developmental neuroimaging, rather than 'snapshots' at isolated points in a life.

Children who are described as being in 'hard to reach' or 'vulnerable' families may attract special effort on the part of outreach workers and practitioners (Boag-Munroe, 2012), particularly in families where parents did not themselves experience warm and sensitive parenting, or where they are experiencing high levels of stress. Some parents may describe their babies as irritable or difficult and, because of anxiety, respond aggressively rather than being able to calm them. Such experiences can lead to low resilience later in life (Hagekull et al., 1993). While alertness and responsiveness to individual risk factors are vital, it is also imperative to exert caution in any interpretation of their (potential) effects. A comprehensive report on the development of a screening tool for health visitors noted that while some outcome predictions may be possible, the influence of different sets of factors vary according to the outcome being considered. From a study of maternal indicators and young children's developmental outcomes, using the Millennium Cohort Data, Kiernan and Mensah (2011: 60) suggest that:

> it may be more appropriate to take a more holistic approach to understanding how families influence their children's development and well-being.

Independence and interdependence

One of the most striking changes during the transition from babyhood to early childhood is a child's growing sense of self (Dunn, 1993). Individual children become aware of how others view them and, as emphasised earlier, it is usually the parent–child relationship that provides the basis for fostering a sense of self-competence and worth. Along with this growing sense of self, the child will be trying to gain a sense of independence, wishing to be seen as capable by others – and told so in words and actions when attempting to be independent. These experiences enable children to learn that they are competent members of society and this promotes their ability to interact successfully with peers throughout middle childhood (Mikulincer and Shaver, 2007). Children develop self-awareness and social awareness in conjunction with a sense of their own agency. When parents and practitioners allow them to assert some power and control over their own lives, they learn to be self-regulating and autonomous. This process will incorporate elements of conflict and its resolution for, as Kernan et al. (2011: 3) explain, young children's relationships encompass:

> understandings and experiences of nurturance, care and learning in interactions and interpersonal relations; conflicts and negotiation; pleasure and rejection; friendships and play; group phenomena; independence and interdependence; and identity and belonging.

By eighteen to twenty-four months old, young children usually recognise themselves in mirrors, begin to use 'I', 'me' and 'mine' and use their own name. They also start to assert their own wishes. A few more months on and they begin to develop their gender identity and to show awareness of racism in their society.

The new Early Years Foundation Stage (DfE, 2012a: 4) states as an overarching principle that ECEC settings should enable young children to 'learn to be strong and independent through positive relationships' (see Chapter 17). Clearly this is a principle we would endorse but we would add that interdependence is also important. While this concept may be embedded in the rhetoric and while we agree that being independent, able to think, act and speak 'bravely' for oneself is important, so too is being able to co-operate and collaborate, listen to, respect and learn from the ideas or contributions of others and to support others in expressing these. Both independence and interdependence are important for the 'common good'.

Belonging

Wrapped up in the process of emotional, social and personal development is the child's sense of 'belonging'. Families today are very different from the families of even a generation ago, and as Jagger and Wright (1999: 3) point out, 'The family is neither a pan-human universal nor a stable or essential entity … Families and family relations are, like the term itself, flexible, fluid and contingent'. However, since research shows how important familiar, loving, significant people are to babies and young children, it is vital that, as a society, we explore ways of ensuring that they feel they are part of a 'family', however it is constituted. Families, like communities, develop their own cultures – ways of being and behaving. Young children are made to feel they belong when they are able to participate in that culture, they know 'what we do and how we behave' (see, for example, Black and Lobo, 2008).

What matters to a young child is the act of parenting, not the gender identity of who does it or if parents are in a heterosexual or same sex partnership/marriage. Despite this, some research has focused on differences between fathers (as males) and mothers (as females), reporting that most fathers behave differently towards their children compared with the mothers. However, as Anderson (1996) points out, it can be the mother who acts as a gatekeeper, either including or excluding the father and thus encouraging or discouraging a meaningful relationship between a father and his child. According to Belsky (1996), fathers whose infants are securely attached to them are usually more extrovert and positive about their home lives than fathers whose children are insecurely attached to them. The strength of attachment to one parent is usually a good indicator of attachment to the other and the relationship between a mother or father and their first-born appears to set the tone for the attachments of later offspring (Brumbaugh and Fraley, 2006). When a new baby joins a family, the older sibling/s may show ambivalence – natural, given that such a newcomer may be usurping the older child's position. However, with family support and encouragement even children younger than three show they can adapt their talk and behave endearingly towards the new baby, picking up cues and modelling by other family members.

The New Zealand Ministry of Education (1996: 54) argues that all children need to have a feeling of belonging, because it 'contributes to inner well-being, security and identity. Children need to know that they are accepted for who they are. They should know that what they do can make a difference and that they can explore and try out new activities'. Meanwhile, McGuire (1991) found that nursery staff in the UK often failed to give additional support to withdrawn children to help them become integrated into a group or to engage in play activities and Anning (1999) observed that three year olds struggling to make sense of themselves as members of a family and a group setting were given insufficient support in dealing with discontinuities between the two contexts.

Mind-reading and mind-mindedness

Mind-reading in this context means having the ability to infer the desires or wishes of another person, usually a person one knows very well. Young children become experts at reading the minds of their parents and siblings, using this knowledge to ingratiate themselves or to tease and annoy. So mind-reading forms part of the social fabric of family life. Of course, all siblings have their quarrels – and sometimes fights. The incidence of fighting between sisters and brothers is higher than that between friends outside the home, although the incidence for boys is roughly the same as that with peers. As Dunn (1984: 144) adds, 'It is because they understand their siblings so well, and because they feel so strongly about them, that their relationship is so significant and so revealing'.

Attendance at an ECEC setting affords babies and young children opportunities to make friends and to play with other children. Again, Dunn (1993) tells us that young children's friendships are important to them and often children as young as four have friends they made when only two. Friends are also important when children move to a new ECEC setting or to school. Those who, on transition, had a friend who moved setting with them fared much better in comparison with those who did not move with a friend, and Dunn found that they remembered that it was the presence of the friend that made them happy in the new setting. She also explored the ways in which family members related to one another and recognised these were reflected in interactions in nurseries. Children who enjoyed high levels of involvement with their mothers were more likely to be conciliatory and to compromise with friends. They also engaged in longer and more elaborate bouts of shared fantasy play and conversations.

A similar effect was found when Howes et al. (1994) explored children's relationships with their ECEC practitioners. Where the practitioners modelled socialisation the children seemed to be more accepting towards each other and when they felt secure in their setting they displayed complex play with other children, with whom they were also more gregarious than children who did not experience positive relationships with staff.

Harris (1989) explains how different cultures build on what may be a universal, innate ability to recognise positive and negative emotional states. He also discusses the ways in which the emotions of guilt and shame are used to socialise children and different cultures use these to varying degrees. By the time they are two years old children are learning the 'scripts' assigned to different emotions by their family or community, that are learned to make one acceptable. Sometimes they will use 'transitional objects' to help them in this regulation of the emotions. These might be dummies, favourite soft toys or comforters that have been self-chosen.

Children who have warm, affectionate relationships with their parents have been found to be more likely to have high self-esteem, to be better socially adjusted and to achieve academically (Mortimer, 2001). In the review of the literature for *Birth to Three Matters* (DfES, 2003a), we used Siegel's (1999) important studies to point out that if parents – and one might surmise this could also apply to practitioners – did not enjoy warm, close relationships with their own parents, then encouraging them to reflect on their narratives of their own childhoods and to understand how they feel can help them become more positive, so that they are able to engage in the loving, sensitive interactions which will benefit their children's emotional wellbeing and personal and social development (David et al., 2003).

For ECEC settings, the issues related to staff relationships with children and the difficulties of shifts, holidays and other complications require debate. Elfer et al. (2011)

advocate the Key Person system to enable close relationships, which the babies and young children need to develop. They suggest that the benefits of the Key Person approach allow for supplementing rather than replacing loving care and learning that children experience at home. It is through the actions and talk of familiar adults, whether family members or staff in an ECEC setting, that young children develop their emotional and social abilities and their physical and cognitive powers. Adults who are capable of being 'mind-minded' – that is, they show they think of young children as 'feeling, intentional and sentient, as opposed to purely physical beings' (Degotardi and Sweller, 2012: 253) – support and encourage such all-round development. They follow each child's interest and try to help individuals achieve their goals, often talking them through their struggles – for example, 'Oh, you're trying to reach the red teddy … (moves red teddy closer) – that's it, now you've got teddy!' In England, Ofsted inspectors are now required to check on children's bonds with their Key Persons (Tassoni, 2013), looking for evidence, such as frequent eye contact, delight in being together, showing they have a strong connection. These are highly desirable features of provision but not always practicable (Goouch and Powell, 2013) and indeed impoverished adult–child ratios may further jeopardise such contingent interactions (Elfer and Page, 2013).

Conclusions: adults' roles, personal qualities, education and training

The main points debated in this chapter have been as follows:

- Early relationships with sensitive, loving others form the model for later relationships; pleasurable interactions during the first two years provide the scripts which children adopt in their later friendships (the adults and older children involved act as models).
- Children who, early in life, have been encouraged by emotionally sensitive parents and carers to explore and enjoy their world will take greater pleasure in goal-directed behaviour later in life and they will persist at difficult tasks; they will also be more competent socially and cognitively.
- Resilient people tend to have, or have had, at least one person in their life to whom they feel they (and what they do) matter.
- Staff in ECEC settings sometimes need to help children integrate into the group and they need to be aware of how friendships can help children cope with transitions.
- Most importantly, as Gerhardt (2004) and we ourselves (David et al., 2003) have urged, babies and young children need to experience unconditional acceptance, respect, continuity of relationships – these can be with several key people – and to bask in interactions and play with those who love and care about them.

Yet what should be said in response to the debate over whether loving staff or well-qualified staff are more essential for ECEC settings? The Effective Provision of Pre-school Education (EPPE) project (Sylva et al., 2004) has provided the main evidence suggesting that staff with higher levels of qualifications are more successful in promoting children's cognitive abilities. Other studies (Degotardi and Sweller, 2012; Meins et al., 2013) show that children also benefit from both parental and ECEC setting staff relationships that are warm and sensitive, so that experiences during the first years of life result in children having fewer anxieties and being more positive in their interactions with other children and adults in their later years. Research suggests that we need to examine current approaches to education and training, since many who have the ability to interact with young children in ways that foster their development and who are empathic, responsive and emotionally attuned, have often acquired these attributes through family modelling. Others may not have been so lucky. Degotardi and Sweller suggest that, rather than content-based workshops, training should involve 'reflective supervision' in which trainees need to be helped to recognise high quality infant experiences and to reflect on their own work-based practices, to link theory to practice, so increasing their ability to appreciate the children's perspectives. Further, these researchers found that staff will often demonstrate greater 'mind-mindedness' when working with older children, thus apparently perceiving babies and toddlers as less capable. Such assumptions could also be challenged in reflective supervision.

Surely therefore, the main question – 'Should ECEC staff be loving or well-qualified?' – should not be an 'either/or' one. Rather, we should ensure babies and young children experience feeling loved and cherished by adults who are appropriately educated and trained to understand their needs holistically – fostering all areas of development.

Questions and exercises

1. How might poverty impact on a young child's social and emotional development?
2. What personal qualities enable an early years practitioner to provide every child in their setting with appropriate experiences to foster their social and emotional development? Can such qualities be taught and if so, how? How do, or could, courses to work in ECEC foster the ability to promote children's social and emotional development?
3. List the practices you have observed in your setting which create barriers to the development of social and emotional development in young children and say how you would set about changing these.

Further reading

We recommend Vasudevi Reddy's *How Infants Know Minds* (2010) on how emotional engagements can show babies' early and increasing awareness of other people's intentions. Similarly focusing on infants and toddlers (birth to two), the Wave Trust (2013) reports 'significant messages about effective parenting and evidenced practice with 0–2s' and particularly mental health and wellbeing. Marion Dowling's (2009) edition of *Young Children's Personal, Social and Emotional Development* links theories of development to practice and to the EYFS. For a culturally sensitive review of attachment research, see John Oates's (2007) edition of *Attachment Relationships*. Finally, Kiernan and Mensah's (2011) article on poverty, family resources and educational attainment highlights the importance of looking beyond poverty headlines, exploring how some parents' behaviours seem to mitigate against economic disadvantage.

8

LANGUAGE DEVELOPMENT IN THE YOUNG CHILD

Thea Cameron-Faulkner

Contents

- Introduction
- Theoretical approaches to language development
- Language development across cultures
- Bilingualism and multilingualism
- Conclusion

Introduction

For decades, researchers from a range of disciplines have been intrigued by the process of language development and the insight it can provide for our understanding of human cognition. The field of child language research is rich with competing theories, all of which aim to address the key question in the field: what are the processes and knowledge base that underlie the development of language in humans? In this chapter I will outline three approaches to the study of language development: the behaviourist approach, the formalist approach and the constructivist approach. While each of these labels subsumes a network of related theories, the categorisation provides a useful starting point. Following the theoretical overview, the discussion will be widened to encompass cross-cultural aspects of language development and their impact on our understanding of the process in general.

Theoretical approaches to language development

In some ways the most logical place to start this discussion is by considering what kind of linguistic knowledge is ascribed to adults. By considering the type of knowledge a child must acquire we can then focus on the manner in which they traverse the path of development from preverbal infants to fully-fledged members of their linguistic community.

The behaviourist approach

In the behaviourist tradition, most typically associated with Skinner (1957), language is situated within the behaviourist rubric of classical and operant conditioning, that is learning evoked through 'stimulus and response' and 'reward/punishment' processes. Classical conditioning is claimed to underlie the child's ability to associate a stimulus (like a noise or object) with an arbitrary verbal sign (a word or phrase). For example, consider a caregiver and child playing with a rattle. The child holds and shakes the rattle and looks towards the caregiver. The caregiver then comments on the object, 'Yes, it's a *rattle*. Do you like the *rattle*?' Over time the child begins to associate the form *rattle* with the object and acquires a new word form. Thus, the early stages of language development involve the child imitating a linguistic form presented in response to a particular stimulus.

The response of the caregiver to the child's utterances further shapes the child's linguistic system through the process of operant conditioning as forms eliciting 'rewards' are retained while forms resulting in 'punishment' are avoided. Thus, if the child produces a linguistic form that approximates a word and is appropriate in a given context, she or he will be rewarded in some way by the adult (such as a positive verbal response 'yes', the presentation of a requested item or the continuation of a conversation). Conversely, if a child produces a form that does not represent the child's target language or is not produced in response to the appropriate stimulus then it is more likely that she or he will not be rewarded (for example, the adult may ignore the utterance, ask for clarification or fail to produce the item that the child attempted to request). So, from the traditional behaviourist perspective, language development was viewed as a process involving imitation of input forms and subsequent shaping of the linguistic system through feedback from more experienced conversational partners.

The formalist approach

Skinner's most famous critic, Noam Chomsky, launched a devastating attack on the behaviourist account to language development in his 1959 review of Skinner's book

Verbal Behavior (1957). Chomsky claimed that the behaviourist characterisation of language was too simplistic and did not capture the underlying complexities of linguistic knowledge. In his review Chomsky proposed that our knowledge of language was highly abstract, consisting of algebraic rules and abstract categories that no child could learn without considerable innate knowledge. Consequently, Chomsky claimed that humans must be endowed with a genetic blueprint of language, known as Universal Grammar (UG). It was claimed that the linguistic information contained within UG went beyond the concrete linguistic expressions produced in everyday speech and captured the underlying rules and regularities which shape all natural languages.

As with all dynamic approaches to theoretical issues, the formalist approach is continually evolving. One of the more recent approaches is the Principles and Parameters theory (Chomsky, 1995) in which UG is claimed to consist of two types of information: first, structural information which equips the child with a set of general linguistic principles, and second a set of parameters ('switches') which allow the child to 'set' certain aspects of their linguistic knowledge to particular values in response to their language of exposure. To take a concrete example, consider the variation in word order across languages.

In English, verbs follow subjects as in (1):

1   It fell.

Whereas in Irish subjects follow verbs (2):

2   Thit sí.

Fell-it.

'It fell.'

Through exposure to their target language the child would subconsciously switch the appropriate parameter in line with the word order patterns attested in their language and thus be said to have acquired the word order (and associated values known as 'headedness') of their native language. In this way the input a child receives acts as a trigger as opposed to the sole source of linguistic evidence available to the child.

Chomsky bolstered his linguistic theory by positing a number of claims pertaining to the linguistic input received by young children. First, Chomsky claimed that the input children receive is degenerate, that is the language children hear contains incomplete utterances, grammatical errors, false starts and many other features of everyday informal speech (Chomsky, 1965). Therefore, if the child's only available source of linguistic knowledge is the ambient language then how could they be sure which utterances were grammatical and which were not? In addition to this, Chomsky and other UG researchers claim that the input does not contain the wide range of structures necessary for a child to work out the underlying categories and rules of their target language:

> People attain knowledge of the structure of their language for which no evidence is available in the data to which they are exposed as children. (Hornstein and Lightfoot, 1981: 9)

Together these two claims are known as the 'Poverty of the Stimulus' argument and are presented as a challenge to any approach to language development in which the input plays a central role.

Chomsky also claimed that children do not receive explicit feedback on the grammaticality of their utterances. For example, a child who produced errors related to negation (*I not do it*) would not be informed consistently of the correct form (*I didn't do it*). This claim is referred to as the 'no-negative evidence' problem and is widely upheld within the formalist tradition:

> I think that the assumption that negative evidence is not available to the child's learning mechanisms is warranted. There are, no doubt, cases in which parents correct their children (e.g., over-regularized affixing). However, there is anecdotal evidence that even in such cases, children are oblivious to such corrections. (Pinker, 1984: 29)

As Pinker points out, even when feedback is on offer there is evidence to suggest that this input is not always positively received as the well-quoted example from McNeill indicates:

Child: Nobody don't like me.

Mother: No, say 'Nobody likes me'

Child: Nobody don't like me.

(dialogue repeated eight times)

Mother: Now listen carefully, say 'Nobody likes me.'

Child: Oh! Nobody don't likes me.

(McNeill, 1966: 69)

In McNeill's example the mother attempts to correct the child's utterance but regardless of instruction the child continues to struggle with the grammaticality of the utterance.

Thus, formalists claim that children could not learn their target language from the input alone and thus must be genetically equipped with some form of linguistic knowledge. Within this framework then the child's task in acquiring their native tongue is to fine tune their innate linguistic knowledge in order to reflect the structural properties of their target language.

The no-negative evidence argument and the Poverty of the Stimulus argument are central to the formalist approach. However, not all researchers agree that children are bereft of feedback or indeed agree on what should be counted as feedback. A number of studies conducted in response to claims about no-negative evidence indicated that caregivers have a tendency to 'recast' their children's ungrammatical utterances as shown in (3) below:

3 Child: fix Lilly

Mother: Oh ... Lilly will fix it.

(Sokolov and Snow, 1994: 47)

In (3) the child produces an ungrammatical utterance and the mother reformulates the gist of the utterance into a grammatical form. The process of recasting can be viewed as a form of feedback; first, the recast indicates to the child that their utterance was ill-formed in some way, and second, the target form is presented in quick succession to the error. This implicit feedback appears to have a positive effect on linguistic development (e.g. Demetras et al., 1986; Bohannon and Stanowicz, 1988). There have also been challenges regarding Chomsky's claims about the linguistic input available to young children (the Poverty of the Stimulus) as researchers investigate the characteristics of Child Directed Speech (CDS) at a fine-grained level. In order to present these arguments I will now move on to discuss a contrasting view of language development broadly referred to in this chapter as the constructivist approach.

The constructivist approach

While researchers working within the formalist tradition focused on the acquisition of linguistic structure and the form of underlying linguistic knowledge, a growing body of developmental linguists and psychologists were shifting attention towards more semantically orientated theories (for example, Bloom, 1970) and frameworks in which the social nature of language provided the backdrop to development (for example, Bates and MacWhinney, 1982; Bruner, 1983; Braine, 1994; Ninio and Snow, 1999). The constructivist approach as described below is an umbrella term for a range of theories (including social interactionist, usage-based and connectionist) which share a common belief that linguistic knowledge is constructed by the child as opposed to being pre-given at birth. Constructivist theories challenge the formalist representation of linguistic knowledge and suggest that adult linguistic knowledge is shaped by experience, that is the language addressed to and used by individual speakers (Hopper and Thompson, 1984; Langacker, 1987; Bybee and Scheibman,

1999; Tomasello, 2000; Croft, 2001). Rather than viewing language as an abstract system of categories and rules, researchers working within constructivist approaches typically view language in terms of linguistic constructions which are tied to specific functions. Thus, in the words of the cognitive linguist Langacker, the grammatical systems of natural languages consist of 'a structured inventory of conventional linguistic units' (1991: 548). This characterisation of language is reflected in the work of many linguists who believe that much of the speech we produce is not stored in terms of abstract linguistic units but instead as 'chunks' of speech with a specific purpose. Coulmas states:

> A great deal of communicative activity consists of enacting routines making use of pre-fabricated linguistic units in a well-known and generally accepted manner. We greet and bid farewell to one another, introduce ourselves and others, apologize and express gratitude, buy groceries and order meals, exchange wishes, make requests, ask for advice or information, report on what we did, and announce what we are about to do. As similar speech situations recur, speakers make use of similar and sometimes identical expressions, which have proved to be functionally appropriate. Thus competent language use is always characterized by an equilibrium between the novel and the familiar. (1981: 1)

This representation of language leads to very different claims regarding the type of knowledge the child has to learn and how they proceed in acquiring it. For example, Tomasello, Lieven and colleagues (see Tomasello, 1992; Lieven et al., 1997; Dabrowska, 2000; Theakston et al., 2001; Lieven et al., 2003) claim that children rely heavily on lexically based constructions in the early stages of language development (for example, *It's a X, want Y*). These units are stored, forming the basis of the child's knowledge of their target language. As more units are stored the child subconsciously extracts the underlying structural patterns that form the fabric of their target language.

Critiques have suggested that constructivist accounts bear a strong resemblance to old fashioned behaviourism; that is, language develops through imitation of the input. However, the constructivist approach differs to behaviourism on two fundamental issues. First, although it is claimed that children are learning from the input, their learning is not straightforward imitation but rather a specific form of cultural learning. As Tomasello states:

> Human children differ from their nearest primate relatives not only in having language but also in being able to imitatively learn other types of social conventions, to communicate with others declaratively, to use material symbols such as pictures and maps, to make and use intentionally defined tools with a history, to collaborate using complementary roles, to teach one another, and to create social institutions such as governments and money. This suggests a fairly general human ability to interact with conspecifics culturally, that is, to create material, symbolic, and institutional artefacts historically and to acquire their use ontogenetically. No other species on the planet has this same propensity for things cultural. (2003: 290)

In the approach to development captured in the above quote Tomasello situates language and its development in children as an intrinsic part of cultural behaviour. Second, children are not limited to input forms but instead move beyond the input by constructing a more schematic representation of language. Therefore, a child learning English will gradually formulate a schema for plural formation which will result in the production of NOUN+s schema. By using this schema a child will produce both correct forms (*cars*, *bikes*, *cakes*) but also from time to time use the schema erroneously (*sheeps*, *feets*). Thus, unlike a behaviourist account, the child is not simply mimicking the input but instead working from the bottom up by learning lexically based constructions and then subconsciously working out the regularities between them.

Within the constructivist approach to language development the linguistic input that children receive is central to the developmental process. What then of the formalist claim that the input that children receive is 'impoverished'? Whether we believe that the language children hear is sufficient for language to develop or not very much depends on the nature of what we think it is that they are acquiring. If the child's task is to discover an abstract and highly rule governed system from the onset of language development then most researchers would agree that the language children typically hear does not contain the vast range of structure necessary for a child to know that '*he*' in (4a) could refer to Jay while in (4b) '*he*' could also refer to someone other than Jay:

4a   When Jay entered the room, he was wearing a yellow shirt.

4b   When he entered the room Jay was wearing a yellow shirt.

(Anderson and Lightfoot, 2002: 19)

However, if we claim that the child's task is to store units of speech and then use these as a basis to gradually extract the patterns of their language then research would indicate that the language children hear is well suited to the task. The specific nature of CDS has been well documented in language development literature. Typically the speech addressed to young children has a specific form of intonation, shorter sentence structure, restricted vocabulary and focuses on the here and now:

The broad outlines of mothers' speech to children – that it is simple and redundant, that is contains many questions, many imperatives, few past tenses, few co- or sub-ordinations, and few dysfluencies, and that it is pitched higher and has an exaggerated intonation pattern – are quite well established. (Snow, 1977: 36)

All these adaptations appear well suited to gaining and maintaining the attention and understanding of young language learners. Studies also indicate that the structures used in CDS are highly repetitive and may thus facilitate the segmentation and abstraction of the lexically based frames which dominate young children's early linguistic systems. For example, Cameron-Faulkner et al. (2003) conducted a lexically based analysis of CDS from twelve mothers. The results demonstrated a high degree of lexical specificity in the speech of the mothers with over half of the CDS sample consisting of a very limited number of lexically based frames (e.g. *Are you …? Look at …, It's a …, What's that?*). Thus, the study indicated that rather than being degenerate, the input addressed to nascent language learners may be well suited to the task at hand.

While studies of CDS indicate the adult may adapt their speech to young children, there are limitations as much of this work is based on a specific sample of the population, namely caregivers living in Western industrialised countries. As a number of researchers have pointed out, CDS is not attested in all cultures. In the next section child language development is discussed within a cross-cultural perspective.

Language development across cultures

Cultural attitudes to language development differ worldwide. In the cultural context of Western, middle-class English-speaking communities, adults tend to employ some form of modified speech when talking to children, as mentioned in the previous section. However, as Lieven (1994) points out, this does not appear to be a universal phenomenon. In a number of cultures adults do not address children directly, for a variety of reasons. Heath (1983) presents an ethnographic study of two rural working-class communities ('Trackton' and 'Roadville') in South Carolina. Trackton is a black working-class area in which the older generations are engaged in farming, while Roadville (only a few miles down the road) is predominantly a white working-class area based around employment in the textile mills. Despite their close proximity, Heath's ethnographic study indicated clear differences within the cultures of the two communities and suggested that these differences are also manifested in caregivers' approach to language development.

In Roadville, Heath comments that: 'When the baby begins to respond verbally, to make sounds which adults can link to items in the environment, questions and statements are addressed to the baby, repeating or incorporating his "word"' (1983: 123), while Heath comments that in Trackton: '[caregivers] do not see babies or young children as suitable partners for regular conversations. For an adult to choose a preverbal infant over an adult as a conversational partner would be considered an affront and a strange behaviour as well' (1983: 86).

Heath claims that in the Roadville community language is viewed as a skill that should be fostered and nurtured by caregivers. Adults modify their speech when addressing young children in order to accommodate the linguistic knowledge of their conversational partners. In contrast, according to Heath, the prevailing ethos in Trackton is that children should discover how the world works for themselves and that this ethos also extends to the acquisition of language. Children are required to find their own way of breaking into the linguistic system of their speech community. However, it is important to note the social environment of the Trackton children:

> Infants are held during their waking hours, occasionally while they sleep, and they usually sleep in the bed with parents until they are about 2 years of age. They are held, their faces fondled, their cheeks pinched, and they eat and sleep in the midst of human talk and noise from the television, stereo, and radio. Encapsulated in an almost totally human world, they are in the midst of constant human communication, verbal and non-verbal. They literally feel the body signals of shifts in emotion of those who hold them almost continuously; they are talked about and kept in the midst of talk about topics that range over any subject. (Heath, 1986: 112)

Thus, while the Trackton children may not have been addressed directly, they were continually exposed to their target language and to the routines and daily activities encoded by it.

Schieffelin (1994) also presents an ethnographic account of language socialisation but this time in among a very different population: the Kaluli community of Papua New Guinea. Schieffelin highlights the lack of CDS attested in the community, but further comments that:

> However, this does not mean that Kaluli children grow up in an impoverished verbal environment and do not learn how to speak. Quite the opposite is true. The verbal environment of the infant is rich and varied, and from the very beginning the infant is surrounded by adults and older children who spend a great deal of time talking to one another. (1994: 485)

The onset of language development is marked by the use of two key words by the child; 'mother' (no) and 'breast' (bo). After this point linguistic interaction between caregiver and child commences as the child is presented with eliciting 'elema' (say like that) constructions such as (5) and (6). The elema are used to inform the child of the appropriate linguistic conventions required within a given context and provide direct instruction to the young language learning child.

5   ni nuwe suke! elema.

My grandmother picked! say like that

6   gi suwo?! elema.

Did you pick?! say like that

(Schieffelin, 1994: 486)

The ethnographic descriptions presented by Heath and Schieffelin are two of many studies which indicate that many children are exposed to language in an indirect way and thus 'tend to participate in communicative interactions in the role of overhearers of non-simplified conversations between others' (Ochs and Schieffelin, 1995: 78). There is a growing body of research that indicates children can and do learn aspects of language through overhearing speech as opposed to being addressed directly. For example, Akhtar et al. (2001) compared the ability of two year olds to acquire novel nouns and verbs when the items were presented direct and indirectly (i.e. with the children overhearing the words in question). The findings of the study indicated that children of around two-and-a-half years found it just as easy to acquire the words in both conditions and thus children can learn words which are not directly addressed to them. The results echoed the perceptions of the parents whose children were involved in the study:

> Many parents reported that their children knew many more words than they had been explicitly taught (including some words that parents would prefer their children had not learned). (2001: 428)

Nevertheless, children from these communities still acquire their native tongue and in addition there is evidence to suggest that children from CDS and non-CDS cultures actually develop language on the same timescale (Ochs, 1985). Such communities are still under-represented in the field of language development. However, it could be argued that in order to fully understand the process of language development it is not only the range of languages that needs to be widened with regard to analysis but also the cultural diversity in which children learn the language of their community.

Bilingualism and multilingualism

The current discussion has centred around children learning one language (i.e. monolingual language development). However, the reality for a large proportion of children and adults across the world is more complex. According to recent estimates more children are raised in bilingual or multilingual environments than monolingual contexts. Within this population the range of learning contexts is vast. For example, some children will be raised as balanced bilinguals with a relatively equal command of two languages; other children may display more advanced skills (or dominance) in one particular language. The social and political perspectives associated with bilingualism and multilingualism are far reaching, however, for the purposes of the current chapter the discussion will focus on aspects of language development within bilingual populations. This section begins with a discussion of some key distinctions made within the field of bilingual language development and then moves on to highlight trends regarding sound and lexical development in bilingual children.

Bilingual language learners are described as either simultaneous bilinguals or sequential bilinguals. Simultaneous bilinguals are exposed to two languages from birth. In cases where the child is brought up in a two parent household it may be the case that they hear one language from their mother and one from their father (one parent, one language), or hear both spoken by both parents. However, as noted by de Houwer (1995) cases of total separation of the languages addressed to children are rare and in most cases children's input will be somewhere on a continuum between separate and mixed. A common question raised by bilingual parents is whether one approach is more effective than the other. Current research appears divided on the issue. For example, while some researchers suggest that the 'one parent one language' approach facilitates native mastery of both languages (see Bain and Yu, 1980), others suggest that the linguistic development of bilingual children is not hindered by caregivers who address their children in more than one language (see García, 1983).

The impact of being raised bilingually on language development and cognitive development more generally is also a key area of debate. There is evidence to suggest the even before the age of twelve months bilingual infants possess different sensitivities to language than their monolingual counterparts. For example, infants around the age of six months are able to distinguish between a wide range of sounds (phonemes) found in both their native and non-native languages. However, over time this ability becomes confined to sounds associated with a speaker's target language only. For example, a Japanese-speaking adult learning English may find it difficult to distinguish the English sound 'r' from 'l' since the two sounds do not serve a meaningful contrast in Japanese. Research on bilingual infants indicates that seven- to eight-month old Spanish-Catalan bilingual infants retain the ability to discriminate between particular vowel sounds, while their monolingual counterparts are no longer able to identify the sounds as different (Albareda-Castellot et al., 2011).

In terms of vocabulary development bilingual children display the same rate of word learning as monolingual peers. That is when the lexical content associated with both languages is combined, bilingual children appear to acquire a comparable number of lexical items to monolingual children (Pearson et al., 1993). However the lexicon of a bilingual child tends to be smaller than age matched peers when considering each language individually (see Mahon and Crutchley, 2006). The grammatical development of bilingual children appears to follow similar trajectories to that of monolingual children. However, there is some evidence to suggest that there may be a lag with regard to some grammatical knowledge but that differences in rates of development reduce over time (see Hoff, 2008 for an accessible and informative overview). As with monolingual children the characteristics of the input play a central role in the language development of bilingual children though, due to the wide range of bilingual and multilingual contexts around the world, determining the role of the input provides unique challenges to child language researchers.

Conclusion

In this chapter, three approaches to language development have been presented. Each approach is informed by a different set of assumptions regarding the nature of linguistic knowledge and as a consequence results in markedly distinct theories of language acquisition. Cross-cultural differences with regard to linguistic input were also discussed with studies indicating that the characteristics of the linguistic environment reflect the cultural beliefs of the community with regard to the transmission of knowledge. The final section focused on language development in bilingual children and outlined some of the key issues of interest to bilingual researchers and parents alike.

Questions and exercises

1. What skills do children bring to the language learning task?
2. To what extent does the presence of CDS facilitate language development?
3. How would the formalist and functionalist approaches account for atypical language learning populations?
4. What contribution could siblings make to the development of language?

Further reading

There is a range of child language textbooks on the market, many of which present the major issues pertaining to language development from a theory neutral perspective, for example, Hoff (2008) *Language Development* and Berko Gleason (2005) *The Development of Language*. Lust (2006) *Child Language: Acquisition and Growth* presents a more formal linguistic approach to the study of language acquisition. For a thorough investigation of the usage-based approach to language development the reader is directed towards Tomasello (2003) *Constructing a Language*. In order to gain an insight into the debate between the innatist and non-innatist approaches to language development useful books are Pinker (1994) *The Language Instinct* and Sampson (2005) *Educating Eve: The 'Language Instinct' Debate*.

9

PLAY AND DEVELOPMENT IN EARLY CHILDHOOD

Justine Howard

Contents

- Introduction
- Why do we play?
- What is play?
- How do children define play?
- Play and development
- Professional play practice
- Cultural differences in children's play
- Conclusion

Introduction

The view that play is important, if not essential for children is something that is often assumed rather than demonstrated (Sutton-Smith, 1997). Play is 'all pervasive yet too vaguely acknowledged as a good thing' (Blenkin and Kelly, 1987: 37). Play scholars span many disciplines (including philosophy, psychology, sociology and anthropology) and their work highlights play's complexity from a historical, cultural and developmental perspective. It would be impractical to attempt an overarching review within an introductory chapter. The purpose here is to highlight the significance of play for development across domains in early childhood and the problems associated with its definition. In particular, the chapter will draw attention to the value of eliciting children's own perceptions of play and emphasise how play's fundamental qualities separate it from other modes of action.

Why do we play?

There have been many attempts to organise accounts of why we play. Strategies range from the popular classical versus dynamic distinction used by Saracho (1991) to the exotic, cross disciplinary rhetorics of Sutton-Smith (1997). The well-used phrase derived from Greek philosophy that there is nothing new under the sun is almost certainly true for organising the literature surrounding play.

Hughes (1999) suggests play theories differ according to whether they emphasise physical, emotional or intellectual development. Earlier accounts focus on one of these domains, for example, philosophical ideas suggest physical reasons for play; psychoanalytic approaches see play as central to emotional health while constructivist theories consider intellectual development. More recently, however, there has been a move towards holistic theories that consider the underlying features of play and its significance across multiple domains.

Early ideas about play

Ellis (1973, cited in Saracho and Spodek, 1998) describes early accounts of play as armchair theories as they come from the philosophical tradition and are largely based on *ideas* about human existence rather than *supporting evidence*. Saracho (1991) presents these theories as competing pairs. Surplus energy versus relaxation, where play either consumes or creates energy, and recapitulation versus pre-exercise, where play either reflects evolutionary extinct behaviours or serves as practice for skills required in adult life (Howard, 2002). The regulatory function proposed by energy theorists is echoed in the arousal modulation of Berlyne (1969). Here children are motivated to play because it provides an optimum means of regulating environmental stimulation. An over-stimulating environment requires exploration (to reduce nervous activity) whereas an under-stimulating environment requires play (to increase nervous activity). The proposition that play allows children to practise essential social skills is an important feature of the bio-cultural approach. This suggests that increased anti-social behaviour in modern society may be a result of reduced free play opportunities and increased adult surveillance, disrupting the development of essential neural pathways and compromising social competence (Jarvis, 2007).

Developmental theories

Whereas philosophical accounts were primarily concerned with why play exists, developmental theories seek to detail the nature and function of this play.

The earliest developmental theories stem from the psychoanalysis of Sigmund Freud (1856–1939) and are concerned with the role of play for social and emotional development. While many of Freud's ideas have been discredited, it is important to recognise the significance of his work, in particular for our appreciation of the unconscious mind and the impact of early experiences. Anna Freud (1968) developed her father's theory and maintained that during play children resolved anxiety and developed coping strategies for future use. Play afforded the opportunity to explore feelings that it would be inappropriate to tackle in everyday life. These ideas were further developed by Erikson (1977) who, in addition to the resolution of trauma, suggested that play provided an opportunity for learning about the self and others. In play children learned about their personality characteristics and the complexity of human relationships. Psychoanalysis continues to make an invaluable contribution to the growing professional fields of therapeutic play and playwork.

Constructivist accounts of play are embedded within broader theories of development and include the work of Piaget and Vygotsky (see Chapter 6). Piaget (1952) maintained that as a species we are motivated to learn in order to ensure that our mental representation of the world matches reality: this he described as equilibrium. To achieve equilibrium we are born with two mechanisms of change: assimilation and accommodation. Of significance is that Piaget saw play as largely assimilative, consolidating existing knowledge rather than being a principal mode of learning. His theory of play was strongly associated with his stage theory of development and he described play as reflecting increased cognitive ability. For Piaget, play was secondary to the business of learning and allowed children to perfect, rather than acquire, developing skills.

Vygotsky maintained that development was driven by our motivation towards social interaction. A central tenet of his work was the zone of proximal development and of significance was his proposition that play itself provides such a zone, where children are able to set their own challenges. Vygotsky argued that in play 'a child always behaves beyond his average age, above his daily behaviour' (1978: 102). This demonstrates his view of the child as both an independent and, critically, a social learner. He was particularly interested in symbolism during imaginative play and it is argued that, for Vygotsky, the ability to allow one thing to stand for something else represents children's first experience with systems, which they will later apply in numeracy and literacy (Whitebread and Jameson, 2005).

Alternative theories describe the holistic value of play rather than focusing on one particular developmental domain (see, for example, Chapter 10). These accounts propose that the value of play lies in its ability to promote adaptive and flexible patterns of behaviour. Bruner (1974) and Sutton-Smith (1979) suggest that play supports behavioural flexibility by freeing children from external goals and opens children's eyes to cognitive alternatives. During play children mix and match behaviours and being in control of the activity minimises the potential to fail and allows them to experiment with combinations fluidly. The power of play to facilitate adaptive and flexible thought is supported by animal analysis of Fagan (1984) who demonstrated that rats who were exposed to enriched, playful environments during infancy showed greater behavioural flexibility. Studies of their brain activity revealed that those who were reared in playful environments had increased neural interconnectivity, indicated by the complex branching and density of synapses. It is suggested that the increase in neural activity occurs because play activity stimulates the production of proteins that are responsible for the growth of important nerve cells (Siviy, 1998). Howard and Miles (2008, in Broadhead et al., 2010) suggest that play enhances children's learning and development because a 'playful state' leads to lower behavioural thresholds, enabling children to try out more complex and purposeful behaviours with minimal fear of failure. A further proposition about the holistic value of play is based on the notion of resilience. Howard and Fearn (2011) propose that playfulness has the power to reduce anxiety and to build and protect esteem which in turn maximises opportunities for learning and development across domains. There is strong empirical evidence to support the beneficial effects of 'playfulness', as is discussed later in the chapter.

What is play?

Holistic theories are exciting as they remind us that there is something unique about play that requires investigation if we are to fully understand its contribution to development. A fundamental problem, however, is agreeing on an operational definition of what play actually is. Providing a definition is important as it ensures we are all talking about the same thing. Attempts to define play can be grouped into those that consider categories, criteria and continuum.

Concordant with his theory of cognition, Piaget (1951) identified three types of play that reflected children's thinking ability: practice play, symbolic play and games with rules (Howard, 2002). These types of play were predominant at particular stages of development (such as practice play during the sensorimotor period) and were dependent on cognitive ability (for example, symbolic play emerging with symbolic thought). Piaget's identification of early sensory play resonates in Goldschmied's work on heuristic play that describes infants' absorption with objects chosen for their sensory and non-prescriptive qualities (see Goldschmied and Jackson, 2003). The proposition that early sensory experience is important for the development of future play skills is a pivotal feature of Jennings's (1999) Embodiment, Projection and Role paradigm (EPR) in therapeutic play. Smilansky (1968) argued that Piaget's typology did not account for certain forms of play and added a category for construction, but for Piaget this represented accommodative rather than assimilative activity. This highlights the issue of subjectivity; what is considered play by one person may not be considered play by another (Howard, 2002). Even the fifteen-category typology of Hughes (1996) may defy this neat categorisation, and all-encompassing typologies, such as the ludic/epistemic distinction made by Hutt et al. (1989), may be too broad. In a review of the literature surrounding play behaviour, Whitebread et al. (2012) propose that play can be divided into five main types, these include: physical play, play with objects, symbolic play, pretence/socio-dramatic play and games with rules.

Criteria approaches suggest that for an activity to be defined as play it must demonstrate intrinsic motivation, positive affect, freedom from rules, non-literality and attention to means over ends (see Rubin et al., 1983). However, there is debate among scholars as to the relative importance of each of these characteristics. Smith and Vollstedt (1985) presented adult raters with video clips of children at play and found that the most common indicators used were non-literality, flexibility and positive affect. Interestingly, intrinsic motivation was not used by the raters despite it being a consistent feature of play within the literature. Smith and Vollstedt subsequently adopted these three principal criteria despite other theorists maintaining that play does not always appear enjoyable or involve pretence (Sutton-Smith and Kelly-Byrne, 1984). The usefulness of the criteria approach is further reduced when we consider that Smith and Vollstedt's adult raters felt that at least two characteristics had to be present before a play judgement was made. Might an activity still be play even though only one characteristic is observed?

Rather than using criteria to make an absolute decision as to whether an activity is or is not play, Pellegrini (1991) suggests that the number of criteria present can be used to place the play on a continuum. More criteria indicate a closer proximity to pure play. As with broad typologies, however, the value of this is questionable. Garvey (1991) presents a dynamic continuum and suggests that during an episode of play, children move in and out of the play frame using different modes of action. This movement in and out of the play frame highlights how difficult it is to make a decision as to whether or not activity is play regardless of whether we adopt a category, criteria or continuum approach as the situation is ever changing. Garvey's work is also interesting as it hints at the significance of play as an attitude or mode of action.

How do children define play?

Animal studies aside, most play research relates to children and it is surprising that only a limited amount of time has been spent investigating their views. As Takhvar comments:

> as play is mostly practiced during childhood, perhaps children themselves could provide a means to define this behaviour, or at least illuminate how far and to what extent they share adults' views. (1988: 238)

Play means different things to different people in different contexts (Guha, 1988; Howard, 2002). By focusing on theories and definitions of play that are the result of adult observations we have arguably been missing the affective elements that render it a powerful developmental media. Winnicott (1971) distinguishes the noun 'play' from the verb 'playing' and proposes that it is the noun, rather than the verb, that warrants investigation. This point is echoed by Lieberman (1977), who separates the behavioural elements of play from its quintessence: the quintessence of play being its essential and defining quality. Recently, there has been renewed interest in children's own perceptions of play in an effort to pinpoint what this illusive quality might be.

Interview studies have revealed that children categorise play according to activity type (including role play, construction activities and outdoor play rather than writing, drawing or reading books), the level of control they are afforded and whether or not an adult is present (see King, 1979; Karrby, 1989). Similarly, using the Activity Apperception Story Procedure (a photographic sorting task), Howard (2002) found that children used cues to categorise play based on who was involved (adult or no adult presence), the activity type (e.g., sand and water versus writing and drawing), whether or not they choose to participate and, in addition, where an activity took place (table or floor). This work and that of Karrby (1989) also demonstrated that children developed these cues as a result of their experiences with both the physical and social environment.

Play and development

The difficulties associated with defining play coupled with the need to isolate play as a causal determinant has meant that empirical support for the developmental potential of play has been limited. Research includes observational, longitudinal and experimental studies, each with its own strengths and limitations.

In the field of language acquisition (see Chapter 8), observational studies show how children play with sounds, nonsensical rhyming patterns and the grammatical construction of sentences (Hughes, 1999). While there are correlations between these acts of play and other skills, for example, children's rhyming ability and reading achievement (Athey, 1984, cited in Hughes, 1999), we cannot infer that this is a direct result of play. During physical play we observe children running, jumping and riding bicycles. These children appear intrinsically motivated and seem to be having fun. There is no doubt that they are developing muscle control, co-ordination, balance and self-awareness but again this is not necessarily a result of the play. For instance, had the children been instructed to ride on the bicycles and in protest rode repetitively back and forth from one end of the yard to the other, the physicality of the activity would remain.

The impressive longitudinal Effective Provision of Pre-school Education (EPPE) project reports that quality, play-based provision in the early years leads to superior social, emotional and cognitive development (Sylva et al., 2004). However, a quality environment is defined via indicators such as the nature of adult–child interaction, and it is questionable whether this is in keeping with the fundamental qualities of play as children often categorise play as being something that does not involve adult participation (see King, 1979; Howard, 2002). The difference between authentic play activities (ones which a child believes to be play) and contrived activities (those which a teacher designs to look like play) is documented by Walsh et al. (2011).

Experimental studies attempt to isolate play as a causal factor but even these do not escape criticism. The classic lure retrieval study by Sylva et al. (1976) is frequently cited as evidence for the relationship between play and problem solving. Children who were allowed to play with materials in a practice session performed better at retrieving an object with clamps and sticks than those who had not engaged in the play beforehand. This study (and others of a similar design) has been criticised, however, for failing to differentiate between play and initial exploration with materials (Sutton-Smith, 1997).

Understanding children's own perceptions of their play has led to significant advances in demonstrating the relationship between playfulness and development. The cues used by children to define play (location, choice and adult involvement) have been used to manipulate experimental conditions in studies designed to measure the impact of playful practice on children's behaviour. These have consistently revealed that playful practice leads to significantly improved performance on problem solving tasks (Ramani, 2005; Thomas et al., 2006; McInnes et al., 2009), deeper concentration and involvement (McInnes et al., 2009) and higher levels of emotional wellbeing (Howard and McInnes, 2012).

Professional play practice

We have come to acknowledge that emotional health lies at the core of children's development and that play is a key way to support this (Howard and Prendiville, 2008). Policy relating to care and education emphasises the importance of wellbeing and many local authorities offer training courses for professionals to learn how to support children's emotional health. Although educational, recreational and therapeutic professionals may encounter play in different settings and experience different pressures in relation to the experiences provided, they are unified by the qualities of play that render it powerful. Rather than seeing play as being qualitatively different across contexts (for example, play as pedagogy or play as therapy) it may be more useful to see this as a spectrum of practice. There is developmental, educational and therapeutic value in all of children's play, although the emphasis placed on these values may differ according to context (Howard and McInnes, 2013). The benefits children accrue in play will vary depending on the depth and nature of the relationships that develop, the child's circumstances and the skills and judgement utilised by the practitioner.

Therapeutic play

The therapeutic power of play is rooted in the psychoanalytic tradition and since the 1920s play has been used to help children express themselves more readily (Landreth, 2002). *Play therapists* harness play to resolve psychosocial difficulties and to make clinical decisions about children's therapeutic needs. They are often, but not always, trained in psychotherapy and their emphasis is on the development of a therapeutic relationship. *Developmental and therapeutic play specialists* use play to enhance children's holistic development, and they work with individuals and groups, facilitating play skills to promote wellbeing and resilience (Howard and Prendiville, 2008). Approaches can be directive, non-directive or integrative. In a directive approach the therapist offers interpretation as to the meaning of the play and may plan specific interventions based on this interpretation. The early psycho-analytic approaches of Anna Freud and Melanie Klein were consistent with this tradition and saw play as an information gathering opportunity. Non-directive approaches are characterised by the active role of the child who essentially leads the session. Carl Rogers instigated a move towards client-led therapies (Hughes, 1999) and this is extended in the work of Virginia Axline (1969), whose approach draws attention to the value of both the therapeutic relationship and the play process. As well as using selected toys, therapeutic play also involves puppetry, story-telling, art, music, drama and dance. This range of media ensures opportunities for multi-sensory experiences, symbolism and role play, all of which are fundamental to the EPR paradigm. This developmental approach to therapeutic play emphasises the successful negotiation of progressive play stages. The process begins with embodied sensory experiences, progresses to symbolism in projective play and cumulates in children's ability to enact roles. Each stage is important, providing 'intrinsic learnings … for life preparation' (Jennings, 1999: 55).

Playwork

The importance of play as a child-directed process and the sensitive nature of adult–child interaction in play are principles shared by therapeutic play and playwork. The parallels between the two professions are particularly evident within the psycholudic approach that draws together the key features of play activity that facilitate healing and development and proposes that, regardless of professional status (e.g., teacher, therapist or playworker), being involved with children during play immerses both the player and adult attendant into a space where healing and development are negotiated (Sturrock, 2003). While playworkers are often associated with recreational play and out-of-school clubs, the range of employment is much wider than this, for example, playworkers may also work in a therapeutic context. Playworkers adhere to a set of principles that are founded on children's right to play and the belief that opportunities for self-directed play are fundamental to development. In particular, they are very aware of the impact adult presence can have on children's play and work hard to ensure that play opportunities remain child-directed. Playworkers understand and respond appropriately to children's play cues, creating stimulating and flexible opportunities that allow children to pursue their own agendas (Brown, 2003). Despite debates surrounding the principles of playwork compared to play in educational settings, many of these objectives are shared by teaching professionals but implementing a play-based approach in educational contexts has proven to be rather more problematic.

Play in early education

Piaget (1951), Vygotsky (1978) and Bruner (1974) have played pivotal roles in the shaping and re-shaping of educational practices and we now acknowledge the importance of child-initiated activity and social interaction for learning and development. While play is clearly embedded within current curriculum initiatives (DCELLS, 2008; DfE, 2012a, EYFS) this is not that new. The Plowden Report clearly advocated the importance of play as a 'principal means of learning in early childhood' (CACE, 1967: 193) as did the curriculum guidance for the foundation stage (QCA, 2000). Despite this, observations of classroom practice demonstrated that play often tended to fulfil a subordinate role, secondary to principal classroom activity (Ofsted, 1993). The reasons for this have been researched widely. Bennett et al. (1997) propose that while teachers may advocate play, the uncertainty among scholars as to its value means that they lack the confidence to utilise it at classroom level. Other difficulties associated with implementing play-based curricula have included increased class size, pressure to account for and measure children's abilities, parental pressure towards the teaching of basic skills and a lack of understanding as to how to become involved in children's play (Sylva et al., 1992; Stipek and Byler, 1997). Prendiville (2008) also found that some teachers were intolerant of the mess associated with some forms of play such as sand and water. Overprescriptive curriculum guidelines and outcome measures have meant that, rather than using their professional skills, teachers have often felt that they have been driving a curriculum van (Edwards and Knight, 2000).

A re-conceptualisation of play that emphasises affective rather than behavioural qualities could ensure the success of curricula that centralise play. Research has shown that children's perceptions of play can be used diagnostically to plan a playful early years environment (Westcott and Howard, 2007; King and Howard, 2012). Understanding the cues children use to signal play as their mode of action allows teachers to create playful environments rather than activities that look like play and also to understand how they can become accepted as co-operative play partners (Rich, 2002; McInnes et al., 2010; 2011). These affective qualities empower practitioners and allow them to celebrate children's many ways of thinking, speaking and listening.

Cultural differences in children's play

Just as there are regional trends towards particular games *within* any given culture, there are also quantitative and qualitative differences in play *across* cultures. The unifying fact is that all children play. Hughes (1999) notes that the main conclusive evidence for cultural differences in children's play relates to competitive and co-operative play behaviour. Children within technologically advanced cultures are more likely to engage in competitive play and children from less affluent, underdeveloped countries are more likely to engage in co-operative games where the emphasis is on sharing and collectivity (see also Chapter 4). From a social constructivist perspective these differences are unsurprising and even before this theoretical approach gained momentum within the social sciences, Lieberman talked of parents and teachers as 'cultural surrogates' (1977: 99) representing the environment at large in encouraging or inhibiting children's play behaviours. Research into children's perceptions of play has demonstrated that children develop an understanding of what it means to play, based on cues from their environment and social interaction (Howard, 2002; Howard et al., 2006).

For play professionals there are many reasons why understanding cultural difference is important. In some cultures, dolls are not regarded positively for religious reasons and the act of dressing up can bring bad luck (Lindon, 2001). Children's play can be influenced by immediate experiences (such as parental separation, war or famine) but also by culturally dependent myth and legend (Jennings, 1999). These differences have implications for practice in therapeutic, educational and recreational play contexts. While a common feature of good early years practice from a white Western view includes opportunities for children to engage in messy play (such as finger painting, clay, sand and water), David and Powell (2005) found that Chinese practitioners had great difficulty understanding the value of this, as it conflicted with their principles of orderliness and cleanliness. Children were afforded opportunities to be playful but these opportunities were different. Indeed, David and Powell note how Chinese practitioners frequently utilised children's natural propensity towards playfulness in their teaching.

It has often been wrongly assumed that the absence of a particular form of behaviour means that it is not essential for children's development. While there are cultural differences in the nature of adult–child interaction during play, the types of play children engage in and the value placed on play for development (Roopnarine et al., 1998), there is little evidence that one particular practice is beneficial over another. Cross-cultural research into children's play warns us against the use of universal, observable behaviour as an indicator of developmental significance. Rather, we should seek to identify and explain the underlying qualities of this behaviour that render it important. It would seem that playfulness is the universal.

Conclusion

This chapter has considered theoretical perspectives as to why we play and the problems associated with defining this complex activity. It has shown how, in our quest to understand play and measure its developmental potential, we became distracted and lost sight of its unique qualities. Understanding children's perceptions draws us back to these qualities and reminds us that play is special. Play affords children the opportunity to learn and to heal and there is potential for these things to occur regardless of the context in which the play activity takes place. That is what makes play unique. Regardless of culture, when playful, children are afforded autonomy, choice and control. Howard and McInnes (2013) propose that there are seven evidenced benefits associated with these characteristics: flexible and adaptive thinking, increased motivation and attention, the development and protection of confidence and esteem, effective communication and the development of healthy attachments and social relationships.

Questions and exercises

1. Why are children's perceptions of play important?
2. What evidence is there for learning through play?
3. Why is an appreciation of cultural difference in play important?

Further reading

There are many general texts on play but I highly recommend the following: Justine Howard and Karen McInnes's (2013) *The Essence of Play: A Practice Companion for Professionals Working with Children and Young People* comprehensively covers the developmental and therapeutic potential of play across contexts and is illustrated with case studies and photographs. Sue Jennings's (1999) *Introduction to Developmental Play Therapy* provides a wonderful insight into therapeutic play, interwoven with beautiful case studies and powerful literary reference. Fraser Brown's (2003) *Playwork: Theory and Practice* is remarkably complex, drawing on the literature from psychology, anthropology, sociology and education, while Marjatta Kalliala's (2006) *Play Culture in a Changing World* offers a fresh and innovative consideration of play over time and across cultures. The latter is one of many insightful books from the Debating Play series edited by Tina Bruce, all of which are highly recommended.

10

CULTURAL-HISTORICAL THEORIES OF CHILD DEVELOPMENT

Marilyn Fleer

Contents

- Introduction
- Cultural development
- The concept of leading activity
- The concept of the social situation of development
- The concept of *perezhivanie*
- The interaction between the ideal and rudimentary in the child's environment
- Cultural-historical model of child development
- Conclusion

Introduction

Previous chapters in this section of the book have examined theories of child development in relation to thinking and cognition, social and emotional development, language development and play. This chapter goes beyond these areas of development and seeks to examine child development from a holistic perspective. To achieve this, it draws upon cultural-historical theory to conceptualise child development.

This chapter specifically foregrounds the cultural rather than the biological nature of children's development. Cultural does not mean ethnicity or race, but rather the higher forms of cultured development that are passed on from one generation to the next, such as values, ethics, morals, concepts and specific ways of thinking about and doing things valued in a particular community. In this conceptualisation, biology is not discounted, but rather the perspective put forward is that the child is shaped by, and shapes, the social and material world in which he or she exits. The child has agency in his or her own development. Child development is not biologically determined, or framed as an unfolding of a natural developmental trajectory (ages and stages), as has been shown in other theories of child development (such as that proposed by Piaget). Rather, child development is framed as a cultural process determined by the society in which the child lives and the child's active engagement in that society.

The chapter begins by illustrating what is meant by these two entangled lines of development – biological and cultural, followed by a discussion of the central concepts of a cultural-historical theory of child development. A model of child development is then presented that draws upon these concepts, illustrating through concrete examples how a cultural-historical theory of child development works in practice.

Cultural development

Shukla is sitting with her four-month-old infant on the grass in the local park. She sees a bird nearby and points to it, exclaiming, 'Look Aarjaw. A beautiful bird'. Aarjaw initially looks at Shukla's face, then when Shukla becomes even more animated, waving her finger and saying, 'Look, look, Aarjaw, quick or you will miss it!', Aarjaw looks at her finger. But he does not look to what Shukla is pointing at until Shukla picks him up and swings him towards the direction of the bird.

The pointing gesture, like many other forms of non-verbal communication, is learned within families and within cultural communities. As a symbolic tool in communication, pointing gestures and facial expressions are particularly important for orienting infants to what matters, and what one should pay attention to within a particular family and community. But the interaction cited above only focuses on communications of the adult towards the infant. It is only half of the picture. It gives no insight into how the pointing gesture itself becomes a tool for the infant to act upon their world. An example of Shukla and Aarjaw earlier in his life gives some clue about how this begins.

Shukla is watching her two-month-old infant, Aarjaw, lying on a soft mat on the floor of their living room. He is surrounded by rattles and soft toys, which are slightly out of reach, but are within view. Aarjaw swings his left arm across towards a toy rabbit. It is a physical movement often observed of young infants who are stretching their bodies without specific purpose. Shukla observes his arm movement and immediately pushes the rabbit towards Aarjaw saying, 'Oh you want the rabbit. Here it is'.

Vygotsky (1994a) famously wrote about a similar case to Aarjaw and Shukla, arguing that this is an example of an infant's actions being given social meaning, where the reflex action is named by the mother as a pointing gesture, allowing for objects in close proximity to be given to the infant. Over time and with repeated experiences such as that shown above, the infant learns that a movement of the arm, and later with more accuracy the finger, will ensure that what it is directed at will be retrieved or at least noticed by the adult. Cultural development and biological development are intertwined. But this narrative of the pointing gesture is illustrative of more than just the development of eye–hand co-ordination or when or what stage an infant can crawl to retrieve an object. The child's development is viewed holistically within their family and community, where the infant's intentions and motives are considered alongside what the adults in the infant's life value and orient the infant towards. As noted by Vygotsky (1994b: 64), 'the organic maturation plays the part of a *condition* rather than a motive power for the process of cultural development' (emphasis added). A maturational view of development, which foregrounds ages and stages, often dissecting the child into the development of language, social skills, emotionality and physicality, is only part of the picture. A cultural-historical view of development explicitly foregrounds the cultural line of development of the child, where the family and societal values and needs frame what a child pays attention to, what they experience and how they appropriate and use the cultural tools of their community to engage with their world, but also how they shape their world.

As noted by Vygotsky (1997: 231):

> cultural development of the child represents a special type of development, in other words, the process of the child's growing into the culture cannot be equated, on the one hand, with the process of organic maturation and on the other hand, it cannot be reduced to simple mechanical assimilation of certain external habits … cultural development, like all other development, is subject to its own patterns, its own stages.

These patterns and complexities of cultural development of the child can be better understood when an analysis of the central concepts of Vygotsky's (1998) theory are examined. I now turn to a close study of the central concepts of a cultural-historical view of child development: 'leading activity', 'social situation of development', '*perezhivanie*' and the 'ideal form'. Please note that these concepts are inter-related. One concept cannot be understood without considering it within a system of concepts about development.

The concept of leading activity

Vygotsky ([1933] 1966) introduced the concept of leading activity through the theoretical work he did in relation to play. He suggested that play was the leading activity of pre-school children. That is, pre-school children readily create imaginary situations when they change the meaning of objects and actions, such as turning a stick into a hobbyhorse, and then engaging in adventures. Children also role play what they have observed in real life (going to the markets with their family) or in fiction/media (e.g. TV, books, tablets), orienting themselves to the rules and roles within society. Play is a special kind of motive that Vygotsky ([1933] 1966) said leads pre-school children's development.

Leontiev (1978) further developed the concept of leading activity in relation to his theory of activity (see also Veresov, 2006), which Elkonin (1999) later conceptualised as a system of leading activities linked to particular periods in a child's life. The periods (infancy, early childhood, pre-school, early school, early adolescence, later adolescence), epochs (early childhood, childhood, adolescence) and phases within periods, each contain a motivational element that represents a unique characteristic of a person's life. Role play is but one of these motivational elements. These periods, epochs and phases parallel Vygotsky's (1998) age periodisation of development. Hedegaard and Fleer (2013: 13–14) state that, 'A child's developmental age period is not the same as the child's biological age. A child's developmental age or age period reflects the child's qualitative relation to his or her environment and depends on the child's motivational orientation'. Leading activities as a central motive in development are always conceptualised as the *relations between the child and the society* within which they live. For example, a child who begins school views him or herself as a *school child* engaged in *school type activities*, with both a motive for formal learning and with a display of certain competencies. The child expects to learn to read and write in this new societal institution of schooling where different kinds of activities take place to home (Hedegaard, 2012; Hedegaard and Fleer, 2013). Transition to school marks the child's leading activity for formal learning. But this does not mean that play is not present, rather a motive for learning becomes more pronounced in the child's hierarchy of motives because they expect to participate in a new type of activity at school that is different from pre-school and home.

In this reading of child development we see development clustered around particular leading activities, such as role play or learning. These leading activities are shown below and should be read as non-linear, or as Elkonin (1999: 29) states, as an 'ascending spiral rather than linearly'.

- Direct emotional communication.
- Manipulation of objects.
- Role playing.
- Learning activity.
- Intimate personal communication.
- Vocational or career-oriented activity.

Elkonin (1999: 27) states that:

> child development is composed, on the one hand, of periods characterized chiefly by assimilation of the objectives, motives, and norms of human relations and, on that basis, by the development of the need-motivational sphere; and, on the other hand, of periods characterized chiefly by the acquisition of socially evolved modes of action with objects and, on that basis, the formation of the child's intellectual and cognitive powers, his operational and technical capabilities.

What this means is that a child's wish for learning in school is different from their motive for play in pre-school. In this theorisation, moving institutions (from pre-school to school) represents a marked change in the child's life and influences their development. Transition from one period to another is marked as a *discrepancy in competence of the child* that realises itself as a *crisis* or as a *critical point in their life*. This happens in different ways when a child begins school. But also we see this later in adolescence, where an adolescent who feels him or herself to be responsible with much competence, and with a motive towards gaining employment, will come into conflict with the adults around him or her if he or she is treated as a child and not an adult. What matters here is (1) the change in the child's life which results from how we organise the institutions or structures in society, and (2) how others around the child treat the child in their social relationships – their expectations in relation to the child's growing competencies and motives for doing different things (like being a school child or an adult).

For the early adolescent period, Elkonin (1999: 25) states:

> The formation of the adolescent personality is greatly influenced by the formation of relations within the peer group based on the code of friendship. Communicative activity, then, is the specific form in which adult relationships are reproduced among adolescents, and the means by which adolescents become more thoroughly versed in the norms that guide adult society. Thus, it is reasonable to assume that the dominant activity during this period is the activity of communication, the activity of building relations with friends on the basis of definite moral and ethical norms that mediate the actions of adolescents.

During this period a high level of self-reflection is evident and a level of social consciousness builds, allowing new motives and objectives to direct later activities towards a future career. But this also happens for the infant whose need for emotional communications with their carer is central for their development.

What is core in *direct emotional communications* in infancy and *intimate personal communications* in early adolescence is the *child–social adult relationship*. What is important here in the central lines of development within the above mentioned periodisation for both *child–social adult relationships* and *child–social object relationships*.

Central lines of development

1. *Child–social adult relationship*: intimate personal communications of the adolescent, although different from the direct emotional communications evident between an infant and an adult, or the communications between play partners in pre-school, do *feature a common 'child–social adult' relationship*.
2. *Child–social object relationship*: the modes of action with objects displayed in early childhood, and again during play in the pre-school years, and learning for the school child and vocational and career oriented actions of the later adolescent, all *represent a 'child–social object' relationship*. We explain this important line of development below using the words of Elkonin (1999).

Elkonin (1999: 26) states:

> what does mastering objective operations involving a spoon or glass have in common with mastering mathematics or grammar? Nonetheless, they have one common feature: they are all elements of human culture. They have a common origin and a common place in the life of society; they all represent the result of a product of history. Through this acquisition of the socially evolved modes of action with objects, the child becomes more fully oriented within the objective world; his [sic] intellectual powers are shaped; he becomes a part of society's productive forces.

In summary, a particular leading activity reflects a child's motive towards particular activities. A change from one leading activity to another, such as role play to formal learning, is reflected as a relation between the ideal form found in society (for example what adults do) and the child's growing competence, needs and motives (what the child brings and is oriented towards). Transitions between leading activities as a form of development is explored further in the next section where we discuss the concept of the social situation of development.

The concept of the social situation of development

Vygotsky (1998), in his theory of child development, stated that at the beginning of each period a unique relation between the child and social reality exits, which he termed the *social situation of development*. He argued that when 'the social becomes the individual' (Vygotsky, 1998: 198) a qualitatively new child emerges. Bozhovich (2009: 61) in describing this 'dialectical leap to a new quality' suggests that Vygotsky wished to deliberately move away from an evolutionary view of child development (ages and stages) and to underscore his revolutionary view of development. Bozhovich (2009) argues that Vygotsky used the metaphor of the caterpillar transforming into a chrysalis, and the chrysalis transforming into a butterfly, to capture the qualitative change in children's development. That is, the child is completely trans-formed into something very different within different periods in childhood. This metaphor also illustrates the *new relationship that the qualitatively different child has to their environment* during different age periods. For instance, how a caterpillar relates to its environment is different from how a butterfly engages with its world – they have different competencies (such as mouths for biting or proboscis for drinking) and different needs (for example, eating leaves or collecting nectar).

Vygotsky (1994b) illustrated the social situation of development by giving an example from clinical work of a mother and three children who are all in the same family situation. The mother when under the influence of alcohol behaves violently towards her children and suffers with periods of psychological disorder, which means that she is unable to adequately care for her children. Each of the three children present a very different case of disrupted development. The young-est child is overwhelmed by the horror of what is happening and is helpless. The second youngest child develops both ambivalence and a painful attachment to the mother, with the co-existence of terror and love. The third child, although exhib-iting some delay in academic capacity, has taken on a very different role. As a ten-year-old child he understands the situation and feels pity for his mother. He in turn nurtures the younger children, taking on the role of the adult. Vygotsky (1994b: 340) asked, 'How can one explain why exactly the same environmental conditions exert three different types of influence on these three different chil-dren?'. The same social situation is interpreted differently because of what each child brings to this specific situation. Vygotsky (1994b: 340–41) argued that in studying development and pedagogy we 'ought to be capable of finding the prism through which the influence of the environment on the child is refracted, i.e. *it ought to be able to find the relationship which exists between the child and its environment, the child's emotional experience [perezhivanie]*, in other words how a child becomes aware of, interprets, [and] emotionally relates to a certain event'. We now turn to the concept of *perezhivanie*.

The concept of *perezhivanie*

According to Vygotsky (1994b) the Russian word *perezhivanie* captures the emotional experience of the child in the course of the child's personal development. *Perezhivanie* represents the unity between the child and their engagement with their social and material environment. Vygotsky (1994b: 341) explained that:

An emotional experience [*perezhivanie*] is a unit where, on the one hand, in an indivis-ible state, the environment is represented, i.e. that which is being experienced – an emotional experience [*perezhivanie*] is always related to something which is found outside the person – and on the other hand, what is represented is how I, myself, am experiencing this, i.e., all the personal characteristics and all the environmental characteristics are represented in an emotional experience [*perezhivanie*]; everything selected from the environment and all the factors which are related to our personality and are selected from the personality, all the features of its character, its constitutional elements, which are related to the event in question. So, in an emotional experience [*perezhivanie*] we are always dealing with an indivisible unity of personal characteristics and situational characteristics, which are represented in the emotional experience [*perezhivanie*].

What is important here is that child development must be viewed as the unity of the child (personal characteristics) and the situational characteristics. They cannot be separated from each other. What Vygotsky (1994b) also strived to capture with his concept of *perezhivanie* is that all aspects of a child's experience and therefore his or her development, are emotionally coloured or charged. He suggested, too, that you cannot separate out cognitive development from emotional development. Educational experiences impact emotionally upon an individual. Social relations are framed as emotional exchanges. Physical activity occurs in relation to how one feels and acts in particular situations and environments. Vygotsky (1994b) argued strongly for the unity of all these dimensions of development, suggesting they could not be separated out from each other. He also suggested that the emotional-motivational dimensions of how a child engages with their social and material environment determine what kind of relationship they have with that environment. When there is a discrepancy, tension, critical point or crisis, then this creates the opportunity for development, as the child seeks to reconcile the new challenge. It is now possible to see why Vygotsky (1994b: 348) argued that the environment is the source of a child's development: 'the environment's role in the development of higher, specifically human characteristics and forms of activity is as a source of development'. But for this to be successful a particular type of interaction between the ideal and rudimentary forms of development is necessary. We now turn our attention to this special type of interaction within the child's environment.

The interaction between the ideal and the rudimentary in the child's environment

This section now considers the concept of the ideal form and the interaction between the ideal and the rudimentary in the child's environment. Vygotsky (1994b) stated that for the environment to be the source of a child's development then what is to be developed must already exist in the child's environment. Vygotsky gave the example of language, where children need to be in rich language environments specific to their society, if they are to learn the dominant language of their community. Families engage infants by communicating with them verbally and non-verbally. Infants are not expected to begin speaking in an ideal form, but are surrounded by people who engage them socially and meaningfully by providing the ideal form of language to them. Having the ideal form in the child's environment affords development of exactly that which is valued and needed to successfully interact. Vygotsky (1994b: 346) noted that, 'Something which is supposed to take shape at the very end of development, somehow influences the very first steps in this development'.

Having the ideal form within the child's environment is also important outside of the family context, such as pre-schools and schools, where different forms of the ideal may exist exerting new demands that have possibilities for further development (see Hedegaard and Fleer, 2013). For example, pre-school children participate in the everyday activities of eating and drinking to sustain life. This is of course a biological need. However, in some families mealtimes are also a source of social learning for particular social protocols, such as sitting still to eat around a kitchen table or bench, or sitting still eating in front of a TV, or as a mobile activity as family members gather food and eat it on the run as they head off for work in the morning, or take food to different areas within the house while playing. When children meet new situations and social protocols in other contexts, such as when attending childcare, this may cause tension for the child.

For instance, in a study of children's everyday lives and transition to school, Fleer (2010) has shown how JJ, a two-year-old child, begins childcare and meets the new demand of sitting at a table to eat. He comes from a home where family meals are served at the kitchen table, but the children are free to take their food and to move about the house to eat with no adult interaction or supervision. In childcare JJ avoids the routine of sitting at the clusters of tables where food is placed for all the children. He is observed hiding under a painting easel. When directed to sit, he places his feet on the table and pushes his chair back, eventually moving the chair several meters from the table. The early childhood educators work hard to help him sit at the table. The ideal form that is valued in the childcare centre is ever present, as all the other children are seated eating their meals. The expert skills acquired at home of eating while moving about are not valued and could not safely be allowed for within a centre where a group of fifteen toddlers have hot lunch. The crisis for JJ of engaging in a new social protocol for eating places huge demands upon him not only to be together with other children to eat, but also to sit still while eating with his feet on the floor and not on the table. This affords the possibilities for development because although the demands are great, the ideal form is visibly present and the educators sensitively and carefully support JJ's transition and eventual development of new competencies and practices.

Cultural-historical model of child development

A holistic view of children's development as theorised through cultural-historical concepts of leading activity, social situation of development, *perezhivanie* and the ideal form are presented together as a model of child development in Figure 10.1. Although a number of models relevant to early childhood years have been empirically presented in the literature (see Fleer, 2010; Hedegaard and Fleer, 2013), only one example is possible within this short chapter. As such, we present a cultural-historical model of child development illustrated through an example from the findings of a study into children's development in everyday life (Fleer, 2010; Fleer and Hedegaard, 2010; Hedegaard and Fleer, 2013). We begin with the observations of Louise in her family over a twelve-month period, over three separate observation periods, followed by the child development model that draws upon the conceptual work of Fleer and Hedegaard (2010), Hedegaard (2012) and Hedegaard and Fleer (2013).

Case example: development in families

Walking to school and childcare: Louise at the beginning of the research was sixteen months old. She lives in a family that is very poor. Because the family does not own a car, the children walk each day for ten kilometres in order to go to childcare, pre-school, school and home again. Louise is pushed in a stroller.

At home: Louise is usually placed in the highchair as dinner is prepared, is held while the adults perform late afternoon chores or supervise outside while the older children play with their bikes or with balls, etc. At sixteen months Louise is often placed in the highchair when the children are outside, or held and moved about as the mother moves about doing things inside or outside the house.

Community services: according to Louise's mother the government agency that supports families in caring for their children expressed concern that Louise was not walking.

Analysis: Louise did not need to walk. She observed all the activity from the vantage point of the stroller, the highchair or the arms of one of the adults – who were also highly mobile – thus affording a dynamic view of all the action occurring within the family (observation period 1).

Three months later, a different kind of observation was noted when the children were given a swing and slide set for Christmas (see Fleer, 2010: 175–80 for further analysis).

Louise sits on the swing: Louise is seated on a swing. She is holding on to the metal bars that support the swing as her father gently moves the swing back and forth. The father explains to the researchers, who have not visited the house for three months, 'She won't go and walk by herself'. The father takes Louise from the swing and places her on her feet.

He continues to hold one hand and walks with Louise saying, 'She will walk around everywhere doing this'. Louise looks to the researchers and smiles as they show appreciation of her walking. The father then explains that if he lets go of her hand, Louise immediately sits down and won't continue to walk (observation period 2, visit 1).

In observation period 3, visit 3 (three months later), Louise is able to walk in the direction of the slide, even though she is unable to climb the ladder.

Louise toddles to the ladder: Louise slowly toddles over to the ladder of the slide. She attempts to lift one leg onto the rung of the ladder – she makes eye contact with an adult who is close by. The adult is visiting the family and notices Louise's repeated attempts to step onto the ladder. The adult lifts Louise to the top of the side. He then supports her body all the way down the slide. He steps back. Louise walks around from the slide to the ladder and again attempts to step onto the rung. After two attempts she looks to the adult, who steps forward and lifts her to the top of the slide and, once again, supports her down the slide. This process continues, with the adult each time giving less support on the slide. Eventually, the adult invites the father to observe Louise going down the slide without adult support, saying, 'She can now do it on her own' (observation period 3, visit 3).

In observation period 3, visit 5, Louise now has the competence to be able to climb up the ladder and slide unaided down the ladder.

Louise climbs to the top of the slide: Louise has climbed to the top of the slide. She is seated on the slide holding onto the rails at the top. She calls to her mother. Her mother is inside and responds with a call, but does not come out to Louise. Louise pushes herself from the top of the slide, sliding down awkwardly, jolting from side to side. She arrives at the bottom of the slide and drops to the ground, knocking herself back as she falls. She rubs her back with her hand and cries. Both her siblings look to her as she cries (observation period 3, visit 5).

Analysis: what we see is a new self-awareness by Louise. The new equipment is enjoyed by her siblings and she too wishes to be on the swing, and later to go on the slide. Her growing strength, along with the need to be able to walk to use the equipment, develops a motive for walking. The introduction of the new slide and swing set was a critical point in Louise's development. The slide and swing set changed the concrete conditions of Louise's everyday world and thus generated an important moment in Louise's development.

We use this example of Louise to show a cultural-historical model of child development, where we specifically conceptualise development holistically, and not as the carving up of the child into social and emotional development, language development, physical development, as has been the case traditionally in early years education programmes and in psychology. As Veresov (2006: 9) notes, 'contemporary developmental psychology is moving away from linear (evolutionary-chronological) towards nonlinear (organic-functional) models of development reflecting the limitations of the former, and venturing into Vygotsky's revolutionary view of development'.

We were able to understand Louise's development by drawing upon a cultural-historical model of early years development shown in Figure 10.1. In using this model we determine that Louise is focused on the object of the slide and swing set. Her leading activity for engaging with objects (see the centre of the model for all leading activities) is supported by her new motive for wanting to walk so she can independently use the slide and swing set when she wishes to do so. The ideal form (the box on right with the central concepts for development shown) of manipulating objects is evident as her siblings competently use the slide and swing set. The event is an emotional experience because over time she successfully challenges herself and gains physical competence in first walking, then sliding and finally climbing. But her physical development could only be understood as a new relation with her environment that was an emotional experience (*perezhivanie*) where a crisis and a level of self-awareness of her own physical competence emerged.

As is understood by the concept of the social situation of development, Louise in the same situation as her siblings engaged with the slide and swing set quite differently because of her unique physical competence. While she observed the ideal forms, she was unable to do the same as her peers until she was able to walk. The model shown in Figure 10.1 allows for a deeper understanding of Louise's

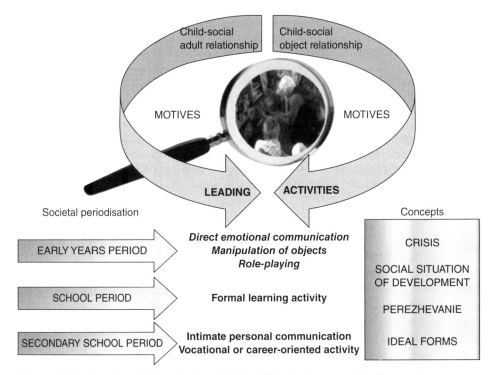

Figure 10.1 A cultural-historical model of child development for the early years

existing unique characteristics. Through using the concepts of the social situation of development, ideal forms, leading activity and *perezhivanie*, it is possible to analyse and understand the cultural nature of Louise's development. Through identifying Louise's motive development, it is possible to go beyond a simple examination of Louise's physical development.

Conclusion

In this chapter we have taken a holistic view of children's development, drawing upon cultural-historical concepts to build a model of child development that allows for the cultural nature of development to be analysed and the outcomes used for supporting pedagogical practices in the early years.

Questions and exercises

Make an observation in an early years setting at the beginning of the semester and then again towards the end of the semester (or beginning of your teaching practice and end of your teaching practice). Observe the same children and situation. Apply the model shown in Figure 10.1 to your observations and determine:

- the ideal form in the first observation and evidence of children showing competence in the ideal form;
- if a leading activity is evident among the children;
- the social situation of development for each of the children observed;
- if *perezhivanie* is evident.

Can you make a statement about the cultural development of the children in the setting you have observed?

Further reading

Fleer's (2010) 'Early learning and development: cultural-historical concepts in play' shows through practical examples how a cultural-historical conception of child development can be drawn upon by educators in the birth to five years period to support learning through play. The idea of conceptual play is introduced as one way to conceptualise learning through play, and to push against the academic drive by some governments to reduce play opportunities in early childhood education programmes because of the belief that children do not learn enough or quickly enough in play-based programmes. This book is a good introduction to the concepts, but you have to read the whole book to gain a full working knowledge of the theory. Hedegaard's (2002) *Learning and Child Development: A Cultural-historical Study* provides a comprehensive presentation of child development conceptualised from a cultural-historical perspective and gives examples of how teachers in the early years of school can work with a cultural-historical conception of child development. This book is rich in practical examples, even though the text explaining the concepts is rather dense. Finally, those interested in reading about how learning and development are conceptualised from a cultural-historical perspective in the early years of school in the Netherlands should have a look at van Oers (2012) 'Developmental education: foundations of a play-based curriculum' in van Oers's edited book *Developmental Education for Young Children: Concept, Practice, and Implementation*. Readers will find that some chapters in this text are more practically oriented, while others present the concepts of 'developmental education' more theoretically. While it is harder to read, this is definitely a good follow-up book for this chapter.

PART THREE

POLICY AND PROVISION FOR YOUNG CHILDREN

This part of the book explores evolving policy and provision for babies and young children, looking at the contemporary political, social and economic motivation for systems and services and tracking some of their historical roots. Throughout this section, the authors highlight in different ways the complex relationship between 'the state' and families and discuss how this impacts on provision and on the beliefs and/or practices of professionals who work with young children and their families. There is a continuation of attention to social constructions of early childhood, to ideas about good enough childcare/parenting – or what constitutes quality in services – and to the positioning of children and childhood in society as policies and provision are developed.

Consideration is also given to ideology and to cultural influence, including the formalisation – sometimes in international charters – of pan-national ideas concerning children's needs, rights and capabilities. These ideas and the inherent value attached to early childhood are reflected in provision that sets, at the very least, a 'bottom line' for babies' and young children's health and wellbeing, safety and welfare, education and care. Many are enshrined in statements about children's rights, which are variously interpreted and supported (or not) in a country's legislation, advocated through associated guidance for professionals (statutory and non-statutory), operationalised in the construction of systems and services and enacted through professional interpretation. The authors show how there can be disjuncture within and across these spheres and how young children can suffer as a consequence.

A recurrent theme in this part of the book is the influence of ideas from other countries and from international bodies, such as the United Nations and the World Health Organization (WHO). Philosophies, principles and practices for the provision of policies and services for children and their families are traced to international declarations and to country-specific examples. This links to the theme of globalisation covered in earlier chapters and again raises the issue of cultural appropriateness in 'policy borrowing' and transplanted professional approaches. It gives rise to questions about the kinds of people suited and equipped to work with young children: how their occupations are viewed, how they are educated and trained, supported and supervised, penalised and rewarded. These issues are picked up implicitly and explicitly across the chapters that follow.

In Chapter 11, Sonia Jackson reviews early years policy and services in the UK. She analyses the development of early years policy and the factors which have shaped it, concluding that there is still some way to go before all young children have access to high quality services appropriate to their age and family circumstances. Compared with other Western European countries, early years services in the UK have been under-funded and split between care and education. Despite government attention and investment between 1997 and 2010, with practical attempts to integrate provision, Jackson argues that little progress has been made towards conceptual integration so that disparities remain in the nature of services, pay and conditions. In addition, childcare as a public service has all but vanished with recent cuts to the welfare budget.

In Chapter 12, Nigel Thomas demonstrates how a growing consensus, which asserts that children have rights, is linked to changes in ideas about their capabilities and adults' responses to these, affecting their relationships with adults – especially their parents – and to the state. He explains the theoretical background to the development of legal (rather than moral) rights and differentiates these from needs or wants while showing the close link between children's welfare and their rights, including their 'liberty' right to participate in decisions affecting their welfare. He traces the development of key legislation governing children's care and upbringing, showing how the law has shifted from being distant and punitive to being protective and increasingly interventionist in the sphere of family life. In so doing, the accountability for children's welfare and for upholding their rights has the potential to be shared between children, family and state, requiring difficult balancing decisions by legal and childcare professionals.

In Chapter 13, Iram Siraj-Blatchford describes the transformative potential involved in young children's early childhood education (ECE) experiences. Provision that exhibits features typical of good quality ECE, which she describes with reference to theory-driven pedagogical models, can make a significant difference to the lives of all young children but especially those from 'disadvantaged' backgrounds. But good quality ECE also enables children to actively contribute to the ongoing process of cultural transformation within their families, communities and societies, through playful activities co-constructed with knowledgeable and sensitive parents and 'pedagogues'. Highlighting the importance of play, she emphasises its role as a context or vehicle for learning and participating in the cultural world around them. Finally, she identifies some of the long-term effects of highly structured ECE environments compared with those that are more open and flexible, seeking to offer young children an emergent curriculum.

In Chapter 14, Dendy Platt picks up the theme of balancing the rights of children with the rights of their families as he details how a child welfare system based on a child protection orientation may arguably prioritise a child's individual rights to protection from harm at the expense of their right to a family life. Resonating with Jackson's argument in Chapter 11, he notes that contextual pressures – such as economic austerity measures leading to reduced capacity in specialist services – together with systemic problems and policy failings may contribute to the difficulty of safeguarding children. He also points out the complexity of identifying and the variability in responding to child maltreatment, principally, though not exclusively, occurring within families. Echoing other contributors to this book, he advocates a more concerted effort to listen to children and take their views or reports seriously; effective inter-professional practice to help prevent abuse and neglect within families or acting in a timely manner if serious maltreatment has occurred; and consideration of the long-term physical and emotional impact for the children concerned.

In Chapter 15, Sally Robinson explains how professionals who work with young children and the context in which people spend their earliest years can make a lifelong difference to their health and wellbeing. Looking back, she traces how deficit beliefs about illness prevention were transformed to become positive concerns about flourishing physically, mentally and socially. Following acknowledgement that economic, political, social and environmental factors play a part in the state of the public's health and wellbeing in a community, and with greater understanding of disease prevention through vaccines and other medicines, the duty of mothers – and mothers alone – to prevent illness in their children waned. Improvements to health and wellbeing through education, communication and empowerment became a shared responsibility involving individuals, communities, health professionals, the state and international bodies such as the WHO. The consequent holistic public health priorities and policies, and the services provided by a range of professionals are explained in relation to the social contributors to health inequalities and to health improvement, protection and illness prevention mechanisms.

In Chapter 16, Siobhan O'Connor challenges the discourse of social inclusion in English policy documentation, arguing that it implies the existence of non-social forms of exclusion, which draw on deficit, medical views of impairment. This has created a dynamic relationship between medical and social constructs of disability, leading to the use of labels such as 'special educational needs'. She argues instead that all forms of inclusion and exclusion are socially constructed and opens a dialogue, which explores the concept of inclusion in association with social justice and equity issues that extend way beyond impairment to encompass poverty, gender, class, ethnicity, sexual orientation, gender identity, religion, beliefs and age. She illustrates her theorising by reference to the Index for Inclusion (Booth and Ainscow, 2011) and its application in the development of education in society, including early childhood provision, which emerges from the establishment of inclusive principles for living and learning with young children.

11

EARLY CHILDHOOD POLICY AND SERVICES

Sonia Jackson

Contents

- Introduction
- Issues in childcare and early education
- Influences on early childhood policy
- Government policy since 1997
- Sure Start and Children's Centres
- Childcare for working parents
- Working towards more integrated services
- Establishing national standards
- Professional development and training
- Conclusion

Introduction

This chapter discusses the development of policy on early childhood care and education in the UK and the influences that have shaped it and continue to do so. Comparisons with other Western European countries highlight the long-term effect of years of political neglect and under-funding (UNICEF 2008; Moss and Lloyd, 2013). The legacy of the historic split between care and education can still be felt throughout our early childhood services and in the thinking of policy makers and practitioners.

However, there has been considerable progress. Few people would now argue, as Margaret Thatcher did, that what happens to children in the years before compulsory schooling is a matter for their families alone. The 1997–2010 Labour government committed itself to a radical transformation of early childhood services with a huge investment of public funding. The Coalition government, in office since 2010, has a different set of priorities but maintains an interest in the early years.

One development to record is that the signs of divergence between the four nations of the UK, already noted in the second edition of this book, have become much more pronounced. Although the main focus in this chapter is on England, reference is made to Wales and Scotland when there are important new initiatives or approaches in those countries. A number of useful websites, listed at the end of the chapter, provide up-to-date information in this period of rapid change.

Issues in childcare and early education

Despite the greatly increased interest in early childhood in government circles, the key policy issues have remained remarkably constant over many decades. Five main issues in early years care and education remain unresolved:

- Since early education (three–five years) has never become an integral part of the free, statutory state education system it is vulnerable to local government cuts.
- Pre-school education and childcare developed along separate lines with differently qualified staff and different conditions of service.
- There is a tension between cost and quality in childcare which results in the children in most need receiving the lowest quality service and leaves many families with no service at all.
- Childcare is mainly staffed by poorly paid women with low levels of education and little prospect of career progression.
- The early age of school entry compared with other European countries raises questions about the suitability of the curriculum and regime for such young children.

Influences on early childhood policy

Early years policy is shaped by a complex interaction of different factors. These include prevailing ideology, historical continuities, educational theories, cultural factors, economic conditions and, more recently, evidence from research.

1 Ideology

A major shift in the debate on working mothers has seen the UK moving much closer to the position in Nordic countries where this is seen as a matter of equal opportunities.

The existing pattern of early childhood education in Britain can be traced back to the Plowden Report, *Children and Their Primary Schools* (CACE, 1967). At the time it was seen as an important advance by campaigners for an extension of nursery education but in retrospect it set early years services on an unfortunate trajectory. In order to expand availability quickly at low cost, the report proposed making all provision part-time and concentrating it in 'deprived' areas. At the time it had the perverse effect of ending most existing full-time nursery education for three to five year olds and making it inaccessible to the poorest children whose mothers had no choice but to work full-time. Consequently, almost all early years education in the UK is still delivered in sessions lasting two-and-a-half hours, which is of limited use as a service for working parents. Moreover the Plowden Report confirmed the perception of day care as a service primarily for children in social need or at risk of abuse or neglect. Even when a nursery school and day nursery existed on the same site, they were usually run completely separately. The 1989 Children Act, which recognised the value of day nurseries and family centres for children 'in need' (but failed to do anything to make them available), was a lost opportunity for creating integrated services.

2 Educational theories

Books about child development often begin by expounding the views of the philosophers John Locke and Jean-Jacques Rousseau, to which many existing schools of pedagogical theory can be traced. Locke believed that a child's mind at birth was a 'tabula rasa', a blank slate, and that all human knowledge and abilities were acquired by learning through teaching and experience. Rousseau, on the other hand, thought that given the right environment, the child's innate capacity would simply unfold through exploration, discovery and imagination (Doddington and Hilton, 2007). The Montessori approach draws its inspiration from this view of childhood in contrast, for example, to an emphasis on adult-directed learning broken up into pre-determined time periods (Nutbrown, 2011).

The nature–nurture debate, as it became known, is now considered rather irrelevant, since contemporary advances in the study of very early brain development have shown that an infant is learning, not only from the moment of birth, but even while still in the womb (see, for example, Legerstee et al., 2013). Genetic and environmental influences are so enmeshed that the attempt to ascribe any individual child's characteristics to one or the other is a fruitless exercise (Schaffer, 2004). Factors such as the mother's diet in pregnancy as well as more obvious negative influences – drug addiction, alcohol misuse or smoking – have been shown to have long-term effects, which are difficult to disentangle either from genetic or postnatal environmental influences (Rayns et al., 2011). Few experts would now dispute that children's earliest experiences have a profound impact on their ability to take advantage of opportunities to learn. However, the debate on how to create the best conditions for learning in the early years is very much alive.

3 Cultural influences

Historical and cultural influences usually remain invisible but they are very important in understanding why things are the way they are. For example, the Second World War had a different impact on countries that experienced it at first hand. One of the strengths of the much-admired Reggio Emilia early childhood service is the political support it has enjoyed. Mayor Bonacci explained to Gunilla Dahlberg that the fascist experience had taught them that people who conformed and obeyed were dangerous. In building a new society it was imperative to nurture and maintain a vision of children who can think and act for themselves (Dahlberg et al., 2007) whereas English schools tend to prefer compliant children who do as they are told and don't ask too many questions. The kinds of people we want children to be and become influences the nature of early years and childcare provision and the beliefs and behaviours of parents, professionals and policy makers towards young children (see Chapter 1).

4 Evidence from research

As far back as the 1980s, analysis of data from the 1970 British Cohort Study (CHES) had quantified the benefits of pre-school education, especially for disadvantaged children (Osborn et al., 1984). However, the first large-scale, systematic research to have a major influence on policy was the Effective Provision of Pre-school Education (EPPE) project, based at the London University Institute of Education. EPPE is a European longitudinal study investigating the effectiveness of early childhood education and care (ECEC) in terms of children's development with a sample of 3,000 children. Unlike any previous research, it looked in detail at the effect of attendance at different types of settings on children's cognitive and social-behavioural outcomes and the interaction between the home and pre-school environment. The findings provided a sound basis for the government's policy of expanding provision and justified the related expenditure (Sylva et al.,

2010). They also provide strong evidence for the need to upgrade the workforce (see Chapter 13).

Government policy since 1997

The election of a Labour government in 1997 was a highly significant turning point. For the first time the state recognised a responsibility for the education and care of its youngest citizens. The National Childcare Strategy (DfES, 1998) also introduced an important change in terminology, with 'childcare' (one word) largely replacing 'day care' in official documents. Another change in terminology is the now general use of 'early years' to cover the period from birth to six years, or in some cases up to eight years. For a time the term 'educare' achieved some popularity, underlining the fact that, especially for very young children, care and education are inseparable. However, this never really caught on, and at the time of writing, the term most used seems to be early childhood education and care.

A series of government initiatives resulted in improved access to early years education over the next few years, supporting developments already in progress and stimulating new forms of provision. At the same time a falling child population created free places in infant schools, which in many areas were filled by admitting four year olds to full-time education. In Wales almost all four year olds were already in school by the year 2000 and by 2013 four, rather than the statutory age of five, has become the usual age of entering primary school reception classes. The government funds part-time nursery places for all three and four year olds in England whose parents want them (fifteen hours a week for thirty-eight weeks) and this is due to be extended to 'vulnerable' two year olds in September 2013, though only under stringent conditions. There is considerable pressure on parents to send four year olds to full-time school as otherwise they risk not getting a place in the primary school of their choice.

The Childcare Act 2006 was another landmark as the first ever piece of legislation to be exclusively concerned with early years and childcare. It was intended to take forward some of the key commitments from the Ten Year Childcare Strategy (HM Treasury, 2004) and was based on the five outcomes set out in *Every Child Matters* (see below) with special reference to early years care and education. The intention of the Act was to bring early years within the mainstream of local authority provision, but its provisions fall far short of the universal full-time nursery education with extended hours of subsidised childcare if needed, available to all children aged three to six years in Nordic countries and in many other parts of Europe. Because it failed to embed pre-school education as a free universal service on the same basis as school-age education, the important reforms introduced by the 1997–2010 Labour government remain highly vulnerable to political changes and budgetary factors.

Sure Start and Children's Centres

The largest new component of Labour's Childcare Strategy was 'Sure Start', the first government programme ever to be targeted at the birth to three age group. Sure Start was an area-based programme providing funds for a variety of different early education, childcare and family support services for children under four in the most disadvantaged areas. An important economic and political motive for the generous funding provided by the Treasury was to enable mothers, especially those on their own, to work instead of being dependent on welfare payments. For this reason every Sure Start scheme had to include a day care component.

Sure Start is generally regarded as one of the major successes of the Childcare Strategy. Evaluation was built in from the beginning and showed small but significant improvements in outcomes for children, for instance enhanced language development (Belsky et al., 2007). More importantly, the Centres were greatly appreciated by the parents who used them and the communities in which they were located (Eisenstadt, 2011).

Children's Centres, which were built on the Early Excellence and family centre models (Whalley, 2000; Draper and Duffy, 2001), filled a gap in early years provision and spread with great rapidity, largely replacing Sure Start centres. They were charged with incorporating high quality nursery education, day care for children of working parents, integration of health and social services support with a strong ethos of partnership with parents. Although many exemplified good and innovative practice, they were still limited by the differing terms and conditions of employment for their staff and by the very low level of training and qualifications (NVQ Level 2) required of those who work directly with young children. These issues were addressed by the review commissioned by the Coalition government from Professor Cathy Nutbrown (see page 155).

Children's Centres might even have become universal but for the change of government in 2010. At their height there were 3,500 throughout the country, but cuts in public services and local authority funding since then have put the process into reverse, with over 400 Centres closing in the first two years of the Coalition government. Even among those that remain open, a high proportion have been obliged to discard the childcare element, originally obligatory, as unaffordable.

Childcare for working parents

A major weakness of all UK government policy statements on ECEC has always been the failure to differentiate between short-term sessional provision and full day care adapted to normal adult working hours. Both are described as childcare, although the practical implications for families are very different.

Day care

The Childcare Act 2006 obliges local authorities in England and Wales to ensure that there are sufficient childcare places to meet the needs of working parents. However, publicly provided childcare in England has almost disappeared. Care for children of working parents is found almost entirely in the private sector, provided either by childminders or in childcare settings run for profit, and increasingly by large commercial chains. Private childcare centres largely serve families where both parents have professional jobs and the fees that they charge often put them out of reach of families on average incomes (Daycare Trust/Family Parenting Institute, 2013). Mothers with fewer educational qualifications are much more likely to work part time and turn to relatives, especially grandmothers, for childcare. Informal care by relatives is still extensively used to fill gaps in provision (Rutter and Evans, 2011).

Playgroups

The playgroup movement started in the 1960s as a response to the acute shortage of nursery places for three to four year olds. Intended as a temporary stopgap, it remained the major form of pre-school provision until schools began to admit four year olds and is still an important element in the patchwork of early years services, especially in rural areas. Though some pre-schools attain standards comparable to nursery schools and classes, the majority have to operate in unsuitable and often shared premises, and staffing depends on the availability of, largely women, prepared to work for token pay or none. On the positive side, this often proved a valuable opportunity for women who had been out of paid employment for several years to build confidence and organisational skills (Henderson, 2011). However pre-schools now have considerable difficulty in finding suitable staff and volunteers as the trend is for women to seek paid jobs at an earlier stage in their children's lives.

Some writers have suggested that the growth of the playgroup movement, which had no parallel in other European countries, and the strength of the Pre-school Playgroups Association, now called the Pre-school Learning Alliance, enabled governments to ignore the campaign for nursery education. There was strong opposition in pre-school circles to the downward extension of the school starting age which meant that pre-schools lost the older age group and were obliged to accept two year olds to remain viable. In Wales, the Welsh-medium playgroups (*Mudiad Ysgolion Meithrin*) played an important role in promoting the Welsh language and were concerned that children might move into English-speaking primary schools before their speech was fully established. However, the evidence suggests that the opposite effect has occurred, creating a growing demand for Welsh-medium primary schools (Siencyn and Thomas, 2007). Recognition of the value of bilingual education has led to a smaller but similar development in Scotland (AcSS, 2010).

In 1998 the government took the bold step of moving responsibility for all early years services from the welfare (social services) to the education sector. This enabled pre-schools in England to apply for education funding provided they meet Ofsted standards for the Early Years Foundation Stage. The greatest significance of this move, however, was the implicit recognition that education begins at birth and not simply at the age of entry into formal schooling.

Childminding

For children under three the most common form of out-of-home care, apart from playgroups and private day centres, is still childminding, known in non-UK countries as family day care. Childminding has a long history and has always been extensively used by poor working mothers, but its existence was not formally recognised in the UK until 1948 with the passing of the Nurseries and Childminders Regulation Act (amended in 1968). The Act made provision for registration of childminders and inspection of premises but was almost entirely concerned with physical safety rather than the suitability of the caregiver.

Research during the 1970s uncovered some shocking conditions, especially among unregistered minders. In response, the National Childminding Association was launched. Renamed as PACEY, it is committed to raising standards of care through training and support as well as acting as an advocacy organisation for its members. It also developed the idea of networks, designed to combat the isolation of childminders, which has always been a problem in the UK. Other countries have better systems for linking family day care workers to provide professional and mutual support and training. The government has now proposed a new system of childminder agencies (DfE, 2013), but these are intended to operate on a commercial rather than a co-operative model and will not address the issue of isolation.

An important landmark for childminding was the belated recognition by the government that childminders are educators as well as carers. All registered childminders in England must now offer the Early Years Foundation Stage curriculum and if they receive government funding are inspected by Ofsted. There continues to be a tension, however, between standards and costs. Childminding is no longer a cheap service for poor parents, and the fees asked by registered childminders are at a similar level to those charged by private day nurseries. The average cost for twenty-five hours of childcare from a childminder is now £98.15 a week (Daycare

Trust/Family Parenting Institute, 2013). The result is that a high proportion of mothers are obliged to give up work when they have a second or third child (Abrams, 2001). Many childminders feel unable to cope with the paperwork required or to meet the requirements of EYFS: numbers of registered childminders have been declining for the past ten years (Daycare Trust/Family Parenting Institute, 2013).

The government's main interest in childcare is to reduce the cost of welfare payments by enabling mothers, especially those without partners, to return to work earlier. In January 2013 they issued a controversial report, *More Great Childcare* (DfE, 2013). It was met by a storm of protest, particularly since it proposed 'relaxing' the adult to child ratios. Many commentators pointed out that it would inevitably lead to children receiving less adult attention and less opportunity for outdoor play, but was unlikely to produce any significant reduction in costs for parents (Daycare Trust/Family Parenting Institute, 2013). In practice, any negative impact is likely to be greatest on children who already receive the lowest quality care. There is already a marked discrepancy between the Ofsted ratings of nurseries and childminders in more advantaged areas compared with others. Among childminders, thirty-nine per cent working in the most disadvantaged areas failed to achieve a 'good' or 'outstanding' rating from Ofsted as compared with only twenty-three per cent in richer areas (Ofsted, 2012b).

Working towards more integrated services

The Laming report (2003) following on the death of Victoria Climbié (see Chapter 14), together with early findings from the EPPE project (see Chapter 13), initiated an innovative policy framework called *Every Child Matters*, designed by a civil servant, John Rowlands. Rather contrary to expectations, this proved extremely helpful to schools as well as pre-school settings. The goals were not just to protect children from harm but to stress their entitlement to five positive outcomes: being healthy, staying safe, enjoying and achieving, making a positive contribution and economic wellbeing. This new, holistic view of children and young people focused on outcomes instead of services and underpinned the ten-year strategy *Choice for Parents, the Best Start for Children* (HM Treasury, 2004). It led to a series of legislative and policy initiatives, some of which survived the 2010 change of government, although *Every Child Matters* has been quietly allowed to fall into abeyance. These included the development of integrated education, health and social care services, extended school hours and targeted services. A related government aim was to eliminate child poverty by 2020, partly by increasing childcare provision enabling more mothers to work. Child poverty is now rising steeply again as a result of a series of measures designed to 'cut the deficit'.

Establishing national standards

The ten-year childcare strategy was designed to rationalise and redesign the existing early years initiatives so that they fitted within the *Every Child Matters* framework and would become a coherent approach to improving the quality of services. Since the government had brought under one legislative umbrella all kinds of early years provision and was investing large sums of public money, it needed to find a way of showing that this was of benefit to the nation. This was the rationale for Ofsted to inspect all services and for all children to be assessed through the Early Years Foundation Stage Profile, effectively a national curriculum for children from birth to five years.

Early Years Foundation Stage (EYFS)

In England, the EYFS became a statutory requirement from September 2008 for every type of early childhood service, including childminders, to be enforced through inspections by Ofsted on a four-year cycle. A review commissioned by the Labour government from Dame Claire Tickell two years after the EYFS was introduced concluded that it had raised standards but endorsed the widespread view that it was far too complicated and burdensome for practitioners. A streamlined EYFS was therefore published in 2012 (see Chapter 17). From a policy point of view, perhaps the most important part of the review was the section on the workforce, which noted that the majority of those attracted to work in the sector were young girls with poor academic qualifications or none. The report went on to state, 'the need to create a strong, resilient and experienced workforce has been a compelling message to this review' (Tickell, 2011, p.42) and urged the government to 'maintain the ambition' for a graduate-led sector.

The new EYFS is generally regarded as an improvement in that it largely endorses a play-based, developmentally appropriate approach to childcare and education for children from birth to five years. However, there is increasing concern about an over-emphasis on preparation for school, exerting backward pressure on early years settings to introduce formal skills too early.

Setting standards in Wales

Proposals for the Welsh Foundation Phase Framework for children aged three to seven years were described by the then First Minister, Rhodri Morgan, as a break with 125 years of British educational practice. Drawing on approaches from, among others, Nordic countries and New Zealand, it adopts an active play-based approach to learning in both indoor and outdoor environments, balancing teacher-led and child-initiated activities (see Maynard et al., 2013). Wales is no less committed to high standards than England, and early years settings are inspected by Estyn (equivalent to Ofsted), but given the approach promoted in the Foundation Phase Framework, there is arguably less downward pressure on services for three and four year olds to institute formal teaching and achieve curriculum goals tied to chronological age.

Wales was the first UK country to appoint a Children's Commissioner and to adopt a rights-based policy (see Chapter 12). Although it has not followed England in joining up care and education formally, the Flying Start programme launched in 2005 lays a strong emphasis on integrating childcare, early learning, parenting and health services.

Professional development and training

Having accepted the main recommendations of the Tickell review, the new government went on to commission a review of early years education and childcare qualifications from Professor Cathy Nutbrown. The final report, *Foundations for Quality*, published in June 2012, was based on very extensive consultation and was widely welcomed. It made nineteen recommendations designed to ensure that staff are as good as they can be and have the skills, knowledge and understanding to make the most of the government's investment in the early years. Nutbrown argues that working in the early years sector should be a recognised and fulfilling career that attracts the very best staff, both men and women (Nutbrown, 2012).

The government claimed that it had accepted most of the recommendations and incorporated them into *More Great Childcare* (DfE, 2013), but Nutbrown herself published an angry response accusing the government of 'Shaking the Foundations of Quality'. She pointed out that the overall thrust of her report had been brushed aside and most of her recommendations had, in effect, been rejected (Nutbrown, 2013). Most importantly, the opportunity to rationalise the educational and career structure of early years work was lost.

Conclusion

After more than thirty years when early childhood policy in Britain essentially stagnated (Jackson, 1993), the year 1997 could be seen as a watershed. For the first time the wellbeing of children under school age was recognised as a legitimate subject of public concern, not simply the responsibility of their own parents. There was a further leap forward in 2004, with the announcement of the National Childcare Strategy and *Every Child Matters*. At the time of writing childcare is once again high on the government's agenda, although principally as a means of reducing the cost of welfare benefits by enabling more mothers to enter the workforce. The concept of childcare as a public service, never strong in the UK, has virtually disappeared. Childcare is only available from private providers, often profit-making chains charging high prices. The dilemma of how to reconcile quality and costs remains as insoluble as ever. Furthermore, cuts in local authority funding have led to severe reductions in availability of support and advice for practitioners and managers of services. At a time of financial stringency any provision that is not statutory is liable to vanish.

During its time in office the Labour government committed billions of pounds to a major reform of early childhood services and the positive effects were seen in communities up and down the country. The vision of Children's Centres combining early years education, family support, childcare, employment advice and health promotion on one site was surely the right one. It is sad to see it diminishing as a result of cuts to local authority funding. More than 400 Sure Start Children's Centres closed during the first two years of the Coalition government, funding overall was cut by a third and a survey by the charity 4Children found that over half had abandoned on-site childcare.

However, not all the progress made during the first years of the century has been lost. The appointment of a Director of Children's Services in every local authority in England is an important step towards the long-term aim of integrating all children's services. There is a commitment to universally available educational provision for three and four year olds, and some two year olds, although still on a part-time basis. National standards have been set for all forms of early years provision receiving state funding. There is growing recognition of the needs of working parents for different forms of childcare more closely matched to the demands of work, and much more awareness of ethnic diversity.

Questions and exercises

1. Why have early education and childcare developed along separate lines in the UK?
2. Do our children start formal schooling too early? What reasons or evidence can you give to support your point of view?
3. How could more high-achieving young women and men be attracted to a career in early childhood care and education?
4. Does Ofsted inspection guarantee the quality of privately provided childcare? What reasons or evidence can you give to support your point of view?

5. How can early years policies balance the needs of working parents and the well-being of young children?
6. What is the impact of family poverty on early learning and development?
7. What important lessons can be learnt from policy and practice in other countries?

A You are a single mother with children aged one and three years. You are offered a job at slightly more than the minimum wage. How will you decide if you should accept it or not?
B Martin, aged five, is often in trouble at school for moving about the classroom and 'bothering' other children. He shows no interests in books or reading. Attention Deficit Disorder has been mentioned. Can you suggest other explanations for his behaviour?

Further reading

Baldock et al.'s (2013) *Understanding Early Years Policy* (3rd edn), provides a useful account of the way early childhood policy is influenced by multiple external factors. It includes an informative timeline of key dates showing the interaction of political changes, economic conditions, legislation and public attitudes. Pugh and Duffy's (2010) *Contemporary Issues in the Early Years* (5th edn) has become a standard text with a 6th edition in press. It combines an excellent introduction to policy and research with many suggestions for improved practice and case studies from leading early childhood centres. Sylva et al.'s (2010) *Early Childhood Matters: Evidence from the Effective Pre-school and Primary Education Project* presents the context and findings from the EPPE longitudinal study in a clear and accessible way. The book is essential reading for understanding why the project was so influential in the formation of government policy, especially after 2004. The Nutbrown Report (2012) *Foundations for Quality* identifies the fundamental workforce problems that hold back the provision of early years care and education in the UK and makes recommendations for reform which may provide a basis for action in the future.

Websites

Main government website: www.education.gov.uk.
Children in Wales – Plant yng Nghymru: www.childreninwales.org.uk.
Children in Scotland: www.childreninscotland.org.uk.
Children in Northern Ireland (CiNI): www.ci-ni.org.uk.
Day Care Trust and Family and Parenting Institute: www.daycaretrust.org.uk.

British Association for Early Childhood Education: www.early-education.org.uk.

National Childminding Association: www.pacey.org.uk.

National Children's Bureau: www.ncb.org.uk.

National Day Nurseries Association: www.ndna.org.uk.

Pre-school Learning Alliance (playgroups): www.pre-school.org.uk.

Effective Provision of Pre-school Education project: www.ioe.ac.uk/eppe.

Early Years Foundation Stage: www.education.gov.uk/schools/teachingandlearn ingcurriculum/eyfs.

12

CHILDREN'S RIGHTS AND THE LAW

Nigel Thomas

Contents

- Introduction
- Theories of rights
- Theories of children's rights
- Declarations of children's rights
- The United Nations Convention on the Rights of the Child (UNCRC)
- Participation rights
- Young children's rights
- How rights are expressed in law
- The development of legal provision for children
- The Children Act 1989
- The Human Rights Act 1998
- The Children Act 2004 and Children's Commissioners
- The Children and Young Persons Act 2008
- Conclusion

Introduction

The aims of this chapter are to introduce some key ideas about children's rights, to show how these are expressed in international instruments such as the United Nations Convention on the Rights of the Child, and then to use this as a foundation to explore the law relating to children, particularly in England and Wales, and how it expresses – or fails to express – children's rights. The chapter concludes with some reflections on the role of Children's Commissioner.

Theories of rights

According to *The Oxford English Dictionary*, a right is 'a justifiable claim, on legal or moral grounds, to have or obtain something, or to act in a certain way'. We can distinguish between legal rights, which are based in law and whose existence is therefore a question of fact, and moral rights, which are based in ethics and whose existence is a question of value.

A right is a claim, entitlement or demand. A right may be absolute – but is not necessarily so. Eleanor Roosevelt captured something of the distinctiveness of rights when she reportedly said, 'A right is not something that somebody gives you; it is something that nobody can take away'. Dworkin (1978) put it another way when he argued that rights 'trump' other values and considerations, as in a card game. Rights are not the same as wants or needs: they have a *fundamental* quality that justifies the force attaching to them. Cranston (1967) and Worsfold (1974) propose three essential criteria for rights – they should be practicable (consistent with conceptions of justice), universal (in that they apply to everyone) and paramount (i.e. important enough to override other considerations).

A distinction is often made between liberty rights, such as the right not to be imprisoned without good cause, and welfare rights, such as the right to a home or to a basic income. Justifications of rights may be based either on 'will', and so linked with membership of a *community of rational autonomous individuals*, or on 'interest', and so based on our membership of a *community who share needs and interests*. Those who favour a justification based on 'will' are likely to be more interested in liberty rights; those who accept a justification based on 'interest' may be prepared to consider welfare rights.

Whichever justification is favoured, rights always appear to be based on some idea of membership of a community. This raises questions about *who is included*. A conception of rights that emphasises rationality and 'will' may exclude adults with severe learning disabilities, or young children, while a conception that emphasises our common needs and interests may also be be more inclusive. Some philosophers believe that animals can have rights too (Singer, 1995); in 2007 the Spanish Parliament extended some rights to certain animals.

Theories of children's rights

The phrase 'children's rights' is a slogan in search of definition. (Rodham, 1976)

Until the twentieth century, discussions of human rights made little if any reference to children, and the extent to which children can be bearers of rights has been much contested since then. Although campaigns to promote rights for children have gathered strength in the past hundred years, there has not always been agreement about what those rights are. A fundamental question is whether children are 'rights-bearers' in the same way as adults, or whether they are in need of special protection that justifies curtailing their freedom.

One way to look at it is this:

1. Children have certain kinds of rights because they are fundamentally the same as adults. This includes rights to make decisions about their own lives.
2. Children have other kinds of rights because they are more vulnerable and dependent than adults. This includes care and protection, and it may include some restrictions on their freedom; but these restrictions must be justified and proportionate.

Consistent with this view, children's rights are sometimes divided into 'participation' rights, which entitle children to take part in social and political life, and 'provision' and 'protection' rights, to ensure that children grow up safe and healthy.

Theoretical objections to the promotion of children's rights take two main forms. One line of argument objects to children having *welfare* and *protection* rights, on the grounds that children indeed ought to be looked after, but that it is misleading to express this in terms of 'rights', rather than adult obligations (O'Neill, 1992). The other objects to children having *participation* rights, on the basis that children are not competent to exercise these rights and must wait until they are adult (Purdy, 1992).

A strong statement of children's rights was made by Holt (1975), who argued 'that the rights, privileges, duties, responsibilities of adult citizens be made available to any young person, of whatever age, who wants to make use of them'. This would include not only the right to vote, but 'the right to be legally responsible for one's life and acts', 'the right to direct and manage one's own education' and the right 'to choose or make one's own home'.

Others are less radical. Archard (2004) distinguishes between 'libertarian' and 'caretaker' interpretations of children's rights, with the former favouring maximum freedom and equality with adults, while the latter is more cautious and protective. Archard himself argues, while not accepting the libertarian case fully, that it is a good starting point as it challenges us to justify any restrictions on children's liberty rather than accepting all restrictions without question.

However, there is a growing consensus that children do have rights and that these include at least some rights that equate to the 'liberty' or 'participation' rights of adults, as well as other rights that assure children care and protection as they grow up. This consensus is forcefully expressed in a series of international agreements, of which the best known and most important is the United Nations Convention on the Rights of the Child.

Declarations of children's rights

Among the foremost advocates of children's rights in the first half of the twentieth century were Eglantyne Jebb and Janusz Korczak. Korczak was a Polish paediatrician and pedagogue who ran child-centred orphanages, with children's parliaments and a children's newspaper (Lifton, 1988). Jebb was the founder of Save the Children, set up to assist child refugees after the First World War. In 1924 she persuaded the League of Nations to adopt a Declaration of the Rights of the Child, by which:

> Men and women of all nations, recognising that mankind owes to the child the best it has to give, declare and accept it as their duty that, beyond and above all considerations of race, nationality or creed:
>
> 1. The child must be given the means needed for its normal development, both materially and spiritually.
>
> 2. The child that is hungry should be fed; the child that is sick should be helped; the erring child should be reclaimed; and the orphan and the waif should be sheltered and succoured.
>
> 3. The child must be first to receive relief in times of distress.
>
> 4. The child must be put in a position to earn a livelihood and must be protected against every form of exploitation.
>
> 5. The child must be brought up in the consciousness that its best qualities are to be used in the service of its fellow men.

In 1948 the United Nations adopted an amended version of Jebb's Declaration, and then in 1959 a more extensive Declaration. In 1979 Poland, inspired by the memory of Korczak, proposed a Convention on the Rights of the Child, which would be a formal treaty and therefore binding on states that ratified it.

The United Nations Convention on the Rights of the Child (UNCRC)

The drafting of the Convention was a long and complex process and the outcome was more detailed and extensive than earlier Declarations. It was adopted by the General Assembly of the United Nations in 1989 and over the next three years was ratified by almost every country in the world (the exceptions to date being the USA and Somalia, and more recently South Sudan). States that ratify the Convention have to report at regular intervals to the Committee on the Rights of the Child on their progress in implementing Convention rights.

The Convention obliges states to make children's best interests a primary consideration. The first forty-one articles set out in detail children's rights to an identity and a family life, to education and health care, to protection from abuse and harm and to participate fully in their cultures and communities. The remaining thirteen articles specify the duties of states to publicise and implement the Convention and the process for ratifying and amending it. The full text of the Convention, can be seen at www.unicef.org/crc/

Participation rights

Unlike earlier statements, the United Nations Convention on the Rights of the Child includes children's rights to participate in decision-making. Article 12 of the Convention says that:

> States Parties shall assure to the child who is capable of forming his or her own views the right to express those views freely in all matters affecting the child, the views of the child being given due weight in accordance with the age and maturity of the child.

The following five articles assert children's rights to freedom of expression, thought and assembly, privacy and access to information. In other words, children are seen as bearers of liberty rights as well as welfare rights.

In the period since 1989 there has been a dramatic increase in the attention paid to children's participation rights, especially by governments and non-governmental organisations. Laws and policies have been reframed to give expression to these rights, at least to some extent. As organisations working for children and young people have shifted the emphasis of their programmes to a 'rights-based' rather than a 'needs-based' approach, participation has become an increasingly prominent feature of that work; and newer organisations have been set up whose primary purpose is to promote participation, some of them led by children and young people. How much difference that participation has yet made to policies and services, or to the reality of children's lives, is not entirely clear.

Young children's rights

For students of early childhood the most important question is how these theories of children's rights apply to children in the earliest years. If one accepts that it makes sense to talk of 'rights' to care, health, education and welfare, then such rights apply regardless of age (and younger children's greater vulnerability may mean that their entitlement has greater urgency). If one takes the view that rights have to be claimed by 'rational autonomous beings', then the door opens to questions about who has sufficient rationality to be included and whether this is limited by age. If rights are something one grows into, when and how does this happen? If rights are something we have from birth, then how are those rights to be exercised by babies and toddlers, who may not know that they have them? A fundamental question is: are young children competent to exercise participation rights?

For a theoretical answer to that question, we can draw on arguments from psychology, and even more from sociology, about how competence is situated in context, achieved and negotiated (see Hutchby and Moran-Ellis, 1998). For a practical response, we should look at evidence from research which shows how very young children, even babies, can express views, preferences and wishes with subtlety, if they are communicated with sensitively, respectfully and imaginatively (see Alderson, 1993; Clark and Moss, 2001; Clark et al., 2005). It is also valuable to consult the General Comment on implementing child rights in early childhood (UNCRC, 2006).

How rights are expressed in law

There are many laws that have an impact on children – in fact, it could be said that all laws do, directly or indirectly. Certainly, laws governing health, housing and welfare benefits have a major impact on children's lives, although they do not directly govern what children do or how their parents look after them. Education and employment law have a more direct effect on children; they spell out who is expected to go to school and what kind of education they should receive, or at what age children may work for payment. Criminal justice law makes specific provision for children and how they should be treated if they are thought to have committed an offence.

However, the laws that have the most profound impact on individual children's lives, and that may affect all children including the very youngest, are the laws governing children's care and upbringing. It is these laws that will be the main focus of this chapter. The legislation of most concern to us will be the Children Act 1989, which is the main provision directly concerned with children's welfare in England and Wales. The Act sets out the framework for the relationship between children, parents and the state. It provides for resolution of disputes between family members and defines the circumstances in which the state may intervene in family life. It lays down the powers and duties of local authorities to provide for children's welfare, and provides safeguards against poor care, whether provided by private individuals and organisations or by state agencies. The equivalent laws in other parts of the UK are the Children (Scotland) Act 1995 and the Children (Northern Ireland) Order 1995, which are based on the same guiding principles but also incorporate significant differences.

The development of legal provision for children

It could be said that until the nineteenth century a child was not a legal entity. A child without property or inheritance was of little interest to the legal system. Children enjoyed no special legal protection and had no rights to plead a case. The only other time the law became interested in them was when they stole or robbed, when the full weight of the law – including imprisonment and capital punishment – might fall upon them.

Laws to protect children developed in the mid-nineteenth century, beginning with factory legislation designed to prevent excesses of exploitation in the work-place, and leading to the novel idea that children should not be working at all. This was followed by laws prohibiting cruelty to children, an important development because it meant a breach in the principle of family privacy and parental (mainly paternal) authority. Laws to provide for children's welfare followed later, with the introduction of state elementary education, then compulsory health surveillance (following alarm at the poor condition of recruits to the army), and finally the extension of duties under the Poor Law to provide for destitute children.

On these foundations developed the modern law relating to children, through a series of landmark Acts of Parliament during the course of the twentieth century. The Children Act 1933 established a juvenile court system, introduced a 'fit person order' – where children could be removed from home without an offence being proved – and established a schedule of offences against children which is still in use today. The Children Act 1948 ended the Poor Law treatment of children, required local authorities to appoint Children's Officers, introduced the provision of care as a service to children and families rather than as a punishment, and improved the supervision of foster homes. The Children and Young Persons Act 1969 reformed the juvenile justice system on welfare principles (although it was never fully implemented) and established non-punitive grounds for children to be removed to local authority care.

It appears that the history of childcare legislation is characterised by an increasing emphasis on children's welfare and a shift away from 'cruelty' to 'care' as the key operating concept. It is also characterised by an increase in mutual accountability between families and the state; the first stage in this was the breaking of the barrier against any intrusion into family privacy or parental authority, while the second stage was bringing parents back into the picture as participants in the decision to provide 'care'.

What is missing up to this point is any real voice for children themselves, who are conceived of as *done to* rather than *doing*. Not until the Children Act 1975 did the law consider a child's wishes and feelings, and then only in a limited way. With the Children Act 1989 the law began to take children seriously as people with the right to a say in their own lives.

The Children Act 1989

Heralded by the Lord Chancellor as 'the most comprehensive and far reaching reform of child law which has come before Parliament in living memory' (HL Deb 06 December 1988 vol 502 cc 487–8), the Children Act 1989, was more wide ranging than any previous legislation because it brought together the *public law*, governing state services to children and child protection, and the *private law*, governing family life and disputes over children's upbringing, in the same statutory framework. The Act reformed the way in which courts intervened in family disputes and the kind of decisions they could make. It reformed the duties and powers of local authorities to children and families, and the way in which services were provided, especially when children are looked after away from home. Finally, it reformed the arrangements for regulation and inspection of childcare services.

Part One of the Act sets out over-arching principles for dealing with children's cases, often referred to as the 'welfare principles':

- That when a court is making a decision about the upbringing of a child it should treat the child's interests as paramount.
- That a court should assume that delay in resolving a case is against the child's interests.
- That a court should not make any order in respect of a child unless satisfied that to do so is better for the child than making another order, or no order at all.
- That in deciding what is in a child's interests the court must have regard to a set of eight factors often referred to as the 'welfare checklist' – the first of which is 'the ascertainable wishes and feelings of the child'.

Other important principles in the Act include:

- The concept of 'parental responsibility', which any legal parent has automatically and which others can acquire. Parental responsibility cannot be taken away from a parent except by the adoption of a child. Parents who separate or divorce are therefore expected to remain part of their child's life and share in the child's upbringing and in decision making. Parents whose children go into care are also expected to remain involved in their lives.
- The 'presumption of contact' – i.e. the presumption that contact is normally in the interests of children and should be positively promoted when they are separated from a parent or other significant person.

Part Two provides for disputes between parents and other relatives to be settled under the above principles. The starting assumption is that children's upbringing will be a matter of agreement between those involved, without the need for court intervention. The court only becomes involved if the parties cannot agree and someone applies for an order to be made. The most common orders are *residence* orders and *contact* orders, which decide whom a child will live with and who will have contact with the child.

Part Three of the Act, which governs services to children and families, defines when a child is 'in need' and the services to which they or their family are entitled (see Chapter 14). These services may include 'accommodation' if, for example, the child's parents are temporarily or permanently unable to provide appropriate care. This normally requires the agreement of a parent (or the child if he or she is over sixteen years). A child accommodated in this way is not 'in care' and the local authority does not have parental responsibility. They are, however, required to assess the child's needs and agree a plan with the parents and child.

Part Four of the Act relates to 'care and supervision' of children. It sets out the circumstances in which children may be removed from their families or the powers of parents restricted, and the process by which this is done. Applications may be made by the local authority or NSPCC. Parents and children have the right to oppose the order and be represented. A 'children's guardian' is appointed to safeguard the child's interests and advise the court. Before making an order the court must be satisfied that: the child is suffering or likely to suffer 'significant harm' if action is not taken. Once this is established, cases are dealt with under the 'welfare principles' and the court is obliged to do what is best for the child. This can include making a care order, which means that the child is committed to the care of the local authority, which then has parental responsibility.

All children who are either accommodated or subject to care orders are 'looked after' within the terms of the Act. Agencies have a duty to safeguard and promote the child's welfare, to consult the child and family before making decisions, to review the child's case at regular intervals and to hear any complaints and representations.

Part Five of the Act deals with protection of children. It provides orders which courts may make in order to protect children from significant harm and sets out the duties of local authorities to investigate situations of risk. Other agencies have duties to assist the local authority with their enquiries – particularly housing, health and education authorities and the NSPCC. This provision is the basis for the 'child protection system', the apparatus of inter-agency work to protect children, including case conferences and child protection registers. This is a distinctively UK response to the problem of how to protect children from harm. Continental approaches tend to be based more on encouraging families to seek help on their own terms. In the UK, as in other English-speaking countries, the emphasis is on investigation, often leading to legal action. In the UK there also is a legal requirement on agencies to work together to investigate abuse, supported by government regulation and guidance which also requires agencies to work together to plan a response to child abuse.

More recently, and specifically in relation to children in the early years, the Childcare Act 2006 placed duties on English local authorities to improve the wellbeing of young children and reduce inequalities between them, in addition to a series of provisions requiring the provision of specific services (see Chapter 11).

The Children Act 1989 and children's rights

The Children Act 1989 aims to strike a balance between the rights of children to autonomy and a voice, their right to care and protection and the rights of parents to bring up their children in the way they see fit. The Act puts into effect some of the key provisions of the UNCRC: the right to live with his or her parents or at least to maintain contact with them; the right to protection from abuse and neglect; the right to suitable care if not able to live with the family. Other legislation in the UK gives some effect to other Convention rights, such as the right to a good education and to participation in recreation and culture, the disabled child's right to care and education to help lead a full and active life, and the right to social security and an adequate standard of living. In each case there are limits on how fully the rights are implemented, which have been well scrutinised in reports such as *Righting the Wrongs* (Save the Children, 2006).

The Article of the UNCRC that has perhaps attracted most attention is Article 12, which gives the child the right to express an opinion and to have that opinion taken into account, in particular in any judicial and administrative proceedings affecting them. The Children Act 1989 makes that right a reality at least for some children – those whose upbringing is being considered by a court and those who are looked after by a local authority. It does not give the same right to children living in their own families. The Children (Scotland) Act 1995 does give parents a duty to take account of their children's wishes in making decisions affecting them, so that children in Scotland have more rights in this respect than those in England and Wales.

The Human Rights Act 1998

The European Convention on Human Rights was signed in 1950 by the Council of Europe (an organisation formed after the Second World War, which has nothing to do with the European Union and which now includes fifty-seven states). The Convention was intended to ensure that the atrocities of the Nazi era could not be repeated. It has become the basis of much European law, under the direction of the European Commission on Human Rights and the European Court of Human Rights in Strasbourg. Human rights under the Convention include the right to life, liberty, fair treatment at law, privacy and respect for family life, freedom of thought, conscience and religion, freedom of expression, assembly and association, and the right to marry and found a family. The Convention prohibits torture, inhuman or degrading treatment, slavery, and also prohibits discrimination in enjoyment of all of the above rights.

By passing the Human Rights Act 1998, Parliament incorporated the European Convention into UK national law. The Act says that a court or tribunal determining any question in connection with a Convention right must take into account any judgment or decision of the European Court or Commission, and that as far as possible national law must be interpreted in a way which is compatible with the Convention. If national law is incompatible with the Convention, the court may make a 'declaration of incompatibility' and the government then has the power to amend the legislation by making an order.

The Human Rights Act also says that it is unlawful for a public authority to act in a way which is incompatible with a Convention right. A person may bring proceedings against a public authority which has acted unlawfully in this way; the court can order the authority to act differently and may also award damages.

Although the Human Rights Act and the European Convention do not mention children directly, they are clearly included. Article 14 prohibits discrimination 'on any ground such as sex, race, colour, language, religion, political or other opinion, national or social origin, association with a national minority, property, birth or other status'. It does not specifically mention age, but there is nothing in the Convention to suggest that all rights do not apply equally to children. Although the Human Rights Act is less comprehensive than the UNCRC, it has more 'teeth' because it can be enforced by the courts (Lyon, 2007).

The Children Act 2004 and Children's Commissioners

The Children Act 2004 contains a number of important reforms to provision for children. One of the key ones is the establishment of the Children's Commissioner for England (following similar appointments in Wales, Northern Ireland and Scotland). Children's Commissioners are there to promote and safeguard the rights of children and young people and to be a voice and champion independent of government. All the Commissioners have slightly different powers and duties; the English Commissioner's duties are weaker, although this is now proposed to change following the Dunford Review (2010).

It remains to be seen how successful the Children's Commissioners will be in advancing the rights and interests of children; however, their introduction arguably represents a major step forward in basing policy and services on children's rights and wishes, rather than simply on their needs as perceived by adults.

The European Union has now begun to take a serious interest in children's rights and across Europe Children's Commissioners and Ombudspersons are working together with the EU and the Council of Europe to promote rights-based approaches (Stalford et al., 2011).

The Children and Young Persons Act 2008

The Children and Young Persons Act 2008 further extended the statutory framework for children in care, aiming to improve the stability of placements and the educational experience and attainment of young people in local authority care. It also strengthened the role of Independent Reviewing Officers, who are expected to ensure that local authorities prioritise children's best interests and take account of their wishes and feelings. This reflects a growing emphasis on the importance of independent people such as visitors, advocates or inspectors in a child's life, particularly when she or he is in care (Thomas, 2008).

Conclusion

I hope that this chapter has served to introduce the theoretical basis for ideas about children's rights, and some of the ways in which they are contested, and has shown how the adoption of the United Nations Convention on the Rights of the Child was a key moment in the development and implementation of these ideas. We have seen that even young children have rights and how UK law attempts, in a rather uneven way, to give expression to children's rights, including the right to take part in decisions. I hope that, in examining key provisions of the Children Act 1989, we have also learned something about the ways in which the law frames childcare policy, including the potential impact of the Human Rights Act 1998. Space has not permitted us to look in similar depth at other areas of law, or at the detailed provisions in Scotland and Northern Ireland, which in some respects are different from those in England and Wales. However, I hope this chapter will have served as an introduction to this field, and that the suggestions for further reading below will help those who wish to take the subject further. I have also included two case examples which readers may like to use in further study.

Questions and exercises

Example 1 – John

John's parents are separated and he lives with his mother. He wants to see his father but his mother is unwilling. She has been insulted and verbally abused by John's father in the past, he does not pay regular maintenance and she does not see why he should visit John and take him out for treats when she is struggling to bring him up on a limited income.

1. What are the options for the parties in this case, and how could it be resolved using the Children Act 1989?
2. What is the relevance in this example of the UNCRC and the Human Rights Act?

Example 2 – Helen

Helen is aged sixteen. She met a man of thirty when she was on holiday in Greece and she wants to marry him. Her mother supports her plan, but her father is opposed.

1. What are the important issues in this case, and how could it be resolved using the Children Act 1989?
2. What is the relevance in this example of the UNCRC and the Human Rights Act?

Further reading

On children's rights useful texts are Alderson (2008), Archard (2004), Flekkoy and Kaufman (1997) and Franklin (2002). Muscroft (1999) is a helpful commentary on the UNCRC. Bainham (2005) and Fortin (2009) are excellent guides to the law relating to children and families and to children's rights. Hershman and McFarlane (2002) is an authoritative source for the Children Act 1989. Stainton-Rogers and Roche (1994) are good on the policy issues and on the relationship between rights and welfare. The Office of the Children's Rights Director for England (shortly to be aborbed into the Office of the Children's Commissioner for England) is a good source of information on children and young people's views of the services they receive when they are living away from home (www.rights4me.org).

13

EARLY CHILDHOOD EDUCATION (ECE)

Iram Siraj-Blatchford

Contents

- Introduction
- An emergent curriculum
- Play and early childhood education
- Effective pedagogy and sustained shared thinking
- International early childhood education models
- Other common pedagogical models of ECE
- Conclusion

Introduction

The United Nations Convention on the Rights of the Child (Article 29, 1) agreed that all children have a right to education:

1   States Parties agree that the education of the child shall be directed to:

   (a)   The development of the child's personality, talents and mental and physical abilities to their fullest potential;

   (b)   The development of respect for human rights and fundamental freedoms, and for the principles enshrined in the Charter of the United Nations;

(c)   The development of respect for the child's parents, his or her own cultural identity, language and values, for the national values of the country in which the child is living, the country from which he or she may originate, and for civilizations different from his or her own;

(d)   The preparation of the child for responsible life in a free society, in the spirit of understanding, peace, tolerance, equality of sexes, and friendship among all peoples, ethnic, national and religious groups and persons of indigenous origin;

(e)   The development of respect for the natural environment. (United Nations General Assembly 1989)

The educational component of early years provision has the potential to transform a child's life and set them on a positive learning trajectory for life. A child's education doesn't miraculously begin when they start 'school'; it is therefore important to recognise that these principles should extend to all children regardless of age. For many children in their earliest years parents provide a rich educational as well as physical and social environment in the home. Unfortunately research shows us that this is not the case for all children. For many children from families disadvantaged by poverty and/or a lack of cultural capital, the quality of the home learning environment is poor and educational provisions of their nursery or playgroup have a significant and long-term influence upon their abilities, learning and life chances (Schweinhart et al., 1993; Siraj-Blatchford and Sylva, 2004; Sylva et al., 2004; Schweinhart et al., 2005). Education begins at birth (some would argue, even earlier) and to understand the nature of education in the first five years of early childhood three concepts are particularly valuable: pedagogy, curriculum and emergent development. The first two of these originate in educational theory and the third is more often applied from developmental psychology. It is important for all those who work with young children to understand the transformative potential of good, early education.

An emergent curriculum

While curriculum may be considered to define the content or product of teaching, the word 'pedagogy' is used by educationalists to describe the form that the teaching takes or the processes that are involved. Pedagogy is defined here following Gage (1977; 1985) as 'the science of the art of teaching' and every capable early educator may certainly be considered to be a *practising artist*. The best early childhood educators creatively draw upon their knowledge of the interests and capabilities of the children in their care, and also upon a wide range of material, cultural and intellectual resources to provide the children with the most effective and rewarding stimulation and hands-on learning experiences possible on a day-to-day basis. And, just as a kind of scientific 'development' may be seen in the work of a great painter (Cezanne comes to mind as a really good example), the performance of an effective early childhood educator also develops as they continually reflect upon, critically evaluate and moderate their practice to achieve excellence. This requires a very good understanding of how children learn, the content of what they could learn – for example, including a good knowledge of the *Early Years Foundation Stage* in England (DfE, 2012a), the *Foundation Phase* in Wales (DCELLS, 2008) or the *Curriculum for Excellence* in Scotland (CRPB, 2006) – and the ability to assess, plan and use the child's social and cultural experiences to help them 'access' the curriculum.

In the context of early childhood education, the term curriculum may be defined broadly as 'all of those experiences, activities and events, whether direct or indirect, intended or otherwise, that occur within an environment designed to foster children's learning and development'.[1] Young children are actively observing and exploring all of the time; they learn from everything that happens in the environment around them. However implicit or *hidden* the curriculum may be in some childcare and education settings, the content of this learning (i.e. the curriculum) is thus always determined by the adults who care for them. The notion of a totally 'free' play environment is really a myth. The material resources (toys, furniture, props) that are selected and the activities, the social interactions and the environments that we offer children define both the opportunities and the limitations for their learning. The linguistic and cultural context in which children are immersed even more fundamentally influences what it is that they learn.

'Emergent development' is actually a philosophical notion that dates back to the very earliest writings in nineteenth-century psychology (Sawyer, 2003). In terms of child development, emergence may be considered to involve processes that occur over time that result in the development of higher order structures of the mind. These may relate to particular intellectual, social and cultural competencies and capabilities – and research has shown that in the early years they are initially developed in social interaction with babies and pre-schoolers – as well as the acquisition of a range of communication and collaboration skills in play (see Siraj-Blatchford, 2008).

However, it is important to recognise that there is much more than any simple process of accumulation of skills involved in this. According to the principles of emergent development, the developmental structures that finally emerge are *irreducible* to their component parts. In fact, from the perspective of emergent development, it is considered impossible to deduce the child's development as a *whole* from any observations of their previously learnt behaviour or behaviours (Sawyer, 2003). This does not mean that we should not learn from our observations of children but that we accept there is a whole lot more going on than can be observed. Emergent

---

[1]Adapted from New Zealand Ministry of Education (1996), p. 10.

development requires an emergent curriculum, that is, content which is experienced but not in the main directly or didactically taught.

'Emergent literacy' was a term first applied in Marie Clay's doctoral dissertation (1966), and Whitehurst and Lonigan (1998) cite Sulzby (1989), Teale and Sulzby (1986) and Sulzby and Teale (1991) in defining the concept as:

> the skills, knowledge, and attitudes that are presumed to be developmental precursors to conventional forms of reading and writing … [as well as] … the environments that support these developments. (op cit: 849)

Clearly this definition may be applied much more widely, with emergent curriculum practices and resources being applied to support young children in learning and experiencing the skills, knowledge and attitudes identified as developmental precursors to a much wider range of curriculum subject areas and communities of practice:[2]

> Rather than individual development being influenced by (and influencing) culture, from my perspective, people develop as they participate in and contribute to cultural activities that themselves develop with the involvement of people in successive generations. People of each generation, as they engage in sociocultural endeavors with other people, make use of and extend cultural tools and practices inherited from previous generations. As people develop through their shared use of cultural tools and practices, they simultaneously contribute to the transformation of cultural tools, practices, and institutions. (Rogoff, 2003: 52)

Often this is how young children are learning in the home, in contingent, embedded contexts that they and their family share, often made more explicit through interactions and making meaning with the child.

Play and early childhood education

Rogoff and others (for example, Maybin and Woodhead, 2003) have shown that a wide range of *playful activities* progressively engage children in the cultural life of adults and their communities (Rogoff et al., 1993; Rogoff, 2003). Play (see Chapter 9) is also widely recognised as a leading context for the child's acquisition of communication and collaboration skills and if we apply our conception of 'emergence', then children's day-to-day learning through play may also be seen as contributing towards,

---

[2]While the subject of science has been studied in depth as a community of practice (Kuhn, 1970), the concept may be applied much more widely to include schools of art and other scholarly communities.

but not itself constituting, the achievement of either a series or continuous process of irreducible restructurings of the young child's mind:[3]

> A child's play is not simply a reproduction of what (s)he has experienced, but a creative reworking of the impressions (s)he has acquired. (Vygotsky, 2004: 11)

For neo-Vygotskians, play is considered to be a 'leading activity' (Leontiev, 1981; Oerter, 1993) but it is important to recognise here that this doesn't mean that play should be considered to predominate in the life of young children, that play is the *only* way that young children learn, or that *all* kinds of play promote development or learning. Play provides an important *context* for learning and development, as Vygotsky put it:

> Only theories maintaining that a child does not have to satisfy the basic requirements of life, but can live in search of pleasure, could possibly suggest that a child's world is a play world. ([1933] 1966: 1)

But:

> The child moves forward essentially through play activity. Only in this sense can play be termed a leading activity that determines the child's development. ([1933] 1966: 1)

In terms of empirical progression we know from decades of research that play begins with solitary play and the child goes on to develop the capability to share, then to co-operate and finally to collaborate in their play (Siraj-Blatchford, 2008). We also know that these developments open up much wider opportunities for learning. But solitary play, shared play, co-operative and collaborative play are not discrete 'stages' that the child works through. Even solitary play serves us well at times throughout our adult learning lives! In most theoretical accounts describing the ways in which these different forms of play open up the possibility of learning, the notion of emergent development is often implicit. For example, when describing play as a 'leading activity', it is only being suggested that it should be seen as a driving force in the child's development of new forms of motivation and action.

Recent contributions from neuroscience have supported the idea that children's early experiences and interactions, including those during play, affect the way the brain develops and helps shape its structure (Bee and Boyd, 2007). Within this research, there is acknowledgement of the importance of play as a:

> scaffold for development, a vehicle for increasing neural structures and a means by which all children practice skills they need in later life. (Isenberg and Quisenberry, 2002: 33)

---

[3]This may be seen as a 'renaissance' of the mind and/or as a gestalt change.

Maude et al. (2006) make the connection between play and the physical environment and stress how play involves gross and fine motor skills as highly important in infants' movement development and any physical education curriculum should be centred around that idea.

Effective pedagogy and sustained shared thinking

The Effective Provision of Pre-school Education (EPPE) research project (Siraj-Blatchford and Sylva, 2004) has provided a large-scale, longitudinal, mixed method research study that has followed the progress of over 3,000 children, from the age of three to eleven. The children started in 141 pre-schools and then entered 800 primary schools across England. The study applied multi-level modelling to investigate the separate effects of personal and social and family background, the quality of the learning support provided in the home, and the quality of the learning environment provided by the children's pre- and primary schools, as well as the effectiveness of the pre- and primary schools. The study has shown that quality pre-school education (as assessed by standardised instruments such as the Early Childhood Environment Rating Scale – Harms et al., 1998; Sylva et al., 2006) can ameliorate the effects of disadvantage by increasing children's learning attainment thereby reducing the effects of social exclusion. High quality ECE can be a strong equaliser for the most disadvantaged children. While all children benefit from high quality ECE, some only get it through pre-school provision rather than in the home.

Sustained shared thinking (SST) was first identified in a qualitative analysis carried out in the *Researching Effective Pedagogy in the Early Years* (REPEY) project undertaken in association with the EPPE project (Siraj-Blatchford et al., 2002; 2003). The REPEY project was developed to identify the most effective pedagogical strategies that are applied in the early years settings to support the development of young children's skills, knowledge and attitudes, and ensure they made a good start at school. The qualitative case studies provided detailed accounts of the learning and teaching that was observed (400 hours of adult observations and 254 episodes of child observations) in twelve of the most effective settings identified by EPPE (from a national sample of 141 settings).

The transcriptions of episodes of SST were subsequently found to provide valuable (concrete) examples of the kinds of effective pedagogy that were needed to develop practice. Sustained shared thinking thus featured in the *Key Elements of Effective Practice (KEEP)* (DfES, 2005) that was distributed to all English pre-school settings, and it has now been included in the national *Early Years Foundation Stage (EYFS)*, a curriculum framework and guidance for England (DfE, 2012a).

The REPEY findings may be summarised as follows:

1. **Adult initiated activity** – effective pedagogues model appropriate language, values and practices. They also encourage socio-dramatic play, and praise, encourage, ask questions and interact verbally with children. Excellent settings tended to achieve a good balance between teacher-led and child-initiated interactions, play and activities. Two-thirds of activities were child-led but in excellent settings half of these were extended with appropriate, guided, cognitive challenge by the adults.

2. **Child initiated but adult extended activities** – this is a particular form of teacher/practitioner initiation that may also be applied in cases where the child initiated. The most effective settings were found to provide both teacher-initiated group work and freely chosen, yet potentially instructive play activities. 'Extension' was included in the definition of 'sustained shared thinking' (see below), and one of the implications clearly identified in the research was that effective pedagogues require a good knowledge and understanding of the curriculum and of how children learn.

3. **The provisions of differentiation and formative assessment** – effective pedagogues assessed children's performance to ensure the provision of challenging yet achievable experiences (i.e. within the zone of proximal development – Vygotsky, 1978) and provide formative feedback. The most effective settings seemed to have shared educational aims with parents supported by regular communication; weekly or monthly dialogues were more effective than termly or annual meetings.

4. **Attention to the relationships between children** – effective settings viewed cognitive and social development as complementary and they supported children in rationalising and talking through their conflicts and resolving problems for themselves with the help of adults. This was not the case where the adults dominated and told the children what to do.

5. **Sustained shared thinking and open-ended questions** – adults and children in the excellent settings were more likely to engage at times in SST: episodes in which two or more individuals 'worked together' in an intellectual way to solve a problem, clarify a concept, evaluate activities or extend narratives, etc. During periods of SST both parties contributed to the thinking and developed and extended the discourse. Associated with SST was also the adult's skilled use of open-ended questioning. These are questions that could genuinely have more than one answer, e.g. 'What do you think?' 'What would you do?' (See Siraj-Blatchford and Manni, 2008 for the analysis of around 6,000 questions asked of children in twelve pre-schools.)

In the UK context, such findings also challenge entrenched beliefs about the value of exclusively encouraging free play and promoting a solely non-interventionist role for early childhood practitioners.

International early childhood education models

An ECE model is an educational system that combines theory with practice. A number of such models may be identified in the UK and overseas that combine a theoretical knowledge base (that may reflect a particular philosophical orientation). The 'qualities' of several particularly popular and 'successful' international ECE models were identified in the *Starting Strong Report* (OECD, 2004) and as Pramling et al. (2004) and Siraj-Blatchford (1999) have observed, a number of interesting commonalities can be found between the most successful (widely replicated) ECE models developed in different countries. Similarly, if we consider the accounts of the three ECE models most clearly identifying their pedagogy in the *Starting Strong Report* (OECD, 2004), we can see that the particular strategies applied according to these accounts of the models (by Ferre Laevers, David Weikart and Carla Rinaldi) match very closely with the REPEY findings, and with additional evidence from the EPPE study (Siraj-Blatchford and Sylva, 2004) that show positive correlations as can be seen in Table 13.1.

In the UK, the Effective Early Learning (EEL) project has drawn upon work carried out by Laevers (1995) in Belgium to provide a professional development

Table 13.1 OECD curriculum outlines

	Teachers' initiating activities	Teachers' extending activities	Differentiation and formative assessment	Relationships and conflict between children	Sustained shared thinking
EEL*	Introducing new activities	Enriching interventions	Observe children	Work out sustaining relations	Engagement
High Scope	Sharing control	Participation as partners	Plan, do, review	Adopt a problem-solving approach	Authentic dialogue
Reggio Emilia	Development of short- and long-term projects	Sustaining the cognitive and social dynamics	Teachers first listen don't talk	Warm reciprocal relationships	Reciprocity of interactions
EPPE/ REPEY	Correlations found with effective practice	Correlations found with effective practice	Correlations found with effective practice	Correlations found with effective practice	Correlations found with effective practice

Source: OECD, 2004

Notes: 'Teacher' also refers to any other adult in early years settings

* 'Effective Early Learning' (EEL) (Pascal and Bertram, 1995), referred to as 'Experiential Education' (EXE) in Praming et al. (2004) taken from the work of Ferre Laevers (1995).

programme that is intended to evaluate and develop quality in early childhood settings (Pascal and Bertram, 1995; 1997). In EEL, effective learning is considered to involve an essentially symbiotic relationship characterised by the 'involvement' of the child and the 'engagement' of the teacher. An involved child is one who has focused their attention and is persistent, is intrinsically motivated, rarely distracted, fascinated and absorbed by their activity. An engaged adult is one who shows sensitivity, stimulation and yet grants enough autonomy for the child to make their own judgements and express their ideas.

Reggio Emilia is a district in Northern Italy where over the last thirty-five years the municipality has developed an extensive network of early childhood services for children from birth to six years, providing for over a third of children under three and nearly all children aged three to six. The city has become world famous for the pedagogical work in these services, attracting many visitors from all over the world (for further reading, see Edwards et al., 1993). The early childhood services in Reggio understand the young child to be a co-constructor of knowledge and identity, a unique, complex and individual subject, engaging with and making sense of the world from birth, but always doing this in relationship with others, both adults and other children. Reggio pre-schools employ specialist staff such as an *atelierista* – a person who runs the atelier, the school's art studio – and a *pedagogista*, who acts as a key worker providing support with documentation and individual planning for a group of children (often across a group of settings) and their families.

The High/Scope approach (Schweinhart et al., 2005), which has also gained considerable popularity in the UK, is based upon an approach originally developed from the practice of Sara Smilansky. The High/Scope daily routine consists of a cycle of 'planning', 'doing' and 'reviewing'. During planning, children decide what activity they will engage in for the session. Once the 'do' part of the routine is complete, the children recall what they have done during review time. A setting organised to provide the High/Scope experience is divided into interest areas to promote active learning and specific kinds of play and the materials are accessible to the children to allow independence. The adult's role is to participate as a partner in the children's activities and there is an emphasis on positive interaction strategies, allowing children to share control and form authentic relationships with other children. In addition, the adult must support children's learning and extend it by helping children to find solutions to problems they encounter.

There is strength to be found in variety and as each of these models is culturally specific it would be a mistake to make any judgement between them. But as suggested above, there are commonalities that may be identified to inform the development of all provisions (Siraj-Blatchford, 1999). To take just one other significant example, the 'documentation' applied in Reggio Emilia and other ECE models provides a means by which children are encouraged to reflect upon their own work and that of their peers. They, therefore, 'become even more curious, interested, and confident as they contemplate the meaning of what they have achieved' (Malaguzzi, 1993: 63). When the children's efforts, intentions and ideas are shown so clearly to be taken seriously by the adults this encourages the children to approach their work with greater responsibly, energy and commitment. Documentation also provides a basis for continuous planning based on the evaluation of work as it progresses; it provides a context for communicating with parents, which often leads them to become more involved in their child's education. High/Scope takes the emphasis on continuous planning and review that is found in Reggio a stage further, providing a more structured and institutionalised approach in the daily plan-do-review routines.

Other common pedagogical models of ECE

A typology of the most commonly applied models of early childhood education has been adapted from a model first developed by Weikart (2000), and is shown in Figure 13.1.

The major organising principles applied in the typology are pedagogy and curriculum (Bernstein, 1981) and the different forms of early childhood practice are distinguished by applying Bernstein's formulation of classification and framing. 'Classification' refers to the strength of the boundaries placed between 'curriculum subjects' – in the early years we might refer to these as *domains of learning*. Where the curriculum content is clearly defined in terms of school subjects we refer to that as *strong* classification. Framing is about who is in control – who it is that selects, sequences or paces the learning. When framing is weak the child has more apparent control, and when it is strong it is the adult or educator who is most clearly in control. So for example, a collaborative, progressive and permissive classroom illustrates weak framing and a traditional didactic one illustrates strong framing.

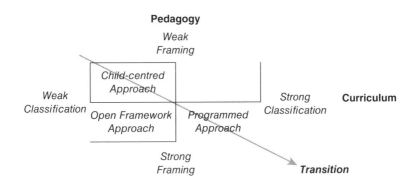

Figure 13.1   Other common models of ECE

Source: Siraj-Blatchford (2008)

In the most extreme applications of the *child-centred approach* in ECE, the teacher responds entirely to the individual child's interests and activities. More often, topic or project themes are adopted that have been chosen especially to appeal to the children's interests. The curriculum emphasis is on encouraging children's independence, their social and emotional growth, creativity and self-expression. The classroom or playroom environment is often rich in stimulus, permissive and provides for open-ended exploration and discovery.

An *open framework approach* provides the educator with a strong pedagogic structure (or framework) that supports the child in their explorations and interactions with, and reflections upon, their learning environment. In this model, the curriculum classification is weaker as the child has a good deal of freedom to make choices between the various learning environments that are on offer. But the optional environments (e.g. sand, water, block play, puzzles) are often provided to achieve particular (usually cognitive or conceptual) curriculum aims, and these aims may be more or less acknowledged by the setting. In some settings children's choices are carefully monitored and a broad and balanced curriculum (including physical, creative, social and academic) is encouraged over the medium or long term.

The *programmed approach* is highly teacher directed providing for little initiative on the part of the child. The rationale for this method is drawn significantly from theories of learning. This pedagogy is usually applied where curriculum objectives may be clearly (and objectively) classified and is likely to be most effective where learning involves the development of simple skills or memorisation. The curriculum content in programmed approaches is often highly structured. This sort of programme has been shown to be detrimental to children's long-term development (Schweinhart and Weikart, 1997).

Some longitudinal studies have shown us that young children provided with programmed instruction sometimes do better than those provided with other forms of pedagogy in the short term (e.g. Karnes et al., 1983; Miller and Bizzell, 1983). But the studies also suggest that even when these effects are apparent, the gains are short lived, with all the significant differences having 'washed out' within a year of the provision ending. Programmed instruction has also been found to result in children showing significantly increased stress/anxiety behaviours (Burts et al., 1990). A more recent and rigorous longitudinal study conducted by Schweinhart and Weikart (1997) showed little difference in the academic performance of young children provided with programmed instruction but significantly more emotional impairment and disturbance leading to special educational provision. More importantly, the Schweinhart and Weikart study showed that in later years the programmed instruction group experienced more suspensions from work and more than double the rate of arrests as either of the other two groups. In terms of serious crimes requiring a custodial sentence, forty-three per cent of the programmed instruction group gained a criminal record, compared with only seventeen per cent of the child-centred group and only ten per cent of the open framework group by the age of twenty-five. Both the Schweinhart and Weikart (1997) study and the High/Scope Perry Pre-school study showed a significant difference in the percentage of young adults married and living with their spouses: while thirty-one per cent of the open framework group and eighteen per cent of the child-centred group were married at the age of twenty-three, none of those experiencing programmed instruction was (Schweinhart and Weikart, 1997).

The England and Northern Ireland EPPE 3–11 has now identified similar patterns: children who attended medium and high quality pre-schools were found to have higher levels of 'self-regulation' in Year 6 (aged eleven, end of primary school) than others. Children who attended high quality pre-schools were also found to display more 'pro-social' behaviour and were less likely to display 'hyperactivity' in Year 6 than children who had attended low and medium quality pre-schools (Sammons et al., 2007). EPPE also shows the importance of having professionals trained specifically in the teaching of young children: graduate teachers as managers of centres or higher proportions of graduate teachers were associated with better outcomes for children. Mixed teams of professionals which included teachers seem to work particularly well (Sylva et al., 2004).

Conclusion

Of course, each of the approaches that are described here and in the *Starting Strong* report remain 'ideal types', and the practices in many settings will involve a combination of all of them. The challenge for early childhood educators is to provide a gradual and supportive transition as the children become more capable, which stimulates learning and development while avoiding any risk of regression or failure. This transition is often reflected in changes in the strength of the classification and framing offered to children as they get older (as shown by the arrow in Figure 13.1).

The EYFS guidance (Early Education, 2012) and the Foundation Phase (DCELLS, 2008) promote a pedagogy which involves negotiating and co-constructing the curriculum through playful processes of SST that may be initiated by either the adult or the child. The question of who initiates this SST is actually less relevant as long as both parties are committed to playing an equal part in determining its focus and direction (its co-construction) in 'collaborative free flow'. In a sense, 'initiation' is taken in turns as different material and symbolic resources are drawn upon, and each play is extended as a more or less unique improvisation. As children develop the capability and are motivated to play with peers, the curriculum guidance in the UK encourages us to continue to provide children with a rich range of experiences and resources to draw upon in collaborative play and to support them in developing a greater awareness of their development and learning. Ultimately, in school, young children take pleasure in learning for its own sake and restrict their play to scheduled playtimes, more disciplined creative activities and their involvement in a variety of games with more formal rules.

Longitudinal studies from America provided early evidence of the effectiveness of pre-school education. The High/Scope Perry Pre-school evaluation showed the substantial benefits that were to be gained through pre-schooling for children brought up in low-income households and at high risk of school failure. Many studies have also shown that social and motivational elements of pre-school programmes are as important as academic outcomes. Early childhood education really matters.

Questions and exercises

1. Why is ECE important in the quest for equality of opportunity?
2. What are the key components of quality programmes?
3. What kinds of professionals are required to support the best outcomes for children? What are the obstacles to this being achieved?
4. What do we know from research about the benefits of ECE?

Further reading

Two publications provide the most comprehensive synthesis of the theory and evidence related to early childhood education currently available. Both of these are US publications, the first comes from the National Research Council and Institute of Medicine (2000) *From Neurons to Neighbourhoods: The Science of Early Childhood Development*, and the second is Bowman et al. (2001) *Eager to Learn*. The EPPE has had a considerable impact on government policy and provided the first robust evidence of the positive effects of pre-school education in the UK. EPPE has shown that high quality pre-school education can help reduce social exclusion and has the potential to break cycles of educational disadvantage. *EPPE Technical Paper 10* (Siraj-Blatchford et al., 2003) provides case study illustrations of good pre-school practices identified through EPPE. In the book *Team Around the Child: Multi-agency Working in the Early Years*, I have a chapter that makes the case for integrating education with care in the early years (Siraj-Blatchford et al., 2007), and my paper, 'Creativity, communication and collaboration: the identification of pedagogic progression in sustained shared thinking' (Siraj-Blatchford, 2007) presents a conceptual model to support further development of good practice in early childhood education.

The *Early Years Foundation Stage* documents can be found online at:

www.education.gov.uk/schools/teachingandlearning/curriculum/a0068102/early-years-foundation-stage-eyfs.

www.education.gov.uk/publications/eOrderingDownload/Development-Matters.pdf (three prime areas).

14

CHILD WELFARE AND PROTECTION

Dendy Platt

Contents

- Introduction
- The extent of the problem
- Child welfare problems in the community
- Responding to serious cases
- Children in the care system
- Adoption
- Inter-professional working
- Policy orientations
- Conclusion

Introduction

The majority of readers embarking on this chapter will approach it from a relatively informed perspective about the needs of children in general, their development and learning, their care and education, and policies aimed at addressing their needs. Many will be less familiar with the more specialist services that respond to children and young people with more significant needs, where sometimes very difficult decisions have to be taken to promote their welfare. This may include removing children from their families, prosecuting offences against children and providing alternative forms of care such as adoption and fostering.

Public awareness of this type of provision has been informed, in recent years, by high profile cases that have attracted press and media attention. Four such cases have been noteworthy. Victoria Climbié, originally from the Ivory Coast, was brought to France and then to England by her aunt, on behalf of her parents, so that she could obtain a good education. Sadly she died in February 2000, aged eight years, as a result of extreme physical abuse and neglect at the hands of the aunt and the aunt's partner. Her situation was the subject of a public inquiry (Laming, 2003). Peter Connelly, originally identified as 'Baby P', died in 2007 aged seventeen months, following abuse and neglect by his mother and her partner (Haringey Local Safeguarding Children Board, 2009). In both these cases, considerable media criticism was directed against the various services involved and particularly the social work profession.

The other two cases offer a contrast to these, with interesting insights that will be explored as this chapter unfolds. Shannon Matthews, at the age of nine years, was imprisoned, drugged and tethered by her mother and an accomplice in the accomplice's flat. The mother then presented the events to the world's media as an abduction, with the apparent intention of (fraudulently) obtaining financial donations to assist with finding Shannon. The case was subject to a serious case review,[1] although the full findings were never published (BBC News, 2010). The last of the four cases is attracting considerable attention at the time of writing. Strictly speaking, it involves separate cases numbering well into the hundreds. They are the sexual crimes, mainly against children and young people, believed to have been committed by Jimmy Savile in his roles as television presenter and charity fundraiser (Gray and Watt, 2013). The allegations have been the subject of police investigations and a number of internal inquiries by the BBC where Savile was employed for a number of years (BBC News, 28 October 2012).

This chapter will use these cases as material in exploring the work undertaken by child welfare services. The concept of child welfare implies a relationship between the state and individual families, whereby the state is required to intervene if the care of the children is seen as unacceptable according to certain defined standards. The chapter will consider how child welfare problems come to light, how and when they receive a response and what is involved in those most serious of interventions, the removal of children from their families or compulsory placement for adoption. The difficulties that come to the attention of services include child abuse and neglect, severe financial problems, disability and learning difficulties, social and behavioural problems, and parents who have serious problems controlling their children's behaviour or managing basic care (e.g. provision of adequate food and clothing). The

---

[1]Serious case reviews are a statutory procedure for the review of serious cases such as a child death or very serious neglect, with a view to local services identifying improvements in practice that may prevent recurrence.

chapter will focus on *social* responses to these problems and will not examine health and educational services. It will analyse policy and service provision in a critical manner and will then consider the broader policy orientations underpinning that service provision. The reader is invited to consider ways in which the many policy dilemmas might be resolved.

The extent of the problem

To consider the prevalence of child welfare problems we can begin with poverty as a general indicator. The latest government statistics show that 3.8 million children[2] in the UK, or twenty-nine per cent of the total child population, were living in poverty in 2009/10 (Adams et al., 2011). The measures used to estimate poverty levels vary, but this figure is based on numbers of children in households earning below sixty per cent of average (median) income after housing costs. Clearly, only a small minority of children in these circumstances will experience the welfare problems with which this chapter is concerned. However, it is well accepted that child welfare problems generally occur within the context of multiple difficulties, often involving or exacerbated by poverty (Parton, 1985; Cawson et al., 2000; Corby et al., 2012). In the cases of Victoria Climbié, Peter Connelly and Shannon Matthews, referred to earlier, it is highly likely that poverty contributed to the problems they faced, although it would have been a background factor rather than the immediate cause.

Regarding child abuse, the World Health Organization uses the term *child maltreatment* to cover all forms of abuse, and its definition of child maltreatment is:

> All forms of physical and/or emotional ill-treatment, sexual abuse, neglect or negligent treatment or commercial or other exploitation, resulting in actual or potential harm to the child's health, survival, development or dignity in the context of a relationship of responsibility, trust or power. (Butchart et al., 2006: 59)

For the purposes of this chapter, we will focus on the first four of these forms of abuse, because they occur mainly in the family context – which in recent decades has been the predominant concern of child welfare services. Accurate figures regarding prevalence of child maltreatment are very difficult to identify, but a recent study suggests that as many as fourteen per cent of adults in the UK may have been victims of severe maltreatment by a parent or guardian while under the age of eighteen years (Radford et al., 2011).

---

[2]A child is defined here as an individual under sixteen years of age, or an unmarried sixteen to nineteen year old in full-time non-advanced education.

Child welfare problems in the community

The ways in which cases of possible child maltreatment come to the attention of services are various. Neighbours may report possible abuse or concerns about poor parenting. Teachers, health visitors, child minders and others may observe children who appear to be having difficulties or may even be injured, and they may hear children's accounts of adverse experiences. The police and children's social work services are among the key organisations to which such reports are directed. The role of the police is to investigate crime and their involvement tends to be restricted to situations where the harm to the child has occurred as a result of a possible criminal offence. The role of social work services, generally part of the local authority, is to assess the needs of children referred to them and to take action where appropriate. Generally, the services prioritise the most serious cases, and the interpretation of seriousness is often related to current policy priorities and resource constraints (Platt and Turney, 2013). For example, with domestic violence referrals, a common pattern is to prioritise only children who are physically harmed during an incident of domestic violence (Stanley et al., 2011) – despite current awareness of the emotional damage to children from witnessing domestic abuse. Successive governments in the UK have adopted an underlying policy position that child welfare and safeguarding children should be the responsibility of whole communities and not simply of specialist services. State intervention is thus seen as a last resort in dealing with child welfare problems.

In the case of Shannon Matthews, before the simulated abduction took place, Shannon appears to have been experiencing neglectful parenting. Neglect involves an ongoing failure to provide the care needed to meet a child's most basic needs. It might become apparent through inadequate nutrition, severe lack of cleanliness, inadequate parental oversight of children, poor clothing and so on. The BBC report (BBC News, 2010) on the serious case review suggests that there was involvement by social workers with the family, but that the problems were never serious enough to warrant court action to remove the children. This finding is a good illustration of the difficulties of responding to neglect cases. Often there is a succession of low-level concerns that, individually, do not add up to a picture of actionable abuse. Services sometimes fail to examine the pattern over time (Daniel et al., 2011), although in Shannon's case, even with hindsight, the evidence prior to her abduction may not have been sufficient to warrant her removal. These limitations in responding to neglect cases affect adolescents as well as children (Hicks and Stein, 2009).

State provision regarding child welfare problems is governed mainly by the Children Act 1989 in England (see Chapter 12). Regarding the other countries of the UK, the arrangements are similar although each country has its own legislation (Stafford et al., 2012); the present account will refer to England, but will draw only on provisions that are substantially the same, in general terms, as those in Scotland,

Wales and Northern Ireland. There are two procedures used by children's social workers in circumstances where there are child welfare concerns such as those facing Shannon Matthews. The first is an investigation of suspected child abuse, under s.47 of the Children Act 1989. The second is a less formal response in which the family's difficulties are assessed and services such as family support may be offered (s.17, Children Act 1989). Such services are often referred to as 'preventive' (aiming to prevent further harm to the child) and may have been provided, unsuccessfully, for Shannon and her family. In both these procedures, emphasis has grown in recent years regarding the importance of focusing on the child and hearing his or her voice.

Another process might have been relevant to Shannon's situation prior to the abduction (although it was introduced after her case came to public attention), and it involves less specialist services. In 2008 the then Labour government introduced a Common Assessment Framework (CAF) in England only, to assess the needs of relevant children and to promote a co-ordinated response. It is targeted on children who have additional needs beyond those of the majority population, and their difficulties are less likely to involve multiple family problems or severe allegations of abuse. The assessment can be used by any professional involved with and concerned for the child, such as health visitor, school nurse, teacher, children centre staff and so forth, and it emphasises preventive interventions. The professionals involved typically meet and co-ordinate the most appropriate form of help from within their own services, and social workers generally become involved only when the problems are more severe. The CAF has had mixed success, with some positive experiences of improved support for families and some difficulties linked to inter-professional working and assessment skills (Holmes et al., 2012). As an approach, it is consistent with the viewpoint that the welfare of children is the concern of whole communities and not something that can be hived off as the responsibility solely of specialists such as social work and children's mental health services.

In the case of Shannon Matthews, there was significant international press and media attention. Yet despite such close monitoring, the newspapers and TV news programmes failed to uncover her mother's lies. If armies of journalists, almost literally camped outside the family home, were so comprehensively deceived, it is illustrative of the very real problems facing child welfare services in assessing children's needs.

Responding to serious cases

Moving on to serious allegations of maltreatment, two children where professionals failed adequately to recognise the problems were Victoria Climbié and Peter Connelly. Had their situations been understood more fully, the local authority in each case should have used the provisions of the Children Act 1989 (see Chapter 12) to remove them from their parents' or guardians' care. In extreme circumstances, the Children Act enables local authorities to apply to the courts for an Emergency Protection Order (s.44) or to use police powers, to allow immediate removal of a child from his or her 'parents' (the term 'parent' is used in this chapter to mean any legal guardian). These are unusual measures, but may well have been applicable, particularly to Victoria Climbié's situation. Once any immediate emergency issues have been resolved, local authorities can apply to the courts for a Care Order (s.31) or Interim Care Order, which will also allow removal of the child(ren), but there is more time and opportunity for assessment, decision-making and for a full court hearing. There are also options to allow the perpetrator of abuse to be excluded from the family home, rather than the child having to be taken away. This course of action is most often used in cases of alleged sexual abuse.

Care Orders may be made in a wide range of situations, not simply those that come with the label 'child abuse'. Parents with severe cognitive or emotional limitations may have difficulties that become insurmountable in bringing up their children; other children may develop behavioural problems that their parents cannot cope with; problems such as parental drug use or criminality may add up to a picture of worsening childcare. Where the harm to the child is significant a Care Order may be the right answer for the child, although appropriate interventions and support may be offered to try to prevent this happening. The widespread image of the social worker walking in to a family's home and removing a child on their own authority is a long way from the truth. Unless a child has been abandoned by his or her parents, court involvement is always necessary. The test applied by the courts is whether the child has suffered (or is likely to suffer) *significant harm* (Children Act, s.31(2)), and whether that harm is attributable to the care given by the parents. Local authorities must present evidence to satisfy the courts on these particular points; legislation and legal precedent provides guidance regarding interpretation. In our examples, it is unlikely that a court would have turned down a Care Order application in respect of Victoria Climbié or Peter Connelly.

Despite the best efforts of child welfare agencies, many children with serious problems are not identified until well into their childhoods or teenage years, and sometimes not at all. Child sexual abuse is a particular case in point. The NSPCC study cited above showed that in thirty-four per cent of cases of contact sexual abuse by an adult, no one else knew about the abuse, and in eighty-three per cent of cases of contact sexual abuse by a peer, no one else knew about it (Radford et al., 2011). Even if someone knew about the abuse, the numbers that come to the attention of the authorities are small. In a previous NSPCC study, ninety per cent of the child sexual abuse identified by the researchers had never been reported (Cawson et al., 2000). The Jimmy Savile case described earlier is one illustration of this difficulty. The allegations only truly came to light after Savile's death, and involved at least 214 recorded crimes, from 1977 through to 2009

(Gray and Watt, 2013). The likelihood, in common with much sexual abuse, is that some of the individuals affected were too frightened to come forward, perhaps because of threats by the perpetrator, and if they had done so they may well not have been believed. For some, there was a lack of trust in the services or in the realistic possibility of successful prosecution. Savile clearly used his celebrity status to hide his activities (Gray and Watt, 2013) and possibly even to make some of his victims feel special at the time. Enabling victims of child sexual abuse to come forward, and ensuring that their voices are heard and adequate responses are made, are among the greatest unresolved policy challenges in this field.

Cases of physical abuse or neglect that lead to fatal consequences are more likely to get press and media coverage than child sexual abuse. Numbers are, thankfully, small. While the press and the media make great play of serious mistakes by child welfare professionals, the overall picture in the UK gives greater cause for optimism (although not complacency). During the thirty years to 2006, there is evidence that numbers of child abuse related deaths in England and Wales fell by eighty-one per cent. This constitutes a reduction that was significantly faster than that of child deaths in general (caused by ill health, accidents, etc.), an achievement that was matched only by a handful of other major developed countries (Pritchard and Williams, 2010). Although it is difficult confidently to attribute these improvements to the success of services – and even a single child death from abuse is one too many – it may be that the work of child protection services made a contribution. A paradox of the child protection system is that professionals operate in a wide range of circumstances and outcomes are affected by a huge number of factors. It is not possible to say that the child protection system is wholly effective, but we can record that there are notable successes as well as notable failings.

Children in the care system

Children may be placed in public care either as a result of a court order or at the request of their parent(s)/carer(s). Even in the case of a request from parents, the child would not be accommodated by the local authority unless the circumstances met the relevant Children Act criteria. Children in both types of situation are referred to collectively as *looked after children*. The older term, 'children in care' is also commonly used. A Care Order empowers the local authority to place a child with foster carers, in residential care, with relatives or in other suitable accommodation. In many cases, after a period in care, an attempt may be made to return a child to his or her family of origin, although where maltreatment of any type has occurred the success rates can be low (Farmer et al., 2011). If a young child cannot return home, adoption or some other means of achieving a permanent and secure future may be the preferred option.

The numbers of children who are looked after by the state have been increasing steadily in recent years (although significant peaks in numbers also occurred in earlier decades). At 31 March 2012 there were 67,050 looked after children in England alone (DfE, 2012d). Of these, seventy-five per cent were in foster care, and during the year up to 31 March 2012, 3,450 looked after children in England were adopted (DfE, 2012d). The overall numbers cited here represents a thirteen per cent increase compared with 31 March 2008. A recent study by the Child and Family Court Advisory and Support Service suggests a number of possible explanations for this increase, in relation to children coming into care via Care Orders (CAFCASS, 2012). One explanation is the effect of the Peter Connelly case. In part, it seems that this case made local authorities and health workers more aware of the need to act in a timely fashion to protect children, and more cases have consequently been brought to court. There may also have been a reluctance to manage risk by supporting families in the community, although the report suggests that, in general, applications for Care Orders were of an appropriate degree of seriousness. The economic slowdown since 2008 may be relevant, in that services to support families in the community, reduced as part of austerity measures, might otherwise have prevented removal to care. And a recent court judgment has placed an expectation on local authorities to accommodate homeless older teenagers in the care system where previously they might simply have been offered housing (G versus the London Borough of Southwark in 2009).

Had Victoria Climbié or Peter Connelly been placed in care, their paths would have differed significantly. Victoria Climbié's birth parents lived in the Ivory Coast and arrangements would probably have been made to return her to their care. In the case of Peter Connelly, if no suitable family carer could be found, given his young age, it is likely he would have been placed in foster care with a view to eventual adoption.

It is important to recognise that the placement of children in these ways is not the end of their story. Children looked after by local authorities will be affected psychologically for the remainder of their lives, by the harm they have experienced and in some cases by both the trauma associated with being removed and their experiences in care. Some overcome these difficulties better than others, and the stability and consistency of the care they receive is crucially important. Attention has been drawn, in the last decade or so, to the alleged failings of the looked after system. Some politicians, for example, have spoken about poor outcomes affecting such children, particularly regarding educational achievement. Recent statistics show that only twenty-five per cent of children in care achieve GCSE qualifications at grades A to C, compared with three-quarters of the general population (Berridge, 2012). One suggestion is that this is because the 'system' has let them down. However, there is growing evidence that educational achievement of children in care is determined by a complex range of factors, including the disadvantages they faced prior to entering the care system and not necessarily by the care system itself. Additional educational support has been introduced recently for children in care, which is likely to lead to improved outcomes in future years (Berridge, 2012). More broadly, research indicating that children, on balance, do well in the care system is increasingly available (Bullock et al., 2006).

Adoption

A key aspiration of those responsible for looked after children is to see them placed on a permanent basis with a single family who can care for them for the remainder of their childhoods. An obvious way to achieve this is to have such children adopted. In the case of Peter Connelly, he might well have been placed in care by the age of twelve months or so, subject to relevant applications to court. Delays – which are detrimental to the children involved – can occur in legal and administrative processes, but it is likely that time savings would be made by what is known as concurrent planning. In other words, the social workers would *at the same time* have worked on the possibilities of both a return home to Peter's birth parents and placement for adoption. If assessment demonstrated that a return home would not meet Peter's needs, then the plans for adoption would all be in place and legal and practical arrangements could be concluded as swiftly as possible.

Unfortunately, the processes outlined here typically can take at least nine months to resolve and for many children cases can go on for more than two years (Sinclair, 2005). Peter Connelly would have been very young if he had been placed for adoption – which, optimistically, might have occurred by the age of eighteen to twenty-four months. A considerable body of research suggests that the chances of successful adoption are reduced incrementally with each additional year of a child's age (Selwyn et al., 2006). This pattern is well supported by child development theory, where the importance of infants achieving secure attachments with key caregivers has long been recognised (see Chapter 7). A wide range of research suggests that the best opportunities to support a child's development occur between birth and approximately the age of four years, and that the earlier intervention occurs to establish a permanent home for a child, the better the outcomes (Brown and Ward, 2012).

The difficulty of achieving adoption at an early stage is compounded by the fact that many child welfare problems do not come to light during the first few years of the child's life, and that fewer prospective adopters want to adopt older children, large sibling groups or those with complex needs. This factor would have made it much more difficult for Shannon Matthews to be adopted since she would have been nine or even ten years by the time decisions of this kind were being addressed. Furthermore, the prospects of adoption for a minority ethnic child, such as Victoria Climbié, would have been worse. There is evidence of poorer quality information being collected for black children and of delays caused by attempts to obtain the best possible ethnic match for the child (Selwyn et al., 2010).

Inter-professional working

This chapter has reviewed the main activities of child welfare services in the UK and has analysed both the potential of these services and the difficulties they face. One area that deserves particular attention is the fundamental role of inter-professional working. Where professionals work together, they can be more effective in co-ordinating a timely response to the child; in building a shared understanding of the child's situation; identifying patterns of care (or lack of care) given to the child; ensuring there is sufficient knowledge of the child to form the basis of a proportionate intervention; and making good decisions by sharing the thinking and the responsibility to do so (See Chapter 19).

Successive inquiries and serious case reviews into child abuse tragedies have endorsed this position. Where things go well, the public don't often hear about it. But where things go wrong, typically there has been a catalogue of major misunderstandings between different professionals, lost documentation, failures to include important people in key meetings and delayed responses to new information. In the case of Victoria Climbié there were significant instances, for example, of information (about possible abuse of Victoria) not being treated with urgency; of concerns not being passed clearly to senior colleagues or other relevant agencies; of failures to interview Victoria alone; of basic poor practices such as incoming faxes being allowed to fall to the floor without being picked up on a regular basis and so on. However, it is important to be aware that these failings often occur in a context of under-resourced, demoralised teams of staff, with difficulties of staff recruitment and retention and inadequate management (Reder and Duncan, 2004).

Successive commentators have identified these as systemic, organisational problems, and that blaming individual professionals for difficulties outside of their control is unlikely to be productive (Munro, 2011). Lord Laming's report was perhaps the first in the UK specifically to hold to account the managers and policy makers responsible for the context in which mistakes were made.

Policy orientations

In all four of the situations explored in this chapter, many would argue that if key people had listened to the *voices of the children* involved, there would have been a much greater chance of preventing further harm from occurring. One way of addressing this and other shortcomings in child welfare services, arguably, is to re-examine the nature of the whole system of provision for vulnerable children. In the past, there has been an often quite polarised debate between a *child protection orientation* and a *family service orientation* (Gilbert et al., 2011). The child protection policy orientation is characterised by a strong focus on responding, often in a legalistic and adversarial way, to reports of child abuse, and a focusing of resources on removing children into the care system when they need to be protected. Systems of this kind are found particularly in English-speaking countries such as the UK, USA and Australia. The family service orientation, by contrast, places greater emphasis on supporting families to retain the care of their children; and services such as family support, parenting education and so on are offered before removal of the children is contemplated. This orientation is more characteristic of continental European and Scandinavian child welfare systems. Arguably, the child protection orientation may emphasise the child's right to protection at the expense of his or her right to a family life. On the other hand the family service orientation may prioritise that right to a family life and indeed the desire to ensure the parents have the best possible chance to bring up their children themselves, but it risks neglecting the safety of the child in the process.

More recently, it has been suggested that a third policy orientation is emerging, the *child-focused orientation*, which acknowledges recent policy developments in a number of countries that have attempted to achieve a middle way between the other two approaches (Gilbert et al., 2011). The child-focused orientation, it is suggested, maintains a clearer focus on the child's needs, promotes the benefits of early interventions to help support the family, but has a clarity in terms of the importance of balancing the rights of the parents with the rights of the child by acting decisively where to do so is warranted. It remains to be seen whether this new orientation will offer greater benefits than the other two.

Conclusion

Child welfare and protection is an emotive topic. This chapter has attempted to describe key aspects of the system in the UK, and at the same time to explore a range of commonplace perceptions of how that system operates. It has, in effect, argued that many of the public criticisms of child welfare services are at best misperceptions and often have been over-exaggerated. There is considerable evidence of good practice, but this occurs alongside significant scope for improvement in the ways in which services operate. If there is one thing I hope the reader will take from this chapter, it is the need for a balanced perspective in a context where personal and political positions often become polarised. In particular, in responding to the needs of the individual child, there is no substitute for clear and careful analytical thinking about how best to deal with the problems. As to whether it is individual practitioners, the organisational systems, the management, the economic context, government policies or the intractability of child welfare problems that are the causes of the difficulties described, I invite the reader to form his or her own judgement.

Questions and exercises

Arrange to interview a social worker in a children and families team, or a family support worker in a voluntary organisation family support project or a Children's Centre. Ask the social worker/project worker:

1. What is the worker trying to achieve in work undertaken with children and families?
2. What are the obstacles to achieving the agency's objectives?
3. How are the agency and worker addressing these obstacles?

Further reading

Corby et al. (2012) covers child protection from a variety of perspectives, and a good source of information about children in the child welfare system is Fahlberg (2012). For an account of how it feels to be a social worker working with children who may have been abused, I recommend Ferguson (2011). Butler and Hickman (2011) is a good general text on child welfare and protection.

15

CHILDREN'S HEALTH AND WELLBEING

Sally Robinson

Introduction

How we improve the health and wellbeing of children cannot be divorced from how we improve the health and wellbeing of the population. This chapter, focusing on England within an international context, shows how the prevention of illness and death first became the business of the state, then of doctors and then a matter for everyone. It explains how the World Health Organization facilitated an understanding of health as an entity in its own right, separate from that of illness. Its holistic and positive definition of health embraces wellbeing and includes all aspects of people's lives. The World Health Organization has simultaneously influenced the methods we use to bring about health improvement, from authoritarian propaganda to education and community empowerment. The chapter introduces health education, health promotion and public health, all of which aim to improve the health and wellbeing of individuals and communities through communication, education and economic, political, social and environmental change. It is through this type of work that the early years workforce has the potential to make a significant impact on children's health and wellbeing which can influence the rest of their lives.

The state takes an interest in health

Understandings about what makes us healthy or ill vary across history, place and culture. In early nineteenth-century England most people believed that illness was both God's will and caused by the foul smelling air. The 1848 Public Health Act aimed to improve the environment, particularly the sanitation, and in so doing clean the air. It heralded the first time that the state intervened in the population's health and formally marked the beginning of the first public health movement, not only in England but in the world (Lupton, 1995). By 1900 the idea of cleanliness being next to Godliness emerged and the state had turned its attention away from the environment towards modifying individuals' behaviour. Children, and their poor physical health, had become more visible to the state thanks to the introduction of universal schooling. School physical education, domestic science, hygiene, the provision of some school meals and medical inspections were introduced (Sutherland, 1987). The state turned its attention to mothers' behaviour because they were seen as the guardians of the next generation's health. It was their duty to produce healthy workers and soldiers for the empire.

As science evolved, mothers were positioned at the forefront of fighting the new enemy: germs. Volunteer lady health missioners, the forerunners of health visitors, were instructed to provide training to mothers about correct infant care and hygiene (Holdsworth, 1988). In this way, formalised health education, in the form of state-led propaganda, began in schools and homes. In a period of fifty years the state's attention to the causes of ill health had moved away from the environment to individuals' behaviour and the germ. The perceived solution had moved away from the provision of long-term, expensive, environmental change paid for by the state to blaming the individual for becoming ill and exhorting them to behave in ways that would prevent illness.

The medical model

Doctors became the masters of both mothers and germs. The scientific study of the human body had been quietly in the ascendant for more than two centuries (Mosley, 2010). Jenner's vaccination for small pox in 1796 raised the prospect that an entire population could be immunised against infectious diseases. By the second half of the nineteenth century Robert Koch and Louis Pasteur proved that germs caused disease (bacteriology); John Snow showed how diseases spread through populations (epidemiology); and Florence Nightingale showed how to communicate complex epidemiological data in easy to understand diagrams. Public health medicine (disease prevention and the monitoring and control of disease in populations by doctors) attracted greater attention than traditional/environmental public health (social and environmental change). The law compelled mothers to vaccinate their babies until 1898 when the anti-vaccinationist movement successfully introduced the concept of 'conscientious objector' into English law (Wolfe and Sharp, 2002). The arrival of penicillin, the 'magic bullet', in the late 1920s created a belief that if disease could not be entirely prevented through immunisation, it could be cured through antibiotics.

The medical model dominated health for most of the twentieth century. It is characterised by a mechanistic understanding of the physical body, an emphasis on objectivity, science, experts and pathology. The model rests on the idea that health is achieved through attaining the 'absence of illness', which is a 'negative definition of health' (Aggleton, 1990). An individual cannot be held responsible for contracting a germ or for a malfunction such as a break or an internal blockage, but he or she is responsible for complying with the advice of the experts in order to make him or herself better. One the legacies of the medical model has been to create an automatic association, in people's minds, that 'health' is synonymous with 'illness'. For example, in 1948 medical science and medical power were perceived as being unimpeachable, and so it was on the basis of these understandings about health and illness that a national service to prevent and treat illness was created and called a National Health Service (NHS). Through it the state continued to expect mothers to take responsibility for the health of their families as well as the nation and to do so without upsetting their husbands. If mothers did not comply with medical advice, and their child became ill, it was their fault (Amos, 1993) regardless of the wider socio-economic environment and poor living conditions over which they usually had no control (Holdsworth, 1988).

Holistic health and wellbeing

The physical and mental trauma of the soldiers who fought in the two World Wars forced a recognition that a person's health was not reflected in their physical body alone, and that if cure was not possible ('absence of illness'), rehabilitation was. The rise of the allied health professionals, such as occupational therapists and speech and language therapists (Wilcox, 2006), along with the contribution of the Quakers (Abbott et al., 2011), were pivotal in helping to bring about the recognition that someone's mental, emotional, social and spiritual state influenced their physical state and vice versa. These advances culminated in a holistic understanding of health as a separate entity to illness, a view which the World Health Organization was keen to emphasise when setting out its own definition of health as not simply about 'attaining the absence of illness', but also as 'physical, mental and social wellbeing' at its inception in 1946 (WHO, 1946; 1947). This is a 'positive definition of health' (Aggleton, 1990) and the inclusion of the word 'wellbeing' was significant. Aristotle, the ancient Greek philosopher, referred to health as biological functioning and to wellbeing as flourishing, happiness, blessedness or prosperity, from the Greek term *eudemonia* (Mehmet, 2011). The creation of the World Health Organization marked the moment that health was formally and internationally recognised as being positive, holistic and incorporating wellbeing.

Community empowerment

By the late 1970s, the limitations of medicine, and the medical model, were becoming apparent. Improvements in population health were found to owe more to improved sanitation and other environmental interventions than to medical care which most of the world could not afford (McKeown, 1976; Stewart et al., 2003). There was an international imperative to prevent disease, promote health and reduce costs. The World Health Organization endorsed the point that health care professionals, while experts in illness, injury and disease, were not, and could not be, the exclusive experts in something as broad as health. The Declaration of Alma Ata (WHO, 1978) made clear that people have the right and duty to participate individually and collectively in their health. The prevention of illness and the promotion of health should be in the community, by the community and for the community. In contrast to the *outcomes*-led medical model, the declaration was saying that the *process* of people's engagement was, in itself, health promoting.

In England, the Black Report in 1980 (Townsend and Davidson, 1982) provided ground-breaking evidence that people's health, their length of life and quality of life, were more significantly influenced by the social and environmental factors around them than health care, and these factors were causing inequalities in health across social classes. If a child was born into a lower socio-economic environment, they would have more ill health and die earlier than a child born into a better socio-economic environment. Poverty was the most significant barrier to achieving health. Health was now a matter for the health, social and economic sectors of society (WHO, 1978).

Studies began to ask what health meant to 'lay' people who were not health professionals, first adults (Calnan, 1987; Cox et al., 1987) and then children. Both revealed that they had positive and holistic views, and aspirations, about health. Noreen Wetton and her colleagues asked children, aged four to eleven, 'What makes you healthy and keeps you healthy?' (Williams et al., 1989). Nearly every child's picture of a healthy person featured a smile. For many, health was, and still is, happiness (The Children's Society, 2011). The children's labelled drawings were positive and holistic including, 'I am work[ing] to make me healthy', 'I am tap dancing', 'God', 'I am playing with my friend', 'fresh air keeps me cool', 'milk' and 'sunshine'. In this era understandings about health were focused on lifestyles and the environment. The physical and social environment needed to be made healthy for the people, and in addition people needed to be given information and skills in order to articulate what they need and want and how to get it. Health became a matter for all government departments including Housing, Transport, Environment, Treasury and Education. The health care services were now an important part of, rather than the whole of, the Department of Health, and they needed to give higher priority to people in the community, rather than hospitals, and to disease prevention (Great Britain NHS and Community Care Act, 1990).

Health education became communication to empower people. This was characterised by a two-way dialogue with an emphasis on understanding people's own aspirations for health, skills development and a recognition of the wider social determinants of health (Hopson and Scally, 1981; Ewles and Simnett, 1985; Downie et al., 1990; Weare, 1992; Green, 2012). *Our Bodies Ourselves*, a seminal publication about women's health first published in 1971, by women and for women, epitomised how health education changed through the 1970s and 1980s. Women were no longer prepared to be simply the recipients of others' instructions nor were they prepared to shoulder all the responsibility for family health. Women's own lives and experiences, which included their children's experiences, began to shape their own health education. *The New Pregnancy Book* and *Birth to Five*, published at this time, included women's own words (Amos, 1993). At a professional level, health education became part of the job role of the multidisciplinary workforce, led by health education specialists who 'up-skilled' the teachers, health care and local authority professionals (see Chapter 19).

The Ottawa Charter for Health Promotion: a new public health

The international community recognised a need to combine health education with the best of traditional/environmental public health and the best of public health medicine. The Ottawa Charter for Health Promotion (WHO, 1986) was a call for a 'new public health' for the world, and it became the bedrock on which all World

Health Organization health improvement policy and action has been based, from then until now. Most governments today have national health policies that reflect much of the Ottawa Charter.

The Ottawa Charter for Health Promotion defines health promotion as:

> The process of enabling people to increase control over, and to improve, their health. To reach a state of complete physical, mental and social well-being, an individual or group must be able to identify and to realize aspirations, to satisfy needs, and to change or cope with the environment. Health is, therefore, seen as a resource for everyday life, not the objective of living. Health is a positive concept emphasizing social and personal resources, as well as physical capacities. Therefore, health promotion is not just the responsibility of the health sector, but goes beyond healthy life-styles to well-being. (WHO, 1986)

It explains that in order to promote health we need to be advocates for health, we need to enable people to achieve their full health potential through equal opportunities and resources. We need to encourage mediation across health, social, economic, non-governmental and voluntary sectors, industry and the media because health cannot be achieved by the health sector alone. Its six priorities were:

1. Build public policies which support health – this means that when public policy is being created, be that financial, educational or social, it should automatically be a health promoting policy. If it is not, then the obstacles need to be identified and removed. Healthy choices should be easy choices.
2. Create supportive environments – this concerns the protection and conservation of our natural and built environments in ways that are conducive to our health and wellbeing.
3. Strengthen community action – this means giving power to the people, strengthening their voices, encouraging local community development by giving community projects information, learning opportunities and support.
4. Develop personal skills – enabling people to access life-long learning including the skills to cope with personal health changes and maximise health potential. This needs to be facilitated by schools, home and community settings.
5. Re-orientate the health services – this calls for health services to move beyond clinical care and cure, and give greater attention to promoting health and to support health professional education in this direction.
6. Moving into the future – the planning, implementation and evaluation of health promotion are activities for everyone to work on together. Caring, holism and ecology are essential ingredients.

The British Conservative government favoured a 'top down', expert-led, disease-focused medical model rather than a more community empowering approach (DH,

1992; National Audit Office, 1996; Baggott, 2011). The social and environmental determinants of health, and action to address health inequalities, moved to centre stage when the Labour government came to power in 1997 (DH, 1998; 2003). These examples serve to remind us that health improvement is inextricably bound with political ideologies (Jones-Devitt, 2011).

Health education, health promotion, public health

Although much of the world has adopted the principles of the Ottawa Charter, there has been much less consensus about what to call the work – health education, health promotion or public health. The health educators were concerned that the education component, which was now part of health promotion, was being trivialised and the word 'promotion' gave the impression that the complex process of health gain was something that could be easily bought and sold, much like a commodity, with no ethical parameters (Williams, 1984). The public health doctors preferred the term 'new public health' (Ashton and Seymour, 1988). Scriven (2010) provides three straightforward definitions:

> Health education comprises planned opportunities for people to learn about health, and to undertake voluntary changes in their behaviour. (2010: 236)

> Health promotion comprises the process of enabling people to increase control over, and improve, their health. (2010: 237)

> Public health comprises preventing disease, prolonging life and promoting health through work focused on the population as a whole. (2010: 239)

Public health always has a clear population focus. Health promotion and health education are terms used for individuals, groups and populations. Health promotion always includes health education. Neither health promotion, health education nor public health includes 'hands on' personal care such as giving injections, dressing and feeding. The World Health Organization's (WHO, 1998) online Health Promotion Glossary can be a useful source of definitions.

England is not typical among the rest of the world. While Europe uses the term health promotion (Speller et al., 2012), current English government policy prefers to use public health as an umbrella term containing four domains:

- Improving the wider determinants of health (social contributors to health inequalities).
- Health improvement (healthy lifestyles and choices).
- Health protection (environmental and medical protection, e.g. vaccinations).
- Health care, public health and preventing premature mortality (preventable illness and death).

The Coalition government's aim for public health in England is to (1) increase life expectancy, taking into account health quality as well as length of life and (2) reduce differences in life expectancy and healthy life expectancy between communities (DH, 2010a; 2011b; 2012a). The policy recognises that the health of the population rests with individuals, local government, the National Health Service, charities/voluntary sector, business, employers and central government. In 2013 the creation of Public Health England (DH, 2012b), as a national and equal sibling to the National Health Service with its own 'ring-fenced' money, marked a significant milestone for the population's health.

Today, public health *specialists* who have a professional responsibility to protect and promote young children's health and wellbeing include health promotion specialists, environmental health specialists, health visitors and school nurses. Public health *practitioners* whose work includes a professional responsibility to protect and promote children's health include teachers, speech and language therapists who work in schools, community child health dieticians and every member of the early years workforce (DH, 2012c).

Measuring and preventing children's illness

The medical model, incorporating the 'negative definition of health' as an 'absence of illness', continues to provide a highly valued approach to treating and preventing illness. Early years practitioners working only with a medical model will measure the health of children by referring to the number who are ill and the range of illnesses. The amount of illness in a population, what epidemiologists call the morbidity rate, is quite easy to measure. Many disease prevention activities such as raising awareness about the importance of immunisations to prevent measles, and pictures to remind children to wash their hands to prevent the spread of germs, can be clearly linked to reduced numbers of sick children (Goldhaber-Fiebert et al., 2010; Burton et al., 2011). This makes this model popular in cases where a practitioner needs to produce clear, measurable outcomes.

Promoting children's health and wellbeing

Promoting a child's health means working with a holistic and 'positive definition', which means not only attaining the 'absence of illness', but also 'physical, mental and social wellbeing'. It is a holistic model that combines the biological, social and psychological determinants of health. Definitions of health encompass fitness, psychosocial wellbeing, energy, personal strengths, freedom, equilibrium, prayer, rituals, morality, genetics, abilities, relationships, resilience and potential (Seedhouse, 1986; Aggleton, 1990; Blaxter, 1990; Earle, 2007). Scriven (2010) breaks health into six dimensions. She explains that physical health is concerned with the body, functioning as a well-oiled machine; mental health comprises thinking clearly and coherently; emotional health is about feelings, expressing these appropriately and coping with difficult feelings such as stress or anxiety; social health is our ability to make and maintain relationships with people; spiritual health concerns personal creeds, morals and may, or may not, be linked to religious beliefs. These five are inter-related (Weare, 2007; Bendelow, 2009; DH, 2010c; Allen, 2011; Stacey, 2011), in that physical activity is known to help with emotional health due to changes in brain chemicals. Mental and emotional health are often conflated as psychological health. Being stressed blocks the neuronal pathways that facilitate learning and thus someone's mental health. People with social health problems often have associated emotional health difficulties, and health inequalities across the British population are recognised to be the result of, and caused by, poor mental health. Aggleton (1990) adds sexual health and sensual health, which includes gender identity and a deep awareness of the senses.

The holistic and positive approach recognises that the individual aspects of a child's health, which are influenced by genetics and personal lifestyles are, in turn, shaped by wider social and environmental determinants. Scriven (2010) calls her sixth dimension societal health. Factors such as poverty, local neighbourhoods, education, support for parents, being in care, commerce, politics, standards of living, investment in early years, employment and climate change also affect children's health (WHO, 2009; Marmot, 2010; Goddard, 2011; Stewart and Bushell, 2011). This is visually represented in social models (Dahlgren and Whitehead, 1991; Barton and Grant, 2006; see Figures 15.1 and 15.2) which, like Bronfenbrenner's bioecological model (Bronfenbrenner and Ceci, 1994), considers the individual at the centre of dynamic biological and social systems (see also Chapter 5).

Over the last thirty years we have seen the 'wellbeing' aspect of health being given more prominence. The word 'health' has expanded to 'health and wellness', 'health and wellbeing' or sometimes just to 'wellbeing' to shake off the entrenched and popular perception from the medical model that health equals illness (and medical care), and to more clearly communicate the broader and current understanding of health so that local authorities, voluntary agencies, community groups, Children's Centres, the public and others can all play their part (DH, 2010b; Walker, 2012a). This chapter is called 'children's health and wellbeing' for this reason. If the chapter had been called 'children's health', I wonder how many readers would have expected to be reading a chapter about children's illnesses. While acknowledging that scholars have produced numerous individual published definitions of health and of wellbeing, each being influenced by the professional and academic disciplines of their authors

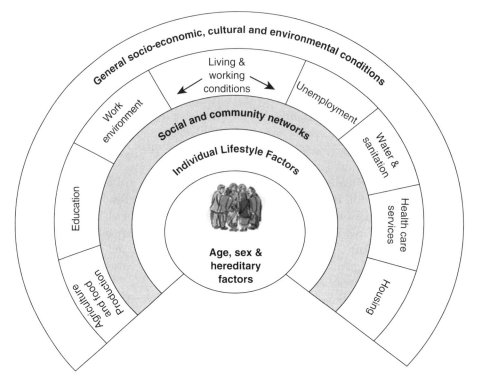

Figure 15.1   A social model of health

Source: Dahlgren G, Whitehead M. (1991). Policies and Strategies to Promote Social Equity in Health. Stockholm, Sweden: Institute for Futures Studies.

(Seedhouse, 1986; Duncan, 2007; Blaxter, 2010; Jones-Devitt, 2011; The Children's Society, 2011; Walker, 2012b), a pragmatic approach informed by the World Health Organization, which defines 'wellness' as the optimal state of health (Smith et al., 2006: 5), is that the words 'health', 'health and wellbeing' and 'wellbeing' all reflect the same positive and holistic goals, and in that sense they are the same.

Measuring children's health and wellbeing

Early years practitioners working with a positive, holistic model of health will quickly find that, unlike working with the medical model, there is no universally agreed way of measuring health because it is a dynamic, and ultimately individual, concept. Practitioners and researchers select a range of subjective and objective measures of physical, mental, social, emotional, spiritual, socio-economic and

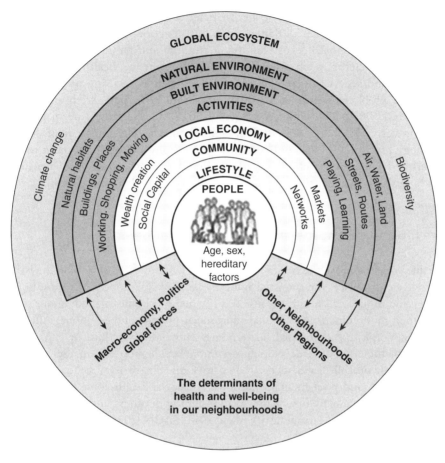

Figure 15.2   A health map for local human habitat

Source: Barton and Grant, 2006

environmental status, in addition to measures of illness. Quantitative and qualitative research, often used in combination, tries to capture the whole. This can
include epidemiological research on illnesses and causes of death; psychosocial
research about children's self-concept, resilience, emotional literacy, social skills,
family relationships and their health related knowledge, attitudes and behaviours;
clinical research such as measuring height and weight or blood tests; socio-economic
research measuring housing conditions, community resources and deprivation.
The annual community health profiles (NPHO, 2012), child health profiles
(CMHO, 2012), recent examples of child public health research (Parry-Langdon,
2008; OECD, 2009; Chamberlain et al., 2010; The Children's Society, 2010; Rees

et al., 2010), child related public health practice and policy (DWP/DfE, 2011; Lewis and Lenehan, 2012) all demonstrate this in action. There is increasing recognition of the importance of identifying children and families' assets, strengths and protective factors, such as esteem, life skills, resilience, healthy behaviours, a safe home and access to play and education, as well as focusing on the deficits, needs and problems (Anda et al., 2010; Marmot, 2010; Ben-Arieh and Frønes, 2012; NICE, 2012; The Children's Society, 2012). In the same way that understanding early childhood draws on disciplines such as physiology, neuroscience, sociology, psychology, social policy, history, philosophy and ethics in order to fully understand children, so children's health draws on these disciplines because a child's health is integral to enabling that child to reach their full potential.

The life course approach to health and wellbeing

The life course approach to health and wellbeing (Marmot, 2010) rests on the wealth of evidence that places the antenatal and early years of childhood as the most important period to invest in health because this is when our bodies, including our brains, are at their most vulnerable to be shaped by social, physical and emotional influences. Socio-economic and emotional surroundings cumulatively reduce or enhance the chances of these children developing common health problems in their later life including: physical ill health such as circulatory diseases, obesity, diabetes, drug and alcohol misuse; and poor mental, emotional and social health concerns such as the inability to empathise, to form happy relationships with others, anti-social behaviour and criminal actions (Marmot, 2010; Allen, 2011; SACN, 2011).

> What a child experiences during the early years lays down a foundation for the whole of their life. (Marmot, 2010: 60)

Promoting the health and wellbeing of children means focusing on children who seem to be fully healthy and well, children who have symptoms of illness or poor health, sick children and dying children. Priorities for young children in England today include: early years nutrition (SACN, 2011); child obesity (Dinsdale et al., 2012; Robinson et al., 2012); mental, emotional health and social health (DH, 2011c; NICE, 2012); bullying (Ofsted, 2012c); the sexualisation of childhood (Bailey, 2011); poverty (DWP/DfE 2011; King, 2011); abuse and neglect (Anda et al., 2010; Radford et al., 2011); intentional injury, accident or trauma (DfE, 2012c); the needs of children in care (DCSF, 2007); the needs of children with life limiting illnesses (DH, 2008); and improving standards of health care for children (Kennedy, 2010; Lewis and Lenehan, 2012). Universal early intervention – promoting the holistic health and wellbeing of all babies and young children – plus more intense targeted early intervention for those with greater needs can reap more benefits for individuals and the population than at any other point of their lives (Marmot, 2010).

Conclusion

Children's health is a holistic and positive concept influenced by social, political, cultural, historical, financial and commercial factors as well as genetics, emotional and other personal experiences. In order to communicate this understanding of health to others, it is acceptable, and perhaps desirable, to use the term children's 'health and wellbeing' or just 'wellbeing'. These influences are at their most potent during the early years as they can have life-long health outcomes. Improving the health and wellbeing of children requires multi-professional, multi-layered approaches which include the views and actions of children, their families and their communities. Early years practitioners are well placed to use communication, education and economic, political, social and environmental change to promote the health and wellbeing of current and future generations.

Questions and exercises

Consider the following quotations taken from this chapter.

1. Studies began to ask what health meant to 'lay' people who were not professionals.

What does health mean to you? Who decides what children's health means?

2. Improvements in population health were found to owe more to improved sanitation and environmental interventions than to medical care.

Consider the ways in which (i) the physical environment of a neighbourhood and (ii) medical care protects, maintains and promotes children's health and wellbeing.

3. Healthy choices should be easy choices.

Consider a place where young children come together. What can this setting do to make healthy choices easy choices for the children?

4. The prevention of illness and the promotion of health should be in the community, by the community and for the community.

When might looking after the community's health conflict with looking after an individual child's health?

Further reading

See what rights children have to health and wellbeing according to the United Nations *Convention on the Rights of the Child* (United Nations General Assembly, 1989). The Nuffield Council on Bioethics (2007) provides ethical guidance about promoting the health and wellbeing of children in chapter 2 of *Public Health Ethical Issues*. In England, note the model of health being used in current government policies such as the *Healthy Child Programme* (DH, 2009); the *Statutory Framework for the Early Years Foundation Stage* (DfE, 2012a) and the *Report of the Young People's Health Outcomes Forum* (Lewis and Lenehan, 2012).

16

INCLUSIVE POLICY AND PRACTICE

Siobhan O'Connor

Contents

- Introduction
- Seeking a definition of inclusion
- Inclusion and social justice
- Social inclusion
- The Index for Inclusion
- Conclusion

Introduction

My sister was born in 1967. My parents knew something was wrong when she didn't meet many of her development milestones within the usual timeframes. It was a relief they said, when their three other children did. My sister was mentally handicapped, a phrase I used throughout my childhood to explain her. It made sense to me. I needed to explain her difference to my friends. My sister was excluded from much of my world as I was from hers. She did not go to my school, nor did she travel to school with me. She was picked up by a bus. I didn't go to her school often, when I did, I wasn't allowed to play in the room with the bubble lamps that made sounds and changed shape and colour when you touched them and where children were allowed to lie on the soft red floor. At my school, I had desks and tables and children didn't lie on the floor.

My sister's behaviour, increasingly challenging, separated our worlds irrevocably. My sister needed the care, support and instruction of professionals within an institution, a different home alongside children and young people who were part of her world and not mine. She came to my home on Sundays, and as I grew older, I spent less time playing a part in what would so often become a chaotic and emotional time. I am not sure whether my sister wanted to see me.

I did see her once on a bus as it stopped at the traffic lights. I knew my brother's and my younger sister's friends, but I didn't know the other people on the bus with her. I stood and waved. My sister did not wave back, no one did, they didn't know me. I pretended my sister had not seen me. I'm not sure, if she had, she would have been able to show me in a way that I was able to recognise and understand.

There was a time when I was told that my sister was not mentally handicapped. She had special needs and then sometime later, profound learning difficulties. But these new ways of explaining my sister held no meaning for me, they were not sufficient in describing what I needed others to understand. Mentally handicapped evoked a depth that surpassed named disabilities or impairments. It touched a relationship that was so profoundly different, confusing and constrained by forces I couldn't even see, let alone grab hold of and change.

The above extract touches briefly on the personal experiences of exclusion, segregation and responses to diversity from my own perspective of loving a sister with profound learning difficulties and multiple impairments. It foregrounds questions that need to be asked in relation to inclusion and exclusion, categorisation and labelling and the complexity of the dynamic inter-relationship between medical and social constructs of disability. The choice to include these words at the start of this chapter marks the beginning of a dialogue that explores the concept of inclusion, not only towards the inclusion of children with impairments, but also as it relates to social justice and equity issues associated with poverty, gender, class, ethnicity, sexual orientation, gender identity, religion, beliefs and age.

As part of this dialogue, I first examine the ways in which the term inclusion is given meaning and then consider perspectives on social justice and dominant conceptions of social inclusion that permeate discourses on inclusion. I next turn to examine discourses of inclusion dominant within the English education system, concerned with children categorised as having 'special educational needs' (SEN). Finally, I review the potential contribution of the Index for Inclusion (Booth and Ainscow, 2011) to the principled development of education and society and the different ways in which the Index has been used in supporting the process of inclusion within a range of educational provision, including early childhood care and education settings and in higher education.

Seeking a definition of inclusion

It is a natural, and surely a proper, feeling that individuals or groups of individuals should not be written off, marginalised, left out of things, cut off from their fellows or sidelined; and that feeling goes along with, or is constituted by, both a sense of justice and a sense of compassion. (Wilson, 2000: 297)

Inclusion can, according to Wilson, 'put these feelings and concepts into some rational and defensible shape' (2000: 297). And yet as Booth (2010: 2) argues, 'Inclusion is a complex notion and its definition cannot be settled in a single sentence with a few well-chosen words'. Rather than seeking a definitive answer to the question 'what does inclusion mean?', the literature commonly refers to a range of ideas associated with the word 'inclusion' and the principles that are characteristic of an inclusive approach. For example, Booth and Dyssegaard recognise inclusion to be concerned with:

> Increasing the participation of all and reducing the exclusion of all;
>
> Increasing the capacity of settings and systems to respond to diversity in ways that value everyone equally;
>
> Putting into action inclusive values. (2008: 42)

At its heart lies a commitment to the values of equality and participation, reducing exclusion and non-discriminatory responses to diversity that respect and value difference within our shared common humanity. Meaning can only be fully understood therefore as these principles or underpinning values are 'played out in particular contexts' (Ainscow et al., 2006: 27).

Inclusion and social justice

Inclusion is closely allied with issues of social justice where the principles of equality and non-discrimination empower every individual 'to pursue a self-determined course of life, and to engage in broad social participation' (Schraad-Tischer, 2011: 11). The concept of social justice is both political and ethical, concerned with individual freedom and the processes by which social inequalities limit the participation of individuals within society and produce unfair outcomes. The Social Justice Index (see Figure 16.1) targets six areas of policy that are fundamental towards developing the principle of social justice (Schraad-Tischer, 2011).

Rather than compensating for exclusion, establishing social justice is dependent on investment in inclusion, with comparisons between OECD member states identifying successful approaches towards achieving greater social justice that fall within a combination of policy areas. For example, increased public expenditure in early childhood programmes may strengthen issues of social justice within the policy areas of labour market inclusion, social cohesion and non-discrimination and intergenerational justice. Parental leave policies and universal, flexible, affordable early childhood care and education services for all children and families not only combine parenting with increased opportunities for participation in the labour market but also contribute towards achieving greater gender equality within the workplace, and home environment.

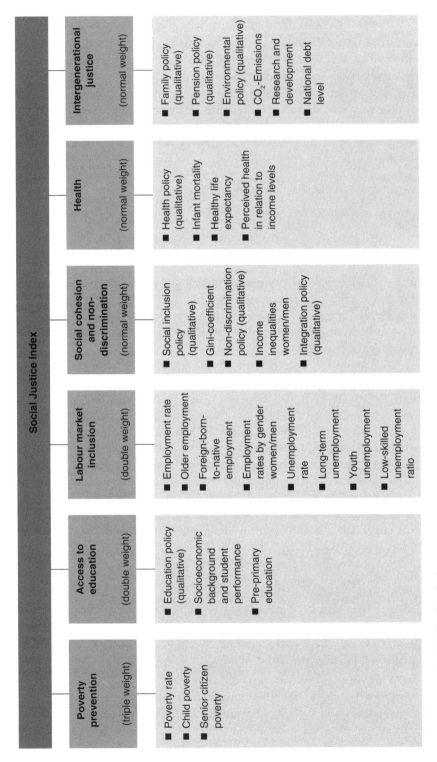

Figure 16.1 Social Justice Index

Source: Schraad-Tischer, 2011

Social inclusion

> Socially inclusive societies are those in which members can: participate meaningfully and actively; have opportunities to join in collective experiences; enjoy equality; share social experiences and attain fundamental wellbeing. (Friendly, 2007: 11)

Closely allied with issues of social justice, the concept of social inclusion is principally concerned with reducing social and economic inequalities and respect for diversity. Early childhood programmes are recognised as fundamental to strengthening social inclusion, or as Hayden (2009: 1) argues:

> I maintain that there is one goal for early childhood programs which transcends all the others: That is ensuring that services model, reflect and 'teach' social inclusion.

Friendly (2007) maintains that early childhood programmes are fundamental to the concept and goals of social inclusion in relation to four key areas. The first of these is associated with the potential contribution of early childhood programmes to enhance all children's development, learning and wellbeing and particularly for children 'with diverse learning rights, whether these stem from physical, mental or sensory disabilities or from socio-economic disadvantage' (OECD, 2006: 17). The Effective Provision of Pre-school Education (EPPE) project (Siraj-Blatchford et al., 2008) (see Chapter 13) continues to examine the effectiveness of early childhood programmes in England, measuring their impact in terms of children's later development and learning and a range of educational and social outcomes. The project has made a significant contribution towards directing government policy in relation to social inclusion:

> Findings have had a considerable impact on Government policy, where it is now recognised that investment in good quality pre-school provision provides an effective means of reducing social exclusion and may help to break cycles of disadvantage. (Siraj-Blatchford et al., 2008: 24–5)

The EPPE researchers refer to the particular benefits for children falling within categories of disadvantage. A range of factors relating to children's family backgrounds are considered to be associated with disadvantage, for example, low socio-economic status, low income, a low level of maternal education and special educational needs. According to these researchers, early childhood programmes can reduce the effects of social disadvantage and act as a preventive measure supporting a reduction in the number of children later categorised as having special educational needs.

According to UNICEF (2011) the challenges to social inclusion as it relates to child poverty and social exclusion 'cannot be overestimated'. Save the Children argues that 'poverty blights children's lives and their futures' and yet, in the UK, it is expected that there will be approximately four million children living in poverty by 2015 (Save the

Children, 2012). Affordable and flexible early childhood programmes that are universally available can support families to overcome disadvantage and social exclusion associated with poverty, unemployment and isolation and can strengthen issues of social justice in relation to gender equality. From 2001, Sure Start was targeted to the thirty per cent most disadvantaged areas throughout England, determined on the basis of having a high concentration of children under four years living in poverty:

> Sure Start is at the heart of our commitment to eradicating child poverty and unlocking the talents and abilities of every single child, giving families new opportunities and aspirations, and improving outcomes for all children. (DCSF, 2008b: 3)

As an integral part of the Sure Start agenda, Children's Centres were established as the ideal form of integrated services for families and young children, providing access within local communities to early childhood care and education provision, family support and outreach services designed to support the participation and engagement of 'hard-to-reach' groups (see Chapter 11). The impact of Sure Start has been associated with less negative parenting styles, improved home-learning environments, higher child immunisation rates, higher levels of positive social behaviour for three year olds and increased use of services for young children and families (DCSF, 2008a). Save the Children (2012) confirms that key successes in reducing child poverty include Sure Start and related increases in parental employment. The Child Poverty Act (2010) aims to dramatically reduce levels of child poverty in the UK (see Chapter 12). However, during periods of economic crises and associated austerity measures, services for young children and their families are at a significant risk of financial cuts at a time when children and families need increased support. While maintaining the commitment to Sure Start, for example, this funding is no longer ring-fenced within financially challenged local authority budgets, thus threatening the future sustainability of such provision.

Finally, social inclusion and respect for diversity are critical in response to increasing diversification within societies. Early childhood is considered a critical period for attitude formation and developing positive responses to difference and diversity. Challenging discriminatory attitudes and negative stereotypes on the basis of perceived differences associated with race, gender, class and religion are therefore fundamental to early childhood programmes, pedagogy and practice and the content of curriculum frameworks.

The Index for Inclusion

The Index for Inclusion (Booth and Ainscow, 2011) sets out in considerable detail the implications for the way adults and children learn together when responses to the diversity of adults and children in society and education value all equally and encourage everyone's participation. Its approach to inclusion is connected to the international context of educational development marked in particular by the Education for All (EFA) movement (UNESCO, 1990) and The Salamanca Statement and Framework for Action signed by the ninety-two participating countries at the Salamanca Conference on Special Needs Education in 1994 (UNESCO, 1994). Supported by the Universal Declaration of Human Rights (UN General Assembly, 1948), and the United Nations Convention on the Rights of the Child (United Nations General Assembly, 1989), EFA recognises that:

> All children, young people and adults have the human right to benefit from an education that will meet their basic learning needs in the best and fullest sense of the term, an education that includes learning to know, to do, to live together and to be. It is an education geared to tapping each individual's talents and potential and developing learners' personalities, so that they can improve their lives and transform their societies. (UNESCO, 2000)

Following the review of EFA at the World Education Forum in Dakar, Senegal (UNESCO, 2000), the Dakar Framework for Action articulated six EFA goals as follows: to expand early childhood care and education; to provide free and compulsory primary education for all; to promote learning and life skills for young people and adults; to increase adult literacy by fifty per cent; to achieve gender equality by 2015; and to improve the quality of education (UNESCO, 2000). With concern directed towards achieving greater equality in educational opportunities, particularly for children most vulnerable to marginalisation and exclusion, explicit references to the vision of EFA as an 'inclusive concept' emerged as fundamental in guiding national government policies in meeting the goals of EFA (UNESCO, 2000).

The Salamanca Statement and Framework for Action is considered by Farrell (2001: 6) to have been 'something of a watershed in enhancing the prospects for inclusion throughout the world'. While committed to EFA, it focused explicitly on both inclusion and participation as 'essential to human dignity and to the enjoyment and exercise of human rights' (UNESCO, 1994). With a view to ensuring that education for all *means* all, the Framework emphasised the development of 'inclusive schools', establishing the foundations on which to build an inclusive society, grounded in the values of community and positive responses to diversity. The concept of inclusion does not therefore refer to a particular group of people; it is about everybody and on this basis the Index for Inclusion challenges the use of the term 'social inclusion' and explicitly rejects the categorisation of children as having SEN.

The discourse of social inclusion found within English policy documentation commonly refers to overcoming the consequences of disadvantage caused by deprivation. This implies that there is an understanding of inclusion that is non-social, rather than a perspective that considers all inclusion and exclusion as socially constructed. In England, this has encouraged the term 'inclusion' to specifically refer to the education of children with impairments or those categorised as having special educational needs. It is a perspective that remains embedded within a medical model of disability, where 'there exists some non-social exclusion which befalls people with impairments which arises naturally as a direct result of their impairment' (Booth, 2010: 2). A focus on deficiency and additional or special needs not only enforces categorisation and labelling towards perceived difference, but also 'forms the basis for segregated and exclusionary provision' (Roberts-Holmes, 2009: 191). The Index proposes therefore that rather than arising from a deficit model of disability and impairment, educational difficulties should be viewed as 'barriers to learning and participation' associated with 'failings in relationships, curricula, approaches to teaching and learning unresponsive to diversity' (Booth, 2010: 1).

The Index adopts a particular perspective on educational development as 'systematic change according to inclusive values', which takes place along three dimensions: creating inclusive cultures, producing inclusive policies and evolving inclusive practices (Booth and O'Connor, 2012: 1). It emphasises the 'elaboration of a framework of values that provides detailed directions for educational development' (Booth, 2010: 1). A model framework is set out in the Index which is concerned with: 'equality, rights, participation, community, respect for diversity, sustainability, non-violence, trust, compassion, honesty, courage, joy, love, hope/optimism and beauty' (Booth, 2011: 33). While not intended as a prescriptive or an exhaustive list, each value heading and accompanying description signifies the beginning of an investigation into what the value may mean for those negotiating a values framework in which actions towards inclusive development can be taken.

The Index is organised according to a series of headings that contribute towards inclusive development. Each heading is related to a series of questions to support reflection, dialogue and for the meaning of inclusion to become clearer by connecting both theory and practice, for example:

Dimension A2: Creating Inclusive Cultures: Establishing Inclusive Values: The school counters all forms of discrimination

Examples of questions:

1. Is it recognised that everyone absorbs prejudices against others which take effort to identify and reduce?
2. Do adults consider their own attitudes to diversity and identify their prejudices so as to better support children to identify and reduce theirs?
3. Is it recognised that institutional discrimination can stem from cultures and policies which devalue the identities of, or otherwise discriminate against, some groups of people?
4. Are legal requirements to reduce 'inequalities' in relation to ethnicity, disability, gender, sexual orientation, sexual identity, religion, belief and age part of comprehensive plans to counter all forms of discrimination?

(Booth and Ainscow, 2011: 93)

The process inherent within the Index is to engage with the ideas behind each of the questions explored. Here, reflection and dialogue may encourage discriminatory attitudes held by adults and children on the basis of negative responses to diversity to be acknowledged and to further understand the dimensions of disadvantage, barriers to participation and oppression that such views give rise to. It may lead to explicit guidance in how negative attitudes to difference can be challenged within the context of children's peer cultures and to understand and comply with the requirements of the Equality Act (2010) to extend inclusive practice.

Examples of the way in which the Index has been used are extremely varied, ranging from whole setting development to the examination of one aspect of inclusive development from particular aspects of cultures, policies and practices. Its use has been documented in Australia and South Africa as a framework for supporting the professional development of educators in response to the notion of an inclusive curriculum and inclusive education (Carrington and Robinson, 2004; Duke, 2009; Oswald, 2010).

The Index for Inclusion has also been used in the design of the Early Childhood Studies (ECS) degree at Canterbury Christ Church University. The module 'Values into Action: a principled approach to the development of early childhood care and education' is associated with three of the Benchmark Excellent Standards for students graduating with a degree with honours in ECS as follows:

> A critical working knowledge and understanding of pedagogical approaches for working with young children and families
>
> Excellent knowledge of issues in relation to rights, diversity, equity and inclusion in relation to working with children and families
>
> A highly developed ability to recognise and challenge inequalities in society and to embrace an anti-bias curriculum. (QAA Higher Education, 2007: 15)

The following extract records students' evaluation of the module:

> I had never really thought about my own beliefs and values, I didn't think that my values were important; it was listening to others and finding out what they believe that has taught me they count and are important especially when thinking about putting values into action.
>
> We do all have different beliefs and values which can influence how we work with anti-discriminatory practice and promote valuing difference and the participation of groups within society. The group has been very inclusive and we have all had the chance to discuss our views. (Booth and O'Connor, 2012: 5)

Students are encouraged to recognise broad alliances for the inclusive transformation of early childhood care and education by linking ideas on inclusion with other principled interventions. For example, the course links inclusion to the anti-bias work promoted by kindergartens by 'Kinderwelten' in Berlin (Derman-Sparks and Olsen Edwards, 2010) and the philosophy of early childhood services established in the Italian city of Reggio Emilia, described by Moss as 'a collective democratic venture' (2011: 2).

Booth (2012) argues that a wide variety of concepts, projects and approaches share a common set of principles and similar aims, such as 'democratic', 'values-based', 'sustainable' or 'anti-bias'. The Index recognises inclusion as a super-ordinate concept standing for a framework of values (Booth, 2011), and in doing so, encourages connections to be made across a range of alliances that share a commitment to the principled development of education and society.

While the 2011 edition of the Index is intended for use in all educational contexts, an earlier version of the Index – *The Index for Inclusion: Developing Play, Learning and Participation in Early Years and Childcare* (Booth et al., 2006) – was designed specifically to support the process of inclusive development within the diverse range of educational and care settings for young children and their families. It has an increased emphasis on play and includes reference to working with children from birth onwards. The use of the Index in early education settings has been documented by Clough and Nutbrown (2007). In reflecting on the experience of using the Index in Early Childhood Care and Education ECCE settings, one early years professional commented:

> I learned loads just reading through the folder – thinking about the questions posed under the different dimensions – there's so much to think about – mind blowing! It's a process that's never actually finished but it feels very good. It is really about developing relationships – that's what it's about – valuing people enough to make relationships with them and then finding ways of working in that richness of diversity. (Clough and Nutbrown, 2007: 156)

The documentation and evaluation of the use of the Index in ECCE settings is, however, limited. Norfolk County Council seeks to address this as part of their 'Index for Inclusion Action Research' project (2013–15) that uses the Index for Inclusion to develop a shared language for educational development based on an explicit values framework and a collaborative approach within the contexts of ECCE settings, schools and further education (Carter, 2013). As part of this project, it is envisaged that a revised edition of the early years Index will be developed by 2014.

Conclusion

Speaking at the opening ceremony of the Paralympic Games in London in 2012, Stephen Hawkins declared that there should be no boundary to human endeavour. In reflecting on the success of the games, Trevor Phillips as Head of the Equalities and Human Rights Commission during the Olympics commented:

Who would have predicted that this summer, through the vast refracting prisms of the Olympics and Paralympics, the world would see revealed such a profound sea change in British attitudes to social diversity.

It remains highly contestable whether the elite sporting endeavours and success of the paralympians contributed towards the valuing of diversity and positive responses to perceived difference. Nor can we assume that positive attitudes to diversity extend towards reducing discrimination on the grounds of ethnicity, sexuality, gender, class, religion, age, disadvantage and poverty. The Index for Inclusion does offer those working with children and their families the support to remove barriers to participation and to respond to diversity in ways that value everyone equally. Inclusion is, however, a never-ending process, 'that involves us in taking responsibility for processes of exclusion experienced by others, and requires our continuous reflection of the values that underlie our actions' (Plate, 2012: 60).

Questions and exercises

1. In reflecting on the extract at the beginning of this chapter, how may labels such as 'mentally handicapped' and 'special needs' contribute towards experiences of exclusion, segregation and negative responses to diversity?
2. Consider any one of the values identified by Booth (2011). Can you identify any barriers that may limit how this value can be put into action?
3. Consider your own personal and/or professional experiences of discrimination. How may an inclusive approach help to reduce discriminatory attitudes?

Further reading

Jennie Lindon's (2012) book provides early years professionals working with young children and their families with theory and research in relation to equality and inclusion, yet links closely with practice, particularly in responding to diversity and removing barriers to participation, while the following website provides information for the Norfolk County Council Index for Inclusion Action Research project (2013–15): www.schools.norfolk.gov.uk/Teaching-and-learning/Indexforinclusion/index.htm. Further information on the Index for Inclusion can be found in texts by Tony Booth and colleagues: see in particular Booth and Ainscow (2011) and Booth et al. (2006). Booth and Dyssegaard (2008) provide a detailed review of available resources for the principled development of education.

PART FOUR

DEVELOPING EFFECTIVE PRACTICE

This final part of the book looks at some of the ways in which theoretical knowledge and understandings can be applied to practice. As Iram Siraj-Blatchford suggested in Chapter 13, this is not a one-off activity. Effective practice is dynamic and is supported by an ongoing consideration of what one sees, hears, believes and understands. This process involves repeatedly challenging oneself (and others) by: drawing on and testing out the validity and appropriateness of theoretical knowledge; listening to children; and reconstructing understandings as they apply to each child, all children and their early childhoods. The emphasis within this part of the book, then, is on critical reflection.

It is important to note that effective planning for practice does not demand constant change. Familiarity and predictability can be important features, particularly for very young children (Page et al., 2013). The many benefits of reflective practice include emotional supervision and support for practitioners themselves, which is particularly important for those experiencing stressful and distressing situations (Loukidou et al., 2009).

McMullen (personal communication, 2012) refers to 'deliberate' practice – deliberating on one's knowledge and understanding in a given situation and doing so with purpose:

> The deliberate early childhood professional is one who always proceeds from a strong philosophical frame, one that is built upon her knowledge and beliefs, as well as her unique capabilities and talents. The beliefs that guide professional decisions should be reasoned beliefs, those that have come from years of deliberation on the

interconnectedness of theory, research and practice, not clouded by our personal outside issues, formed out of convenient habit or based on unexamined assumptions. (cited in Goouch and Powell, 2012)

In the chapters that follow, the authors examine this interconnectedness and show how critical reflection supports the development of effective, ethical practice across the early childhood professions.

In Chapter 17, Helen Moylett emphasises how observation plays a vital part in the reflective process of planning for, working with and understanding young children over time. She describes different observation processes and techniques and their relationship to assessment. In so doing she also reminds us of the situatedness of observations, the importance of the resourcing and context in which these occur and the culturally embedded nature of taken-for-granted assumptions we may perpetuate while observing and the role of reflection in challenging and potentially reconstructing the truisms that we have seen, heard and believed.

In Chapter 18, Alison Clark's focus is on research 'with' rather than 'on' children: that is, research in which children are viewed as active participants in the research process. Clark notes that there are particular challenges for those wanting to undertake research of this kind with young children, particularly those relating to language and power. Clark provides two case studies of research studies which set out to listen to children's perspectives before commenting on the impact this kind of research has for the roles adopted by adults and children.

In Chapter 19, Angela Anning draws on her extensive research into multi-agency work to examine the theories, policies and practice of multi-professional and integrated service development and asks, 'Is working together working?' She explains how socio-cultural theory helps to clarify links between policy and practice and how Activity Theory can help in exploring how organisational knowledge is generated and sustained by members of a professional community and how it can be used as a framework to encourage and support professionals from different agencies to reflect on their perspectives and develop and own new, shared understandings. She highlights three dilemmas that commonly surface when different kinds of professionals work together and provides examples concerning their composite identities (Who I am), sharing information, knowledge and beliefs (What I know) and professional territorialism (What I do). She concludes that serious commitment to professional education and training for working together is needed to overcome these kinds of dilemmas, especially in a climate that prioritises early intervention.

Finally, in Chapter 20, Carol Aubrey discusses effective leadership in early years settings, focusing on the ways in which early childhood leaders may have an impact on worthwhile outcomes for young children. Aubrey begins by examining existing literature before drawing upon research she and her colleagues undertook with early childhood leaders who were willing to explore their own leadership practice. Aubrey draws from this some emergent themes and emphasises, in particular, the current lack of opportunity for continuing professional development in relation to early childhood leadership.

17

OBSERVING CHILDREN TO IMPROVE PRACTICE

Helen Moylett

Contents

- Introduction: thinking about observation
- The importance of observation in the early years
- The role of context
- The purposes of observation
- Observation methods (participant and non-participant methods)
- From observation to assessment
- From assessment to planning
- Recording assessment
- Limitations of observation – links to effective practice and provision
- Conclusion

Introduction: thinking about observation

A teacher asks a five-year-old girl what she is doing.

'I'm drawing God', she says.

'But nobody knows what God looks like', retorts the teacher.

'They will in a minute', replies the child.

If that story amuses you, you are not alone. I have been told various versions of it – and told it myself and always met with laughter. It seems to have originated in the United States. Sir Ken Robinson told it during a TED (Technology, Entertainment, Design) talk in 2006, introducing it as, 'I heard a great story recently'. His is the most viewed TED talk of all time, so perhaps that's why the story has gained popularity. Adults laugh when they hear it in recognition of the way in which we can be caught out by a child's creative thinking – the child does not share the fixed mindset of the practitioner, who takes it as a given that nobody knows what God looks like. Some of the adults who laugh at this tale may also be laughing at the child's ignorance – but that only means that they share the belief of the teacher that nobody knows what God looks like. In fact, in seeking to represent God to her own satisfaction, the girl is fol-lowing the artistic, creative and cultural traditions of many centuries and her belief in her power to make such a representation is a 'taken for granted' powerful enough to challenge the teacher's.

The story starts this chapter because it is essentially a story about thinking and captures some important issues involved in observing children.

- Observation is never value free – you bring who you are, your beliefs and your habits of mind to it, even when you stand back.
- An adult observer who is standing back (non-participant) only uses her or his brain and therefore her or his perceptions – not the child's.
- Adult brains work differently from those of young children – your brain is about half as active as theirs.
- Never assume you know what the child's purpose is – your 'taken for granted' may not be theirs.
- Even the most experienced practitioner will sometimes be surprised by young children's thinking if they maintain an open mind and pay attention!

In the story about the child drawing God, the teacher is not engaging in formal observation of the child; it is an everyday interaction. So what is the difference between this sort of interaction and observation in an early years setting? The short answer is – sometimes not a lot.

Early years practitioners are not experimenters and do not observe children in laboratory conditions but use naturalistic observation methods which include every-day activities. Sometimes, for instance, if they use a particular approach to pedagogy such as the Effective Early Learning (EEL) programme (Pascal et al., 2001), are taking part in a research project, are hosting students undertaking a degree in early child-hood studies or are closely observing a particular child or group about whom they are concerned, settings may use non-participant observation methods. Both partici-pant and non-participant observers may use informal conversations as well as more structured methods such as time sampling, photos, video recording, sticky notes, record sheets and profiles. The rest of this chapter looks at why observation is so important in the early years as well as how observations may be recorded and used to assess children's progress and plan next steps in learning.

The importance of observation in the early years

'Observation is important because it provides adults with a lens through which to study the child's world' (Langston, 2011). It is this perceived need to observe children that has informed early years education and care for centuries. Linda Pound (2011), introducing a book on learning theories ranging from the seventeenth century to the present day, points out observation's pivotal importance:

> Theories can be rooted in research and experimentation or they may be philosophical and hypothetical. Whatever their basis, the importance of observation is a common strand in the work of many theorists who were interested in finding out how children learn. Some were academics who became interested in children – others were experienced in working with children and developed theories to help them understand their experience. What is interesting is how often ideas which were based purely on observation are now supported by developmental theory. (Pound, 2011: 2)

So it is not surprising that all current curriculum models stress the importance of observation; this is often seen as an essential part of adopting a 'child-centred' approach.

The role of context

Learning and development from birth to five years are not context free. They occur as the result of a complex interaction between children and their experiences within relationships and within particular environments. This process is described in the literature as occurring within the interactionist tradition that conceives of development as located within nested social contexts (Bronfenbrenner in Evangelou et al., 2009). In England the Bronfenbrenner model is reflected in the themes of the Early Years Foundation Stage (EYFS) which positions the unique child at the centre of the framework enabled by positive relationships and enabling environments which support the child's learning and development. It is represented thus (see Figure 17.1) in the EYFS non-statutory guidance *Development Matters* (Early Education, 2012).

All these themes emerge from the ideas underpinning Bronfenbrenner's early model of three ecological domains: the family, the settings attended, and the community in which the child lives (see Chapter 5). Bronfenbrenner's theory has been extended and developed (Bronfenbrenner, 2005; Swick and Williams, 2006) but the simpler model, as modified by Myers (Myers and Bronfebrenner 1992), was used by

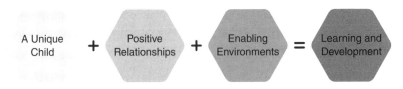

Figure 17.1   The four themes of the EYFS

Source: Early Education (2012) Development Matters in the Early Years Foundation Stage, London: Early Education, Crown copyright. [Online] Available at www.early-education.org.uk and for download at www.foundationyears.org.uk/early-years-foundation-stage-2012/ (accessed 20/12/2012).

Evangelou et al. (2009). This helpfully identifies how value systems and beliefs mediate these ecological domains. These factors come together in the social context and impact on the child's learning. Evangelou et al. (2009) represent this interplay in the diagram below with the arrows operating in all three domains (see Figure 17.2)

The importance of context explains why the statutory framework for the EYFS makes it clear that observations are not the sole preserve of setting-based practitioners: 'In their interactions with children, practitioners should respond to their own

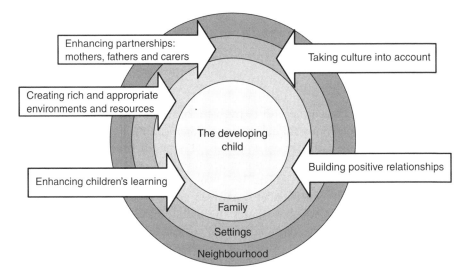

Figure 17.2   The contexts of children's development

Source: Evangelou, M., Sylva, K., Kyriacou, M., Wild, M. and Glenny, G. (2009) Early Years Learning and Development Literature Review Department for Children, Schools and Families, Research Report No. DCSF-RR176 [Online] Available at www.gov.uk/government/publications/early-years-learning-and-development-literature-review (accessed 16/09/2013).

day-to-day observations about children's progress, and observations that parents and carers share' (EYFS Statutory framework 2.1, DfE, 2012a).

So observation is important in helping practitioners to understand children. When carried out in collaboration with parents it may set the child's learning not just in the context of the setting but of their family, cultural, social and community background. How effectively or authentically this happens will depend on a range of factors – not least the relationship established between staff and parents.

The purposes of observation

The diagram (Figure 17.3) from *Development Matters* (Early Education, 2012) demonstrates how observation does not stand alone but is the starting point in the 'observation, assessment and planning' cycle. The main purpose of observation in most early years settings is to enable practitioners to begin to get to know the children and what

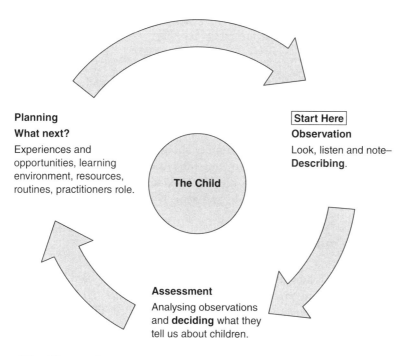

Figure 17.3   Observation, assessment and planning

Source: Early Education (2012) Development Matters in the Early Years Foundation Stage, London: Early Education, Crown copyright. [Online] Available at www.early-education.org.uk and for download at www.foundationyears.org.uk/early-years-foundation-stage-2012/ (accessed 20/12/2012).

they can do, assess children's progress and plan accordingly for their next steps in learning. It also helps them to assess whether their practice and provision is appropriate. Putting together observation evidence from the setting with evidence from parents (and sometimes other professionals involved with the child) also aims to help practitioners and parents develop a rounded, holistic picture of the child.

Langston (2011: 16) illustrates the importance of this sharing with parents.

> A practitioner watched as a boy selected block after block, creating a 3m by 0.5m structure, until finally he ran out of floor space when his construction reached a wall.
>
> The practitioner was amazed to note the care with which the boy fitted smaller blocks against the wall so that no gaps were left between the wall and what she assumed was his 'path'. He then began to walk carefully along the 'path', stopping from time to time to stamp his heels firmly on certain blocks. Interested in the boy's imagination and concentration, the practitioner discussed his 'path' with him, photographed the construction and made a note about his precision and attention to detail.
>
> Some time later she showed her photographs and observations to the boy's father who revealed, to her amazement, that the boy's construction was not a path but a parquet floor! It turned out that the boy had seen his father, a floor-layer, at work and had been imitating his actions, building a floor and compressing the tightly fitting blocks by stamping his heels on them.

This is also an example of how adult conversations with children are not always democratic dialogues in that children may want to please or be reluctant or unable to reveal the true extent of their thinking. If we think back to the story which started this chapter, the child showed great, possibly, unusual, belief in her idea and confidence in challenging the teacher's certainty about the impossibility of the task. (It is also worth considering, in relation to Langston's example above, how you might have approached the conversation with the boy making the 'path', in order to find out more about his thinking and what he was actually doing.)

Observation methods

If practitioners are following the cycle illustrated in Figure 17.3 it is important that observations are not just random or repetitive, but capture significant moments in children's thinking, learning or development because these observations are used as the first step in this important cyclical process. So what are the best ways to observe?

The EYFS statutory framework is very clear that:

> Assessment should not entail prolonged breaks from interaction with children, nor require excessive paperwork. Paperwork should be limited to that which is absolutely necessary to promote children's successful learning and development (EYFS Statutory Framework, 2.2, DfE, 2012a).

It appears that several things underpin successful observation: real interest in noticing what the child says and does; knowledge of child development; and observers' willingness to be aware of their own pre-conceptions. These are much more important than getting the right format – although that can help! There are some useful methods which minimise paperwork and support effective observation and which are utilised in many settings.

Participant observations

Sticky notes

For most of the time practitioners should be interacting with children but as we have seen, that does not stop them from observing learning. Many settings use sticky notes or labels for these incidental observations which can be dated and then be stuck in a child's folder and/or shared with other staff. Practitioners only record things which are different or new for the child and which they regard as significant. In the example below (Figure 17.4), although this is an informal note, the practitioner has included the child's name, date, where the observation took place and added his or her initials at the end. This note was given to Connor's key person who added it to his folder, thought about how she could encourage his interest and new-found skill in future, and shared the information with his mother when she collected him.

Digital photography and video recording

The use of photographs and video has reduced the need for writing copious notes. Photographs can capture some of the process of children's learning as well as the product. For instance, a series of photographs can show Jessica, aged three, carefully

---

Connor M

17.10.12

Craft area

Connor tried again to make cuts in the edge of
paper unaided and succeeded for the first time.
He shouted 'Look, Look' to everyone as he
repeated his success several times. DH

Figure 17.4   Post-it note observation

placing beads and twigs on a piece of paper, her careful outlining of her structure with a purple felt pen and then her proud smile when she declares, 'It is finished!'. Video could enrich the observation even further by enabling her verbal communication and body language to be recorded.

Many settings now have access to small cameras and smartphones with excellent recording capacity. In some settings young children are used to being photographed and filmed – and taking their own photographs and making their own films – as well as watching the results on the whiteboard or laptop. Digital cameras and videos will date photographs and film and they can easily be shared with parents and other professionals. Settings often upload photos, film and other observations to secure sites for this purpose. All settings should have policies and procedures for seeking parental permission to take photographs and film footage of their children as well as policies on the safe use of the internet. You might want to reflect on how practitioners might obtain informed consent from children to use or share video and photographic images and why this may be important.

Non-participant observations

The types of observation methods discussed above are very useful but often happen 'as and when' rather than having a specific focus. The result may be that practitioners have more information about some children than others. Many settings try to ensure that all children are observed in a more formal and focused way at regular intervals. Where there are concerns about a child's learning and development this may occur every week or even every day.

These observations may take various forms. It may be that each key person observes each child in their group as a non-participant observer on a rolling programme and as the term or the year progresses chooses different foci to ensure that the child has been observed across a wide variety of activities or contexts. It is important to observe play or a freely chosen activity as it is in these that the child will best demonstrate what they can do and how they think.

Sometimes practitioners will be using particular observation frameworks with all the children to inform them about aspects of their provision and/or children's wellbeing and involvement. This combination of wellbeing and involvement as an important indicator of children's learning has been developed by Ferre Laevers at Leuven university in Belgium and extensively used by Chris Pascal and Tony Bertram in the UK as part of the EEL and Baby Effective Early Learning (BEEL) programmes (Pascal et al. 2001; Bertram and Pascal, 2006).

The Leuven Involvement Scale uses five levels as a framework for observing children's involvement. This is a brief version adapted from Laevers (1994) and Robson (2006).

Table 17.1 Adapted Leuven Scale

Level	Activity
1	No activity. The child may appear to be mentally absent.
2	Actions with many interruptions for approximately half the time of the observation.
3	More or less continuous activity. The child is doing something but lacks concentration, motivation and pleasure in the activity. In many cases the child is functioning at a routine level.
4	Activity with intense moments. The activity matters to the child and involvement is expressed for as much as half the observation time.
5	Sustained intense activity. The child's eyes are more or less uninterruptedly focused on the activity. Surrounding stimuli barely reach the child and actions require mental effort.

Any scale that attempts to categorise another person's involvement will be open to many layers of interpretation. You may be interested in the case studies around this in Moylett (2013). A child may not appear to be engaged in the task that the practitioner has asked him or her to do but is very involved in some other learning. Think, for example, about the child who is not engaging with the adult set task because he or she and a friend are negotiating and planning a course of action for when they go outside.

Target child observation

If practitioners have concerns about a particular child's development or behaviour they may want to carry out a series of structured observations. An example is the Antecedents, Behaviour, Consequences (ABC) approach (see, for example, Drifte, 2004). In this a non-participant observer spends some time focusing on what triggers the behaviour causing concern (the antecedents) then what actually happens and the consequences. Below and in Table 17.2, readers will find an example of a format for this form of observation:

After carrying out a series of these observations, practitioners and parents may reflect on the following questions to make an assessment:

- What do you think the child is communicating?
- How do you think child might be feeling?
- What usually happens next?
- What do you think the child might be getting out of behaving this way?
- What do you think the other children might be getting out of him or her behaving in this way?

Table 17.2 Example of format for ABCs of behaviour observation

ABCs of Behaviour			
Child's Name:	**Group/Key Person:**	**Recorded by:**	
Date Time	**Antecedents**	**Behaviours**	**Consequences**
	Who was the child with? Activity? What were adults doing/ saying? Resources available? What happened immediately before the behaviour?	What exactly does the child do that causes concern?	What does practitioner do/say? What does child do/ say? What do other children do/say? What do other adults do/say?

It is always important to bear in mind the fact that we are all biased observers, and this can be particularly significant when reflecting on children's behaviour. Many of the children, for instance, will have been brought up in a different culture than the observer's and their family and community may have different expectations regarding behaviour. Politeness rituals such as saying please and thank you, for example, are not universal. Some children may have been positively discouraged from making eye contact with adults as it is seen as disrespectful (Lane, 2008: 134).

Time sampling

Time sampling involves watching a child for a specific period of time, e.g. ten minutes at regular intervals throughout the day. Ideally this would be repeated at least once more in the same week. As well as giving information about a child, this form of observation can be helpful in finding out more about provision.

During their work on the *Every Child a Talker* programme (DCSF, 2009a), for instance, a nursery school in a very disadvantaged area had become increasingly concerned about language delay among the afternoon group of boys. In order to begin to understand their needs two types of observation were undertaken over a period of about one week. The observation methods included:

- Recording how the boys were using the environment, and where and when they interacted with adults.
- Language observations recording the purposes of language children were using.

The results are represented in Figure 17.5.

Observations

Spider tracking	Conclusions
creative area adult literacy area role play **garden** water **construction** small world	• The boys' activities centred in a few areas, with a main pathway between the construction area and the garden. • Boys rarely chose to access the literacy and creative areas. • Adults were deployed at planned activities but boys usually opted out of these and joined in only with encouragement. • Boys rarely approached adults – fewer than one interaction with an adult per boy each session. Where this did take place it was usually with their group leader (key person). • Boys therefore had limited exposure to skilled adult support for developing language.

Language observations		Conclusions
Communicate preferences, choices, wants or needs	✓(22)	• The boys used little language, for a limited range of purposes. • Little language was used to join play activities – the boys would first watch, then play alongside, then join without words. • A leader organised the play, and was the only one to plan the activity and assign roles. • Play was divided between girls and boys – conflict arose if groups of girls and boys were accessing the same activity.
Enter play or join an activity	✓(16)	
Plan, develop, or maintain play or group activity	✓(5)	
Resolve or avoid conflict	–	
Entertain, describe past events, tell or retell story	–	
Find things out, wonder, hypothesize	–	

Figure 17.5   Observations and assessment

Source: DCSF, 2009a

The staff realised that the observations were telling them as much about their own provision and practice as about the children and they responded by making pedagogical changes in four main areas:

• Organisation
• Physical environment
• Interactions
• Experiences (DCSF, 2009a: 15–18).

From observation to assessment

The next part of the cycle according to the diagram from Early Education (2012) (Figure 17.3 on page 231) is assessment. There are two types of assessment:

- Formative assessment, also known as assessment for learning – where assessment is part of and supports learning and teaching as well as building up a gradual picture over time.
- Summative assessment – the periodic summary of formative assessments, which makes statements about children's achievements. Its purpose is to check a child's development and progress at regular intervals. An example of summative assessment is the EYFS Profile completed at the end of reception class.

In the assessment part of the cycle practitioners reflect on what they have observed the child doing and/or saying. As well as standing back and observing, practitioners will usually have been interacting with the children, and these interactions will also have contributed to the picture. This stage can be described as a process of 'putting the clues together' to understand more about who the child is. These clues may reveal something about the child's:

- Feelings – pleasures, fears, excitements, security and so on.
- Preferences.
- Interests and current pre-occupations in what they are learning.
- Ways of approaching the world around them.
- Ways of thinking and learning.
- Skills and knowledge.

Deciding what the observation might say about a child is the practitioner's assessment. In order to make this assessment the practitioner draws on many aspects of professional knowledge and skill, including knowledge of child development and knowledge of likely learning pathways within and across different areas of learning. Moylett and Stewart (2012: 43) note:

> A good assessment also depends on using emotional intelligence, as well as awareness of the context, the culture, family and home experiences. What parents and carers share about the child outside of the setting provides crucial information to help practitioners and parents together to understand and interpret what they observe.

Effective assessment is never drawn from just one observation but is grounded in growing awareness of the whole child. Formative assessment is ongoing because new observations often link to earlier ones and children's interests shift, sometimes in unpredictable ways. Observations need to be thought about and analysed in order to make decisions about both 'how' and 'what' the child is learning.

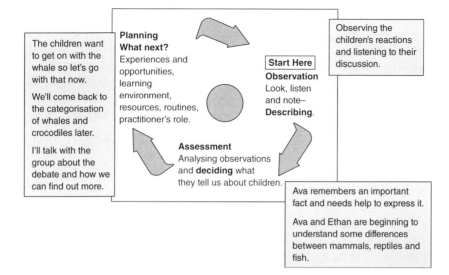

Figure 17.6   The observation, assessment and planning cycle in action – what the practitioner is thinking about and noting at each stage

Source: Moylett, 2013

Sometimes observation, assessment and planning happen 'in the moment' and may only be 'recorded' in the practitioner's mind:

Babies and young children, however, are experiencing and learning in the here and now, not storing up their questions until tomorrow or next week. It is in that moment of curiosity, puzzlement, effort or interest – the 'teachable moment' – that the skilful adult makes a difference. By using this cycle on a moment-by-moment basis, the adult will be always alert to individual children (observation), always thinking about what it tells us about the child's thinking (assessment), and always ready to respond by using appropriate strategies at the right moment to support children's well-being and learning (planning for the next moment). (DCSF, 2009b)

An example of the observation, assessment and planning cycle

Figure 7.6 illustrates an example of a practitioner observing and assessing the learning of a group of children.

A group of four three and four year olds are engaged in discussion about making a whale to go with some other sea creatures they have talked about and made. The practitioner's process is important but not recorded until after the event when she makes a brief note about her planning for later.

From assessment to planning

The next stage in the cycle is planning and we saw the practitioner both assessing and planning 'in the moment'. Planning involves deciding how best to respond to, support and extend the children's wellbeing, interests, ways of learning, current competence and confidence, or their progress in skills and knowledge. Settings will have their own approaches to short-term planning. Some arrange regular planning sessions where team members share observations and assessment and discuss ways forward for individuals and groups – sometimes knows as PLODs – Possible Lines of Direction.

Recording assessment

As we saw in the discussion about making the whale, not all assessment is recorded but some of it must be in order to help children learn and provide evidence of progress which can be discussed and thought about with the children, their parents and other professionals. Many settings create learning journeys, learning stories, learning diaries and/or other forms of documentation. The purpose of these varies depending on the setting. Some settings develop learning stories with and for the children that become a significant part of the child's life, with contributions from children, staff and parents. These are often based on the ideas of Margaret Carr (see the further reading section at the end of this chapter). Other settings develop learning journeys or portfolios that are available for parents to see if they wish and are not regularly discussed with the children. Others illustrate and display the processes of learning and assessment on the wall as a public celebration of learning and development. Often these settings are influenced by the Reggio Emilia pre-schools approach to documentation. Rinaldi (Project Zero and Reggio Children, 2001: 83) describes their documentation as 'visible listening, the construction of traces (through notes, slides, videos and so on) that not only testify to the children's learning paths and processes, but also make them possible because they are visible' (see also Chapter 13).

Limitations of observation – links to effective practice and provision

Although Ofsted is often cited as the reason for excessive paperwork, the inspection framework for early years settings (Ofsted, 2012a) has a renewed emphasis on learning rather than administration. In 2009, Ofsted reported on the common features of outstanding providers. This report included reference to observation, assessment and planning. That is, staff:

- know children well because they regularly talk about the observations they make in all areas of children's learning;

- make sure the learning environment meets the needs of each child, taking account of the range of abilities and learning styles;
- systematically monitor and evaluate how inclusive the setting is;
- observe children skilfully and discuss sensitively with parents and carers to identify and plan at an early stage for any additional support children may need. (Ofsted, 2009)

However, even in an outstanding setting the potential benefits of observation, assessment and planning can be limited by the approach to pedagogy that is employed. Judith Stevens (2013) explores an interesting example:

> The practitioner plans an activity, based on observations of the children, identifying a learning intention of 'Counts up to three or four objects by saying one number name for each item'. Building on the children's interests in rhymes, the practitioner provides five green speckled frogs, a log and some crepe paper 'lily pad' leaves. The children engage in counting the frogs, some counting three or four frogs, saying one number name for each. The children are engaged, the practitioner makes observations and assesses their achievement in that particular aspect of learning and development.

Reading this you may think it sounds perfectly acceptable, but Stevens points out the limitations of the activity and how they can be avoided.

> If the children are fascinated by the number rhyme 'Five Little Speckled Frogs', then make a collection of all sorts of frogs – wooden, fabric, plastic, in different shapes, sizes and colours. Introduce these in wicker baskets, alongside logs and natural objects. Observe how the children investigate and explore the resources.
>
> Sabiha: Notice the descriptive and comparative language Sabiha uses as she sorts the frogs. Notice the words she uses to compare the size of the sets she creates 'there are more green frogs, there's millions. No, not millions, one, two, three … eleven.' Notice also, how she puts the frogs into sets, starting with materials, then realizing this is too complex, debates size and moves on to colour – green, and 'not green'. She plans, makes decisions about how to approach her self identified task, solves the problem and reaches her goal.
>
> Eddie: Notice how Eddie lines the frogs up and counts them, then how he throws them all in the air and tries to count them where they land. When he gets to 'seven', notice his satisfaction: 'That's my brother, that is – seven. I be seven too after Christmas'. Notice too how he makes predications and keeps on trying, showing a belief that a different approach will pay off.
>
> (Stevens, 2013)

Stevens brings us back to where this chapter started with a story about thinking that illustrates the fact that while observation can be informal it is never value free. It is also very dependent on what we notice or attend to. We are all biased observers who will interpret children's actions through the lens of our own experience and perspectives. Stevens (2013) shows us that it is not just these 'in observer' factors that influence what we observe but also what we provide for children because that deeply influences the children's learning and behaviour. Remember the observations in the nursery school cited previously where concerns about boys' under-achievement led to changes in practitioner practice. If you want to explore what we notice (and don't notice) in more depth try reading Chabris and Simons (2011) and/or watching 'The Monkey Business Illusion' (www.youtube.com/watch?v=IGQmdoK_ZfY) which is both amusing and challenging!

Conclusion

We have seen in this chapter that observation is about both watching and listening to make learning visible. Children need adults beside them who are fascinated by their 'thinking in action' and use their observations to support and extend those children's learning. Nancy Kline (1999) links the quality of our attention-giving skills to the creation of space to think. She states: 'The quality of your attention determines the quality of other people's thinking … Attention, the act of listening with palpable respect and fascination, is the key to a Thinking Environment' (1999: 36 and 37). When adults pay that sort of attention to children they not only support children, but open themselves up to becoming what Tina Bruce (1999) has called 'long-term-forever-learner' kinds of practitioners.

Questions and exercises

1. In the example given by Langston (2011) above, how would the practitioner's observation have been strengthened by involving the child?
2. What sort of recording of assessment have you seen in early years settings?
3. How do parents contribute to observation and assessment?
4. How do visitors to the settings you know find out about children's progress and achievements?

Further reading

Margaret Carr's (2001) *Assessment in Early Childhood Settings: Learning Stories* is a useful guide to the philosophy and practice of observing and documenting children's learning through learning stories. If you are working within the EYFS framework and want to know more about possible ways to support and extend children's learning through effective observation, assessment and planning then you may find Vicky Hutchin's (2007) *Supporting Every Child's Learning in the EYFS* extremely helpful. Finally, Sharne Rolfe's (2001) chapter on 'Direct observation' provides a rigorous academic guide to doing research in the early years that is specifically written for beginner researchers.

18

UNDERTAKING RESEARCH WITH CHILDREN

Alison Clark

Contents

- Introduction
- Research 'with' not 'on' children
- Research with young children
- Case studies
- Roles in research
- Conclusion

Introduction

This chapter sets out to provide an introduction to undertaking research with children and, in particular, with young children under five years old. The focus will be on qualitative research methods. The chapter will discuss some of the characteristics of research 'with' rather than 'on' children. This will be followed by a brief exploration of a number of challenges and possibilities of carrying out research with young children. A chapter of this length cannot give a comprehensive investigation of this important subject but is intended as a pointer to a number of key issues which can be followed up in volumes dedicated to research with children (for example, Greene and Hogan, 2005; Christensen and James, 2008; Harcourt et al., 2011) and to individual research studies referred to in the text.

Research 'with' not 'on' children

Continuing interest in the sociology of childhood (see Chapter 3) has led to an increasing number of research studies which seek to understand children's own experiences of their everyday lives (for example, Thomas and O'Kane, 1998; Davis et al., 2008). This research paradigm focuses on research 'with' rather than 'on' children (Fraser, 2004). The differences are rooted in how children are viewed in the research process. Do researchers view children as passive research objects on whom research is carried out or do researchers view children as active participants in the research process, sharing, for example, in what is being studied, the control of research tools and in what happens next as a result of the research?

Woodhead and Faulkner (2008) in their discussion of children and research within developmental psychology investigate a range of views about children which have been adopted within this influential discipline. They identify two of the approaches as the 'closely observed child' and the 'test tube child' (2008: 17–19). The 'closely observed child' might be the focus of intense observation in the same way as a wild-life documenter might observe animals from a hide:

> Observers may be found backed up against the corner of a classroom or playground trying to ignore children's invitations to join in the game, kidding themselves they can appear as a metaphoric fly on the wall. (Woodhead and Faulkner, 2008: 17)

A researcher setting out to observe three and four year olds would probably encounter particular difficulties in trying to convince an enquiring group of young children that the researcher was in fact 'not there'. This particular form of non-participant observation is only one of a number of ways in which to undertake observations of children. Different approaches to observation will be discussed later in this chapter.

Woodhead and Faulkner illustrate their second category, the 'test-tube child' in which children are placed under a research 'spotlight' under laboratory conditions. They encapsulate this way of viewing children in research by referring to a photograph of the developmental psychologist Arnold Gessell undertaking research on a baby. The young child is seated within a glass dome. Gessell is standing in front of the child, dressed in his white laboratory coat. The photograph shows two other adults within the frame: a note taker and a cameraman (in addition to the photographer who captured this image). Two of the questions to be asked in interpreting such a scene might be: whose world is being explored here? Who is on strange territory, the researcher or the child?

Research which sets out to undertake research 'with' rather than 'on' children might be identified as research in which the researcher sets out to understand more about children's worlds by entering unfamiliar territory. This can involve learning directly from children on their own 'home ground' which may include a range of environments including a nursery (for example, Clark and Moss, 2005; Clark and Moss, 2011), a residential children's home (Emond, 2005) or a local neighbourhood (for example, Hart, 1979; Percy-Smith, 2002).

Research with young children

There are particular challenges for those who are setting out to involve young children in research. This section will examine some of these challenges. The issues discussed are not unique concerns to the field of early childhood research. There are many other research groups whose ways of communicating challenge research strategies based on the written communication. One such example is non-literate communities in the majority world (for example, Holland and Blackburn, 1998). However, the factors discussed below can be accentuated in the case of young children, particularly if the research participants are pre-verbal or with limited apparent verbal skills.

Languages

Establishing modes of communication between the researcher and the research participant is central to many qualitative research studies (Fraser, 2004; Christensen and James, 2008). Carrying out an interview, for example, relies on the researcher being able to express her or his questions in a way which conveys their meaning clearly without forcing a hoped-for response (Hatch, 1990). Misunderstandings can abound whatever the age group of the participant but there are particular complexities related to the thinking and language skills of young children.

The following is an example of misunderstanding taken from a research study with a group of three to five year olds about their outdoor play space (Clark, 2005; Clark and Moss, 2005). The researcher was interviewing a group of children while they were all sitting outside in a play house:

> The question was: 'What is missing outside at [your pre-school]?' Some of the children's responses were more literal than anticipated. Children … answered 'the window'. The perspex was missing because a vandal had broken the pane and it had been removed. (Clark and Moss, 2005: 102)

This was a sensible answer in the context in which the researcher had asked the question but was a very different response than was anticipated. The research question appeared simple but was in fact asking the children to understand the term 'missing' in a particular way: 'In view of your experience of this and other play spaces what resources or opportunities should be added to this preschool's outdoor space?' (Clark and Moss, 2005: 102).

This last example illustrates the link between language and context in establishing meaningful communication between young children and researchers. A child who appears to be 'non-verbal' or using few words in the research environment may in fact be talkative at home or in another setting (see, for example, Wells, 1986). This may especially be the case for children for whom English is an additional language (see, for example, Brooker, 2002). Cousins (1999) in her research which focused on listening to four year olds, discusses several examples where the children's spoken contributions to the research were influenced by where the conversations took place. She describes a four-year-old boy, Dean, who had not talked to anybody during his first two weeks in his reception class:

> By chance, I watched him in the playground and saw Dean bend down and peep through the railings to look longingly at his old nursery. The children were just going out for a walk and I could see big tears rolling silently down his cheeks. (1999: 25)

Cousins asked Dean if he would like to visit his old nursery and with the permission of his teacher the researcher and child made a visit together:

> The change in Dean when we stepped through the nursery door was instantaneous and I captured it all on my mini-tape recorder.
>
> The children were still out having their walk, so Dean rushed round and round the nursery touching familiar toys and looking in cupboards and on shelves. He talked non-stop and when he spotted the indoor pond full of fish and tadpoles he remembered all the details of going to collect them and building the pond with his nursery nurse. (1999: 25)

These examples highlight the importance of how language is used and in what context to enable young children to be involved in research (see Hill et al., 1996, and Alderson and Morrow, 2011 for a discussion of the importance of context when conducting research with older children). This leads to the question of whether babies and older non-verbal children can be active participants in research rather than passive research objects. An important starting point in such cases is to begin by establishing the modes of communication used by each individual child, whether this is a baby or an older child with disabilities. This tuning in to each child's preferred ways of communicating may require considerable effort, patience and imagination on the part of the researcher (see, for example, Davis et al., 2008).

These concerns draw attention to the importance of respect within the research relationship between the researcher and the research participant. This notion of respect is one of the characteristics of research which sets out to work 'with' rather than 'on' children.

Power

Research can be understood in many ways. One interpretation is to see research as being about the revealing and handling of knowledge which in turn has an impact on the creators, gatherers and distributors of that knowledge. Research involving young children has the added complication of involving a generational imbalance of power between adult and child (Robinson and Kellett, 2004; Greene and Hill, 2005). When a researcher walks into a setting to begin a study he or she carries the twin advantage of being an adult and also a 'knowledge collector', the bearer perhaps of a notebook or laptop and audio recorder. This impression can be heightened, the younger the age group of the research participants. Awareness of the power divide can be the starting point for efforts to attempt to lessen these gaps in order for more honest communication to take place (see below). However, adult researchers still remain the most powerful players in the research process. This highlights the importance of considering the ethical implications of undertaking research with young children. Alderson and Morrow (2011) stress how this reflection on ethics applies throughout the research process from an early planning stage to dissemination.

Case studies

This next section draws on examples of two research studies with young children. The studies illustrate different ways of engaging with the challenges of language and power posed by undertaking research with young children. Both studies seek to listen to young children's perspectives about their everyday lives. The first carried out by a Danish researcher, Hanne Warming, explores participant observation as a means of listening to young children (Warming, 2005). The second study involving the Mosaic approach uses participatory, visual methods to involve young children in the process of reviewing and changing early childhood provision.

Case study one: participant observation

Observation can cover a range of different approaches to research ranging from a detached 'invisible' observer described earlier to a 'total immersion' strategy whereby the observer seeks to join in or participate in the lives of those being observed. Warming describes the aim of 'participant observation' as to 'learn about "the other" by participating in their everyday life' (2005: 51). This is one of a number of interpretations of 'participant observation' (Adler and Adler, 1987; Atkinson and Hammersley, 1998).

The aim of Warming's study was to find out from young children about what an ideal life in early childhood provision would look like. She decided in this study to choose participant observation as the research method which fitted her research aims:

> Participant observation would allow me to study children's interactions with each other, with pedagogues and with the physical surroundings, whereas interviews would only allow me to study narratives about these interactions, producing a construction of children's cognitive perceptions of *det gode børneliv* contextualised by the interview process itself. (2005: 54)

The study carried out in a bornehave or kindergarten in Denmark involved Warming joining in the children's everyday lives. Warming explains:

> This participant role means the researcher makes an effort to participate in the children's everyday life in the kindergarten, and as far as possible in a way like the children do: play with the children, submit to the authority of the adult carers, abdicating from one's own adult authority as well as from one's own adult privileges. (2005: 59)

This approach can been seen as choosing to take a 'least adult' role (Corsaro, 1985; Mandell, 1991; Thorne, 1993; Mayall, 2000). This is one way of engaging with the question of power in relation to undertaking research with young children. However, as Warming states, the differences between adults and children cannot be removed but perhaps reconsidered and renegotiated through this research approach.

Spending time in the research setting immersed in the everyday routines of the young children's lives revealed several different sources of information for piecing together what were the significant ingredients of a 'good life' for the children in the setting. These pieces relied on different languages or modes of communication. Several sources of research material emerged from listening to children's talk with each other and their pedagogues together with conversations with the researcher. However, how children moved around the space and expressed their feelings through a range of non-verbal communication also formed a rich source of information. Warming describes this as 'listening with all the senses' (2005: 55). Participant observation thus provided more than one method for engaging with the research question.

Listening to young children through participant observation can be seen as one way of addressing the questions of power and language discussed. Warming presents the case for listening through participant observation as a form of giving voice to young children's perspectives in contrast to listening as a way of understanding:

> Giving voice involves listening, whereas listening does not necessarily involve giving voice. Listening as a tool requires hearing and interpreting what you hear, whereas giving voice further requires 'loyal' facilitation and representation, making common cause with children. (Warming, 2005: 53)

Case study two: the Mosaic approach

This second case study illustrates another possible research strategy for undertaking research with young children. The Mosaic approach is a framework for viewing young children as competent, active explorers of their environment. It has been developed by Alison Clark and Peter Moss as a research tool for listening to young children's perspectives (see, for example, Clark and Moss, 2005; Clark, 2010). The approach has since been adopted by other researchers and practitioners in the UK and abroad (for example, see Einarsdóttir, 2005). There are links between this approach and the idea of 'documentation' promoted in the pre-schools of Reggio Emilia in Northern Italy (Clark, 2005: 29–49) (see also Chapter 13).

The Mosaic approach is based on the following view or understanding of children and childhood:

- Young children as 'experts in their own lives' (Langsted, 1994)
- Young children as skilful communicators
- Young children as rights holders
- Young children as meaning-makers. (Clark and Moss, 2005: 5–8)

The Mosaic approach uses several different ways of listening to young children – the tools of observation and interviewing together with participatory tools. These are tools in which the children are actively involved in expressing their perspectives. These include using cameras to take their own photographs, making books of their images, taking adults on tours and recording the tours themselves, making maps and responding to images of other spaces (the magic carpet). The approach is designed to be flexible to allow for other methods to be used according to individual children's strengths or needs. The emphasis is placed on the researcher adjusting to the modes of communication preferred by the children rather than those in which the researcher is most comfortable.

The adoption of digital photography as one of the research tools controlled by the children is one example of how young children have been 'placed in the driving seat'. During the first study in which the Mosaic approach was developed during 1999 and 2000, children took their photographs using single-use cameras. However, by the third study which began in 2004 many of the young children involved became more confident in using the digital camera and photo printer than the researcher. The introduction of visual methods, using both types of camera, opened up different possibilities for young children to document their experiences. Part of the value appears to relate to the cultural status of photographs:

> Cameras offer young children the opportunity to produce a product in which they can take pride. Children who have seen members of their family taking photographs, poured

over family albums or looked at photographs in books and comics, know that photographs have a value in the 'adult world'. This is not always the case for children's own drawings and paintings. (Clark and Moss, 2011: 28)

One of the research tools in the Mosaic approach is map-making using children's own photographs and drawings (see, for example, Clark and Moss, 2005: 39–43; Clark and Moss, 2011: 30–2). This documentation can make children's perspectives visible in a way which can open up conversations with peers, practitioners, researchers and parents. The following example is taken from the Spaces to Play project, the second study undertaken by the authors of the Mosaic approach to involve young children in the redesign of an outdoor play space (Clark, 2005; Clark and Moss, 2005; Clark, 2007). Two three year olds, Ruth and Jim, had been engaged in leading the researcher on a tour of their play space while they recorded the tour with photographs. Ruth and Jim met shortly after the tour to make a map using their chosen images and drawings.

During this activity a visitor came to see the study in action:

Ruth: This is a very pretty map.

Researcher: It's a very pretty map. You know, it tells me such a lot about outside. Shall we see what Gina can see on our map? Gina, what do you think about our outside …

Gina: I can see that Ruth and Jim have very special things outside. I can see that you chose the prams and the buggies, and I can even see you in the picture so I know you like playing with those things, maybe. And, Jim, your favourite thing … I think your favourite thing outside might be the train. Yes? And can we have a picture of you outside with the train.

Ruth: What do I like?

Gina: You tell me what you like. Do you like Heather [member of staff] with the climbing frame?

Ruth: No, I like going on …

Gina: Oh, you like going on the climbing frame.

(Extract from Clark, 2005: 43–4)

Ruth relished the opportunity to be in control of the conversation and the meaning-making. She had been the one to ask the visitor for her interpretation of what she saw and took delight in contradicting the adult's interpretation. The power differences between adults and children are not removed by conducting research with children in this way but spaces are created within the research encounters which enable children to demonstrate their expertise.

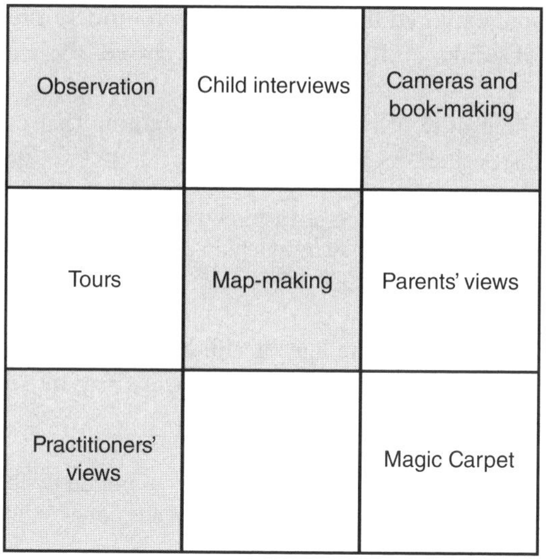

Observation	Child interviews	Cameras and book-making
Tours	Map-making	Parents' views
Practitioners' views		Magic Carpet

Figure 18.1   An example of methods brought together in the Mosaic approach

Source: Clark, 2005

Roles in research

This final section raises some questions about the roles of children and adults when research is undertaken with children. If the roles which children play within research are expanded there is a subsequent impact on the role of the researcher, other adults and, at times, the research audience.

The roles of children in research

The case studies above have raised some possible ways in which children can be active participants during fieldwork. Alderson and Morrow (2011) have been among those to raise the question of how children – including young children – can be actively involved before and after fieldwork takes place – in setting the research agenda and in the analysis, writing up and dissemination. Kellett's work on children as researchers (for example, Kellett, 2005; 2010) has raised new possibilities for how children can take responsibility throughout the research process. When the research participants are under five years the term 'children as co-researchers' may be inter-preted differently. The aim would not be to make young children into mini–adult researchers but to reinterpret the role in ways which demonstrated young children's competencies. In terms of setting research agendas it is far easier for young children

251

to influence the topic explored in an action research model of research in which the local knowledge of adults and children is valued (see, for example, Reason and Bradbury, 2006).

There needs to be a note of caution here in assuming that every child will want to be engaged with research. As Roberts remarks:

> It cannot be taken for granted that more listening means more hearing or that the cost benefits to children of participating in research on questions which they may or may not have a stake is worth the candle. (2008: 264)

This warning applies whatever the age of children involved. A research study may not be of particular interest to individual children or may be seen as an invasion of their time. Roberts continues:

> we need to be clear when it is appropriate for us to ask young people to donate time – one of their few resources – to researchers and when it is not. (2008: 271)

Role of the researcher

Undertaking research with young children can release researchers from some responsibilities but at the same time can add new dimensions to their role. A researcher who shares power with children is relinquishing the need to 'know all the answers'. This can be a relief, realising that research seen in this way is not about gathering further evidence of what is known but expecting new ways of understanding to emerge. This role as 'adult as enquirer' may be at odds with the role children expect of adults. If the research context is one which highlights the role of adults as experts then this contrast may be marked. This may be the case for many children who take part in research in educational and health settings if the adults in these institutions are seen as the 'experts'.

A further freedom for researchers may emerge through the use of a wider range of 'languages' within the research process. Visual methods, for example, described in the second case study above, may open up new modes for communication for the researcher as well as for the research participants (see, for example, Thomson, 2008; Mitchell, 2011). This may lead to alternative approaches for researchers to record their research experience and to disseminate their findings.

However, undertaking research with young children places different ethical responsibilities on researchers (for example, see Harcourt et al., 2011). One particular concern with working with young children rests on how research findings are disseminated. Sharing conference platforms with young children may not be an appropriate use of their skills and time. However, this increases the importance of the researcher's role as mediator of the children's experiences.

Role of practitioners and parents

Research with young children needs to be viewed in context. Young children spend the majority of their time with adults and therefore research which seeks to understand their lives will also encounter adults, whether they are family members, practitioners or friends. There is a particular advantage of involving parents and practitioners in research with the youngest children, those under three years, as their knowledge of the fine details of children's lives will add important perspectives to research undertaken (for example, see the case study of Toni, age twenty-two months in Clark and Moss, 2011: 38–41).

Research into the everyday lives of young children in early childhood environments raises questions about the experiences of practitioners. These spaces are shared spaces in which adults and children spend many hours together each week. One possibility is that the principles which can be applied for engaging with young children in participatory research can also be explored with practitioners. Such ideas have been investigated in a three-year study, Living Spaces, which set out to involve young children and adults in the design and review of a nursery and Children's Centre (Clark, 2010). Here the visual, participatory methods have supported teachers, early years professionals, health workers and students to explore the question, 'What does it mean to be in this place?' This perhaps indicates that rather than discussing the need for child-friendly methods it is more a question of seeking 'participant-friendly methods' which enable participants of different ages and abilities to communicate their perspectives (Fraser, 2004: 25).

Conclusion

This chapter has considered some of the ways in which children, particularly young children, can be involved in research. It has highlighted two areas in particular which need to be addressed in undertaking research with young children, those of language and power. These, in turn, raise issues concerning the ethics of research. Once children are involved in research the roles of adults are changed in some way, whether they are acting as researchers, practitioners or as a research audience. This is one indication of why developments in this area may have wide implications for the undertaking of social research in general. Early childhood researchers, practitioners and students have important contributions to make to these debates.

Questions and exercises

1. How can researchers 'play to the strengths' of young children in developing methods which enable young children to communicate their views and experiences?
2. What research strategies would you suggest to take into account the power divide between researchers and young children?
3. What possible disadvantages for young children can you see if more research is conducted which elicits their views and experiences?

Further reading

Lewis et al. (2004) *The Reality of Research with Children and Young People* is an accessible volume which seeks to ground discussions about how to carry out research with children and young people with specific case studies written by researchers. Each chapter is accompanied by a short reflective commentary. Clark and Moss (2005) *Spaces to Play: More Listening to Young Children Using the Mosaic Approach* is a short volume which offers a way in to undertaking research with young children. The process of using a multi-method approach is demonstrated from the initial design stages of a project through to how to document research findings. The final section discusses ethical and methodological questions arising from this study about conducting research with young children.

19

IS WORKING TOGETHER WORKING?

Angela Anning

Contents

- Introduction
- Multi-agency working
- Theoretical perspectives
- Examples from the real world
- Conclusion

Introduction

Over the last two decades both Labour and Coalition governments' policies have promoted integrated services delivered by multi-agency teams for families with young children. As Sonia Jackson outlined in Chapter 11, early years services have been at the cutting edge of innovation in implementing the policies. It has been both the 'best and worst of times' to be a professional who works with young children and their families.

There are ideological differences between the two governments' approaches to public services. The New Labour vision was encapsulated in the famous 'onion' diagram (see Figure 19.1).

The Labour government invested massively in early years services (e.g. extending the hours of universal free education for all three and four year olds), intervention programmes (such as Sure Start), workforce reform (e.g. Early Years Professionals)

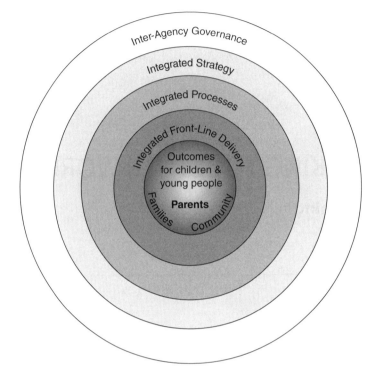

Figure 19.1   The New Labour model of integrated services

Source: DfES, 2004: 6

and the expansion of childcare (e.g. Neighbourhood Nurseries). The role of the state was central to addressing social exclusion, cycles of deprivation and poverty. Local authorities and settings charged with delivering services were audited by government regulation, targets and inspections (Anning et al., 2010).

The Coalition government is operating in a climate of economic austerity; sometimes it is hard to disentangle ideological from economic imperatives in their policies. The policy of Results Based Accountability is generating a raft of performance related measures for all settings and agencies delivering services. Payment by results systems were introduced into Children's Centres in 2012. Results are linked to value for money and renewed funding. This system, though draconian, may result in the analysis of data being fed back into revised practices. At the same time, the Coalition government's vision is to decentralise and deregulate. There is to be less red tape and bureaucracy. The focus is local solutions and diversity in services with a greater role for the voluntary and private sector. Further, its vision to achieve social justice is a Big Society, where volunteer and community based groups work alongside paid professionals to deliver services. Local authorities are responsible for strategic thinking and commissioning and for delivering statutory services. The 'nanny' state is to be rolled back from the private space of family life. Unless they are identified as 'at risk' or in need of authoritarian treatment, families are to take responsibility for their own futures.

Despite different ideologies, Labour and Coalition governments are united by a strong commitment to early intervention and partnerships with parents, to address poverty by tackling parental unemployment, to increase efficiency by systemic changes, to rely on evidence-based practice and to continue with 'joined up thinking' in the design and delivery of services.

Multi-agency working

A definition of multi-agency working from the DfE website is:

- a team around a particular child or family (TAC/TAF)
- a panel dealing with needs of individual children or families based on an area or establishment
- where services work together within a single unit, either co-located or virtual
- regular meetings across services (e.g. once a month). (DfE, 2012b)

Multi-agency working could involve anyone whose job or voluntary work puts them in contact with children, young people and their families and is likely to include professionals from social work, health, education, 'Early Years', youth work, playwork, guidance and counselling, police and youth justice.

The benefits are intended to include:

- early identification and intervention
- easier or quicker access to services or expertise
- improved achievement in education and better engagement in education
- better support for parents
- children, young people and family's needs addressed more appropriately
- better quality services
- reduced need for more specialist services. (DfE, 2012b)

One can read into these statements the underpinning vision of the Coalition government outlined above. This vision builds on the theme of prevention which was central to New Labour's social exclusion task force policy and continues to underpin the importance of early intervention in improving young children's life chances and trajectories.

Theoretical perspectives

Government policies all over the world have shifted from considering the child in isolation from societal, community and familial contexts to a clear understanding that all these features of a child's life are inter-related. The application of socio-cultural theory to this construct of childhood has informed our thinking on how changes in social policy impact on those who both deliver and receive integrated services.

In the United Kingdom integrated services have developed from the distinct and separate histories and traditions of social services, the National Health Service and education. Of particular relevance to inform our understanding of the impact of policy changes are two socio-cultural-historical theoretical frameworks (see Chapter 10). I have found these helpful in trying to understand how the policy of multi-agency working has impacted on early years practitioners and service users.

First, Wenger's (1998) seminal work on *communities of practice* explores how knowledge is generated and shared in the world of work. Some knowledge is conceptual, learned in training or from propositional knowledge, e.g. psychology or sociology. Some is experiential, learned in the daily routines of working, often embedded in actions. Knowledge gained from experience is mostly tacit. We are rarely required to make it explicit or justify it to clients. Wenger argues that new members of a community are introduced to this kind of knowledge through *legitimate peripheral participation* alongside more experienced practitioners. This kind of knowledge may generate habits or rituals which are seen as 'normal' within a community of practice. Practitioners from different agencies are trained and experienced in distinct practices – e.g. working as a family support worker or as a teacher – and use different languages or styles of discourse to exchange information in their daily work. These ways of acting and talking within a particular community can exclude others, including service users, and may be problematic when groups of professionals are required to work together in multi-agency teams.

Wenger's model of how knowledge is created in communities of practice defines two complementary processes: *participation* and *reification*. Participation involves the daily, situated interactions and shared experiences of members of the community working towards a common goal. Staff in a Children's Centre bring together the previous histories, cultures and activities of nursery education and day care to an integrated setting where they are required to work together delivering seamless services. Reification involves the explication of these versions of knowledge into representations. These may be embodied in the artefacts in a centre (for example, alphabet friezes and floor cushions), documents (for example, children's profiles on the Early Years Foundation Stage Curriculum and daily notes on young children's diets for their parents) and rules and rituals (for example, all children must 'do' an educational activity each day and key workers must always 'hand' the child to the person who collects them at the end of the day). The problem is that workers from day care settings may have made very different uses of artefacts than workers from educational settings. A book or paper and pencil may be used in informal, play-based activities by day care staff – storying and drawing. In educational settings they may be used in formal, didactic activities – learning about letters and practising writing one's name – in preparation for 'school readiness', which is advocated by the current government (DfE, 2013). Rules and rituals around eating and toilets may be dominated by health and safety concerns by care workers, but by the exigencies of 'the school day' by teachers. New members of the communities, such as trainees or children, are encultured into the activities, acquiring the relevant discourse and habits as they learn how to be professionals or pupils. It is unlikely that staff from either agency would have been expected to justify their rites and rituals to anybody. It is just what they do.

A second theoretical perspective I have found useful is Engeström's *activity theory*. In activity theory (Engeström, 1999) a key concept is that new knowledge is created within work organisations through collaborative activities each of which may form *parallel activity systems*. The *subject* of an activity system is the agent from whose point of view an analysis of the work activity is perceived. The *object* is the raw material (overweight children) or problem space (poor educational standards) at which the activity system is directed. The *outcomes* may be intentional – improvements in children's health or educational outcomes – or unintentional – dissatisfaction of parents with clinical services 'telling them' how to feed their children or three year olds becoming alienated from 'school' learning. The *instruments* utilised to work towards outcomes include powerful tools such as health visitor records, immunisations procedures or the developmental assessments of two year olds, 'school readiness' equipment and training, or informal notes on children's interests and achievements. The *community* comprises the many individuals and groups who share the common aim of servicing the welfare, health and educational needs of a locality. Their *division of labour* is premised on both horizontal division of tasks across services and vertical division of tasks through power and status of individuals within services. Finally, *rules* underpin all activity systems and regulate the way members of the community allocate time to tasks, record their actions, are appraised for their efficiency and are allocated rewards and promotions.

An activity will look very different to a health visitor, family support worker or an early years professional, though they may share the same intended outcomes of the health, development and wellbeing of a child. An important premise in Engeström's model is that since subjects within a team construct objects in an activity system differently, conflict is likely to arise as tasks are redefined, reassigned and divided differently within changing organisations. Different perspectives or 'voices' meet, collide and eventually merge into new versions of knowledge. His premise is that these conflicts must be brought out into the open and articulated in debates if any progress is to be made towards creating new forms of knowledge appropriate for new social/political/historical situations and contexts. Through contradictions within and between activity systems being articulated and evidenced, connections can be used creatively to create strategies for managing change. Engeström describes how these connections should be anchored up to a vision for the future and down to actions that are 'real'. His research methods for eliciting understandings of knowledge creation in working organisations include taking evidence of work activities (photographs, films or written descriptions) to meetings to confront subjects with different perspectives (for example, those of doctors, nurses and patients), recording their dialogues and transcribing their interactions for subsequent analysis and reflection. In turn these analyses of what has been said are fed back to the members of organisations or communities to support them in articulating and refining an extended, shared knowledge base. They are then able to design and 'own' new activities which exemplify or represent the team's extended, shared knowledge.

Examples from the real world

Throughout the last two decades I have observed professionals grappling with the realities of multi-agency working. I have evaluated Centres of Excellence, Sure Start Local Programmes (SSLPs) and vulnerable/at risk two year olds in day care programmes. Within these different socio-cultural-political contexts I have observed common dilemmas. I have grouped a discussion of these dilemmas into three sections: *Who I am*, *What I know* and *What I do*.

Who I am

Some early years practitioners were recruited into multi-agency teams such as those who applied for jobs in SSLPs (many of which morphed into Children's Centres in 2005). These early adopters were 'volunteers'. They had seen for themselves the limitations of children's services operating in silos and welcomed the opportunity to develop new ways of working. But others found that their workplace settings were transformed by government/local authority edicts into integrated service settings. These workers were 'conscripts' to the vision of integrated services, grouped into multi-agency teams at a discomforting rate, often with little preparation or training.

Individuals brought to the teams the baggage of their own 'tribal' affiliations to a particular agency such as social services, education, health or welfare. They brought their personal histories of the status and hierarchies of particular disciplines within agencies – teachers and nursery officers, speech therapists and health visitors, social workers and family support workers, psychologists and doctors. Their identities, values and beliefs were different. An example was the way they explained the causes of family dysfunctions or attributed 'blame' for problems. A social worker might blame a family crisis on the inequalities inherent in a divided society; a teacher might blame parents' lack of aspirations and education; a health visitor might blame poor parenting and children 'failing to thrive'. Each 'tribe' had its own language and preferred ways of 'treating' problems. It is no surprise that, as Engeström's theory predicts, the 'voices' of these disparate groups of practitioners collided.

Often members of multi-agency teams found their professional identities destabilised by these collisions (Anning et al., 2010). Most had excellent track records in their jobs; that is why they were appointed to innovative services. They were anxious when they saw responsibilities at which they had traditionally excelled being handed to, as they saw it, 'less well qualified' professionals. For example, a health visitor said of outreach work in a SSLP, 'Sometimes I get anxious when family support workers seem to be taking on work that I see is my role in families'. A speech therapist in a nursery for children with disabilities expressed concern that she was asked to 'train' nursery officers to work with children with language delay in the 'classrooms' rather than delivering the specialist treatment herself in clinics (though appointments were often missed).

Blurring of professional roles was confounded by labels assigned to them in revised staffing structures. A teacher in a Children's Centre told us that being rebranded as a generic 'nursery worker' and expected to take on routine care work with under three year olds had made her feel under-valued: 'I don't know if I'm a nursery nurse or a teacher any more'. A care worker expressed unease at being expected 'to act like a teacher and deliver a curriculum these days – I'm not a teacher'. A worker in a child mental health team said: 'First of all we called ourselves project workers, which I absolutely hated, because it says that we could be someone who had been employed as a volunteer you know, off the streets, without any qualifications … Now we've got this new ghastly generic label and I can never say it without stumbling over it and people have no idea what it means'.

The complications of differing pay and conditions of work exacerbated tensions. A teacher in a Children's Centre, working 'traditional' school hours and with school holiday entitlements is likely to earn more than their manager who works under less generous social services day care conditions, pay structures and holiday entitlements. An early years professional, trained to graduate level, with responsibility for early learning within a setting, is paid far less than a teacher. It takes determined leadership and skilful management to disentangle these inequalities, anxieties and resentments about professional identities and changing roles and responsibilities. A key imperative is that team members support both the emergent team as a unit and at the same time individuals who are struggling with new working practices that make them feel insecure or uncomfortable. Leaders in settings who understood this imperative were much more likely to translate a vision of integrated services into practices that 'worked' (Anning et al., 2007).

What I know

Sharing knowledge is critical to making multi-agency team work effective. But it takes time and infinite patience to listen to and learn about what colleagues from other agencies know, and time is a precious commodity. Making time for meetings is problematic; as one practitioner said, 'Who looks after the children while we sit and talk to each other?' A further complication is that many peripheral but essential members of multi-agency teams are seconded or employed on a part-time basis. Time for attending meetings is not costed into their hourly contracts. Managers struggle to find times when all staff members are able to attend.

As I observed teams struggling to understand other professionals' perspectives, values, language and knowledge it became clear that some strategies *are* productive in sharing and redistributing knowledge. Managers and leaders need to set up robust and reliable systems for sharing core knowledge and current information. Strategic information and policy-based knowledge/updates can be shared electronically. But deep knowledge exchange requires a different approach. When staff join the team, annual dates and times for regular, well-chaired, whole team meetings (monthly) and more reflective away days (when the settings are closed on dates to which parents are alerted well in advance) need to be mandatory and costed into hourly contracts. For groups within settings, the most effective way of sharing knowledge is for sub-groups to meet to share evidence of their daily activities (what Wenger called 'participation'). Participants bring to the meetings work schedules, notes of encounters with parents, children's work or records or specific case studies to use as the stimulus for exchange of ideas (Anning and Edwards, 2006). For individuals within teams, work shadowing or delivering services with colleagues from different agencies, observing their 'reifications' of practice, are productive. Implicit knowledge is made explicit as professionals work alongside each other. However, time needs to be set aside in staff/team meetings to tease out, discuss and make explicit this kind of knowledge. This is best done by openly sharing examples of critical incidents or observations of practice from the team's workplaces. This kind of collaboration provides fertile ground for teams to work together to co-construct 'expanded' versions of their professional knowledge.

A further challenge is sharing professional knowledge with volunteers. In 2012 the Coalition government funded Parent Champions in Liverpool. The project was in response to evidence from evaluations of early intervention programmes of low take up of services by many of the most vulnerable families. In the Parent Champions project parent volunteers from local communities were trained to reach out to parents whose children were not participating in early learning. Value was placed on the parents' own local knowledge and sharing knowledge between professionals and parent champions became a two-way process. The intention is to roll the programme out nationally.

Partnership with parents requires new ways of redistributing and co-constructing knowledge. Evidence from the National Evaluation of Sure Start (NESS, 2011) (see www.ness.bbk.ac.uk/ for reports) and The Effective Pre-School and Primary Education 3–11 Project (EPPE 3–11) (Sylva et al., 2008) reinforced the importance of actively involving families in the development, health and wellbeing of children. The quality of the home learning environment – measures such as access to books, amount of story reading, paper and pencils, use of libraries, everyday opportunities for learning about numbers, shapes and sizes – predicted better than expected cognitive outcomes for children, regardless of the socio-economic status of their family. It is more important what parents do with their children than who they are. This kind of evidence sits uneasily with systems based on socio-economic indicators as predictors of children's potential attainments.

For professionals to work in true partnership with parents requires courage and new skills. The most radical SSLPs had a vision of *empowering parents* and redistributing knowledge to the local community. They encouraged local parents to volunteer, train, then gain employment in local services. For these programmes, the redistribution of professional knowledge was a democratic aim, crucial to capacity building in the local community and in common with a 'funds of knowledge' orientation to community engagement (e.g. Moll et al., 1992). An evaluation officer said:

> Our early years, speech and language and occupational specialists are willing to share expertise, because they acknowledge that so much of what they do is not rocket science. It is the ethos of this Sure Start that those things can be shared. It's encouraging people to come from the community to be trained.

Such a radical approach to the redistribution of knowledge brings with it the challenges of maintaining quality and the threat of deskilling professionals. It is hard to get the balance right. A speech and language therapist expressed this dilemma:

> We are cascading information down, because this is our model. We like to get the community and parents working on the programme. We can teach them practically how you do it, we can teach them the words to say, but there are all the other things, like the professionalism, that isn't there. We are now trying to make sure that these people have the right kind of training, that they've got confidence in their own skills, but they're not over confident and they don't think, I know everything there is to know about speech and language. I've found that quite difficult. (Anning et al., 2005: 45–6)

A final challenge is how professionals from different agencies, volunteers and parents as partners share information about families and children. The Common Assessment Framework (CAF) is designed to collate information about families with additional or complex needs. A team of professionals who are in contact with the family, including family members themselves, meet to contribute perspectives on the family's needs. The administration and responsibility for enacting the CAF is co-ordinated by a Lead Professional (a Special Educational Needs Co-ordinator (SENCO), teacher, health visitor or family support worker) who acts as the single point of contact for the team around the family (TAF). The policy of the Coalition government is that such protocols and systems enable multi-agency teams to *develop outcomes-focused plans for time-limited interventions that are owned by the families themselves.* These aspirations sound neat and efficient; but in the real world of communities with complex needs, issues of confidentiality trouble practitioners. Volunteers have to be trained in how to deal with confidential information. Health professionals and social workers have anxieties about handling sensitive information inherited from the disciplines of their own agencies. In one SSLP the manager's attempt to get her team to share administrative space and work stations to promote better communications and more efficient use of space was thwarted when the health visitor moved her files into a locked cabinet and her work station into a cupboard. She refused to budge.

What I do

Without a shared vision and good leadership multi-agency teams retreat back into their preferred, single agency ways of working. Engeström calls them '*parallel activity systems*'.

The ways in which professionals and parents use spaces is a metaphor for how people are able to change what they do. During the decades when SSLPs and Children's Centres were flagship exemplars of 'joined up' thinking and practice, costly, new buildings were designed and built with single, non-stigmatised reception areas, multi-purpose service delivery suites and shared staffrooms. Yet I observed spaces designed for generic purposes re-shaped into separate zones, cupboards and shelving used to screen off sections of shared areas and doors shut. A popular 'Stay and Play' area for children and parents attending pre- and postnatal clinics was closed down during clinic hours because health staff complained that it was too noisy. Community cafés where parents and young children met to socialise in a relaxed and safe space were converted into offices by managers on 'health and safety' grounds. A parent said: 'They shut our café down because they said it was too risky to have hot drinks where there were kids around'.

Some services did offer genuinely new ways of working. As the speech therapist quoted above said, these activities were not 'rocket science'; but they were informed by a different kind of understanding. Two examples are given.

EXAMPLE 1

A teacher was seconded to an intervention project designed to promote early literacy and language in an area where many children started school with poor communication skills and little experience of books/reading. She worked in a range of settings such as pre-school playgroups in church halls, sessional care for children whose parents attended literacy and numeracy training and Children's Centres. She was used to working in the ethos of a nursery school and found the 'chaotic' nature of the sessions in her new peripatetic role unsettling. She found herself retreating into 'teacherly' behaviours – sitting with groups of children in the corner focusing on books/storying and emergent writing activities. She was polite to the parents; but they tended to sit around the edges of the rooms talking and drinking coffee, enjoying rare opportunities to talk with like-minded adults. The teacher saw the children and their development as her prime responsibility and the parents were equally preoccupied with their own priorities.

During a particularly 'chaotic' stay and play session, the teacher made a quick decision to staple onto a parents' notice board drawings of their families that the children had done with her that day. Parents crowded around the board to look at the drawings. The teacher stood with them and chatted informally. She used the 'object' of the display to anchor down to realities of their own children's drawings and anchor up to general talk about the development of children's mark-making, drawing and writing.

She recalled later that this intuitive action marked a turning point in what she did in all her subsequent work. Having gained a way of talking with parents, she was able to build up a rapport with them. She encouraged them to make and enjoy scrap books of their own child's mark-making at home and in setting sessions. A group of parents recreated the local Post Office in the role play area to encourage their children to talk and 'write'. Two fathers made scrap books with the children from magazines about football and cars. Parents began taking a real interest in story books they borrowed from the setting, making puppets with the children to act out the stories and enjoying reading to their children. The pivotal moment for this professional was when she connected with the parents. It turned her relationship with the parents into one of mutual co-operation for the benefit of the children's development as eager learners of early literacy.

EXAMPLE 2

A speech therapist struggled to get parents of children referred to her to attend appointments in the brand new Children's Centre. A family support worker, who had worked in the multi-cultural community for many years, suggested that they might try running joint sessions in a long-established church hall with a tradition of inclusion of local events, regardless of the race and faith of attendants. The focus of the activity was

(Continued)

(Continued)

'early intervention with a family focus'; but it was advertised to parents as fun. The sessions included a choice of snacks for children and parents, a lively mixture of singing and dancing together, and some well-loved games such as 'Going on a Bear Hunt' and playing with a parachute.

The sessions *were* fun and attendance rates were high. There were scarves and fabrics for the children and adults to whirl and musical instruments to play. The music was a mixture of nursery rhymes and current pop favourites and culturally specific songs and dances – something for everyone. During the snack times the two professionals moved quietly among the families chatting to them; and through these informal exchanges the speech therapist coaxed reluctant attendees of her specialist sessions to understand how she could help and support their children's speech and language development. She listened carefully to how and when the families were able to attend her sessions and adjusted the places and times of appointments to suit their needs. Using this common-sense strategy, the two professionals pooled their respective strengths and offered a rich mixture of specialist and generalist activities that were responsive to the local community. As the family worker said: 'We try and do it the other way round now. We'll say, 'What do you want? What do you need? And what can we do to make that a possibility?'

Conclusion

What evidence is there that working together works? NESS reported that SSLPs improved some parent outcomes, but not child outcomes. Where health worked closely with SSLPs, their well-tried systems for home interventions and record keeping enhanced the effectiveness of services for young children. These results encouraged the adoption in the UK of Family Nurse Partnerships (DH, 2011d) to work with young teenage parents.

It was disappointing that the educational outcomes of the target SSLP children were not 'better than expected'. It is likely that the emphasis on universal free early education for all three and four year olds in the control groups accounted partly for this finding. The good news was that most young children in the UK were benefitting from free early education. However, the influential EPPE project reported that educational outcomes were better when children had access to high quality teaching. Qualified teachers are too expensive for many settings, many employ graduate level EYPs instead who are less well paid. Evaluation of EYP impact suggests that, especially if they are managers, they can improve the quality of provision for over three year olds but not for two year olds (Mathers et al., 2011). This problem will need to be addressed, when, by 2014, forty per cent of the most disadvantaged two year olds in poorer areas will be offered fifteen hours a week of free 'education'. Funding will be available for start up costs for new nurseries and childminders in these areas. The most recent government proposals (DfE, 2013) concerning the mix of staff qualifications, the quality of provision and staff–child ratios is currently an area of contention and concern and the process and effects of their operationalisation are uncertain (see also Chapter 20).

The future of Children's Centres, though less well funded, looks assured. Their role is to improve outcomes for young children and their families, with particular focus on more disadvantaged families. Multi-agency teamwork, though in many respects unproven, is to be a key source of early intervention. Each centre will have a named health visitor to provide advice and run services and a named social worker to help build confidence in child protection. Outreach systems leaders will be trained and appointed to manage home-based interventions.

However, without a serious commitment to developing in the workforce the knowledge, skills and attitudes to make working together work, the kinds of dilemmas outlined in this chapter will not go away.

Questions and exercises

1. How would you describe multi-agency teamwork?
2. What are the barriers to early years professionals working together?
3. What strategies might work in your own setting to overcome the barriers?
4. Who wins and who loses in the delivery of integrated services and why?
5. In ten years' time how do you think working together in early years services might look?

Further reading

For up-to-date information on government policy on multi-agency work access the DfE website at www.education.gov.uk. For a range of professional perspectives on the practicalities of making multi-agency team work happen read Michael Gasper (2010) *Multi-Agency Working in the Early Years: Challenges and Opportunities*. For information on research methods and the theory underpinning this chapter read Anning et al. (2010) *Developing Multi-Professional Teamwork for Integrated Children's Services* (2nd edn).

20

EFFECTIVE EARLY CHILDHOOD LEADERSHIP

Carol Aubrey

Contents

- Introduction
- Changing policy context
- Research evidence on effective early childhood leadership
- A case study of early childhood leadership
- Conclusion

Introduction

This chapter focuses on effective early childhood (EC) leadership. It will consider the role that EC leaders play in the improvement of outcomes for very young children that include being healthy, staying safe, enjoying and achieving (DfES, 2003b). It will not linger on generic leadership and management skills but will attempt to identify ways that early childhood leaders may have an impact on worthwhile outcomes for children. It will examine what existing policy requires and what early childhood leadership literature reveals. It will also draw upon EC leadership research carried out by the writer and colleagues with EC leaders, willing to explore their own leadership and interrogate their own leadership practice. The chapter will end with an exploration of emergent themes that may shed further light on effective EC leadership practice.

Changing policy context

The government's *Ten Year Strategy for Childcare*, Department for Education and Skills (HM Treasury, 2004) pledged to create 3,500 Children's Centres for 2010 with access for all families; a commitment to extend free early education places for three and four year olds to fifteen hours a week; a goal to extend this to twenty hours a week; and affordable school-based childcare between 8 a.m. and 6 p.m. for all five to eleven year olds by 2010. Also pledged was a new duty on local authorities (LAs) to ensure that quality affordable childcare was available where families lived and a new legal framework for the regulation and inspection of early education and childcare by 2008, thus creating a single system for all services. This was delivered through the Childcare Act (DfES, 2006). The strategy also created a Transformation Fund of £125 million per annum from April 2006, intended to support investment by LAs in quality affordable and sustained childcare, at the same time, pledging a single quality framework for children from birth to five years, through an integrated approach to care and education. In terms of financial support, the strategy also increased maximum eligible costs in the childcare element of the Working Tax Credit. There was an increase in the proportion of childcare costs covered by the tax credit from seventy to eighty per cent.

Next steps for early learning and childcare, building on the Ten-Year Strategy

The Department for Children, Schools and Families (DCSF, 2009c) provided an update on progress on the strategy and set out new steps to improve early years and childcare provision in the future years. This included a gradual extension of the number of free places for two year olds, originally to around twenty per cent, and subsequently to be extended to forty per cent. Relevant to this chapter, a commitment was made for all existing staff and new recruits to the sector to be supported to achieve a minimum of a full and relevant NVQ Level 3 qualification by 2015, with a graduate practitioner – an early years professional (EYP) – to provide leadership in every childcare setting by 2015, two per setting in the most disadvantaged areas. Meanwhile, the Apprenticeships, Skills, Children and Learning Act (DCSF, 2009d) included provision to establish Children's Centres on a statutory footing to ensure they became an element of early years provision.

In its 2011 policy statement, *Supporting Families in the Foundation Years* (DfE and DH, 2011), the Coalition government outlined its vision for supporting children and families from pregnancy to five years. This came in the wake of major policy recommendations from Marmot (2010) to increase expenditure allocated to EC in order to reduce health inequalities (see also Chapter 15). This was reinforced by Field (2010) who stressed the need for early intervention to support the poorest and most disadvantaged families since life chances are heavily predicated upon development in the first five years; by Allen (2011) who argued for early intervention to create high levels of 'school readiness' for all children regardless of family income; and by Munro (2011) who also emphasised the effectiveness of early intervention with children and families in respect of safeguarding. A review of the Early Years Foundation Stage (EYFS) by Tickell (2011) led to a new Statutory Framework for the EYFS from the Department for Education (DfE, 2012a, EYFS) mandatory for all early years (EY) providers from the beginning of September, 2012.

The Nutbrown Review (Nutbrown, 2012) of early education and childcare qualifications reinforced the view that all staff should be qualified to a minimum 'full and relevant Level 3', with Level 2 qualifications in English and mathematics required before training began. Clear routes to progress to more senior roles should be available, with all early years practitioners able to aspire to become pedagogical leaders as EYPs, with a specialist route to qualified teacher status (QTS) for those who wish to achieve this. This echoed Tickell (2011: 7) who emphasised the importance of a 'strong, well-qualified EY workforce with a Level 3 and a graduate ambition'. As at September 2012, there were 10,400 EYPs with a further 2,688 in training and a programme funded to continue until March 2015 (Crabbe, 2012). There has also been a three-year, two-cohort pilot programme *New Leaders in EY* that aims to attract high-calibre graduates onto a programme offering Early Years Professional Status (EYPS), a Masters in EC with extensive work placement and mentoring.

Overall, it is clear from the Nutbrown Report (Nutbrown, 2012: 5) that high quality early education and childcare is regarded as central to a positive long-term impact on children's later learning and achievements and 'staff with the necessary knowledge and understanding are a crucial element of that quality'. It is also emphasised that 'research has shown the huge positive impacts of graduate leadership on areas of child development such as early literacy and social development' (Nutbrown, 2012: 8).

The government's response (DfE, 2013) to the Nutbrown Report (2012) in turn emphasised that graduate leadership was the best way to improve outcomes for young children. While those with EYPS were graduates trained specifically to work with babies and children from birth to five years, equivalent to the new Early Years Teachers being introduced, it was noted that the Early Years Teachers were to 'lead the further improvements in quality' (DfE, 2013: 44). In line with raising the status and quality of the workforce, improvements were to be made to the Ofsted regulatory regime. Since September 2012, inspections had focused on three central judgements related to how well the provision met the needs of the range of children attending; its contribution to children's wellbeing; and its leadership and management. It was also expected that providers would justify the staffing structure they used, its flexibility and the way it helped to deliver better outcomes for children.

Research evidence on effective early childhood leadership

Throughout this period, effective leadership has been widely accepted as a vital ingredient in achieving institutional improvement. Research evidence from different countries and different educational contexts has shown the powerful impact of leadership in securing organisational development and change (Harris et al., 2002). While leadership research in the school sector is established, driven largely by the National College, research on leadership in EC, though burgeoning, is still quite limited and dominated by a relatively small number of researchers (e.g. Rodd, 1996; 2006). This provided a stimulus to our own systematic review of research on EC leadership (Muijs et al., 2004). Increased accountability and financial constraints in the sector, greater competition and frequent changes in government policy have been seen to require more sophisticated leadership and management skills (Hayden, 1997; Rodd, 1997).

In the English context, with the introduction of the National Childcare Strategy and integrated approaches to early education and care, the situation has become more complex and the need for effective leadership even greater. The range of providers registered to deliver education and childcare, however, may have contrasting philosophies and values, as well as different structures, despite being driven by a common inspection remit. One distinction between EC education and other fields in which leadership has been studied is the extent to which women occupy the leadership roles, in contrast to the business world. Some have suggested that the leadership styles used by women are very different from those used by male leaders, though recent studies do not support gender differences in leadership style (Evetts, 1994; Coleman, 2001).

The relative absence of research in the field has been matched by the absence of leadership development programmes. The National Professional Qualification for Integrated Centre Leaders (NPQICL), for Sure Start Children's Centre leaders and their deputies, with National Standards for Children's Centre Leaders, was introduced in 2007. These standards are distinct from, but complementary to, those recently introduced for the EYPs (CWDC, 2006; Teaching Agency, 2012) as it is not assumed or intended that an EYP should lead and manage multi-agency, multidisciplinary Children's Centres. The NPQICL is designated as an equivalent qualification to the National Professional Qualification for Head teachers (NPQH). Head teachers of maintained nursery schools can thus choose either qualification.

As noted above, EC programmes have been found to have both short-term and long-term benefits in terms of academic achievement, lower levels of grade retention, higher graduation rates and lower levels of delinquency later in life. For example, Stipek and Ogano's review (2000) highlighted that children who attended higher quality EC centres in the United States context showed better academic outcomes, more positive student–teacher relationships, better academic behaviour and social skills. A key factor of quality EC provision was identified as leadership, alongside factors such as creating a language-rich environment, sensitive teachers, child-focused communication with the child's home, higher levels of teacher/carer education, smaller child–adult ratios and lower staff turnover. In an Australian study (Hayden, 1997), a high quality early childhood programme was found to be related to lower levels of staff turnover, which in turn related to scores on childhood development and social and emotional skills scales. These studies point to the importance of leadership. A US evaluation of Head Start programmes found that competent and stable leadership exerted a powerful influence on the effectiveness of programme implementation and was one of the main distinguishing factors between the most and least successful programmes (Ramey et al., 2000). Unsuccessful programmes were characterised as having less experienced leadership – leaders who were less skilful at training and supervising staff, less good at working with schools and the community and less involved and committed.

An important leadership role in EC lies in co-ordination between the various actors and agencies, such as family, school and community, which need to work together to maximise the benefits. Nowhere is this more apparent than in the multi-agency English Sure Start Children's Centres. An audit of multi-agency working by Atkinson et al. (2001; 2002) that included a Sure Start Local Programme (SSLP) as one of a number of case studies revealed that a key factor in the success of such work was effective leadership. Turning specifically to the National Evaluation of SSLPs (NESS) (Belsky et al., 2007), effective leadership/management was one of eighteen identified domains of implementation that, collectively, significantly discriminated between groups of more or less effective programmes. Determining which features of SSLP proficiency might be principally responsible for such an effect, however, proved more difficult to determine.

Much of the existing research in EC leadership has focused on self-report of leaders on elements of leadership such as roles, attributes, skills and competencies of leaders, informed by systematic literature searches of relevant databases. As this chapter has already shown, a paucity of research in the area, despite high potential, serves as a limitation. Moyles (2006) developed a list of EC leadership attributes from the literature and then worked with a focus group of two consultants and sixteen practising heads to develop a typology of leadership and management roles of effective management and leadership (ELMS). The ELMS document went through several iterations as the group undertook activities such as keeping diary records and holding monthly meetings. The completed ELMS exemplification materials, including cameos and other stories, were composed of: leadership skills; management skills; professional skills and attributes; and personal characteristics and attitudes, with accompanying sets of questions and intended as a tool for evaluation purposes.

Effective Provision of Pre-school Education (EPPE, Sylva et al., 2004) and Researching Effective Pedagogy in the Early Years (REPEY, Siraj-Blatchford et al., 2002) (see Chapter 13) had already found that individual pre-schools varied in their effectiveness for influencing a child's development, and that children made better all-round progress in settings where there was strong leadership and relatively little staff turnover, where a trained teacher acted as manager and a good proportion of the staff were graduates, though the majority of characteristics identified were associated with effective pedagogy to support cognitive and social development rather than effective leadership. Following re-analysis of the REPEY case studies (Siraj-Blatchford and Manni, 2007), supported by research educational literature, progressive engagement with the data and in consultation with a specialist EC focus group, 'categories of effective leadership practice' were identified. A fundamental requirement for leading for learning was contextual leadership that shows awareness of and takes account of operating within a dynamic environment, commitment to collaboration and improvement of children's learning, each quality being found strongly represented in the effective settings studied. Also identified were:

- Identifying and articulating a collective vision.
- Ensuring shared understandings, meanings and goals.
- Effective communication.
- Encouraging reflection.
- Monitoring and assessing practice.
- Commitment to ongoing, professional development.
- Distributed leadership.
- Building a learning community and team culture.
- Encouraging and facilitating parent and community partnerships.
- Striking the balance between leading and managing.

These, it was argued, might be considered valuable in the development of leadership training.

Sharp et al. (2012) used a similar methodology for their study of highly effective Children's Centre leadership. They undertook a systematic literature search; collected LA documentation related to models of leadership being used; carried out twenty-five case studies of Children's Centres that involved interviews with LA staff, centre leaders and staff, and staff from other agencies and parents; validated findings and developed recommendations through practitioner workshops.

They explored new organisational models, such as clustering of centres, and considered the main leadership challenges in a context of changing external environment. Case studies involved five 'highly effective' and five 'good' category single-centre settings, based on Ofsted reports, and fifteen settings using new and emerging models of leadership, such as self-improving 'system' leadership drawn from school leadership literature. Eight core behaviours of highly effective leaders and seven core behaviours for system leadership were specified. Current and future leadership skills and training needs, challenges and solutions at a time of continuing change and scarce resources were explored. Core behaviours, underpinned by key knowledge, skills and attributes were:

- Having a clear vision to improve outcomes for children and families.
- Engaging responsively with families.
- Using evidence to drive improvements in outcomes.
- Using business skills strategically.
- Facilitating open communication.
- Embracing integrated working.
- Motivating and empowering staff.
- Being committed to their own learning and development.

Core behaviours bear resemblance to the National Standards for heads of Children's Centres and define the knowledge, skills and understanding needed to fulfil them: leading learning and development; stronger families, stronger communities; being accountable and responsible; shaping the present and creating the future; managing the organisation; and building and strengthening teams. Ways that the concept of 'system leadership' (Hargreaves, 2010), developed in the school sector, might be applied to the Children's Centre or 'foundation years' were considered as a means of developing a self-improving system.

What these recent studies attempt to do is to address the hesitance of earlier researchers in the sector to engage with concepts of leadership and ensure that their research is well informed by theory and research in the broader field of leadership studies. They attempt to focus on identification of what effective EC leadership is in the context of the broader field of leadership concepts.

Viviane Robinson (2006), however, pointed out that educational leadership research has produced limited evidence about links between leadership and learning and to date even that evidence is very inconclusive. She argued that educational leadership should be grounded in the best evidence about effective teaching that has a positive impact (or in the case of early childhood leadership, ensuring that children also stay healthy, safe and secure). The next step, she maintained, is a backward mapping process in specifying the processes and policies; in this case, within the EC setting that facilitates these conditions. The challenge is to strengthen those conditions that enable the setting to function effectively and weaken the impact of those conditions that inhibit or prevent the setting from functioning effectively.

A case study of early childhood leadership

In the interests of linking reported views and experiences of English EC leaders to observed practice, the author and colleagues decided to plan an investigation of EC leadership through an initial seminar with twenty-five local leaders that led to an in-depth study of twelve leaders and colleagues through a survey, interviews and 'day-in-the-life' observations (Aubrey, 2011; Aubrey et al., 2013).

The seminar

Leaders were selected on the basis of their effective practice, identified by the local adviser and confirmed by Ofsted reports. They were asked to answer five key questions:

1. What does leadership mean in your setting? Here the leaders stressed having a clear vision and working towards it. To them, this meant having an awareness of the wider social, political and educational context. It entailed raising the profile of early education and care and developing a shared philosophy. Fundamental to this was a recognition of its multidisciplinary nature, valuing learning and having a commitment to ongoing professional development.
2. What factors contributed to the effectiveness of this role? Promoting early years across a range of agencies was regarded as prerequisite, with a firm commitment to working towards specific outcomes. Again, commitment to ongoing professional development and support for staff was thought to contribute to effective leadership.
3. What factors hindered effectiveness in this role? It was felt that the state of change and development over a number of years had created a real lack of clarity about EC care and education. This was coupled with a general lack of knowledge about childhood at all levels, a lack of status, a lack of resources in terms of staffing, time and materials and a lack of professional development. In turn, it could lead to a sense of isolation and low levels of responsibility.
4. What were the training needs? The need for more general accreditation of EC leadership and management at varying levels and with appropriate funding was emphasised.
5. How could capacity be built in the field? It was felt there were distinct training and development needs in the sector. This sentiment resonated through their responses. Valuing learning was at the core, with a commitment to working towards specific outcomes and promoting EY across a range of agencies.

The survey

Twelve leaders and exemplar settings continued to work with us in investigating the full range of EC provision that included three private nursery and day care settings; two voluntary family centres; four nursery and reception classes in infant and primary schools (foundation stage units for children aged three to five years; three Children's Centres providing a range of services for children from birth to four years, their families and community).

One hundred and ninety-four practitioners responded to our survey of views on EC leadership that included the majority of leaders and middle leaders and a range of practitioners working in and around the centres concerned. In terms of demographics, the workforce was mainly female (four males responded), aged between twenty and forty-eight years old. The majority who responded had at least a diploma in nursery nursing or National Vocational Qualification (NVQ) Level 3 or equivalent. Respondents in foundation stage units and Children's Centres predominantly had a first degree or postgraduate qualification, while private and voluntary day care workers were more likely to have on-the-job NVQs at Levels 2 and 3. Two-thirds had original training that covered the period from birth upwards, while disproportionately respondents from foundation units had not trained to work with very young children.

In terms of roles and responsibilities, there was high agreement that the most important aspect of the leader's role was to deliver a quality service. By contrast, nobody ranked first an 'entrepreneurial approach, mindful of competition with others'.

With respect to personal characteristics of effective leaders, a more sophisticated analysis of responses suggested that respondents with postgraduate qualifications tended to favour warmth, rationality, knowledgeability, assertiveness, goal orientation, coaching, mentoring and guiding, which we described as *leaders as guides*. Those with NVQs tended to favour vision, warmth, professional confidence, systematic planning, proactivity and empowerment, which we described as *leaders as motivators*. Those with so-called 'other qualifications' who had been trained for professions other than education, such as the library service, health-related professions, play leadership or social work tended to favour systematic planning, risk-taking, influence, proactivity, vision and empowerment, which we described as *leaders as strategists*. Finally, those with post-graduate qualifications were also likely to favour influence, authority, economic competitiveness, business awareness and risk-taking, which we described as *business oriented*.

While there was some overlap between these categories there was at least some indication that leaders with different qualifications, coming from different professional heritages and working in different types of setting regarded a different set of characteristics and emphases as important to effective EC leadership. Given different job descriptions and role specifications among the range of leaders, this was scarcely surprising. It does, however, indicate the existence of many different types of EC leader and the need for a 'best fit' approach that is derived from organisational development theory (e.g. Handy, 1993) and that takes account of leader, followers, task and environment. It may also go some way to understanding participants' response to the question – who makes the decisions? Many differences were found in the weight given to 'all staff', 'appropriate individuals', 'children' and 'parents'. Middle and senior management were regarded as unimportant and the child was reported overall as having least input. Given the current emphasis on children's participation and voice, this finding was surprising, though private and voluntary providers were more likely to say decisions were made by children 'all the time', which might reflect a stronger emphasis on 'client' expectations. Children's Centre leaders were more likely to say that parents made decisions 'all the time', in line with original programme practice that they should be locally driven and responsive to the needs of families.

Interviews with leaders and staff groups

Perceptions and definitions of EC leadership were wide-ranging and diverse when probed in more depth through interview. The role of previous experience, role models and academic study were all identified by leaders as important and a variety of training models were considered that included peer mentoring, developing critical friends and paired visits to peers' settings. Staff groups collectively reported no experience of leadership training but mentioned the influence on them of role models and the more ad hoc picking up of 'nuggets of what people said'. Leaders acknowledged that general leadership theory and principles were common across sectors but what was distinctive about EC leadership was its being female-led, its emotional involvement and its caring. That is not to say that males make ineffective leaders but rather, as Blackmore (1989) emphasised, organisational theorists have characterised leadership by masculine traits of aggression, competition and independence, while Shakeshaft (1989) in the US revealed women's leadership as focused on collaboration, power-sharing, caring and relationships. Shakeshaft also noted women leaders were consultative, creating a nurturing and non-hierarchical culture that reflected Gilligan's (1982) 'ethic of caring'. Court (1994) in the New Zealand context described women in leadership positions who 'empowered' or shared power with others and created organisational cultures based on collaboration, communication and shared decision-making. In England, Hall (1996) identified an organisational culture created by women school leaders as one of trust, openness and commitment. In terms of our own respondents, staff inevitably stressed the leadership qualities that impacted on them as followers, and leaders commented on the role of followers in shaping their practice.

In terms of roles and responsibilities, high quality education and care and children's achievements were emphasised by leaders and staff alike. Views of leaders and staff on business and entrepreneurial skills were again mixed but interviews uncovered a deep unease about 'for profit motives in a sector so poorly paid'. One respondent stated: 'I came from the private sector because I did not like the idea of making a profit … exploiting those on low wages'. In terms of decision-making, there was recognition of 'top-down' LA decision-making but nevertheless retention of a collaborative culture within the organisation. Overall, respondents felt that their organisations were hierarchically organised at the strategic level but collaborative at the operational level.

A typical 'day-in-the-life' or EC leadership in action

A typical 'day-in-the-life' was consistent with leaders' previous reports and included rich and varied activities. Leaders working in foundation stage units had very demanding roles, balancing teaching, administration and pedagogical leadership. Leaders observed in private and voluntary organisations were more likely to lack administrative support and to be preoccupied with low-level administrative tasks. Leaders in Children's Centres were seen working on complex and large-scale projects that might entail substantial financial and administrative responsibility for new buildings, developing new policy through consultation with the public, private and voluntary sector that represented a variety of professional groups. At the same time, there was a blurring of distinctions between private, voluntary and state, as new Children's Centres were being formed and extended schooling developed. This meant that leaders were finding themselves taking on new major operational tasks, calling for financial and administrative or technical expertise that they must learn 'on-the-job'.

Robinson's earlier advice to employ backward mapping that involved working backwards from positive impacts on children to tease out leader influence provided a useful frame for examining observed practice. This revealed the high intensity of foundation stage leaders' roles in working both directly with children and with other professionals and para-professionals that they worked alongside. The same intensity of focus on high quality learning and teaching was observed in those Children's Centres, state, voluntary and private provision, who were observed to coach staff in planning, teaching and profiling of young children's work, supporting and challenging their practice in order to raise the quality of provision provided. The strong focus of attention was observed to be on play, learning and childcare experiences with a range of other indirect activities being carried out around core services of support for families and communities.

There was laughter when leaders shared their own video highlights with one another. They exclaimed at their evident tiredness, the long hours and the intensity of their work, what Evans et al. (1994) first termed the 'culture of over-conscientiousness' of EC practitioners. They applauded their capacity to deliver the new childcare strategy. They celebrated their ability to 'hold focus' in spite of underlying emotions and uncertainties and indeed, were willing to articulate their own feelings of inadequacy at times as well as their outstripping in expertise of their LA line managers.

The need for and celebration of 'upskilling' in the workforce was very apparent in the displays of newly acquired NVQs, the welcoming, greeting and supporting of new staff. These all marked the new pathways into the EC workforce. Leaders bemoaned the lack of leadership training available, accentuating the gap in training opportunity between those least and most qualified. Indeed, the need for new skills, knowledge and understanding across the sector was a feature of the video footage. The scale of workforce reorganisation highlighted, the reported low status accorded to EC work and the variability of qualifications across the sector identified by the survey, threw into relief the lack of opportunity for EC leadership training.

Conclusion

Ebbeck and Waniganiyake (2000: 28) considered that definitions of EC leadership lacked clarity, coherence and comprehensiveness due to a 'failure to take into account the circumstances and consequent evolution of roles and responsibilities'. Viviane Robinson (2006) argued that we need theories of educational leadership that are firmly grounded in knowledge of the conditions that teachers (and carers) need to promote their children's learning (health, wellbeing and safety). There are important mismatches between the context in which leaders currently work and the conditions that would enable them to be stronger instructional leaders. One mismatch concerns the leader's current job and the intensity of focus that is required to lead or oversee a successful programme of instructional improvement. Most leaders already have a heavy workload with administrative duties taking up considerably more hours per month than those of instructional leadership, as observations in our study confirmed. If raising standards and hence instructional leadership are the policy priority then how will the existing workload be reorganised to make this a reality? In order to address this question, we need theories of leadership that are firmly grounded in knowledge of the conditions that practitioners need to promote children's learning. Whether or not the qualities of good leadership identified by such theories are the same as those identified by generic theories will not be answered until research on leadership and research on effective teaching and learning are more closely aligned.

Questions and exercises

1. Note down what kinds of knowledge and understanding you think are needed to lead improvement in the quality of teaching and learning in an EC setting you know of?
2. Talk to the leader of that EC setting about what evidence they would provide to an Ofsted inspector to demonstrate the effectiveness of leadership and management in that setting.

Further reading

If you want to find out more about different concepts and characteristics of EC leadership, as well as the roles and responsibilities, you might want to look at Carol Aubrey's (2011) *Leading and Managing in the Early Years*. A short technical report of this work can be found in Aubrey et al. (2013).

REFERENCES

Abbott, M.P., Chijioke, M.E., Dandelion, P. and Oliver, J.W. (2011) *Historical Dictionary of the Friends (Quakers)*. Maryland: Scarecrow Press.

Abebe, T. and Aase, A. (2007) 'Children, AIDS and the politics of orphan care in Ethiopia: the extended family revisited', *Social Science and Medicine*, 64: 2058–69.

Abrams, R. (2001) *Three Shoes, One Sock and No Hairbrush: Everything You Need to Know about Having Your Second Child*. London: Cassell.

ACPF (2011) *The Africa Report on Child Wellbeing. Budgeting for Children*. Addis Ababa: Africa Child Policy Forum.

AcSS Academy of Social Sciences (2010) *Making the Case for the Social Sciences*, No.7 Scotland. London: Sage.

Adams, N., Barton, A., Johnson, G. and Matejic, P. (eds) (2011) *Households Below Average Income: An Analysis of the Income Distribution 1994/95–2009/10*. London: Department for Work and Pensions.

Adler, P. and Adler, P. (1987) *Membership Roles in Field Research: Qualitative Research Methods Series* (Vol. 6). Thousand Oaks, CA: Sage Publications.

Aggleton, P. (1990) *Health*. London: Routledge.

Ainscow, M., Booth, T. and Dyson, A. (2006) *Improving Schools, Developing Inclusion*. London: Routledge. [Online] Available at: http://arrts.gtcni.org.uk/gtcni/bitstream/2428/49039/1/Ainscow.pdf (accessed 31/12/2012).

Akhtar, N., Jipson, J. and Callanan, M. (2001) 'Learning words through overhearing', *Child Development*, 72: 416–30.

Alanen, L. and Mayall, B. (2001) *Conceptualising Child–Adult Relations*. London: Routledge Falmer.

Albareda-Castellot, B., Pons, F. and Sebastián-Gallés, N. (2011) 'The acquisition of phonetic categories in bilingual infants: new data from a new paradigm', *Developmental Science*, 14(2): 395–401.

Alderson, P. (1993) *Children's Consent to Surgery*. Buckingham: Open University Press.

—— (2008) *Young Children's Rights: Exploring Beliefs, Principles and Practice* (2nd edn). London: Jessica Kingsley Publishers.

Alderson, P. and Morrow, V. (2011) *Ethics of research with Children and Young People: a practical handbook*. London: Sage

Allen, G. (2011) *The Report of the Independent Review of Poverty and Life Chances. Early Intervention: The Next Steps*. London: Her Majesty's Stationery Office.

Amos, A. (1993) 'In her own best interests? Women and health education: a review of the last fifty years', *Health Education Journal*, 52(3): 141–50.

Anda, R.F., Butchart, A., Felitti, V.J. and Brown, D.W. (2010) 'Building a framework for global surveillance of the public health implications of adverse childhood experiences', *American Journal of Preventive Medicine*, 39(1): 93–8.

Anderson, A.M. (1996) 'Factors influencing the father–infant relationship', *Journal of Family Nursing*, 2(3): 306–24.

Anderson, S. and Lightfoot, D. (2002) *The Language Organ: Linguistics as Cognitive Psychology*. Cambridge: Cambridge University Press.

Anning, A. (1999) 'The influence of socio-cultural context on young children's meaning making', paper given at the BERA (British Educational Research Association) Conference, Sussex University, England, 2–5 September.

Anning, A., Chesworth, E. and Spurling, L. (2005) *The Quality of Early Learning, Play and Childcare Services in Sure Start Local Programmes*. Research Report 09. Nottingham: Department for Education and Skills (DfES) Publications.

Anning, A., Cottrell, D., Frost, N., Green, J., Robinson, M. (2010) *Developing Multi-Professional Teamwork for Integrated Children's Services: Research, Policy and Practice* (2nd edn). Maidenhead: Open University Press.

Anning, A. and Edwards, A. (2006) *Promoting Young Children's Learning from Birth to Five: Developing the New Early Years Professional* (2nd edn). Maidenhead: Open University Press.

Anning, A. and members of the NESS implementation team (2007) *Understanding Variations in Effectiveness amongst Sure Start Local Programmes*. Research Report 024. Nottingham: DfES Publications.

Archard, D. (2004) *Children: Rights and Childhood* (2nd edn). London: Routledge.

Ariès, P. (1962) *Centuries of Childhood: A Social History of Family Life*. New York: Vintage.

Ashton, J. and Seymour, H. (1988) *The New Public Health*. Milton Keynes: Open University Press.

Atkinson, M., Wilkin, A., Stott, A., Doherty, P. and Kinder, K. (2002) *Multi-agency Working: A Detailed Study*. Slough: National Foundation for Educational Research.

Atkinson, M., Wilkin, A., Stott, A. and Kinder, K. (2001) *Multi-agency Working: An Audit of Activity*. Slough: National Foundation for Educational Research.

Atkinson, P. and Hammersley, M. (1998) 'Ethnography and participant observation and interviewing', in N. Denzin and Y. Lincoln (eds), *Strategies of Qualitative Inquiry*. Thousand Oaks, CA: Sage Publications, pp. 110–13.

Aubrey, C. (2011) *Leading and Managing in the Early Years* (2nd edn). London: Sage Publications.

Aubrey, C., Godfrey, R. and Harris, A. (2013) 'How do they manage? An investigation of early childhood leadership', *Educational Management, Administration and Leadership*, 41(1): 5–29.

Austin, L.M. (2003) 'Children of childhood: nostalgia and the romantic legacy', *Studies in Romanticism*, 42(1): 75–98.

Axline, V. (1969) *Play Therapy*. New York: Ballentine Books.

Baggerman, A. and Dekker, R.M. (2009) *Child of the Enlightenment: Revolutionary Europe Reflected in a Boyhood Diary*, Vol. 1. Brill: Academic Pub.

Baggott, R. (2011) *Public Health Policy and Politics* (2nd edn). London: Palgrave.

Bailey, R. (2011) *Letting Children Be Children. Report of an Independent Review of the Commercialisation and Sexualisation of Children*. London: Department for Education.

Bain, B. and Yu, A. (1980) 'Cognitive consequences of raising children bilingually: "one parent, one language"', *Canadian Journal of Psychology*, 34: 304–13.

Bainham, A. (2005) *Children: The Modern Law* (3rd edn). Bristol: Family Law.

Baldock, P., Fitzgerald, D. and Kay, J. (2013) *Understanding Early Years Policy* (3rd edn). London: Paul Chapman.

Baron-Cohen, S. (2011) *Zero Degrees of Empathy: A New Theory of Human Cruelty*. London: Allen Lane.

Barton, H. and Grant, M. (2006) 'A healthy map for the local human habitat', *Journal of the Royal Society for the Promotion of Health*, 126(6): 52–253.

Bates, E. and MacWhinney, B. (1982) 'A functionalist approach to grammatical development', in E. Wanner and L. Gleitman (eds), *Language Acquisition: The State of the Art*. Cambridge: Cambridge University Press.

BBC News (2010) *Shannon Matthews: Kirklees Social Services Cleared*. [Online] Available at: www.bbc.co.uk/news/10323906 (accessed 28/10/2012).

—— (2012) *Jimmy Savile Abuse Allegations: Timeline*. [Online] Available at: www.bbc.co.uk/news/uk-19921658 (accessed 28/10/2012).

Beatty, B., Cahan, E.D. and Grant, J. (2006) *When Science Encounters the Child: Education, Parenting, and Child Welfare in 20th-century America*. New York: Teachers College Press.

Bee, H.L. and Boyd, D.G. (2007) *The Developing Child* (11th edn). Boston MA: Pearson.

Belsky, J. (1996) 'Parent, infant and social-contextual antecedents of father–son attachment security', *Developmental Psychology*, 32(5): 905–13.

Belsky, J., Barnes, J. and Melhuish, E. (2007) *The National Evaluation of Sure Start. Does Area-based Early Intervention Work?* Bristol: The Policy Press.

Ben-Arieh, A. and Frønes, I. (2012) 'Taxonomy for child well-being indicators: a framework for the analysis of the well-being of children', *Childhood*, 18(4): 460–76.

Bendelow, G. (2009) *Health, Emotion and the Body*. Cambridge: Polity Press.

Bennett, N., Wood, E. and Rogers, S. (1997) *Teaching through Play: Teachers' Thinking and Classroom Practice*. Buckingham: Open University Press.

Berk, L.E. (2008) *Child Development* (8th edn). Boston, MA: Allyn and Bacon.

Berko Gleason, J. (2005) *The Development of Language.* Boston: Pearson Education Inc.

Berlyne, D.E. (1969) 'Laughter, humour and play', in G. Lindzey and E. Aronson (eds), *Handbook of Social Psychology.* Reading, MA: Addison-Wesley.

Bernier, A., Carlson, S.M. and Whipple, N. (2010) 'From external regulation to self-regulation: early parenting precursors of young children's executive functioning', *Child Development*, 81: 326–39.

Bernstein, B. (1981) 'Codes, modalities and the process of cultural reproduction: a model', *Language and Society*, 10: 327–63.

Berridge, D. (2012) 'Educating young people in care: what have we learned?', *Children and Youth Services Review*, 34(6): 1171–75.

Bertram, T. and Pascal, C. (2006) *The Baby Effective Early Learning Programme* (BEEL). Birmingham: Amber Publishing.

Bjorklund, D.F. (2011) *Children's Thinking: Cognitive Development and Individual Differences* (5th edn). Belmont, CA: Wadsworth.

Black, K. and Lobo, M. (2008) 'A conceptual review of family resilience factors', *Journal of Family Nursing*, 14(1): 33–55.

Blackmore, J. (1989) 'Educational leadership: a feminist critique and reconstruction', in J. Smyth (ed.), *Critical Perspectives on Educational Leadership.* London: Falmer.

Blair, C. (2002) 'School readiness: integrating cognition and emotion in a neurobiological conceptualization of children's functioning at school entry', *American Psychologist*, 57: 111–27.

—— (2010) 'Stress and the development of self regulation in context', *Child Development Perspectives*, 4(3): 181–8.

Blair, C. and Razza, R.P. (2007) 'Relating effortful control, executive function, and false-belief understanding to emerging math and literacy ability in kindergarten', *Child Development*, 78: 647–63.

Blaxter, M. (1990) *Health and Lifestyles.* London: Routledge.

—— (2010) *Health* (2nd edn). Cambridge: Polity Press.

Blenkin, G. and Kelly, A. (1987) *The Primary Curriculum.* London: Harper and Row.

Bloch, C. (2007) 'Foreign language learning in South Africa early childhood education', in M. Cochran and R. New (eds), *Encyclopedia of Early Childhood Education*, 4: 1224–26

Bloom, L. (1970) *Language Development: Form and Function in Emerging Grammars.* Cambridge, MA: MIT Press.

Boag-Munroe, G. (2012) 'Engaging "hard-to-reach" families: a view from the literature', in T. Papatheodorou (ed.), *Debates on Early Childhood Policies and Practices.* London: Routledge, pp.183–92.

Bohannon, N. and Stanowicz, L. (1988) 'The issue of negative evidence: adult responses to children's language errors', *Developmental Psychology*, 24: 684–9.

Boland, A.M., Haden, C.A. and Ornstein, P.A. (2003) 'Boosting children's memory by training mothers in the use of an elaborative conversational style as an event unfolds', *Journal of Cognition and Development*, 4: 39–65.

Booth, T. (2010) 'How should we live together? Inclusion as a framework of values for educational development'. Unpublished essay.

——— (2011) 'Curricula for the common school: what shall we tell our children?', *FORUM*, 53(1): 31–48.

——— (2012) *Introducing the Index for Inclusion*. Martin-Luther-Universität Halle-Wittenberg, 12 January. [Online] Available at: http://vimeo.com/37953068 (accessed 23/05/2012).

Booth, T. and Ainscow, M. (2011) *Index for Inclusion: Developing Learning and Participation in Schools*. Bristol: CSIE.

Booth, T. and Dyssegaard, B. (2008) *Quality Is Not Enough*. Copenhagen: Ministry of Foreign Affairs of Denmark, Danida. [Online] Available at: www.danidadevforum. um.dk/en/menu/Topics/QualityIsNotEnough.htm (accessed 05/05/2012).

Booth, T. and O'Connor, S. (2012) *Lessons from the Index for Inclusion: Developing Learning and Participation in Early Years and Childcare*. [Online] Available at: www. migration-boell.de/web/diversity/48_3380.asp (accessed 28/03/2013).

Booth, T., Ainscow, M. and Kingston, D. (2006) *Index for Inclusion: Developing Learning, Participation and Play in Early Years and Childcare* (2nd edn). Centre for Studies on Inclusive Education.

Bornstein, M.H. and Bruner, J.S. (eds) (1989) *Interaction in Human Development*. Hillsdale, NJ: Erlbaum.

Boseley, S. (2012) 'Ban under-threes from watching television, says study', *Guardian*, 9 October. [Online] Available at: www.guardian.co.uk/society/2012/oct/09/ban-under-threes-watching-television (accessed 19/12/2012).

Bossard, J. and Boll, E. (1966) *The Sociology of Child Development*. New York: Harper and Row.

Bourdieu, P. (1992) *The Logic of Practice*. Cambridge: Polity Press.

Bowlby, J. (1951) *Maternal Care and Mental Health. Report to the World Health Organization*. Geneva: World Health Organization.

——— ([1953] 1965) *Child Care and the Growth of Love*. Harmondsworth: Penguin.

——— (1988) 'Developmental psychiatry comes of age', *American Journal of Psychiatry*, 145: 1–10.

Bowman, B., Donovan, S. and Burns, S. (eds) (2001) *Eager to Learn: Educating our Preschoolers*. Washington, DC: National Academy Press.

Bozhovich, L.I. (2009) 'The social situation of child development', *Journal of Russian and East European Psychology*, 47: 59–86.

Braine, M. (1994) 'Is nativism sufficient?', *Journal of Child Language*, 21: 9–31.

Brannen, J., Heptinstall, E. and Bhopal, K. (2001) *Connecting Children: Care and Family Life*. London: Routledge Falmer.

Braungart-Rieker, J.M., Garwood, M.M., Powers, B.P. and Wang, X. (2001) 'Parental sensitivity, infant affect, and affect regulation: predictors of later attachment', *Child Development*, 72(1): 252–70.

Brehony, K.J. (2000) 'Montessori, individual work and individuality in the elementary school classroom', *History of Education*, 29(2): 115–28.

Britten, B. and Savill, R. (2008) 'Police fear internet cult inspires teen suicides', *Daily Telegraph*, 24 January. [Online] Available at: www.telegraph.co.uk/news/main. jhtml?xml=/news/2008/01/23/nsuicide123.xml (accessed 28/01/2012).

Broadhead, P., Howard, J. and Wood, J. (2010) *Play and Learning in the Early Years: From Research to Practice*. London: Sage Publications.

Bronfenbrenner, U. (1979) *The Ecology of Human Development*. Cambridge, MA: Harvard University Press.

—— (1986) 'Ecology of the family as a context for human development: research perspectives', *Developmental Psychology*, 22: 723–42.

—— (2005) *Making Human Beings Human: Bioecological Perspectives on Human Development*. Thousand Oaks, CA: Sage Publications.

Bronfenbrenner, U. and Ceci, S.J. (1994) 'Nature-nurture reconceptualised in developmental perspective: a bioecological model', *Psychological Review*, 101(4): 568–86.

Bronfenbrenner, U. and Morris, P.A. (1998) 'The ecology of developmental processes', in W. Damon (series ed.) and R.M. Lerner (vol. ed.), *Handbook of Child Psychology: Vol. 1. Theoretical Models of Human Development* (5th edn). New York: Wiley, pp. 993–1028.

Brooker, L. (2002) *Starting School – Young Children's Learning Cultures*. Buckingham: Open University Press.

Brown, F. (2003) *Playwork: Theory and Practice*. Buckingham: Open University Press.

Brown, R. and Ward, H. (2012) *Decision-making within a Child's Timeframe: An Overview of Current Research Evidence for Family Justice Professionals Concerning Child Development and the Impact of Maltreatment*. London: Childhood Wellbeing Research Centre.

Bruce, T. (1999) 'In praise of inspired and inspiring teachers', in L. Abbott and H. Moylett (eds), *Early Education Transformed*. London: Falmer.

Brumbaugh, C.C. and Fraley, R.C. (2006) 'The evolution of attachment in romantic relationships', in M. Mikulincer and G.S. Goodman (eds), *The Dynamics of Romantic Love: Attachment, Caregiving, and Sex*. New York: Guilford Press, pp. 71–101.

Bruner, J. (1974) 'Child's play', *New Scientist*, 62: 126–8.

—— (1983) *Child's Talk: Learning to Use Language*. Oxford: Oxford University Press.

—— (2000) 'Foreword', in J. DeLoache and A. Gottlieb (eds), *A World of Babies: Imagined Childcare Guides for Seven Societies*. Cambridge: Cambridge University Press.

Bruns, A. (2006) 'Towards produsage: futures for user-led content production', in F. Sudweeks, H. Hrachovec and C. Ess (eds), *Proceedings: Cultural Attitudes towards Communication and Technology 2006*. Perth: Murdoch University, pp. 275–84. [Online] Available at: http://snurb.info/files/12132812018_towards_produsage_0. pdf (accessed 02/03/2011).

Buckingham, D. (2000) *After the Death of Childhood: Growing Up in the Age of Electronic Media*. Cambridge: Polity Press.

—— (2007) 'Childhood in the age of global media', *Children's Geographies*, 5(1–2): 43–54.

Bullock, R., Courtney, M., Parker, R., Sinclair, I. and Thoburn, J. (2006) 'Can the corporate state parent?', *Children and Youth Services Review*, 28(11): 1344–58.

Burke, P. (2000) *A Social History of Knowledge: From Gutenberg to Diderot*. Cambridge: Polity Press.

Burke, A. and Marsh, J. (eds) (2013) *Children's Virtual Play Worlds: Culture, Learning and Participation*. New York: Peter Lang.

Burton, M., Cobb, E., Donachie, P., Judah, G., Curtis, V. and Schmidt, W.P. (2011) 'The effect of handwashing with water or soap on bacterial contamination of hands', *International Journal of Environmental Research and Public Health*, 8(1): 97–104.

Burts, D., Hart, C., Charlesworth, R. and Kirk, L. (1990) 'A comparison of frequency of stress behaviours observed in kindergarten children in classrooms with developmentally appropriate versus developmentally inappropriate instructional practices', *Early Childhood Research Quarterly*, 5: 407–23.

Busza, J., Castle, S. and Diarra, A. (2004) 'Trafficking and health', *British Medical Journal*, 328: 1369–71.

Butchart, A., Putney, H.T.F. and Kahane, T. (2006) *Preventing Child Maltreatment: A Guide to Taking Action and Generating Evidence*. Geneva: World Health Organization.

Butler, I. and Hickman, C. (2011) *Social Work with Children and Families: Getting into Practice* (3rd edn). London: Jessica Kingsley.

Bybee, J. and Scheibman, J. (1999) 'The effect of usage on degrees of constituency: the reduction of don't in English', *Linguistics*, 37: 575–96.

CACE (Central Advisory Council for Education) (1967) *The Plowden Report: Children and their Primary Schools*. Central Advisory Council for England. London: HMSO.

CAFCASS (2012) *Three Weeks in November … Three Years On … Cafcass Care Application Study 2012*. London: CAFCASS.

Calnan, M. (1987) *Health and Illness: The Lay Perspective*. New York: Tavistock.

Cameron-Faulkner, T., Lieven, E. and Tomasello, M. (2003) 'A construction based analysis of child directed speech', *Cognitive Science*, 27: 843–73.

Cannella, G.S. (1997) *Deconstructing Early Childhood Education: Social Justice and Revolution. Rethinking Childhood, Volume 2*. New York: Peter Lang.

Carlson, S. and Moses, L. (2001) 'Individual differences in inhibitory control and children's theory of mind', *Child Development*, 72: 1032–53.

Carr, M. (2001) *Assessment in Early Childhood Settings: Learning Stories*. London: Paul Chapman.

Carrington, S. and Robinson, R. (2004) 'A case study of inclusive school development: a journey of learning', *The International Journal of Inclusive Education*, 8(2): 141–53.

Carter, J. (2013) *School Improvement for all in Norfolk*. [Online] Available at: www.schools.norfolk.gov.uk/Teaching-and-learning/Indexforinclusion/index.htm (accessed 14/03/2013).

Cawson, P., Wattam, C., Brooker, S. and Kelly, G. (2000) *Child Maltreatment in the United Kingdom*. London, NSPCC.

Chabat, A. (Originator) and Balmes, T. (Director) (2009) *Babies*. France: StudioCanal.

Chabris, C. and Simons, D. (2011) *The Invisible Gorilla*: *And Other Ways our Intuition Deceives Us*. London: HarperCollins.

Chamberlain, T., George, N., Golden, S., Walker, F. and Benton, T. (2010) *Tellus4 National Report*. London: Department for Children, Schools and Families.

Children's Society (2010) *Understanding Children's Well-Being. A National Survey of Young People's Well-Being*. London: The Children's Society.

—— (2011) *How Happy Are Our Children?* London: The Children's Society.

—— (2012) *Promoting Positive Well-Being for Children. A Report for Decision-Makers in Parliament, Central Government and Local Areas*. London: The Children's Society.

Chomsky, N. (1959) 'A review of B.F. Skinner's "Verbal Behavior"', *Language*, 35: 26–58.

—— (1965) *Aspects of the Theory of Syntax*. Cambridge, MA: MIT Press.

—— (1995) *The Minimalist Program*. Cambridge, MA: MIT Press.

Christensen, P. and James, A. (eds) (2008) *Research with Children: Perspectives and Practices* (2nd edn). London: Routledge Falmer.

Clark, A. (2005) 'Ways of seeing: using the Mosaic approach to listen to young children's perspectives', in A. Clark, P. Moss and A. Kjørholt (eds), *Beyond Listening: Children's Perspectives on Early Childhood Services*. Bristol: Policy Press, pp. 29–49.

—— (2007) 'View from inside the shed: young children's perspectives of the outdoor environment', *Education 3–13*, 13(4): 349–63.

—— (2010) *Transforming Children's Spaces: Children's and Adults' Participation in Designing Learning Environments*. London: Routledge.

—— (2013) *Childhoods in Context*. Bristol: Policy Press

Clark, A. and Moss, P. (2001) *Listening to Young Children: The Mosaic Approach*. London: National Children's Bureau.

—— (2005) *Spaces to Play: More Listening to Young Children Using the Mosaic Approach*. London: National Children's Bureau.

—— (2011) *Listening to Young Children: The Mosaic Approach* (2nd edn). London: National Children's Bureau.

Clark, A., Moss, P. and Kjørholt, A. (eds) (2005) *Beyond Listening: Children's Perspectives on Early Childhood Services*. Bristol: Policy Press

Clay, M.M. (1966) 'Emergent reading behavior', unpublished doctoral dissertation, University of Auckland, New Zealand.

Clough, P. and Nutbrown, P. (2007) *A Student's Guide to Methodology* (3rd edn). London: Sage.

CMHO (Child and Maternal Health Observatory) (2012) *Child Health Profiles*. [Online] Available at: www.chimat.org.uk/profiles (accessed 23/11/2012).

Cockburn, T. (2013) *Rethinking Children's Citizenship*. Basingstoke: Palgrave Macmillan.

Cohen, S. (1987) *Folk Devils and Moral Panics: The Creation of the Mods and Rockers* (2nd edn). Oxford: Blackwell.

Coleman, M. (2001) *Women's as Head Teachers: Striking the Balance:* London: Trentham.

Corby, B., Shemmings, D. and Wilkins, D. (2012) *Child Abuse: An Evidence Base for Confident Practice*. Maidenhead, Open University Press.

Corsaro, W. (1985) *Friendship and Peer Culture in the Early Years*. Norwood, NJ: Ablex.

—— (2011) *The Sociology of Childhood* (3rd edn). London: Sage Publications.

Coulmas, F. (ed.) (1981) *Conversational Routine*. The Hague: Mouton.

Court, M. (1994) *Women Transforming Leadership*. Palmerston North, New Zealand: ERDC Press.

Cousins, J. (1999) *Listening to Four-year-olds*. London: National Early Years Network.

Cox, B.D., Blaxter, M., Buckle, A.L.J., Fenner, N.P., Golding, J.F., Gore, M., Huppert, F.A., Nickson, J., Roth, M., Stark, J., Wadsworth, M.E.J. and Whichelow, J.J. (1987) *The Health and Lifestyles Survey*. London: Health Promotion Trust.

CRPB (Curriculum Review Programme Board) (2006) *A Curriculum for Excellence: Progress and Proposals*. Edinburgh: Scottish Executive.

Crabbe, T. (2012) Early Years Graduate Leadership. *Presentation to the Early Childhood Studies Degrees Network*, 2 December, 2012. London: South Bank University. Unpublished presentation.

Cranston, M. (1967) 'Human rights, real and supposed', in D.D. Raphael (ed.), *Political Theory and the Rights of Man*. Bloomington, IN: Indiana University Press.

Croft, W. (2001) *Radical Construction Grammar: Syntactic Theory in Typological Perspective*. Oxford: Oxford University Press.

Cunningham, H. (2005) *Children and Childhood in Western Society since 1500* (2nd edn). Harlow: Pearson Press.

CWDC (Children's Workforce Development Council) (2006) *Early Years Professional Standards*. London: CWDC.

Dabrowska, E. (2000) 'From formula to schema: the acquisition of English questions', *Cognitive Linguistics*, 11: 1–20.

Dahlberg, G., Moss, P. and Pence, A. (2007) *Beyond Quality in Early Childhood Education and Care: Languages of Evaluation* (2nd edn). London: Routledge.

Dahlgren, G. and Whitehead, M. (1991) *Policies and Strategies to Promote Social Equity in Health*. Stockholm: Institute for Futures Studies.

Daniel, B., Taylor, J., Scott, J., Derbyshire, D. and Neilson, D. (2011) *Recognizing and Helping the Neglected Child: Evidence-based Practice for Assessment and Intervention*. London, Jessica Kingsley.

David, T. and Powell, S. (2005) 'Play in the early years: the influence of cultural difference', in J. Moyles (ed.), *The Excellence of Play*. Buckingham: Open University Press.

David, T., Goouch, K., Powell, S. and Abbott, L. (2003) *Birth to Three Matters: A Review of the Literature* (DFES Research Report No. 444). London: Department for Education and Skills (DFES).

Davidson, C. (2009) 'Young children's engagement with digital texts and literacies in the home: pressing matters for the teaching of English in the early years of schooling', *English Teaching: Practice and Critique*, 8(3): 36–54.

Davies, D. (1999) *Child Development: A Practitioner's Guide*. New York: Guilford Press.

Davis, J., Watson, N. and Cunningham-Burley, S. (2008) 'Disabled children, ethnography and unspoken understandings: the collaborative construction of diverse communities', in P. Christensen and A. James (eds), *Research with Children: Perspectives and Practices* (2nd edn). London: Routledge Falmer, pp. 220–38.

Daycare Trust and Family Parenting Institute (2013) *Childcare Costs Survey 2013*. London: Daycare Trust and Family Parenting Institute. [Online] Available at: www.daycaretrust.org.uk/data/files/Research/costs_surveys/Childcare_Costs_Survey_2013.pdf (accessed 01/03/2013).

DCELLS (Department for Children, Education, Lifelong Learning and Skills) (2008) *Framework for Children's Learning for 3- to 7-year-olds in Wales*. Cardiff: Welsh Assembly Government.

DCSF (Department for Children, Schools and Families) (2007) *Statutory Guidance on Promoting the Health and Well-being of Looked After Children*. Nottingham: DCSF.

—— (2008a) *Social and Emotional Aspects of Development*. Nottingham: DCSF.

—— (2008b) *The Sure Start Journey: A Summary of Evidence*. Nottingham: DCSF.

—— (2009a) *Every Child a Talker: Guidance for Consultants and Early Language Lead Practitioners, Third Instalment, Destination: Every Child a Talker*. Nottingham: DCSF.

—— (2009b) *Learning, Playing and Interacting – Good Practice in the Early Years Foundation Stage*. Nottingham: DCSF.

—— (2009c) *Next Steps for Early Learning and Childcare. Building on the Ten-Year Strategy*. Nottingham: DCSF.

—— (2009d) *Apprenticeships, Skills, Children and Learning Act*. London: HMSO.

De Houwer, A. (1995) 'Bilingual language acquisition', in P. Fletcher and B. MacWhinney (eds), *The Handbook of Child Language*. Oxford: Blackwell, pp. 219–50.

De Lange, A. (2005) 'Observations on Burkina Faso', unpublished paper presented at Childhoods in Emerging and Transforming Societies, 29 June–3 July, University of Oslo.

Degotardi, S. and Sweller, N. (2012) 'Mind-mindedness in infant child-care', *Early Childhood Research Quarterly*, 27: 253–65.

Demetras, M., Post, K. and Snow, C. (1986) 'Feedback to first language learners', *Journal of Child Language*, 13: 275–92.

DfE (Department for Education) (2012a) *Statutory Framework for the Early Years Foundation Stage. Setting the Standards for Learning, Development and Care for Children from Birth to Five.* London: DfE.

—— (2012b) *Multi-Agency Working.* [Online] Available at: www.education.gov.uk/childrenandyoungpeople/strategy/integratedworking/a0069013/multi-agency-working (accessed 01/03/2013).

—— (2012c) *Child Death Reviews: Year Ending 31 March 2012.* London: DfE.

—— (2012d) *Children Looked After by Local Authorities in England (Including Adoption), Statistical First Release*, SFR20/2012. [Online] Available at: www.education.gov.uk/researchandstatistics/statistics/allstatistics/a00213762/children-looked-after-las-england (accessed 25/11/2012).

—— (2013) *More Great Childcare. Raising Quality and Giving Parents More Choice.* London: DfE.

DfE and DH (Department for Education and Department of Health) (2011) *Supporting Families in the Foundation Years.* London: DfE.

DfES (Department for Education and Skills) (1998) *National Childcare Strategy.* London: HMSO.

—— (2003a) *Birth to Three Matters.* Nottingham: DfES.

—— (2003b) *Every Child Matters.* Green Paper. London: HMSO.

—— (2004) *What Works in Promoting Children's Mental Health.* Nottingham: DfES.

—— (2005) *Primary National Strategy Key Elements of Effective Practice (KEEP).* Nottingham: DfES /Sure Start.

—— (2006) *Childcare Act.* London: HMSO.

DH (Department of Health) (1992) *Health of the Nation. A Strategy for Health in England.* London: HMSO.

—— (1998) *Independent Inquiry into Inequalities in Health.* London: DH.

—— (2003) *Tackling Health Inequalities: A Programme for Action.* London: DH.

—— (2008) *Better Care: Better Lives – Improving Outcomes and Experiences for Children, Young People and their Families living with Life-Limiting and Life-Threatening Conditions.* London: DH.

—— (2009) *Healthy Child Programme. Pregnancy and the First Five Years of Life.* London: DH.

—— (2010a) *Healthy Lives, Healthy People. Our Strategy for Public Health in England.* London: DH.

—— (2010b) *Our Health and Wellbeing.* London: DH.

—— (2010c) *Confident Communities, Brighter Futures. A Framework for Developing Wellbeing.* London: DH.

—— (2011a) *Health Visitor Implementation Plan 2011–15. A Call to Action.* London: DH.

—— (2011b) *Healthy Lives, Healthy People. Update and Way Forward.* London: DH.

—— (2011c) *No Health without Mental Health.* London: HMSO.

—— (2011d) *The Evidence Base for Family Nurse Partnership*. [Online] Available at: http//fnp.dh.gov.uk/category/evidence-research/ (accessed 01/03/2013).

—— (2012a) *Improving Outcomes and Supporting Transparency. Part 1: A Public Health Outcomes Framework for England, 2013–2016*. London: DH.

—— (2012b) *Structure of Public Health England*. London: Public Health Transition Team, DH.

—— (2012c) *Healthy Lives, Healthy People: Towards a Workforce Strategy for the Public Health System*. London: DH.

Derman-Sparks, L. and Olsen Edwards, J. (2010) *Anti-bias Education for Young Children and Ourselves*. Washington, DC: National Association for the Education of Young Children.

Diamond, A., Barnett, W.S., Thomas, J. and Munro, S. (2007) 'Preschool program improves cognitive control', *Science*, 318:, 1387–8.

Dinsdale, H., Ridler, C. and Rutter, H. (2012) *National Child Measurement Programme: Changes in Children's Body Mass Index between 2006/7 and 2010/11*. Oxford: National Obesity Observatory.

Doddington, C. and Hilton, M. (2007) *Child-centred Education: Reviving the Creative Tradition*. London: Sage.

Dominici, G. ([1401] 1927) *On the Education of Children*. Washington DC: Catholic University of America.

Douglas, M. (1966, reissued 2006) *Purity and Danger: An analysis of concept of pollution and taboo*. Abingdon: Routledge Classics

Dowling, M. (2009) *Young Children's Personal, Social and Emotional Development* (3rd edn). London: Sage.

Downie, R.S., Fyfe, C. and Tannahill, A. (1990) *Health Promotion. Models and Values*. Oxford: Oxford University Press.

Draper, L. and Duffy, B. (2001) 'Working with parents', in G. Pugh (ed.), *Contemporary Issues in the Early Years*. London: Paul Chapman, pp. 151–62.

Drifte, C. (2004) *Encouraging Positive Behaviour in the Early Years*, London: Paul Chapman.

Duke, J. (2009) 'The use of the index for inclusion in a regional educational learning community' (Unpublished). [Online] Available at: http://eprints.qut.edu.au/29400/1/c29400.pdf (accessed 23/05/2012).

Duncan, G.J., Claessens, A., Huston, A.C., Pagani, L.S., Engel, M., Sexton, H., Dowsett, C.J., Magnuson, L., Klebanov, P., Feinstein, L., Brooks-Gunn, J., Duckworth, K. and Japel, C. (2007) 'School readiness and later achievement', *Developmental Psychology*, 43: 1428–46.

Duncan, P. (2007) *Critical Perspectives on Health*. London: Palgrave.

Dunford, J. (2010) *Review of the Office of the Children's Commissioner (England)*. London: The Stationery Office.

Dunn, J. (1984) *Sisters and Brothers*. London: Fontana.

—— (1993) *Young Children's Close Relationships: Beyond Attachment*. Newbury Park, CA: Sage Publications.

—— (1999) 'Mind reading and social relationships', in M. Bennett (ed.), *Developmental Psychology*. London: Taylor and Francis, pp. 55–71.

Dworkin, R. (1978) 'Liberalism', in S. Hampshire (ed.), *Public and Private Morality*. Cambridge: Cambridge University Press, pp. 113–43.

DWP/DfE (Department for Work and Pensions and Department for Education) (2011) *A New Approach to Child Poverty: Tackling the Causes of Disadvantage and Transforming Families' Lives*. London: HMSO.

Eade, J. and Valkanova, Y. (2009) *Accession and Migration: Changing Policy, Society and Culture in an Enlarged Europe*. Farnham: Ashgate.

Earle, S. (2007) 'Exploring Health', in S. Earle, C.E. Lloyd, M. Sidell and S. Spurr (eds), *Theory and Research in Promoting Public Health*. Milton Keynes: The Open University, pp. 37–66.

Early Education (2012) *Development Matters in the Early Years Foundation Stage*. London: Early Education, Crown copyright. [Online] Available at: www.early-education.org.uk and for download at: www.foundationyears.org.uk/early-years-foundation-stage-2012/ (accessed 20/12/2012).

Ebbeck, M. and Waniganayake, M. (2000) *Early Childhood Professionals: Leading Today and Tomorrow*. Eastgardens, NSW: McLennan and Petty.

Edwards, A. and Knight, P. (2000) *Effective Early Years Education – Teaching Young Children*. Buckingham: Open University Press.

Edwards, C., Gandini, L. and Forman, G. (1993) *The Hundred Languages of Children: The Reggio Emilia Approach to Early Childhood Education*. Norwood, NJ: Ablex Publishing.

Einarsdóttir, J. (2005) 'Playschool in pictures: children's photographs as a research method', *Early Childhood Development and Care*, 175(6): 523–42.

Eisenstadt, N. (2011) *Providing a Sure Start: How Government Discovered Early Childhood*. Bristol: The Policy Press.

Elfer, P. and Page, J. (2013) *Nursery Ratios and Babies Under 12 Months in Nursery*. London: Roehampton University.

Elfer, P., Goldschmied, E. and Selleck, D. (2011) *Key Persons in the Early Years. Building Relationships for Quality Provision* (2nd edn). London: Routledge.

Elkin, F. (1960) *The Child and Society: The Process of Socialisation*. New York: Random House.

Elkonin, D.B. (1999) 'Toward the problem of stages in the mental development of children', *Journal of Russian and East European Psychology*, 37(6): 11–30.

Elman, J.L. (2005) 'Connectionist models of cognitive development: where next?', *TRENDS in Cognitive Sciences*, 9: 111–17.

Emond, R. (2005) 'Ethnographic research methods with children and young people', in S. Greene and D. Hogan (eds), *Researching Children's Experience: Approaches and Methods*. London: Sage Publications, pp. 123–40.

Engeström, E. (ed) (1999) *Perspectives on Activity Theory*. New York: Cambridge University Press.

Erikson, E.H. (1977) *Toys and Reasons: Stages in the Ritualisation of Experience*. New York: Norton.

—— (1995) *Childhood and Society.* Vintage Books.

Erlandsson, K. and Fagerberg, I. (2005) 'Mothers' lived experiences of co-care and part-care after birth, and their strong desire to be close to their baby', *Midwifery*, 21: 131–8.

Evangelou, M., Sylva, K., Kyriacou, M., Wild, M. and Glenny, G. (2009) *Early Years Learning and Development Literature Review* Department for Children, Schools and Families, Research Report No. DCSF-RR176 [Online] Available at www.gov.uk/government/publications/early-years-learning-and-development-literature-review

Evans, L., Packwood, A., Neill, St. J. and Campbell, R.J. (1994) *The Meaning of Infant Teachers' Work*. London: Routledge.

EveryChild (2012) *Making Social Work Work: Improving Social Work for Vulnerable Families and Children Without Parental Care Around the World.* London: EveryChild.

Evetts, J. (1994) 'The new headteacher: the changing work culture of secondary headship', *School Organisation*, 14(1): 37–47.

Ewles, L. and Simnett, I. (1985) *Promoting Health. A Practical Guide*. London: Elsevier.

Fagan, R.M. (1984) 'Play and behavioural flexibility', in P.K. Smith (ed.), *Play in Animals and Humans.* Oxford: Basil Blackwell, pp. 159–73.

Fahlberg, V. (2012) *A Child's Journey through Placement*. London, Jessica Kingsley.

Farah, M.J., Shera, D.M., Savage, J.H., Betancourt, L., Giannetta, J.M., Brodsky, N.L., Malmud, E.K. & Hurt, H. (2006) 'Childhood poverty: Specific associations with neurocognitive development', *Brain Research*, 1110: 166–74.

Farmer, E., Sturgess, W., O'Neill, T. and Wijedasa, D. (2011) *Achieving Successful Returns from Care: What Makes Reunification Work?* London, BAAF.

Farrell, P. (2001) 'Special education in the last twenty years: have things really got better? British Journal of Special Education, 28(1): 3-9.

Fass, P. (2007) *Children of a New World: Society, Culture and Globalization*. New York: New York University Press.

Fass, P. (Ed.) (2013) *The Routledge History of Childhood in the Western World.* Abingdon: Routledge.

Fenwick, J., Barclay, L. and Schmied, V. (2008) 'Craving closeness: a grounded theory analysis of women's experiences of mothering in the Special Care Nursery', *Women and Birth*, 21: 71–85.

Ferguson, H. (2011), *Child Protection Practice*. Hampshire, Palgrave Macmillan.

Field, F. (2010) *The Foundation Years: Preventing Poor Children Becoming Poor Adults. The Report of the Independent Review on Poverty and Life Chances*. London: HM Government.

Fildes, V. (1995) 'The culture and biology of breastfeeding: an historical review of Western Europe', in P.S. Macadam and K.A. Dettwyler (eds), *Breastfeeding: Biocultural Perspectives.* New York: Aldine, pp. 101–26.

Fleer, M. (2010) *Early Learning and Development: Cultural-Historical Concepts in Play.* Cambridge: Cambridge University Press.

Fleer, M. and Hedegaard, M. (2010) 'Children's development as participation in everyday practices across different institutions', *Mind Culture and Activity*, 17: 149–68.

Flekkoy, M. and Kaufman, N. (1997) *The Participation Rights of the Child: Rights and Responsibilities in Family and Society.* London: Jessica Kingsley.

Ford, R.M., McDougall, S.P. and Evans, D. (2009) 'Parent-delivered compensatory education for children at risk of educational failure: improving the academic and self-regulatory skills of a Sure Start pre-school sample', *British Journal of Psychology*, 100: 773–97.

Fortin, J. (2009) *Children's Rights and the Developing Law* (3rd edn). London: Butterworth.

Fox, J.L., Diezmann, C.M. and Grieshaber, S.J. (2011) 'Teachers' and parents' perspectives of digital technology in the lives of young children', in S. Howard (ed.), *AARE Annual Conference 2010*, 28 November–2 December 2010, Melbourne, Australia. [Online] Available at: http://eprints.qut.edu.au/41179/ (accessed 01/03/2013).

Franklin, B. (ed.) (2002) *The New Handbook of Children's Rights.* London: Routledge.

Fraser, S. (2004) 'Situating empirical research', in S. Fraser, V. Lewis, S. Ding, M. Kellett and C. Robinson (eds), *Doing Research with Children and Young People.* London: Sage.

Freud, A. (1968) *The Psychoanalytic Treatment of Children.* New York: International Universities Press.

Freud, S. (1924) 'The loss of reality in neurosis and psychosis', *Standard Edition*, 19: 183–87.

Friendly, M. (2007) 'How ECEC programmes contribute to social inclusion in diverse societies', *Early Childhood Matters*, June: 11–14.

Frith, U. and Frith, C. (2001) 'The biological basis of social interaction', *Current Directions in Psychological Science*, 10: 151–5.

Gage, N. (1977) *The Scientific Basis for the Art of Teaching.* New York: Teachers College Press.

—— (1985) *Hard Gains in the Soft Science: The Case of Pedagogy.* Bloomington: Phi Delta Kappa CEDR Monograph.

García, E.E. (1983) *Early Childhood Bilingualism.* Albuquerque: University of New Mexico Press.

Garcia, M., Pence, A. and Evans, E. (eds) (2008) *Africa's Future, Africa's Challenge: Early Childhood Care and Development in Sub-Saharan Africa.* Washington: World Bank.

Garon, N., Bryson, S.E. and Smith, I.M. (2008) 'Executive function in preschoolers: a review using an integrative framework', *Psychological Bulletin*, 134: 31–60.

Garvey, C. (1991) *Play* (2nd edn). London: Fontana.

Gasper, M. (2010) *Multi-Agency Working in the Early Years: Challenges and Opportunities*. London: Sage.

Gauvain, M. (2001) *The Social Context of Cognitive Development*. New York: Guilford Press.

—— (2005) 'With eyes to the future: a brief history of cognitive development', *New Directions for Child and Adolescent Development*, 109: 119–126.

Geary, D.C. and Bjorklund, D.F. (2000) 'Evolutionary developmental psychology', *Child Development*, 71: 57–65.

Geertz, C (1973) *The Interpretation of Cultures*. New York: Basic Books.

Gerhardt, S. (2004) *Why Love Matters*. London: Taylor and Francis.

Giddens, A. (1976) *New Rules of Sociological Method: A Positive Critique of Interpretive Sociologies*. London: Hutchinson.

—— (1993) *Sociology*. Cambridge: Polity Press.

Gilbert, N., Parton, N. and Skivenes, M. (2011) 'Changing patterns of response and emerging orientations', in N. Gilbert, N. Parton and M. Skivenes (eds), *Child Protection Systems: International Trends and Orientations*. New York, Oxford University Press, pp.243-257.

Gilligan, C. (1982) *In a Different Voice: Psychological Theory and Women's Development*. Cambridge, MA: Harvard University Press.

Goddard, B. (2011) 'Education and wellbeing', in A. Knight and A. McNaught (eds), *Understanding Wellbeing. An Introduction for Students and Practitioners of Health and Social Care*. Banbury: Lantern, pp. 214–226.

Goldhaber-Fiebert, J.D., Lipsitch, M., Mahal, A., Zaslavsky, A.M. and Salomon, J.A. (2010) 'Quantifying child mortality reductions related to measles vaccination', *PLoS ONE*, 5(11): e13842. doi:10.1371/journal.pone.0013842.

Goldschmied, E. and Jackson, S. (2003) *People under Three: Young Children in Day Care*. London: Routledge.

Goleman, D. (2004) *Emotional Intelligence and Working with Emotional Intelligence*. London: Bloomsbury.

—— (2007) *Social Intelligence: The New Science of Human Relationships*. London: Arrow Books.

Goody, J. (1982) *Cooking, Cuisine and Class*. Cambridge: Cambridge University Press.

Goouch, K. and Powell, S (2013) *The Baby Room. Principles, Policy and Practice*. Maidenhead: Open University Press.

Goouch, K. and Powell, S. (2012) 'Who in the world cares for babies?' Keynote presentation at the *TACTYC Annual Research Conference*, Birmingham International Conference Centre, November 2012.

Gopnik, A. and Wellman, H. (1992) 'Why the child's theory of mind is really a theory', *Mind and Language*, 7: 145–71.

Gottleib, A. (2004) *The Afterlife Is Where We Come From: The Culture of Infancy in West Africa*. Chicago: University of Chicago Press.

Graves, R. (1960) *The Greek Myths. Vol. 1.* New York: Penguin.

Gray, D. and Watt, P. (2013) *Giving Victims a Voice: Joint Report into Sexual Allegations Made Against Jimmy Savile.* London: NSPCC and Metropolitan Police.

Green, L. (2010) *Understanding the Life Course: Sociological and Psychological Perspectives.* Cambridge: Polity Press.

—— (2012) 'Educating for health', in L. Jones and J. Douglas (eds), *Public Health: Building Innovative Practice.* Milton Keynes: Sage Publications/The Open University, pp. 277–314.

Greene, S. and Hill, M. (2005) 'Researching children's experience: methods and methodological issues', in S. Green and D. Hogan (eds), *Researching Children's Experience: Approaches and Methods.* London: Sage, pp. 1–21.

Greene, S. and Hogan, D. (eds) (2005) *Researching Children's Experience: Approaches and Methods.* London: Sage.

Guha, M. (1988) 'Play in school', in G. Blenkin and A. Kelly (eds), *Early Childhood Education.* London: Paul Chapman.

Guo, Yuhua (2000) 'Food and family relations: the generation gap at the table', in Jun Jing (ed.), *Feeding China's Little Emperors. Food, Children and Social Change.* Stanford, CA: Stanford University Press, pp. 94–113.

Hagekull, B., Stenberg, G. and Bohlin, G. (1993) 'Infant–mother social referencing interactions: description and antecedents in maternal sensitivity and infant irritability', *Early Development and Parenting*, 2(3): 183–91.

Halford, G.S. and Andrews, G. (2010) 'Information–processing models of cognitive development', in U. Goswami (ed.) *Wiley-Blackwell Handbook of Childhood Cognitive Development* (2nd edn). Oxford: Wiley-Blackwell.

Hall, V. (1996) *Dancing on the Glass Ceiling: A Study of Women Managers in Education.* London: Paul Chapman.

Handy, C. (1993) *Understanding Organisations* (4th edn). London: Penguin.

Harcourt, D., Perry, B. and Waller, T. (eds) (2011) *Researching Young Children's Perspectives: Debating Ethics and Dilemmas Of Educational Research with Children.* London: Routledge.

Hardman, C. (1978) 'Can there be an anthropology of children?' *Journal of the Anthropological Society Oxford*, 4(1): 85–99.

Hargreaves, D. (2010) *Creating a Self-Improving School System.* Nottingham: National College for School Leadership.

Haringey Local Safeguarding Children Board (2009) *Serious Case Review: Baby Peter. Executive Summary*, London: Haringey Children's Services Department.

Harms, T., Clifford, R.M. and Cryer, D. (1998) *Early Childhood Environmental Rating Scale* (revised edn) (ECERS-R). New York: Teachers College Press.

Harris, A., Day, C., Hadfield, M., Hopkins, D., Hargreaves, A. and Chapman, C. (2002) *Effective Leadership for School Improvement.* London: Routledge.

Harris, P. (1989) *Children and Emotion: The Development of Psychological Understanding.* Oxford: Blackwell.

Hart, R. (1979) *Children's Experience of Place*. New York: Irvington Publishers.

Hashim, I.M. (2006) *The Positives and Negatives of Children's Independent Migration: Assessing the Evidence and the Debates*. Sussex: Centre for Migration Research Working Paper T16. [Online] Available at: www.migrationdrc.org/publications/ working_papers/WP-T16.pdf (accessed 31/12/2012).

Hatch, J. (1990) 'Young children as informants in classroom studies', *Early Childhood Research Quarterly*, 5: 251–64.

Hayden, J. (1997) 'Directors of early childhood services: experience, preparedness and selection', *Australian Research in Early Childhood*, 8(1): 49–67.

—— (2009) *Our Advocacy Message: Early Childhood for Social Inclusion*. Australia: Bernard van Leer Foundation/ Macquarie University.

Heath, S.B. (1983) *Ways with Words*. Cambridge: Cambridge University Press.

—— (1986) 'What no bedtime story means: narrative skills at home and school', in B. Schieffelin and E. Ochs (eds), *Language Socialization Across Cultures*. Cambridge: Cambridge University Press, pp. 97–126.

Hedegaard, M. (2002) *Learning and Child Development: A Cultural-Historical Study*. Aarhus: Aarhus University Press.

—— (2012) 'Analyzing children's learning and development in everyday settings from a cultural-historical wholeness approach', *Mind Culture and Activity*, 19: 1–12.

Hedegaard, M. and Fleer, M. (2013) *Play, Leaning and Children's Development: Everyday Life in Families and Transition to School*. Cambridge University Press: New York.

Henderson, A. (ed.) (2011) *Insights into the Playgroup Movement: Equality and Autonomy in a Voluntary Organisation*. Stoke on Trent: Trentham Books.

Hendrick, H. (2003) *Child Welfare: Historical Dimensions, Contemporary Debates.* Bristol: Policy Press.

Hendry, J. (2008) *An Introduction to Social Anthropology: Sharing our Worlds* (2nd edn). Basingstoke: Palgrave MacMillan.

Hershman, D. and McFarlane, A. (2002) *Children Act Handbook*. Bristol: Family Law.

Heymann, J. (2002) 'Social transformations and their implications for the global demand for ECCE', *UNESCO Policy Brief 8*. [Online] Available at: www.unesco. org/education/ecf/briefs (accessed 06/03/2009).

Heywood, C. (2001) *A history of childhood: children and childhood in the West from medieval to modern times*. Cambridge: Polity Press.

Hicks, L. and Stein, M. (2009) *Neglect Matters: A Multi-agency Guide for Professionals Working Together on Behalf of Teenagers.* London: Department for Children, Schools and Families.

Hill, M. and Tisdall, K. (1997) *Children and Society*. Harlow: Longman.

Hill, M., Laybourn, A. and Borland, M. (1996) 'Engaging with primary-aged children about their emotions and well-being: methodological considerations', *Children and Society*, 10: 129–44.

HM Government (1989) *The Children Act*. London: HMSO.

—— (2004) *The Children Act*. London, HMSO.

HM Treasury (2004) *Choice for Parents, the Best Start for Children: A Ten Year Strategy for Childcare*. London: The Stationery Office.

Hoff, E. (2008) *Language Development* (4th edn). Belmont, CA: Wadsworth Publishing.

Holdsworth, A. (1988) *Out of the Dolls House*. London: BBC Books.

Holland, J. and Blackburn, J. (eds) (1998) *Whose Voice? Participatory Research and Policy Change*. London: Intermediate Technology Publications.

Holloway, S. and Valentine, G. (2000) *Children's Geographies: Playing, Living, Learning*. London: Routledge.

Holmes, L., McDermid, S., Padly, M. and Soper, J. (2012) *Exploration of the Costs and Impact of the Common Assessment Framework*. London: Department for Education.

Holt, J. (1975) *Escape from Childhood: The Needs and Rights of Children*. New York: Penguin.

Hopper, P. and Thompson, S. (1984) 'The discourse basis for lexical categories in universal grammar', *Language*, 60: 703–52.

Hopson, B. and Scally, M. (1981) *Lifeskills Teaching*. Maidenhead: McGraw-Hill.

Hornstein, D. and Lightfoot, N. (1981) *Explanations in Linguistics*. London: Longman.

Howard, J. (2002) 'Eliciting young children's perceptions of play, work and learning using the activity apperception story procedure', *Early Child Development and Care*, 127: 489–502.

Howard, J. and Fearn, M. (2011) 'Play as resource for children facing adversity: an exploration of indicative case studies', *Children and Society*, 26(6): 456–68.

Howard, J. and McInnes, K. (2012) 'The impact of children's perceptions of an activity as play rather than not play on emotional well-being', *Child: Care, Health and Development*, 6 June, DOI: 10.1111/j.1365-2214.2012.01405.x.

—— (2013) *The Essence of Play: A Practice Companion for Professionals Working with Children and Young People*. London: Routledge.

Howard, J. and Prendiville, E. (2008) 'Developmental and therapeutic play', *Ip-Dip: For Professionals in Play*, 5: 16–17.

Howard, J., Jenvey, V. and Hill, C. (2006) 'Children's categorisation of play and learning based on social context', *Early Child Development and Care*, 176: 379–93.

Howes, C., Hamilton, C.E. and Matheson, C.C. (1994) 'Maternal, teacher and child care history correlates of children's relationships with peers', *Child Development*, 65(1): 264–73.

Hughes, B. (1996) *A Playworker's Taxonomy of Play Types*. London: Playlink.

Hughes, C., Jaffee, S., Happe, F., Taylor, A., Caspi, A. and Moffitt, T. (2005) 'Origins of individual differences in theory of mind: from nature to nurture?', *Child Development*, 76: 356–70.

Hughes, F. (1999) *Children, Play and Development*. Boston, MA: Allyn and Bacon.

Hummel, S., Chilcott, J., Rawdin, A. and Strong, M. (2011) *Economic Outcomes of Early Years Programmes and Interventions Designed to Promote Cognitive, Social and Emotional Development among Vulnerable Children and Families. Part 2: Economic Model*. School of Health and Related Research, University of Sheffield.

Hutchby, I. and Moran-Ellis, J. (eds) (1998) *Children and Social Competence: Arenas of Action*. London: Falmer.

Hutchin, V. (2007) *Supporting Every Child's Learning in the EYFS*. London: Hodder Education.

Hutt, S.J., Tyler, S., Hutt, C. and Christopherson, H. (1989) *Play, Exploration and Learning*. London: Routledge.

Inhelder, B. and Piaget, J. (1958) *The Growth of Logical Thinking from Childhood to Adolescence: An Essay on the Construction of Formal Operational Structures*. New York: Basic Books.

Isenberg, J.P. and Quisenberry, N. (2002) *Play: Essential for all Children: A Position Paper of the Association for Childhood Education International*. [Online] Available at: www.ci.pleasanton.ca.us/services/recreation/gb/gb-playessentials.html (accessed 01/03/2013).

Jackson, B. and Jackson, S. (1979) *Childminder: A Study in Action Research*. London: Routledge.

Jackson, M. (1987) 'Making sense of school', in A. Pollard (ed.), *Children and Their Primary Schools: A New Perspective*. Lewes: Falmer, pp.81-5.

Jackson, S. (1993) 'Under-fives: thirty years of no progress?', in G. Pugh (ed.), *Thirty Years of Change for Children*. London: National Children's Bureau, pp. 19–114.

Jagger, G. and Wright, C. (eds) (1999) *Changing Family Values*. London: Routledge.

James, A. and James, A. (2012) *Key Concepts in Childhood Studies.* London: Sage.

James, A. and Prout, A. (1996) 'Strategies and structures: towards a new perspective on children's experiences of family life', in J. Brannen and M. O'Brien (eds), *Children in Families: Research and Policy.* London: Falmer, pp.41-52.

—— (eds) ([1990] 1997) *Constructing and Reconstructing Childhood: Contemporary Issues in the Sociological Study of Childhood*. London: Falmer.

James, A., Jenks, C. and Prout, A. (1998) *Theorizing Childhood*. Cambridge: Polity Press.

James, P. (2006) *Globalism, Nationalism, Tribalism. Bringing Theory Back In: Towards a Theory of Abstract Community, Volume 2*. London: Sage.

Jarvis, P. (2007) 'Monsters, magic and Mr Psycho: rough and tumble play in the early years of a primary school, a biocultural approach', *Early Years*, 27: 171–88.

Jenks, C. ([1996] 2005) *Childhood*. London: Routledge.

Jennings, S. (1999) *Introduction to Developmental Play Therapy*. London: Jessica Kingsley.

Johnson, G.M. (2010) 'Young children's internet use at home and school: patterns and profiles', *Journal of Early Childhood Research*, 8: 282–93.

Jones, N. with Vilar, E. (2008) 'Situating children in international development policy: challenges involved in successful evidence-informed policy-making', *Evidence and Policy*, 4(1): 31-51.

Jones-Devitt, S. (2011) 'Wellbeing and health', in A. Knight and A. McNaught (eds), *Understanding Wellbeing. An Introduction for Students and Practitioners of Health and Social Care*. Banbury: Lantern, pp. 23–36.

Kagan, J. (2010) *The Temperamental Thread*. New York: Dana Foundation.

Kalliala, M. (2006) *Play Culture in a Changing World*. Buckingham: Open University Press.

Karmiloff-Smith, A. (2010) 'Neuroimaging of the developing brain: taking 'developing' seriously. *Human Brain Mapping*, 31(6): 934–41.

Karnes, M., Shwedel, A. and Williams, M. (1983) 'A comparison of five different approaches for educating young children from low-income homes', in M. Kames, A. Shwedel and M. Williams (eds), *As the Twig Is Bent … Lasting Effects of Pre-school Programmes*. Hillsdale, NJ: Erlbaum. pp. 133–70.

Karras, R.M. (2003) *From Boys to Men: Formation of Masculinity in Late Medieval Europe*. Philadelphia: University of Pennsylvania Press.

Karrby, G. (1989) 'Children's conceptions of their own play', *International Journal of Early Childhood Education*, 21(2): 49–54.

Katz, C. (2004) *Growing Up Global: Economic Structuring and Children's Everyday Lives*. Minnesota: University of Minnesota Press.

Keck, M.E. and Sikkink, K. (1998) *Activists Beyond Borders*. New York: Cornell University Press.

Kehily, M.J. (2009) 'Children, young people and sexuality', in H. Montgomery and M. Kellett (eds), *Children and Young People's Worlds: Developing Frameworks for Integrated Practice*. Bristol: Policy Press, pp.219-236.

Kellett, M. (2005) *How to Develop Children as Researchers: A Step by Step Guide to Teaching the Research Process*. London: Paul Chapman.

—— (2010) *Rethinking Children and Research: Attitudes in Contemporary Society*. London: Continuum.

Kelly, C. (2007) *Children's World: Growing Up in Russia 1890–1991*. New Haven: Yale University Press.

Kennedy, I. (2010) *Getting it Right for Children and Young People: Overcoming Cultural Barriers in the NHS so as to Meet their Needs*. London: Department of Health.

Kenway, J. and Bullen, E. (2001) *Consuming Children: Education – Entertainment – Advertising*. Buckingham: Open University Press.

Kernan, M., Singer, E. and Swinnen, R. (2011) 'Introduction', in M. Kernan and E. Singer (eds), *Peer Relationships in Early Childhood Education and Care*. London: Routledge, pp. 1–14.

Kiernan, K. and Mensah, F. (2011) *PREview: Maternal Indicators in Pregnancy and Children's Infancy that Signal Future Outcomes for Children's Development, Behaviour and Health: Evidence from the Millennium Cohort Study*. Yorkshire and Humber: CHIMAT.

Kinder, M. (1993) *Playing with Power in Movies, Television, and Videogames: From Muppet Babies to Teenage Mutant Ninja Turtles*. Berkeley: University of California Press.

King, L. (2011) *Telling it Like it Is. Children and Young People Speak Out About Their Experiences of Living in Poverty in the UK Today*. London: Save the Children.

King, P. and Howard, J. (2012) 'Children's perceptions of choice in relation to their play at home, in the school playground and at the out-of-school club', *Children and Society*, DOI:10.1111/j.1099-0860.2012.00455.x.

King, R. (1979) *All Things Bright and Beautiful? A Sociological Study of Infant Classrooms*. Bath: Wiley.

Kjørholt, A.K. (2007) 'Childhood as a symbolic space: searching for authentic voices in the era of globalisation', *Children's Geographies*, 5(1–2): 29–42.

Klapisch-Zuber, C. (1987) *Women, Family and Ritual in Renaissance Italy*. London: University of Chicago Press.

Kline, N. (1999) *Time to Think, Listening to Ignite the Human Mind*. London: Ward Lock.

Kuhn, T. (1970) *The Structure of Scientific Revolutions* (2nd edn). Chicago, IL: University of Chicago Press.

Laevers, F. (1995) *An Exploration of the Concept of Involvement as an Indicator for Quality in Early Childhood Education*. Dundee: Scottish Consultative Council on the Curriculum.

—— (ed.) (1994) *The Leuven Involvement Scale for Young Children* (manual and video), Experiential Education Series, No.1. Leuven: Centre for Experiential Education.

Laming, Lord (2003) *The Victoria Climbié Inquiry: Report of an Inquiry by Lord Laming*. Cmnd 5370. London: The Stationery Office. [Online] Available at: www.dh.gov.uk/prod_consum_dh/groups/dh_digitalassets/documents/digitalasset/dh_110711.pdf (accessed 15/3/2013).

Landreth, G. (2002) *Play Therapy: The Art of the Relationship*. London: Brunner-Routledge.

Landry, S.H., Smith, K.E., Swank, P.R. and Guttentag, C. (2008) 'A responsive parenting intervention: the optimal timing across early childhood for impacting maternal behaviors and child outcomes', *Developmental Psychology*, 44(5): 1335–53.

Lane, J. (2008) *Young Children and Racial Justice*. London: National Children's Bureau.

Langacker, R.W. (1987) *Foundations of Cognitive Grammar: Theoretical Prerequisites*. Stanford, CA: Stanford University Press.

—— (1991) *Concept, Image, and Symbol: The Cognitive Basis of Grammar*. Berlin and New York: Mouton de Gruyter.

Langsted, O. (1994) 'Looking at quality from the child's perspective', in P. Moss and A. Pence (eds), *Valuing Quality in Early Childhood Services: New Approaches for Defining Quality*. London: Paul Chapman, pp.28-42.

Langston, A. (2011) 'A guide to the revised EYFS: part 2 – observation and planning', *Nursery World*, 4 October.

Lankshear, C. and Knobel, M. (2011) *New Literacies: Everyday Practices and Classroom Learning* (3rd edn). Maidenhead, Berkshire: Open University Press.

Lareau, A. (2000) 'Social class and the daily lives of children: a study from the United States', *Childhood*, 7(2): 155–71.

—— (2003) *Unequal Childhoods: Class, Race and Family Life*. Berkeley, CA: University of California Press.

Larson, J. and Marsh, J. (2012) *The Sage Handbook of Early Childhood Literacy* (2nd edn). London: Sage.

Lee, N. (2001) *Childhood and Society: Growing Up in an Age of Uncertainty*. Buckingham: Open University Press.

Legerstee, M., Haley, D..and Bornstein, M. (eds) (2013) *The Infant Mind: Origins of the Social Brain,* New York: Guilford Press.

Leontiev, A.N. (1978) *Activity, Consciousness and Personality*. Englewood Cliffs, NJ: Prentice Hall.

—— (1981) *Problems of the Development of Mind*. Moscow: Moscow University Press.

LeVine, R.A. and New, R. (eds) (2008) *Anthropology and Child Development: A Cross-cultural Reader*. Oxford: Blackwell.

Levy, R. (2011) *Young Children Reading at Home and at School*. London: Sage.

Lewis I. and Lenehan, C. (chairs) (2012) *Report of the Young People's Health Outcomes Forum*. London: Department of Health.

Lewis, J. (2012) 'The failure to expand childcare provision and to develop a comprehensive childcare policy in Britain during the 1960s and 1970s', *Twentieth Century British History*, DOI:10.1093/tcbh/hws011.

Lewis, M.D. (2000) 'The promise of dynamic systems approaches for an integrated account of human development', *Child Development*, 71: 36–43.

Lewis, V., Kellett, M., Robinson, C., Fraser, S. and Ding, S. (eds) (2004) *The Reality of Research with Children and Young People*. London: Sage.

Liebel, M. (2004) *A Will of Their Own: Cross Cultural Perspectives on Working Children*. London: Zed Books.

Lieberman, J.N. (1977) *Playfulness: Its Relationship to Imagination and Creativity*. London: Academic Press.

Lieven, E. (1994) 'Crosslinguistic and crosscultural aspects of language addressed to children', in C. Gallaway and B.J. Richards (eds), *Input and Interaction in Language Acquisition*. Cambridge: Cambridge University Press, pp. 56–73.

Lieven, E., Pine, J.M. and Baldwin, G. (1997) 'Lexically based learning and early grammatical development', *Journal of Child Language*, 24: 187–219.

Lieven, E., Behrens, H., Spears, J. and Tomasello, M. (2003) 'Early syntactic creativity: a usage-based approach', *Journal of Child Language*, 30: 333–70.

Lifton, B. (1988) *King of Children: A Biography of Janusz Korczak*. New York: Farrar, Straus and Giroux.

Lindon, J. (2001) *Understanding Children's Play*. Cheltenham: Nelson Thomas.

—— (2012) *Equality and Inclusion in Early Childhood* (2nd edn). Oxon: Hodder Education.

Livingstone, S. (2002) *Young People and New Media*. London: Sage.

Lloyd, E. and Penn, H. (2013) *Childcare Markets: Can They Deliver an Equitable Service?* Bristol: Policy Press.

Loukidou, E., Ioannidi, V. and Kalokerinou-Anagnostopoulou, A. (2009) 'Nursing as emotional labour: a specialised pedagogical approach as the new challenge and innovative educational intervention for health promotion', *17th International Conference on Health Promoting Hospitals and Health Services (HPH)*, Hersonissos, Crete, Greece, 6–8 May.

Lowe, R. (1980) 'Eugenics and education: a note on the origins of the intelligence testing movement in England', *Educational Studies*, 6(1): 1–8.

Luke, A. and Luke, C. (2001) 'Adolescence lost/childhood regained: on early intervention and the emergence of the techno-subject', *Journal of Early Childhood Literacy*, 1: 91–120.

Lupton, D. (1995) *The Imperative of Health: Public Health and the Regulated Body*. London: Sage.

Lust, B. (2006) *Child Language: Acquisition and Growth*. Cambridge: Cambridge University Press.

Lyon, C. (2007) 'Interrogating the concentration on the UNCRC instead of the ECHR in the development of children's rights in England?' *Children & Society*, 21(2): 147–153.

Mabbott, J. (2010) 'The "reading war" in early childhood education: a Marxist history', unpublished EdD thesis, The University of Sheffield.

MacFadyen, U. (2010) 'Do babies have rights?', *Action for Sick Children (Scotland) Conference*, Glasgow Royal Concert Hall, 14 September.

Mahon, M. and Crutchley, A. (2006) 'Performance of typically-developing school-age children with English as an additional language (EAL) on the British Picture Vocabulary Scales II (BPVS II)', *Child Language Teaching and Therapy*, 22(3): 333–53.

Makhmalbaf, H. (2007) *Buddha Collapsed Out of Shame*. Iran: Makhmalbaf Film Studio.

Malaguzzi, L. (1993) 'History, ideas and basic philosophy', in C. Edwards, L. Gandini and G. Forman (eds), *The Hundred Languages of Children: The Reggio Emilia Approach to Early Childhood Education*. Norwood, NJ: Ablex Publishing, pp. 41–89.

Malkovich, A. (2013) *Charles Dickens and the Victorian Child: Romanticizing and Socializing the Imperfect Child*. New York: Routledge.

Mandell, N. (1991) 'The least-adult role in studying children', in F.C. Waksler (ed.), *Studying the Social Worlds of Children: Sociological Readings*. London: Falmer, pp. 38–59.

Manzo, K. (2005) 'Exploiting West Africa's children: trafficking slavery and uneven development', *Area*, 37(4): 393–401.

Marcus, I.G. (1996) *Rituals of Childhood: Jewish Acculturation in Medieval Europe*. New Haven, CT: Yale University Press.

Marmot, M. (2010) *Fair Society, Healthy Lives: A Strategic Review of Health Inequalities in England Post-2010*. London: University College of London.

Marsh, J. (2005) (ed.) *Popular Culture, Media and Digital Literacies in Early Childhood*. London: Routledge Falmer.

—— (2010a) 'Young children's play in online virtual worlds', *Journal of Early Childhood Research*, 8: 23–39.

—— (2010b) 'New literacies, old identities: young girls' experiences of digital literacy at home and school', in C. Jackson, C. Paechter and E. Reynolds (eds), *Girls and Education 3–16: Continuing Concerns, New Agendas*. Buckingham: Open University Press, pp. 197–209.

—— (2011) 'Young children's literacy practices in a virtual world: establishing an online interaction order', *Reading Research Quarterly*, 46(2): 101–18.

Marsh, J., Brooks, G., Hughes, J., Ritchie, L. and Roberts, S. (2005) *Digital Beginnings: Young Children's Use of Popular Culture, Media and New Technologies*. Sheffield: University of Sheffield. [Online] Available at: www.digitalbeginings.shef.ac.uk/ (accessed 19/12/2012).

Mathers, S., Ranns, H., Karemaker, A., Moody, A., Sylva, K., Graham, J. and Siraj-Batchford, I. (2011) *Evaluation of the Graduate Leader Fund: Final Report (RR144)*. London: DfE Publications.

Maude, P., Whitehead, M. Cushing, A. and Crisp, M. (2006) *Observing and Analysing Learners' Movements*. Worcester: Tacklesport Consultancy Ltd.

Mayall, B. (ed.) (1994) *Children's Childhoods: Observed and Experienced*. London: Falmer.

—— (2000) 'Conversations with children: working with generational issues', in P. Christensen and A. James (eds), *Research with Children*. London: Routledge Falmer.

—— (2002) *Towards a Sociology for Childhood: Thinking from Children's Lives*. Buckingham: Open University Press.

Maybin, J. and Woodhead, M. (eds) (2003) *Childhoods in Context*. Chichester: John Wiley.

Maynard, T., Taylor, C., Waldron, S., Smith, R., Power, S. and Clement, J. (2013) *Evaluating the Foundation Phase: Policy Logic Model and Programme Theory*, Cardiff: Welsh Government Social Research. [Online] Available at: http://wales.gov.uk/about/aboutresearch/social/latestresearch/evaluating-foundation-phase-policy-logic-model-programme-theory/?lang=en (accessed 01/03/2013).

McGuire, J. (1991) 'Social interactions of young, withdrawn children in day nurseries', *Journal of Reproductive and Infant Psychology*, 9: 169–79.

McInnes, K., Howard, J., Miles, G.E. and Crowley, K. (2009) 'Behavioural differences exhibited by children when practising a task under formal and playful conditions', *Educational and Child Psychology*, 26(2): 31–9.

—— (2010) 'Differences in adult–child interactions during playful and formal practice conditions: an initial investigation', *The Psychology of Education Review*, 34(1): 14–20.

—— (2011) 'Differences in practitioners' understanding of play and how this influences pedagogy and children's perceptions of play', *Early Years: An International Journal of Research and Development*, 31(2): 121–33.

McKeown, T. (1976) 'The medical contribution', reproduced in B. Davey, A. Gray and C. Seale (eds) (2001) *Health and Disease: A Reader* (3rd edn). Buckingham: Open University Press.

McMullen, M. (2012) 'The deliberate professional' (a personal communication) cited in K. Goouch and S. Powell (forthcoming), 'Who do we think they are? Roles, responsibilities and identities of baby room staff working in full daycare settings in England', *International Journal of Early Years Education*.

McNeill, D. (1966) 'The creation of language by children', in J. Lyons and R.J. Wales (eds), *Psycholinguistic Papers: The Proceedings of the 1966 Edinburgh Conference*. Edinburgh: Edinburgh University Press.

Mead, M. (1954) *Growing Up in New Guinea*. Louisiana: Pelican.

Mehmet, N. (2011) 'Ethics and wellbeing', in A. Knight and A. McNaught (eds), *Understanding Wellbeing. An Introduction for Students and Practitioners of Health and Social Care*. Banbury: Lantern, pp. 37–49.

Meins, E., Munoz Cenlifanti, L.C., Fernyhough, C. and Fishburn, S. (2013) 'Maternal mind-mindedness and children's behavioural difficulties: mitigating the impact of low SES', *Journal of Abnormal Child Psychology*, doi: 10.1007/s10802-012-9699-3.

Messenger, W. (2012) 'the influence of professional cultures on collaborative working in children's centres', unpublished PhD thesis, University of Worcester.

Mikulincer, M. and Shaver, P.R. (2007) *Attachment in Adulthood: Structure, Dynamics, and Change*. New York: Guilford Press.

Miller, R. and Bizzell, R. (1983) 'The Louisville experiment: a comparison of four programmes', in M. Karnes, A. Shwedel and M. Williams (eds), *As the Twig Is Bent … Lasting Effects of Pre-school Programmes*. Hillsdale, NJ: Erlbaum, pp. 171–200.

Mintz, S. (2004) *Huck's Raft: A History of American Childhood*. Cambridge, MA: Belknap Press.

Mitchell, C. (2011) *Doing Visual Research*. London: Sage.

Moll, L.C., Amanti, C., Neff, D., Gonzalez, N. (1992) 'Funds of knowledge for teaching: using a qualitative approach to connect homes and classrooms', *Theory into Practice*, 31(2): 132–41.

Montessori, M. ([1949] 1967) *The Absorbent Mind*. New York: Dell.

Mortimer, H. (2001) *Special Needs and Early Years Provision*. London: Continuum.

Morrow, V. (1998) *Understanding Families: Children's Perspectives*. London: National Children's Bureau.

Mosley, M. (2010) *The Story of Science. Power, Proof and Passion*. London: Mitchell Beazley, Octopus Publishing.

Moss, P. (2011) *Democracy as First Practice in Early Childhood Education and Care.* [Online] Available at: www.child-encyclopedia.com/documents/MossANGxp1.pdf (accessed 23/05/2012).

Moss, P. and Lloyd, E. (2013) 'Is England really near the top of the league?', *Nursery World*, 8–12 April.

Moyles, J.K. (2006) *Effective Leadership and Management in the Early Years.* Maidenhead: Open University Press.

Moylett, H. (2013) *Learning and Teaching in the Early Years: Active Learning.* London: Practical Pre-School Books/MA Education.

Moylett, H. and Stewart, N. (2012) *Understanding the Revised Early Years Foundation Stage.* London: Early Education

Muijs, D., Aubrey, C., Harris, A. and Briggs, M. (2004) 'How do they manage? Research in leadership in early childhood', *Journal of Early Childhood Research*, 2(2): 157–70.

Munck, T. (2000) *The Enlightenment. A Comparative Social History, 1721–1794.* London: Hodder Education.

Munro, E. (2011) *The Munro Review of Child Protection. Part One: A Systems Analysis.* London: Department for Education.

Muscroft, S. (ed.) (1999) *Children's Rights: Reality or Rhetoric? The UN Convention on the Rights of the Child – The First Ten Years.* London: Save the Children.

Myers, R. and Bronfenbrenner, U. (1992) *The Twelve Who Survive: Strengthening Programmes of Early Childhood Development in the Third World.* Abingdon: Routledge

Nardi, B.A. and O'Day, V.L. (1999) *Information Ecologies: Using Technology with Heart.* The MIT Press, Cambridge.

National Audit Office (1996) *Health of the Nation. A Progress Report.* London: HMSO.

National Research Council and Institute of Medicine (2000) *From Neurons to Neighbourhoods: The Science of Early Childhood Development*, ed. J. Shonkoff and D. Phillips. Washington, DC: National Academy Press.

Nederveen Pieterse, J. (2004) *Globalization and Culture: Global Melange.* Oxford: Rowman and Littlefield.

NESS (National Evaluation of Sure Start (2011) *The Impact of Sure Start Local Programmes on Five Year Olds and Their Families. Report of the Longitudinal Study of 5-year-old Children and Their Families.* London: Department for Education.

NESSE (Networks of Experts in Social Sciences of Education and training) (2012) *Mind the Gap: Education Inequality Across EU Regions.* [Online] Available at: www.nesse.fr/nesse/activities/reports/mind-the-gap-1 (accessed 01/03/2013).

New Zealand Ministry of Education (1996) *Te Whariki: Every Childhood Curriculum.* Wellington, NZ: Learning Media Ltd.

NICE (National Institute for Health and Care Excellence) (2012) *NICE Guidance on Social and Emotional Wellbeing – Early Years*. London: National Institute for Health and Care Excellence.

NICHD Early Child Care Research Network (2006) 'Infant–mother attachment classification: risk and protection in relation to changing maternal caregiving quality', *Developmental Psychology*, 42(1): 38–58.

Nieuwenhuys, O. (1996) 'The paradox of child labour and anthropology', *Annual Review of Anthropology*, 25: 237–51.

Ninio, A. and Snow, C. (1999) 'The development of pragmatics: learning to use language appropriately', in T.K. Bhatia and W.C. Ritchie (eds), *Handbook of Language Acquisition*. New York: Academic Press, pp. 347–86.

Noble, K.G., Tottenham, N. and Casey, B.J. (2005) 'Neuroscience perspectives on disparities in school readiness and cognitive achievement', *The Future of Children*, 15: 71–89.

Norfolk County Council Index for Inclusion Action Research project (2013–2015). [Online] Available at: www.schools.norfolk.gov.uk/Teaching-and-learning/Indexforinclusion/index.htm (accessed 01/03/2013).

Noriuchi, M., Kikuchi, Y. and Senoo, A. (2008) 'The functional neuroanatomy of maternal love: mother's response to infant's attachment behaviors', *Biological Psychiatry*, 63: 415–23.

NPHO (Network of Public Health Observatories) (2012) *Health Profiles*. [Online] Available at: www.apho.org.uk/default.aspx?RID=49802 (accessed 23/11/2012).

Nuffield Council on Bioethics (2007) *Public Health Ethical Issues*. Cambridge: Cambridge Publishers.

Nutbrown, C. (2011) *Key Concepts in Early Childhood Education and Care*. London: Sage.

—— (2012) *Foundations for Quality: The Independent Review of Early Education and Childcare Qualifications*. London: Department for Education.

—— (2013) *Shaking the Foundations of Quality? Why 'Childcare' Policy Must Not Lead to Poor Quality Early Education and Care*. Sheffield: University of Sheffield.

Oates, J. (ed.) (2007) *Attachment Relationships*. Milton Keynes. The Open University.

O'Brien, M., Alldred, P. and Jones, D. (1996) 'Children's constructions of family and kinship', in J. Brannen and M. O'Brien (eds), *Children in Families: Research and Policy*. London: Falmer, pp. 84–100.

Ochs, E. (1985) 'Variation and error: a sociolinguistic approach to language acquisition in Samoa', in D.I. Slobin (ed.), *The Crosslinguistic Study of Language Acquisition, Vol. I*. Hillsdale, NJ: Erlbaum.

Ochs, E. and Schieffelin, B.B. (1995) 'The impact of language socialization on grammatical development', in P. Fletcher and B. MacWhinney (eds), *The Handbook of Child Language*. Oxford: Blackwell, pp. 73–94.

OECD (Organisation for Economic Co-operation and Development) (2004) *Starting Strong: Curricula and Pedagogies in Early Childhood Education and Care: Five*

Curriculum Outlines. Paris: OECD Directorate for Education. [Online] Available at: www.oecd.org/dataoecd/23/36/31672150.pdf (accessed 06/03/2009).

—— (2006) *Starting Strong II: Early Childhood Education and Care.* Paris: OECD Publications. [Online] Available at: www.oecd.org/newsroom/37425999.pdf (accessed 31/12/2012).

—— (2009) *Doing Better for Children.* Paris: OECD Publishing.

—— (2011) *Doing Better for Families. United Kingdom.* OECD Publishing.

—— (2012) *OECD Internet Economy Outlook 2012.* Paris: OECD Publishing, 11 October 2012. [Online] Available at: www.oecd.org/sti/interneteconomy/ieout-look.htm (accessed 19/12/2012).

Oerter, R. (1993) *The Psychology of Play: An Activity Oriented Approach.* Munich: Quintessenz.

Ofcom (2012) *Children and Parents: Media Use and Attitudes Report. October 2012.* [Online] Available at: http://stakeholders.ofcom.org.uk/binaries/research/media-literacy/oct2012/main.pdf (accessed 19/12/2012).

Ofsted (Office for Standards in Education) (1993) *First Class: The Standards and Quality of Education in Reception Classes.* London: HMSO.

—— (2005) *Firm Foundations.* [Online] Available at: www.ofsted.gov.uk (accessed 01/03/2013).

—— (2009) *Childcare Groups: A Passion to Be Outstanding,* No. 090108. Manchester: Office for Standards in Education.

—— (2012a) *Annual Report 2011–12.* London: Department for Education.

—— (2012b) *Evaluation Schedule for Inspections of Registered Early Years Provision,* No. 120086. Manchester: Office for Standards in Education.

—— (2012c) *No Place for Bullying.* London: Office for Standards in Education.

O'Neill, O. (1992) 'Children's rights and children's lives', in P. Alston, S. Parker and J. Seymour (eds), *Children, Rights and the Law.* Oxford: Oxford University Press, pp. 24–42.

Osborn, A., Butler, N.R. and Morris, A.C. (1984) *The Social Life of Britain's Five-year-olds.* London: Routledge and Kegan Paul.

Oswald, M. (2010) 'Teacher learning during the implementation of the index for inclusion in a primary school', unpublished dissertation. Stellenbosch University.

Oswell, D. (2013) *The Agency of Children: From Family to Global Human Rights.* Cambridge: Cambridge University Press.

Owusu-Bempah, K. (2007) *Children and Separation. Socio-genealogical Connectedness Perspective.* London: Routledge.

Page, J., Nutbrown, C. and Clare, A. (2013) *Working with babies and young children from birth to three* (2nd edition). London: Sage.

Palmer, S. (2006) *Toxic Childhood.* London: Orion Press.

Palmieri, M. ([1429] 1825) *Della vita civile* [*Civil Life*] (Vol. 160). G. Silvestri. 1825.

Parry-Langdon, N. (ed.) (2008) *Three Years On: Survey of the Development and Emotional Well-Being of Children and Young People.* London: The Office for National Statistics.

Parton, N. (1985) *The Politics of Child Abuse*. Basingstoke, Macmillan.

Pascal, C. and Bertram, A. (1995) *Evaluating and Developing Quality in Early Childhood Settings: A Professional Development Programme*. Worcester: Amber Publishing Co. Ltd.

—— (1997) 'A conceptual framework for evaluating effectiveness in early childhood settings', in M.K. Lohmander (ed.), *Researching Early Childhood, Vol. 3, Settings in Interaction*. Gothenburg: Göteborg University, Early Childhood Research and Development Centre. pp. 125–50.

Pascal, C., Bertram, A., Ramsden, F. and Saunders, M. (2001) *Effective Early Learning Programme* (EEL) (3rd edn). University College Worcester: Centre for Research in Early Childhood Education.

Pearce, D. (1978) 'The feminization of poverty: women, work, and welfare', *Urban and Social Change Review*, 11: 28–36.

Pearson, B.Z., Fernandez, S.C. and Oller, D.K. (1993) 'Lexical development in bilingual infants and toddlers: comparison to monolingual norms', *Language Learning*, 43: 93–120.

Pellegrini, A. (1991) *Applied Child Study: A Developmental Approach* (2nd edn). Hillsdale, NJ: Lawrence Erlbaum Associates.

Penn, H. (2005) *Unequal Childhoods: Young Children's Lives in Poor Countries*. London: Routledge.

—— (2008) 'Working on the impossible: early childhood policies in Namibia', *Childhood*, 15(3): 379–95.

—— (2011) 'Travelling policies and global buzzwords: how international non-governmental organizations and charities spread the word about early childhood in the global South', *Childhood*, 18(1): 94–113.

—— (2013) *Understanding Early Childhood, Issues and Controversies*. London: Oxford University Press.

Percy-Smith, B. (2002) 'Contested worlds: constraints and opportunities growing up in inner and outer city environments of an English Midlands town', in L. Chawla (ed.), *Growing Up in an Urbanizing World*. London: Earthscan.

Perner, J. (1991) *Understanding the Representational Mind*. Cambridge, MA: MIT Press.

Peterson, C. and Siegal, M. (1995) 'Deafness, conversation, and theory of mind', *Journal of Child Psychology and Psychiatry*, 36: 459–74.

Piaget, J. (1951) *Play, Dreams and Imitation in Childhood*. London: Routledge and Kegan Paul.

—— (1952) *The Origins of Intelligence in Children*. New York: Norton.

—— (1965) *The Child's Conception of Number*. New York: Norton.

—— (1969) *The Child's Conception of the World*. Totowa, NJ: Littlefield and Adams.

Pinker, S. (1984) *Language Learnability and Language Development*. Cambridge, MA: Harvard University Press.

—— (1994) *The Language Instinct: How the Mind Creates Language*. London: Penguin Books.

Plate, E. (2012) 'Staff support for inclusion: an international study', unpublished thesis, Canterbury Christ Church University.

Plato, B.J.T. (2009) *The Republic*. Boston: MobileReference.

Platt, D. and Turney, D. (2013) 'Making threshold decisions in child protection: a conceptual analysis', *British Journal of Social Work*, DOI:10.1093/bjsw/bct007.

Plowman, L., Stephen, C. and McPake, J. (2010) *Growing Up With Technology: Young Children Learning in a Digital World*. London: Routledge.

Pollard. A. (ed.) (1987) *Children and Their Primary Schools: A New Perspective*. Lewes: Falmer.

Popkewitz, T. (2004) 'Foreword', in G. Steiner-Khamsi (ed.), *The Global Politics of Educational Borrowing and Lending*. New York: Teachers College Press, pp.vii-xii.

Postman, N. (1985) 'The disappearance of childhood', *Childhood Education*, 61(4): 286–93.

Pound, L. (2011) *Influencing Early Childhood Education: Key Figures, Philosophies and Ideas: Key Themes, Philosophies and Theories*. Maidenhead: Open University Press.

Pramling, I., Sheridan, S. and Williams, P. (2004) 'Chapter 2: key issues in curriculum development for young children', in OECD, *Starting Strong Curricula and Pedagogies in Early Childhood Education and Care: Five Curriculum Outlines*. Paris: OECD Directorate for Education. [Online] Available at: www.oecd.org/dataoecd/23/36/31672150.pdf (accessed 06/03/2009).

Prendiville, S. (2008) 'Bringing the beach indoors: a study investigating sand and water play opportunities in infant classrooms in the Republic of Ireland', unpublished Masters thesis, University of Limerick.

Prensky, M. (2001) 'Digital natives, digital immigrants', *On the Horizon*, 9(5): 1–6.
Pritchard, C. and Williams, R. (2010) 'Comparing possible "child-abuse-related-deaths" in England and Wales with the major developed countries 1974 – 2006: signs of progress?', *British Journal of Social Work*, 40: 1700–18.

Pritchard, C. and Williams, R. (2010) 'Violent deaths of children are going down', *Every Child Journal*, 1(5): 24–29.

Project Zero and Reggio Children, Italy. (2001). *Making learning visible: Children as individual and group learners*. Reggio Emilia, Italy: Reggio Children S.r.l. and Reggio Children/USA.

Prout, A. (2005) *The Future of Childhood*. London: Routledge Falmer.

Prout, A. and James, A. (1990) 'A new paradigm for the sociology of childhood? Provenance, promise and problems', in A. James and A. Prout (eds), *Constructing and Reconstructing Childhood: Contemporary Issues in the Sociological Study of Childhood*. London: Falmer, pp.7-32.

Pugh, G. and Duffy, B. (eds) (2010) *Contemporary Issues in the Early Years* (5th edn). London: Sage.

Purdy, L. (1992) *In Their Best Interest? The Case Against Equal Rights for Children*. Ithaca, NY: Cornell.

QAA Higher Education (2007) *Benchmark Standards for Early Childhood Studies Degrees*. Mansfield: The Quality Assurance Agency for Higher Education.

QCA (Qualifications and Curriculum Authority) (2000) *Curriculum Guidance for the Foundation Stage*. London: QCA, Reference QCA 00/587.

Qvortrup, J. (2005) 'Varieties of childhood', in J. Qvortrup (ed.), *Studies in Modern Childhood: Society, Agency, Culture*. Basingstoke: Palgrave Macmillan, pp. 1–20.

Qvortrup, J., Bardy, M., Sgritta, G. and Wintersberger, H. (eds) (1994) *Childhood Matters: Social Theory, Practice and Politics*. Aldershot: Avebury.

Radford, L., Corral, S., Bassett, C., Howat, N. and Collishaw, S. (2011) *Child Abuse and Neglect in the UK Today*. London: NSPCC.

Rai, R. and Pannar, K. (2010) *Introduction to Culture Studies*. Mumbai: Himalaya Publishing House.

Ramani, G.B. (2005) 'Co-operative play and problem solving in pre-school children', unpublished Doctoral thesis, University of Pittsburgh.

Ramey, S.L., Ramey, C.T., Phillip, M.M., Lanzi, R.G., Brezausek, C., Katholi, C.R., Snyders, S. and Lawrence, E.L. (2000) *Head Start Children's Entry into Public School: A Report on the National Head Start/Public School Early Childhood Transition Demonstration Study*. Birmingham, AL: Curtan International Research Centre.

Rayns, G., Dawe, S. and Cuthbert, C. (2011) *All Babies Count: Prevention and Protection for Vulnerable Babies: A Review of the Evidence*. London: NSPCC.

Reason, P. and Bradbury, H. (2006) *Handbook of Action Research*. London: Sage.

Reddy, V. (2010) *How Infants Know Minds*. Cambridge, MA: Harvard University Press.

Reder, P. and Duncan, S. (2004) 'Making the most of the Victoria Climbiè Report', *Child Abuse Review*, 13: 95–114.

Rees, G., Goswami, H. and Bradshaw, J. (2010) *Developing an Index of Children's Subjective Well-Being in England*. London: The Children's Society.

Rich, D. (2002) 'Catching children's stories', *Early Education*, 36: 6.

Rideout, V. and Hamel, E. (2006) *The Media Family: Electronic Media in the Lives of Infants, Toddlers Preschoolers and their Parents*. California: Kaiser Family.

Rideout, V.J., Vandewater, E.A. and Wartella, E.A. (2003) *Zero to Six: Electronic Media in the Lives of Infants, Toddlers and Preschoolers*. Washington: Kaiser Foundation.

Riesman, P. (1992) *First Find Your Child a Good Mother: The Construction of Self in Two African Communities*. NJ: Rutgers University Press.

Riggs, N.R., Jahromi, L.B., Razza, R.P., Dillworth-Bart, J.E. and Mueller, U. (2006) 'Executive function and the promotion of social-emotional competence', *Journal of Applied Developmental Psychology*, 27: 300–9.

Rimm-Kaufman, S., Pianta, R.C. and Cox, M. (2000) 'Teachers' judgments of problems in the transition to school', *Early Childhood Research Quarterly*, 15: 147–66.

Ritzer, G. (2008) *Sociological Theory* (7th edn). New York: McGraw-Hill Higher Education.

Roberts, H. (2008) 'Listening to children: and hearing them', in P. Christensen and A. James (eds), *Research with Children: Perspectives and Practices*. London: Routledge Falmer, pp.260-75.

Roberts-Holmes, G. (2009) 'Inclusive policy and practice', in T. Maynard and N. Thomas (eds), *An Introduction to Early Childhood Studies* (2nd edn). London: Sage Publications, pp. 190–201.

Robinson, C. and Kellett, M. (2004) 'Power', in S. Fraser, V. Lewis, S. Ding, M. Kellett and C. Robinson (eds), *Doing Research with Children and Young People*. London: Sage, pp. 81–96.

Robinson, K. (2006) 'Schools kill creativity', TED Talks. [Online] Available at: www.ted.com/talks/ken_robinson_says_schools_kill_creativity.html (accessed 01/03/2013).

Robinson, S. (2006) *Healthy Eating in Primary Schools*. London: Paul Chapman.

Robinson, S., Yardy, K. and Carter, V. (2012) 'The development of obesity in infancy and childhood', *Journal of Child Health Care*, 14 September.

Robinson, V.M. (2006) 'Putting education back into educational leadership', *Leading and Managing*, 12(1): 62-75.

Robson, S. (2006) *Developing Thinking and Understanding in Young Children*. Oxford: Routledge.

Rodd, J. (1996) 'Towards a typology of leadership in the early childhood professional of the 21st century', *Early Child Development and Care*, 120: 119–26.

—— (1997) 'Learning to be leaders: perceptions of early childhood professionals about leadership roles and responsibilities', *Early Years*, 18(1): 40–6.

—— (2006) *Leadership in Early Childhood: The Pathway to Professionalism*. Buckingham: Open University Press.

Rodham, H. (1976) 'Children under the law', in A. Skolnick (ed.), *Rethinking Childhood: Perspectives on Development and Society*. Boston: Little, Brown.

Rogoff, B. (1989) 'The joint socialization of development by young children and adults', reprinted in P. Light, S. Sheldon and M. Woodhead (1991), *Learning to Think. Child Development in Social Context 2*. London: Routledge.

—— (1990) *Apprenticeship in Thinking: Cognitive Development in Social Context*. New York: Oxford University Press.

—— (1992) 'Three ways to relate person and culture: thoughts sparked by Valsiner's review of *Apprenticeship in Thinking*', *Human Development*, 35: 316– 20.

—— (2003) *The Cultural Nature of Human Development*. Oxford: Oxford University Press.

Rogoff, B., Chavajay, P. and Matusov, E. (1993) 'Questioning assumptions about culture and individuals. Commentary of Michael Tomasello, Ann Cale Kruger and Hilary Horn Ratner', *Behavioural and Brain Sciences*, 16: 533–4.

Rolfe, S. (2001) 'Direct observation', in G. MacNaughton, S. Rolfe, S and I. Siraj-Blatchford (eds), *Doing Early Childhood Research, International Perspectives on Theory and Practice*. Buckingham: Open University Press, pp. 224–39.

Roopnarine, J., Lasker, J., Sacks, M. and Stores, M. (1998) 'The cultural contexts of children's play', in O. Saracho and B. Spodek (eds), *Multiple Perspectives on Play in Early Childhood*. New York: New York Press, pp. 194–219.

Rose, L. (1991) *The Erosion of Childhood: Childhood in Britain 1860–1918*. London: Routledge.

Rousseau, J.J. (1964) *Jean Jacques Rousseau: His Educational Theories Selected from Emile. Julie and Other Writings.* New York: Barron's Educational Series.

Rubin, K.H., Fein, G.G. and Vandenberg, B. (1983) 'Play', in P.H. Mussen and E.M. Hetherington (eds), *Handbook of Child Psychology, Vol. 4.* Basel: S. Karger.

Rueda, M.R., Rothbart, M.K., McCandliss, B.D., Saccomanno, L. and Posner, M.I. (2005) 'Training, maturation, and genetic influences on the development of executive attention', *Proceedings of the National Academy of Sciences*, 102: 14931–6.

Ruffman, T., Slade, L. and Crow, E. (2002) 'The relation between children's and mothers' mental state language and theory-of-mind understanding', *Child Development*, 73: 734–51.

Rutter, J. and Evans, B. (2011) *Informal Childcare: Choice Or Chance? A Literature Review*. London: Daycare Trust.

SACN (Scientific Advisory Committee on Nutrition) (2011) *The Influence of Maternal, Fetal and Child Nutrition on the Development of Chronic Disease in Later Life*. London: SACN.

Sammons, P., Sylva, K., Melhuish, E., Siraj-Blatchford, I., Taggart, B. and Barreau, S. (2007) *Effective Pre-school and Primary Education 3–11 Project (EPPE 3–11): Influences on Children's Attainment and Progress in Key Stage 2: Social/Behavioural Outcomes in Year 5. Full Report*. London: Institute of Education, University of London.

Sampson, G. (2005) *Educating Eve. The 'Language Instinct' Debate*. New York: Continuum International.

Saracho, O. (1991) 'Educational play in early childhood', *Early Child Development and Care*, 66: 45–64.

Saracho, O. and Spodek, B. (1998) *Multiple Perspectives on Play in Early Childhood*. New York: New York Press.

Savage, M. (2012) 'Home literacy and agency: an ethnographic approach to studying the home literacy practices of six multiliterate children in Qatar', unpublished EdD Thesis, University of Sheffield.

Save the Children (2006) *Righting the Wrongs: The Reality of Children's Rights in Wales*. Cardiff: Save the Children.

—— (2012) *Child Poverty in 2012: It Shouldn't Happen Here*. London: Save the Children.

Sawyer, R. (2003) 'Emergence in creativity and development', in R. Sawyer, V. John-Steiner, S. Moran and D. Feldman (eds), *Creativity and Development*. Oxford: Oxford University Press, pp. 12–60.

Schaffer, H.R. (2004) *Introducing Child Psychology*. Oxford: Blackwell.

Schieffelin, B. (1994) 'Language acquisition and socialization: three developmental stories and their implications', in B. Blount (ed.), *Language, Culture, and Society*. Illinois: Waveland Press Inc., pp.470-512

Scholl, B. and Leslie, A. (1999) 'Modularity, development and theory of mind', *Mind and Language*, 14: 131–53.

Schön, D. (1983) *The Reflective Practitioner: How Practitioners Think in Action*. New York: Basic Books.

Schraad-Tischer, M. (2011) *Social Justice in the OECD: How Do the Member States Compare*. Berlin: Bertelsmann Stiftung.

Schweinhart, L.J. and Weikart, D.P. (1997) 'The High/Scope Preschool Curriculum Comparison Study through age 23', *Early Childhood Research Quarterly*, 12: 117–43.

Schweinhart, L.J., Barnes, H.V. and Weikart, D.P. (1993) *Significant Benefits: The High/Scope Perry Preschool Study Through Age 27* (Monographs of the High/Scope Educational Research Foundation, 10). Ypsilanti, MI: High/Scope Press. PS 021 998.

Schweinhart, L.J., Montie, J., Xiang, Z., Barnett, W., Belfield, C. and Nores, M. (2005) *Lifetime Effects: The High/Scope Perry Preschool Study Through Age 40*. Ypsilanti, MI: High/Scope Press.

Scott, K. (2010) *That Deadman Dance*. London: Bloomsbury.

Scriven, A. (2010) *Promoting Health. A Practical Guide*. London: Bailliere Tindall.

Searle, G.R. (1976) *Eugenics and politics in Britain, 1900–1914 (Vol. 3)*. Leyden, The Netherlands: Springer.

Seedhouse, D. (1986) *Health. The Foundations for Achievement*. Chichester: John Wiley.

Selwyn, J., Quinton, D., Sturgess, W. and Baxter, C. (2006) *Costs and Outcomes of Non-infant Adoptions*. London: British Association for Adoption and Fostering.

Selwyn, J., Harris, P., Quinton, D., Nawaz, S., Wijedasa, D. and Wood, M. (2010) *Pathways to Permanence for Black, Asian and Mixed Ethnicity Children*. London, BAAF.

Serpell, R. (1993) *The Significance of Schooling: Life Journeys in an African Society*. Cambridge: Cambridge University Press.

Seung Lam, M. and Pollard, A. (2006) 'A conceptual framework for understanding children as agents in the transition from home to kindergarten', *Early Years: Journal of International Research and Development*, 26(2): 123–41.

Shakeshaft, C. (1989) *Women in Educational Administration*. Beverley Hills, CA: Sage Publications.

Sharp, C., Lord, P., Handscomb, G., Macleod, S., Southcott, C., George, N. and Jeffes, J. (2012) *Highly Effective Leadership in Children's Centres*. Nottingham: National College for School Leadership.

Sheridan, M.D., Howard, J. and Alderson, D. (2011) *Play in Early Childhood. From Birth to Six Years* (3rd edition). Abingdon: Routledge.

Shonkoff, J.P. and Phillips, D.A. (eds) (2000) *From Neurons to Neighborhoods: The Science of Early Childhood Development*. Washington DC: National Academy Press.

Shore, A. (2011) *The Science of the Art of Psychotherapy*. New York: Norton.

Siegel, D. (1999) *The Developing Mind*. New York: Guilford Press.

Siegler, R.S. (2000) 'The rebirth of children's learning', *Child Development*, 71: 26–35.

Siegler, R.S., DeLoache, J. and Eisenberg, N. (2010) *How Children Develop: International Edition* (3rd edn). New York: Worth.

Siencyn, S.W. and Thomas, S. (2007) 'Wales', in M.M. Clark and T. Waller (eds), *Early Childhood Education and Care: Policy and Practice*. London: Sage, pp. 135–66.

Sigelman, C.K. and Rider, E.A. (2008) *Life-Span Human Development* (6th edn). London: Thomson Wadsworth.

Sinclair, I. (2005) *Fostering Now: Messages from Research*. London, Jessica Kingsley.

Singer, P. (1995) *Animal Liberation* (revised edn). London: Pimlico.

Singer, P. (2001) Unsanctifying Human Life: Essays on Ethics. Oxford: Blackwell.

Siraj-Blatchford, I. (1999) 'Early childhood pedagogy, practice, principles and research', in P. Mortimore (ed.), *Understanding Pedagogy and its Impact on Learning*. London: Paul Chapman, pp. 20–45.

—— (2007) 'Creativity, communication and collaboration: the identification of pedagogic progression in sustained shared thinking', *Asia-Pacific Journal of Research in Early Childhood Education*, 1(2): 3–23.

—— (2008) 'Understanding the relationship between curriculum, pedagogy and progression in learning in early childhood in Hong Kong', *Journal of Early Childhood Education*, 7(2): 6–13.

Siraj-Blatchford, I. and Manni, L. (2007) *Effective Leadership in the Early Years Sector. The ELEYS Study*. London: Institute of Education, University of London.

Siraj-Blatchford, I. and Manni, L. (2008) '"Would you like to tidy up now?" An analysis of adult questioning in the English Foundation Stage', in *Early Years: An International Journal of Research and Development*, 28(1), 5-22.

Siraj-Blatchford, I. and Sylva, K. (2004) 'Researching pedagogy in English pre-schools', *British Educational Research Journal*, 30(5): 713–30.

Siraj-Blatchford, I., Clarke, K. and Needham, M. (2007) *Team Around the Child: Multi-agency Working in the Early Years*. Stoke on Trent: Trentham Books.

Siraj-Blatchford, I., Sylva, K., Muttock, S., Gilden, R. and Bell, D. (2002) *Researching Effective Pedagogy in the Early Years: DfES Research Report 356*. London: Department for Education and Skills.

Siraj-Blatchford, I., Sylva, K., Taggart, B., Sammons, P. and Melhuish, E. (2003) *Technical Paper 10: Case Studies of Practice in the Foundation Stage*. London: Institute of Education.

Siraj-Blatchford, I., Taggart, B., Sylva, K., Sammons, P. and Melhuish, E. (2008) 'Towards the transformation of practice in early childhood education: the Effective Provision of Pre-school Education (EPPE) project', *Cambridge Journal of Education*, 38(1): 23–36.

Siviy, S.M. (1998) 'Neurobiological substrates of play behaviour in the structure and function of mammalian playfulness', in M. Berkoff and J.A. Byers (eds), *Animal Play: Evolutionary, Ecological and Comparative Perspectives*. Cambridge: Cambridge University Press, pp. 221–42.

Skelton, C. and Francis, B. (2012) 'The "Renaissance child": high achievement and gender in late modernity,' *International Journal of Inclusive Education*, 16(4): 441–59.

Skinner, B.F. (1957) *Verbal Behavior*. New York: Appleton-Century-Croft.

Smart, C., Neale, B. and Wade, A. (2001) *The Changing Experience of Childhood: Families and Divorce*. Cambridge: Polity Press.

Smilanksy, S. (1968) *The Effects of Sociodramatic Play on Disadvantaged Preschool Children*. New York: Wiley.

Smith, B.J., Tang, C.T. and Nutbeam, D. (2006) 'WHO Health Promotion Glossary: new terms', *Health Promotion International*, 21(4): 340–5.

Smith, P.K. and Vollstedt, R. (1985) 'On defining play; an empirical study of the relationship between play and various play criteria', *Child Development*, 56: 1042–50.

Smuts, A.B. and Smuts R.W. (2006) *Science in the Service of Children, 1893–1935*. New Haven, CT: Yale University Press.

Snow, C.E. (1977) 'Mothers' speech research: from input to interaction', in C.E. Snow and C.A. Ferguson (eds), *Talking to Children: Language Input and Acquisition*. Cambridge: Cambridge University Press, pp. 31–49.

Sokolov, J. and Snow, C. (1994) 'The changing role of negative evidence in theories of language development', in C. Gallaway and B.J. Richards (eds), *Input and Interaction in Language Acquisition*. Cambridge: Cambridge University Press, pp. 38–55.

Soni, A. (2012) 'Promoting emotional well-being or mental health in England', in T. Papatheodorou (ed.), *Debates on Early Childhood Policies and Practices*. London: Routledge, pp. 172–82.

Soyinka, W. (1989) *Ake: The Years of Childhood*. London: Vintage Books.

Speier, M. (1976) 'The adult ideological viewpoint in studies of childhood', in A. Skolnick (ed.), *Rethinking Childhood: Perspectives on Development and Society*. Boston, MA: Little Brown, pp. 168–86.

Speller, V., Parish, R., Davison, H. and Zilnyk, A. (2012) *The CompHP Professional Standards for Health Promotion Handbook*. Paris: International Union for Health Promotion and Education.

Springhall, S. (1999) *Youth, Popular Culture and Moral Panics: Penny Gaffs to Gangsta-Rap, 1830–1996.* New York: St. Martin's Press.

Stacey, C. (2011) 'Psychoneuroimmunology and wellbeing', in A. Knight and A. McNaught (eds), *Understanding Wellbeing. An Introduction for Students and Practitioners of Health and Social Care.* Banbury: Lantern, pp. 67–77.

Stafford, A., Parton, N., Vincent, S., Smith, C. (2012) *Child Protection Systems in the United Kingdom: A Comparative Analysis.* London: Jessica Kingsley.

Stainton-Rogers, W. and Roche, J. (1994) *Children's Welfare and Children's Rights: A Practical Guide to the Law.* London: Hodder and Stoughton.

Stalford, H., Thomas, N. and Drywood, E. (2011) 'Editorial: the European Union and children's rights', *International Journal of Children's Rights*, 19(3): 375–9.

Stanley, N., Miller, P., Richardson Foster, H. and Thomson, G. (2011) 'A stop–start response: social services' interventions with children and families notified following domestic violence incidents', *British Journal of Social Work*, 41(2): 296–313.

Stearns, P.N. (2011) *Childhood in World History.* Abingdon: Routledge.

Steedman, C. (1995) *Strange Dislocations: Childhood and the Idea of Human Interiority, 1780–1930.* Cambridge, MA: Harvard University Press.

Steiner-Khamsi, G. (ed.) (2004) *The Global Politics of Educational Borrowing and Lending.* New York: Teachers College Press.

Stern, D.N. (1985) *The Interpersonal World of the Infant.* New York: Basic Books.

Stevens, J. (2013) 'Observing, assessing and planning for how young children are learning', in H. Moylett (ed.), *Characteristics of Effective Early Learning: Helping Young Children Become Learners for Life.* Maidenhead: Open University Press.

Stewart, J. and Bushell, F. (2011) 'Built environment and wellbeing', in A. Knight and A. McNaught (eds), *Understanding Wellbeing. An Introduction for Students and Practitioners of Health and Social Care.* Banbury: Lantern, pp. 201–13.

Stewart, J., Bushell, F. and Habgood, V. (2003) *Environmental Health as Public Health.* London: Chadwick House.

Stipek, D.J. and Byler, P. (1997) 'Early childhood education teachers: do they practice what they preach?', *Early Childhood Research Quarterly*, 12: 305–25.

Stipek, D.J. and Ogano, T. (2000) *Early Childhood Education.* Los Angeles, CA: UCLA: Center for Healthier Children, Families and Community.

Sturrock, G. (2003) 'Towards a psycholudic definition of playwork', in F. Brown (ed.), *Playwork: Theory and Practice.* Buckingham: Open University Press, pp. 81–97.

Sulzby, E. (1989) 'Assessment of writing and of children's language while writing', in L. Morrow and J. Smith (eds), *The Role of Assessment and Measurement in Early Literacy Instruction.* Englewood Cliffs, NJ: Prentice- Hall, pp. 83–109.

Sulzby, E. and Teale, W. (1991) 'Emergent literacy', in R. Barr, M. Kamil, P. Mosenthal and P.D. Pearson (eds), *Handbook of Reading Research (Vol. 2).* New York: Longman, pp. 727–57.

Sutherland, I. (1987) 'History and background'. In Sutherland, I. (ed) *Health Education. Perspectives and Choices*. Chicago: NEC publications, pp.1-38.

Sutton-Smith, B. (1979) *Play and Learning*. New York: Gardner Press.

—— (1997) *The Ambiguity of Play*. Cambridge, MA: Harvard University Press.

Sutton-Smith, B. and Kelly-Byrne, D. (1984) 'The idealisation of play', in P.K. Smith (ed.), *Play in Animals and Humans*. Oxford: Basil Blackwell, pp. 305–21.

Swick, K.J, and Williams, R. (2006) 'An analysis of Bronfenbrenner's Bio-ecological perspective for early childhood educators: implications for working with families experiencing stress', *Early Childhood Education Journal*, 33(5): 305–27.

Sylva, K., Blatchford, P. and Johnson, S. (1992) 'The impact of the National Curriculum on pre-school practice', *International Journal of Early Education*, 21(1): 41–51.

Sylva, K., Bruner, J.S. and Genova, P. (1976) 'The role of play in the problem solving of young children 3–5 years old', in J.S. Bruner, A. Jolly and K. Sylva (eds), *Play: Its Role in Development and Evolution*. Penguin: New York, pp.244-261.

Sylva, K., Siraj-Blatchford, I. and Taggart, B. (2006) *Early Childhood Environmental Rating Scale – Extension (ECERS-E)* (2nd edn). Stoke on Trent: Trentham Books.

Sylva, K., Melhuish, E.C., Sammons, P., Siraj-Blatchford, I. and Taggart, B. (2004) *The Effective Provision of Pre-School Education (EPPE) Project: Final Report*. London: Department for Education and Skills/Institute of Education, University of London.

—— (2008) *Effective Pre-School and Primary Education 3–11 Project (EPPE 3–11): Report from the Primary Phase: Pre-school, School and Family Influence on Children's Development during Key Stage 2 (Age 7–11)*. London: Department for Children, Schools and Families, Research Report 061.

—— (eds) (2010) *Early Childhood Matters: Evidence from the Effective Pre-School and Primary Education Project*. London: Routledge.

Takhvar, M. (1988) 'Play and theories of play: a review of the literature', *Early Child Development and Care*, 39: 221–44.

Tassoni, P. (2013) 'Settling in,', *Nursery World*, 14–27 January:16–17.

Taylor, P.H., Exon, G. and Holley, B. (1972) *A Study of Nursery Education*. London: Schools Council/ Methuen.

Teaching Agency (2012) *Early Years Professional Standards from September 2012*. London: The Teaching Agency.

Teale, W. and Sulzby, E. (eds) (1986) *Emergent Literacy: Writing and Reading*. Norwood, NJ: Ablex.

Theakston, A., Lieven, E., Pine, J. and Rowland, C. (2001) 'The role of performance limitations in the acquisition of verb argument structure', *Journal of Child Language*, 28: 127–52.

Thomas, A. (2010) 'Digital literacy: the state of play', paper presented at the New Media Consortium, Anaheim, CA, June 9–12.

Thomas, L., Howard, J. and Miles, G. (2006) 'The effectiveness of playful practice for learning in the early years', *The Psychology of Education Review*, 30(1): 52–8.

Thomas, M. (ed.) (2011) *Deconstructing Digital Natives: Young People, Technology and the New Literacies.* New York: Routledge.

Thomas, N. (2002) *Children, Family and the State: Decision-making and Child Participation.* Bristol: Policy Press.

—— (2005) *Social Work with Young People in Care.* London: Palgrave MacMillan.

—— (2008) 'Consultation and advocacy', in B. Luckock and M. Lefevre (eds), *Direct Work: Social Work with Children and Young People in Care.* London: British Association for Adoption and Fostering.

—— (2009) *Children, Politics and Communication: Participation at the Margins.* Bristol: Policy Press.

Thomas, N. and O'Kane, C. (1998) *Children and Decision-making: A Summary Report.* Swansea: University of Wales Swansea, International Centre for Childhood Studies.

Thomas, N. and Percy-Smith, B. (2010) *A Handbook of Children and Young People's Participation: Perspectives from Theory and Practice.* London: Routledge.

Thomson, P. (ed.) (2008) *Doing Visual Research with Children and Young People.* London: Routledge Falmer.

Thorne, B. (1993) *Gender Play: Girls and Boys in School.* New Brunswick, NJ: Rutgers University Press.

Tickell, Dame C. (2011) *The Tickell Review of the Early Years Foundation Stage.* London: Department for Education.

Timimi, S. (2009) 'The commercialization of children's mental health in the era of globalization', *International Journal of Mental Health*, 3: 5–27.

Tomasello, M. (1992) *First Verbs. A Case Study of Early Grammatical Development.* New York: Cambridge University Press.

—— (2000) 'Do young children have adult syntactic competence?', *Cognition*, 74: 209–53.

—— (2003) *Constructing a Language: A Usage-based Theory of Language Acquisition.* Cambridge, MA: Harvard University Press.

Tomasello, M., Carpenter, M., Call, J., Behne, T. and Moll, H. (2005) 'Understanding and sharing intentions: the origins of cultural cognition', *Behavioral and Brain Sciences*, 28: 675–91.

Townsend, P. and Davidson, N. (eds) (1982) *Inequalities in Health: The Black Report.* London: Penguin.

Trevarthen, C. (2009) 'Why attachment matters in sharing meaning', keynote address. *SIRCC Seminar*, 11 September, Glasgow Marriott Hotel. [Online] Available at: www.iriss.org.uk (accessed 11/02/2013).

Turkle, S. (2011) *Alone Together.* Cambridge, MA: MIT Press.

Twum-Danso, A. (2009) 'International children's rights', in H. Montgomery and M. Kellett (eds), *Children and Young Peoples Worlds: Developing Frameworks for Integrated Practice*. Bristol: The Open University and Policy Press, pp.109-126.

UNCRC (United Nations Committee on the Rights of the Child) (2006) *General Comment No.7, Implementing Child Rights in Early Childhood*, CRC/C/GC/7. [Online] Available at: www.refworld.org/docid/460bc5a62.html (accessed 14/05/2013).

UNESCO (1990) *World Declaration on Education for All and Framework for Action to Meet Basic Learning Needs*. Jomtien: UNESCO.

—— (1994) *The Salamanca Statement and Framework for Action*, Paris: UNESCO.

—— (2000) *The Dakar Framework for Action. Education for All: Meeting Our Collective Commitments*. Dakar: UNESCO

UN General Assembly (1948) *Universal Declaration of Human Rights*, 10 December, 217 A (III). [Online] Available at: www.unhcr.org/refworld/docid/3ae6b3712c.html (accessed 28/03/2013).

—— (1989) *Convention on the Rights of the Child, General Assembly Resolution 44/25*. [Online] Available at: www.refworld.org/docid/460bc5a62.html (accessed 14/05/2013).

UNICEF (2008) *The Child Care Transition. Innocenti Report Card 8*. Florence: The United Nations Children's Fund. [Online] Available at: www.refworld.org/docid/460bc5a62.html (accessed 14/05/2013).

—— (2011) *Preventing Social Inclusion through the Europe 2020 Strategy: Early Childhood Development and the Inclusion of Roma Families*. UNICEF and the European Social Observatory in collaboration with the Belgian Federal Planning Service (Ministry) for Social Integration. [Online] Available at: www.ecdgroup.com/pdfs/Preventing-Social-Exclusion.pdf (accessed 01/03/2013).

Valkanova, Y. (2009) 'The passion for educating the "new man": debates about pre-schooling in Soviet Russia, 1917–1925', *History of Education Quarterly*, 49(2): 211–21.

Valkanova, Y. and Brehony, K.J. (2006) 'The gifts and "contributions": Friedrich Froebel and Russian education (1850–1929)', *History of Education*, 35(2): 189–207.

Van Oers, B. (2012) 'Developmental education: foundations of a play-based curriculum', in B. van Oers (ed.), *Developmental Education for Young Children. Concept, Practice, and Implementation*. The Hague, The Netherlands: Springer, pp. 13–26.

Vandenbroeck, M. (2007) 'Beyond anti-bias education: changing conceptions of diversity and equity in European early childhood education', *European Early Childhood Education Research Journal*, 15(1): 21–35.

Veresov, N. (2006) 'Leading activity in developmental psychology: concept and principle', *Journal of Russian and East European Psychology*, 44(5): 7–25.

Vincent, C. and Ball, S. (2007) 'Making Up' the Middle-Class Child: Families, Activities and Class Dispositions. *Sociology*, 41(6): 1061-1077.

Vygotsky, L.S. ([1926]1997) *Educational Psychology*. Florida: CRC Press.

—— ([1933] 1966) *Play and Its Role in the Mental Development of the Child*, Voprosy psikhologii, No. 6, trans. C. Mulholland, Psychology and Marxism Internet Archive 2002. [Online] Available at: www.marxists.org/archive/vygotsky/works/1933/play.htm (accessed 06/03/2009).

—— (1978) *Mind in Society: The Development of Higher Mental Processes*. Cambridge, MA: Harvard University Press.

—— (1986) *Thought and Language*. Cambridge, MA: MIT Press.

—— (1994a) 'The problem of the cultural development of the child', in R. van der Veer and J. Valsiner (eds), *The Vygotsky Reader*. Oxford: Blackwell, pp. 57–72.

—— (1994b) 'The problem of the environment', in R. van der Veer and J. Valsiner (eds), *The Vygotsky Reader*. Oxford: Blackwell, pp. 338–50.

—— (1997) *The Problem of Cultural Age. The Collected Works of L.S. Vygotsky: Vol. 4*. New York: Plenum.

—— (1998) *Child Psychology. The Collected Works of L S. Vygotsky: Vol. 5*. New York: Plenum.

—— (2004) 'Imagination and creativity in childhood', *Journal of Russian and East European Psychology*, 42(1): 4–84.

Waksler, F.C. (ed.) (1991) *Studying the Social Worlds of Children: Sociological Readings*. London: Falmer.

—— (1996) *The Little Trials of Childhood and Children's Strategies for Dealing with Them*. London: Falmer.

Walker, P. (2012a) 'On public health and wellbeing', in P. Walker and M. John (eds), *From Public Health to Wellbeing. The New Driver for Policy and Action*. Basingstoke: Palgrave, pp. 1–20.

—— (2012b) 'Wellbeing: meaning, definition, measurement and application', in P. Walker and M. John (eds), *From Public Health to Wellbeing. The New Driver for Policy and Action*. London: Palgrave, pp. 21–46.

Wall, K. (2010) *Autism and Early Years Practice* (2nd edn). London: Sage.

Walsh, G., Sproule, L., McGuinesss, C. and Trew, K. (2011) 'Playful structure: a novel image of early years pedagogy for primary school classrooms', *Early Years*, 31(2): 107–19.

Wang, C.C.D.C. and Mallinckrodt, B.S. (2006) 'Differences between Taiwanese and U.S. cultural beliefs about ideal adult attachment', *Journal of Counselling Psychology*, 53(2): 192–204.

Warming, H. (2005) 'Participant observation: a way to learn about children's perspectives', in A. Clark, P. Moss and A. Kjorholt (eds), *Beyond Listening: Children's Perspectives on Early Childhood Services*. Bristol: Policy Press, pp. 51–70.

Wave Trust (2013) *Conception to Age 2. The Age of Opportunity*. London: DfE publications.

Weare, K. (1992) 'The contribution of education to health promotion', in R. Bunton and G. Macdonald (eds), *Health Promotion: Disciplines and Diversity*. London: Routledge, pp. 66–85.

—— (2007) 'Delivering health education: the contribution of social and emotional learning', *Health Education*, 107(2): 109–13.

Weikart, D. (2000) *Early Childhood Education: Needs and Opportunity*. Paris: UNESCO: International Institute for Educational Planning.

Wellman, H. (2002) 'Understanding the psychological world: developing a theory of mind', in U. Goswami (ed.), *Handbook of Childhood Cognitive Development*. Oxford: Blackwell, pp. 167–87.

Wellman, H. and Gelman, S.A. (1998) 'Knowledge acquisition in foundational domains', in W. Damon (gen. ed.), D. Kuhn and R.S. Siegler (vol. eds), *Handbook of Child Psychology, Vol. 2: Cognition, Perception and Language*. New York: Wiley, pp. 523–73.

Wells, G. (1986) *The Meaning Makers: Children Learning Language and Using Language to Learn*. London: Hodder and Stoughton.

Wenger, E. (1998) *Communities of Practice*. Cambridge: Cambridge University Press.

Westcott, M. and Howard, J. (2007) 'Creating a playful classroom environment', *Psychology of Education Review*, 31(1): 27–34.

Westerman, W. (2001) 'Youth and adulthood in children's and adults' perspectives', in C. Erricker, C. Otta and J. Erricker (eds), *Spiritual Education, Cultural, Religious and Social Differences: New Perspectives for the 21st Century*. Brighton: Sussex Academic Press, pp. 248–259.

Whalley, M. and the Pen Green Team (2000) *Involving Parents in Their Children's Learning*. London: Paul Chapman.

Whitebread, D. and Jameson, H. (2005) 'Play, storytelling and creative writing', in J. Moyles (ed.), *The Excellence of Play*. Buckingham: Open University Press, pp. 59–71.

Whitebread, D., Basilio, M., Kuvalja, M. and Verma, M. (2012) *The Value of Children's Play*. A report written for the Toy Industries of Europe. University of Cambridge.

Whitehurst, G. and Lonigan, C. (1998) 'Child development and emergent literacy', *Child Development*, 69(3): 848–72.

WHO (World Health Organization) (1946) *Constitution of the World Health Organization*. Adopted by the International Health Conference, New York 19 June–22 July.

—— (1947) *Development and Constitution of the WHO. Chronicle of the World Health Organization, 2(1–2)*. [Online] Available at: http://whqlibdoc.who.int/hist/chronicles/chronicle_1947.pdf (accessed 15/12/2012).

—— (1978) *Declaration of Alma-Ata. International Conference on Primary Health Care*. Alma-Ata, USSR, 6–12 September.

—— (1986) *The Ottawa Charter for Health Promotion*. Ottawa: WHO.

—— (1998) *Health Promotion Glossary*. Geneva: WHO.

—— (2009) *Global Plan of Action for Children's Health and the Environment 2010–2015*. Geneva: WHO. [Online] Available at: www.who.int/ceh/cehplanaction10_15.pdf (accessed 16/11/2012).

Wilcox, A.A. (2006) *An Occupational Perspective of Health*. New Jersey: Slack.

Williams, G. (1984) 'Health promotion – caring concern of slick salesmanship?', *Journal of Medical Ethics*, 10: 191–5.

Williams, T., Wetton, N. and Moon, A. (1989) *A Picture of Health. What Makes You Healthy and Keeps You Healthy?* London: Health Education Authority.

Wilson, J. (2000) 'Doing justice to inclusion', *European Journal of Special Needs Education*, 15(3): 297–304.

Wimmer, H. and Perner, J. (1983) 'Beliefs about beliefs: representations and constraining function of wrong beliefs in young children's understanding of deception', *Cognition*, 13: 103–28.

Winnicott, D.W. (1971) *Playing and Reality*. London: Routledge Classics.

Wohlwend, K. (2009) 'Early adopters: playing new literacies and pretending new technologies in print-centric classrooms', *Journal of Early Childhood Literacy*, 9: 117–40.

Wolfe, R.M. and Sharp, L.K. (2002) 'Anti-vaccinationists past and present', *BMJ*, 325(7361): 430–2.

Wolfe, S. and Flewitt, R.S. (2010) 'New technologies, new multimodal literacy practices and young children's metacognitive development', *Cambridge Journal of Education*, 40: 387–99.

Wood, D., Bruner, J.S. and Ross, G. (1976) 'The role of tutoring in problem-solving', *Journal of Child Psychology and Psychiatry*, 17: 89–100.

Woodhead, M. (1999) 'Reconstructing developmental psychology: some first steps', *Children and Society*, 13(1): 3–19.

Woodhead, M. and Faulkner, D. (2008) 'Subjects, objects or participants? Dilemmas of psychological research with children', in P. Christensen and A. James (eds), *Research with Children: Perspectives and Practices* (2nd edn). London: Routledge Falmer, pp. 10–39.

Woodhead, M., Ames, P., Vennam, U., Abebe, W., and Streuli, N. (2009). *Equity and quality? Challenges for early childhood and primary education in Ethiopia, India and Peru*. Bernard van Leer Foundation, The Hague, Netherlands.

Worsfold, V.L. (1974) 'A philosophical justification for children's rights', *Harvard Educational Review*, 44(1): 142–59.

Wyness, M. (2012) *Childhood and Society: An Introduction to the Sociology of Childhood* (2nd edn). Basingstoke: Palgrave Macmillan.

Yelland, N., Lee, L., O'Rourke, M. and Harrison, C. (2008) *Rethinking Learning in Early Childhood Education*. Buckingham: Open University Press.

Zelazo, P.D., Carlson, S.M. and Kesek, A. (2008) 'The development of executive function in childhood', in C. Nelson and M. Luciana (eds), *Handbook of Developmental Cognitive Neuroscience* (2nd edn). Cambridge, MA: MIT Press, pp. 553–74.

Zelazo, P.D., Qu, L. and Muller, U. (2005) 'Hot and cool aspects of executive function: relations in early development', in W. Schneider, R. Schumann-Hengsteler and B. Sodian (eds), *Young Children's Cognitive Development: Interrelationships Among Executive Functioning, Working Memory, Verbal Ability and Theory Of Mind*. New Jersey: Lawrence Erlbaum Associates, pp. 71–95.

Zelitzer, V.A. (1985) *Pricing the Priceless Child: The Changing Social Value of Children*. New York: Basic Books.

Zener, R.S. (1999) 'Revisiting the process of normalization', *NAMTA Journal*, 24(1): 87–105.

INDEX